Edited & designed by
The Information & Technology
Publishing Co Ltd
PO Box 500024
Dubai
United Arab Emirates
Tel +971 4 210 8000
Fax +971 4 210 8080
www.itp.com

For
Time Out Guides Limited
Universal House
251 Tottenham Court Road
London W1T 7AB
Tel + 44 (0)20 7813 3000
Fax + 44 (0)20 7813 6001
Email guides@timeout.com
www.timeout.com

Editorial
Managing Editor Justin Etheridge
Editors Rob Orchard, Marcus Webb
Proofreader Simon Coppock
Indexer Jackie Brind

Editorial/Managing Director Peter Fiennes
Series Editor Ruth Jarvis
Deputy Series Editor Lesley McCave
Business Manager Gareth Garner
Guides Co-ordinator Holly Pick
Accountant Kemi Olufuwa

Design
Designers Philip Bunting, Dalton Butler
Art Director Scott Moore

Advertising
Group Sales Manager Victoria Hazell
Advertisement Manager Tim Calladine
Sales Director Mark Phillips
International Sales Manager Ross Canadé
International Sales Executive Simon Davies
Advertising Assistant Lucy Butler

Marketing
Marketing Director Mandy Martinez
Marketing & Publicity Manager, US Rosella Albanese

Production
Production Manager Kyle Smith
Production Director Mark Lamond
Production Controller Marie Howell

Time Out Group
Chairman Tony Elliott
Managing Director Mike Hardwick
Group Financial Director Richard Waterlow
Group Commercial Director Lesley Gill
Group General Manager Nichola Coulthard
Group Circulation Director Jim Heinemann
Group Art Director John Oakey
Online Managing Director David Pepper
Group Production Director Steve Proctor
Group IT Director Simon Chappell

Contributors
Contributing Editors Matthew Lee, James Montague, Lyndsey Steven, John Thatcher.

Introduction Justin Etheridge. **History** Antonia Carver. **Dubai Today** Antonia Carver. **Architecture** Antonia Carver. **Culture & Customs** Antonia Carver. **Where to Stay** Lyndsey Steven. **Sightseeing** Lucy Monro (*Hatta, Pool position, Big Red* Shelley Frost). **Restaurants** Matthew Lee. **Cafés & Bars** Marcus Webb, Matthew Lee. **Shops & Services** James Montague. **Festivals & Events** Marcus Webb. **Children** Antonia Carver. **Film & Theatre** Marcus Webb. **Galleries** Antonia Carver. **Nightlife** Marcus Webb. **Spectator Sports** Steve Hill. **Participation Sports** Steve Hill. **Health & Fitness** Steve Hill. **Abu Dhabi** John Thatcher. **Northern Emirates** Lyndsey Steven. **East Coast** Lyndsey Steven. **Directory** Lyndsey Steven.

Maps JS Graphics (john@jsgraphics.co.uk). Maps based on material supplied by Net Maps.

Photography Victoria Calaguian & Christopher Manson. Additional photography Sevag Davidian, Wadih El-Najjar, Hywell Waters and courtesy of the Al Bustan Rotana Dubai, Al Raha Beach Hotel, Arabian Court Hotel, Dubai Municipality, the Dusit Dubai, Emirates Palace Hotel, Hatta Fort Hotel, Hilton Dubai, Jumeirah International, Le Meridien Al Aqah, Oasis Beach Hotel, TheOne&Only Royal Mirage, the Ritz-Carlton Dubai, Nakheel, the Shangri-La Dubai, the Sheraton Creek Dubai and Voyagers Xtreme. Pages 13, 184, 201, 233 staff/getty; pages 17 US Navy/Getty Images; pages 19, 21, 24, 25, 26, 68 Rabih Moghrabi/Getty Images; page 33 Jimin Lai/Getty Images; page 74 Craig Willers; page 143 Mike Hewitt/Getty Images; pages 147, 185 Julian Herbert/Getty Images; page 156 Dave Hogan/Getty Images; pages 3, 157, 189 Nasser Younes/Getty Images; pages 184, 196 David Cannon/Getty Images; page 186 Andrew Redington/Getty Images; page 188 Ezra Shaw/Getty Images; page 193 Chung Sung-Jun/Getty Images; page 194 Clive Brunskill/Getty Images; page 199 Joe Raedle/Getty Images; page 217 Ross Kinnaird/Getty Images; page 227 Paul Lakatos/Getty Images

The Editors would like to thank Kit Ballantyne, Charlotte Butterfield, Simon Coppock, Jessica Gliddon, Arsalan Mohammad, Ananda Shakespeare, Anna Wright.

Dubai

timeout.com/dubai

Published by Time Out Guides Ltd, a wholly owned subsidiary of Time Out Group Ltd.
Time Out and the Time Out logo are trademarks of Time Out Group Ltd.

© Time Out Group Ltd 2005
Previous edition 2004

10 9 8 7 6 5 4 3 2

This edition first published in Great Britain in 2005 by Ebury Publishing
Ebury Publishing is a division of The Random House Group Ltd,
20 Vauxhall Bridge Road, London SW1V 2SA

Random House Australia Pty Limited 20 Alfred Street, Milsons Point, Sydney, New South Wales 2061, Australia
Random House New Zealand Limited 18 Poland Road, Glenfield, Auckland 10, New Zealand
Random House South Africa (Pty) Limited Isle of Houghton, Corner Boundary
Road & Carse O'Gowrie, Houghton 2198, South Africa

Random House UK Limited Reg. No. 954009

Distributed in USA by Publishers Group West
1700 Fourth Street, Berkeley, California 94710

Distributed in Canada by Penguin Canada Ltd
10 Alcorn Avenue, Toronto, Ontario, Canada M4V 3B2

For further distribution details, see www.timeout.com

ISBN 1-904978-90-8

A CIP catalogue record for this book is available from the British Library

Colour reprographics by Icon, Crowne House, 56-58 Southwark Street, London SE1 1UN

Printed and bound in Germany by Appl

Papers used by Ebury Publishing are natural, recyclable products made from wood grown in sustainable forests

All rights reserved. No part of this publication may be reproduced, stored in a retrieval system, or transmitted in any
form or by any means, electronic, mechanical, photocopying, recording or otherwise, without prior permission from the
copyright owners.

Contents

Introduction

Dubai's transformation from sleepy trading post to buzzing cosmopolitan city in under half a century is nothing short of remarkable. From a desolate sandpit, the city has become an incredibly popular tourist hotspot, with over five million people visiting in 2004 alone. And there's no sign of the momentum letting up: dozens of luxury hotels and 'super-projects' are planned to rise out of the sand in the near future as the ultra-ambitious authorities chase their goal of attracting ten million visitors a year by 2010.

It's an unlikely success story. It's easy to forget that before 1971, when the UAE achieved its independence, today's modern city was mostly sand. Even a few years ago, Europeans jetting off to Dubai for a timely break in the sun would probably have been greeted by snorts of derision from bemused neighbours. Yet today the city comes top of many holiday wishlists.

The city's meteoric rise has changed local people's lives beyond recognition. Where one or two generations ago Bedouin families eked out a hand-to-mouth existence in the sand, they now live in luxury villas and drive 4x4s. New hotels, shopping malls, residential properties, offshore islands and vast office spaces transform the skyline on a seemingly daily basis. Dubai's wealth is still based in part on oil, but the fresh force of tourism is increasingly driving the new economy.

So what are the attractions? Well, you needn't look far to find them. The coast is crammed with hotels, each with their own private beach offering turquoise waters and perpetually blue skies. OK, so the city's cultural infrastructure may be underdeveloped – there are few historical sights and a dearth of local theatre but if mornings on the beach, afternoons in the malls and evenings in excellent restaurants are what you're after, then Dubai is your place.

For a taste of old Arabia, travel to Fujairah on the east coast, surrounded on one side by the Hajjar mountains and on the other by the Gulf of Oman. With traditional villages stretching along the shoreline, natural wadis snaking through mountains and waterfalls, it feels a million miles away from Dubai.

Many people question whether the city can maintain its breakneck pace of expansion, but the truth is that Dubai Inc. is, for now and the foreseeable future, continuing to defy expectations. Dubai's undoubted achievements and grand schemes have generated such a buzz that winter-breakers who would never have previously considered a Middle Eastern holiday are now flocking to the City of Gold... and leaving singing its praises.

ABOUT THE TIME OUT CITY GUIDES

Time Out Dubai is one of an expanding series of Time Out City Guides, now numbering 45, produced by the people behind London and New York's successful listings magazines. Our guides are written and updated by resident experts, in this case the same team that produces the monthly listings magazine *Time Out Dubai*. We have striven to provide you with all the most up-to-date information you'll need to explore the city, whether you're a local or first-time visitor.

THE LOWDOWN ON THE LISTINGS

Above all, we've tried to make this book as useful as possible. Addresses, phone numbers, transport information, opening times, admission prices, websites and credit card details are all included in our listings. And, as far as possible, we've given details of facilities, services and events, all checked and correct at the time we went to press. However, since owners and managers can change their arrangements at any time, we always advise readers to phone and check opening times and other particulars. While every effort has been made to ensure the accuracy of the information contained in this guide, the publishers cannot accept responsibility for any errors it may contain.

PRICES AND PAYMENT

We have noted whether venues such as shops, hotels and restaurants accept credit cards or not but have only listed the major cards – American Express (**AmEx**), Diners Club (**DC**), MasterCard (**MC**) and Visa (**V**). Many businesses will also accept other cards and travellers' cheques.

The prices we've supplied should be treated simply as guidelines. Fluctuating exchange rates and inflation can cause charges, in shops and restaurants particularly, to change rapidly. If prices vary wildly from those we've quoted, please write and let us know. We aim to give

the best and most up-to-date advice, so we always want to know if you've been badly treated or overcharged.

THE LIE OF THE LAND

The city of Dubai is roughly divided in two halves by the Creek, forming the basic areas of Deira, to the north, and Bur Dubai, to the south. Many Dubaians refer to locations as being Deira-side or Bur Dubai-side respectively. Beyond Bur Dubai lies Jumeirah, the stretch of golden shoreline now home to opulent hotels and wealthy expats. Each of these areas has its own chapter within the Sightseeing section, and each is further subdivided into loosely defined areas such as Karama. In this guide, in chapters not already divided by area, these districts are included within the addresses. Wherever possible, a map reference is provided for places listed.

TELEPHONE NUMBERS

The international code for Dubai is 9714; the first three digits designate the country of the UAE, while the remaining '4' indicates the emirate of Dubai (each of the emirates – and other significant areas – have a corresponding number; international calls to Abu Dhabi, for example, should begin with 9712). Add '0' before this emirate-specific digit to create an area code (eg 04), but this is necessary only when dialling from one emirate to another. All phone numbers are seven digits. For more on telephones, see p259.

ESSENTIAL INFORMATION

For all the practical information you might need for visiting the city – including visa and customs information, emergency phone numbers, useful websites and the local transport network – turn to the **Directory** chapter at the back of this guide. It starts on p246.

MAPS

The maps section at the back of this book, which starts on p273, includes overview maps of Dubai and the UAE, as well as street maps of the city. There is a map of Abu Dhabi on pp214-215. Bookshops such as Book Corner (see p124) and Magrudy's (see p125) also sell fairly useful maps of the UAE, covering major roads and highways.

LET US KNOW WHAT YOU THINK

We hope you enjoy *Time Out Dubai*, and we'd like to know what you think of it. We welcome tips for places that you consider we should include in future editions and take notice of your criticism of our choices. You can email your comments to us at guides@timeout.com.

There is an online version of this book, along with guides to 45 other international cities, at **www.timeout.com**.

WIN PRIZES WORTH
Dhs. **1,500,000**

1st Prize Dhs. **1,000,000**

OR ONE OF 10
FABULOUS PRIZE

Entry tickets only
Dhs. **500**

In Context

History

Pearls, smuggling and trade – the seeds of Dubai's global ambition were sown early.

Witnessing the frenzied construction in 2005 of commercial powerhouses like the Dubai International Financial Centre and Gold & Commodities Exchange, you might be forgiven for thinking that the sleepy emirate had suddenly discovered the notion of trade. In fact, settlements dating from as early as the 5th and 6th centuries AD have been found in Jumeirah – modern Dubai's upmarket suburb – an indication that with the advent of Islam, the Ummayad and then Abbasid Islamic dynasties, Dubai was already established as a stop-off point for business for the caravans serving the Islamic epicentre of the day, Iraq. But it was the lure of pearl-trading that would put Dubai on the international map: Venetian jeweller Gasparo Balbi made the first written reference to 'Dibei' in 1580, during a search of the East to uncover a lucrative source of the precious stones.

SETTLING THE 'PIRATE COAST'

Dubai, strategically located on a ten-kilometre (six-mile) creek, started its remarkable evolution from a small, sleepy fishing village some time during the 18th century. The town was wedged between two powerful clans who held sway over the lower Gulf: the Bani Yas of Liwa Oasis, who had gone on to settle in Abu Dhabi (the modern capital of the UAE), and the Qawasim, based in the northern emirates and parts of modern-day Oman.

The Qawasim's powerful navy had already triggered the ire of the British empire's ruling classes. The area had become known as the 'Pirate Coast', owing to the presence of agile, armed Arab dhows which plundered ships from the British East India Company. The disruption to British commercial interests prompted a show of superior British naval power that brought the ruling families of this part of the Arabian coastline to their knees. Britain, fearing attempts from Russia and France to challenge its dominance of the region, then signed exclusivity treaties with the leaders of the 'Trucial States', offering protection and non-interference in local politics on the condition that leaders didn't even correspond with other global powers. Dubai and the rest of the Trucial Coast were thus brought firmly within the sphere of British influence.

RISE OF THE MAKTOUMS

In 1833, the era of Maktoum family rule began, probably as a result of an internal quarrel among the Bani Yas of Abu Dhabi, when 'violent conduct' on the part of its leader Sheikh Khalifa prompted the emigration of around 800 members of the Al Bu Falasah branch of the tribe. There was little resistance in Dubai to Obaid bin Said and Maktoum bin Butti, who took over the then village-sized settlement along the Creek. With Obaid's death a few years later, Maktoum took the reigns of power, ushering in the bloodline that continues to rule Dubai today.

The Maktoums based themselves in Shindagha, which provided easy access to the sources of Dubai's wealth: the Gulf for pearling and fishing, and the Creek for trade. In 1820 Mohammed bin Hazza, then ruler of Dubai, signed the trading village's first preliminary truce with London, all too aware of the superior manpower of neighbouring Abu Dhabi and the Qawasim, who controlled much of the northern emirates and modern-day Oman.

Under the protection of the British navy, which helped to stamp out the hitherto constant disruptions to trade caused by raids among the various tribes along the Trucial Coast, Dubai concentrated on making money. Like the other city-ports that went on to form the United Arab Emirates, Dubai evolved around its creek, an inlet from the Persian Gulf (known on this side of the water – make no mistake – as the Arabian Gulf). Like the other creeks along the northern coast, Dubai's suffered from sandbars formed at its entrance by strong tides – but at least it was much longer than those of its neighbours. With the seas pacified, the pearling industry thrived and its wares were exported both to India and to Europe. Trade with India and Persia encouraged more foreign traders to open up shop in the city-port, which was already developing a reputation as a town not only open for business, but one that warmly welcomed non-Arabs to take their share.

In the mid 19th century, Shindagha may have been the preserve of around 250 Arab homes, but its neighbouring community Bur Dubai was the base for almost 100 houses belonging to Indian traders. Across the Creek, Deira boasted 1,600 compounds, housing Arabs, Persians and Baluchis from modern-day Pakistan. Deira souk was also thriving, with around 350 shops.

INTO THE 20TH CENTURY

It was the liberal, open-minded Maktoum bin Hashar, whose rule began in 1894, who capitalised most fully on Dubai's emergence as a business and commercial centre. In a foreshadowing of the modern-day obsession with a tax-free environment, Dubai in the late 19th century exempted almost half of the men who worked in the pearling industry from taxes. Although more divers worked the pearl banks in Dubai than in any other Trucial State, the ruler ended up receiving only half the revenue of neighbouring Abu Dhabi.

No matter: Dubai's population exploded. As the pearling industry continued to bring more wealth to the town, Sheikh Maktoum deftly implemented business-oriented policies that attracted traders from Lingah, the Persian port on the other side of the Gulf. Run by the Qawasim family, Lingah had, through the 1800s, acted as the main entry point for goods coming into the Persian Gulf. The Persians, desperate for tax revenue, wrested control of the port from the Arabs at the turn of the century, replacing Arab officials with Persians and then Belgians, whose rigid bureaucracy and high tariffs persuaded merchants to head off in search of cheaper trade environments on the Arab side of the Gulf.

As the 20th century began, Sheikh Maktoum made Dubai a free zone by abolishing commercial taxes. The leader also courted the big players in the Persian warehousing trade, offering important Indian and Persian traders cheap land. With these trade giants drawn into the city, others duly followed. In the first two decades of the 20th century, Dubai's population doubled to around 20,000, rapidly catching up with Sharjah, its larger neighbour and sometime trade rival.

Traders who had reckoned on a temporary sojourn in Dubai settled in the city once it became clear that taxes and regulations in Persia were there to stay. The pearling industry was now booming. Many people emigrated from the Persian district of Bastak, part of the Arab-dominated province of Lars, naming their new-found home on the Creek after their homeland; Bastakia soon became another thriving commercial area.

Sheikh Maktoum's power rose with the fortunes of his city-state. He began the process of building bridges between the rival sheikhdoms of the coast, calling a meeting of the Trucial leaders in 1905, which foreshadowed the creation of the federation, agreed just under 70 years later.

RECESSION HITS THE GULF

After experiencing years of growing prosperity, Dubai and the rest of the Gulf fell prey to the worldwide recession of the 1930s – a warning to its leaders of how the trade-based city's fortunes would ebb and flow with the tide of

Sheikh Zayed, architect of the UAE

The UAE stands as a model of success in a region fraught with misunderstanding, corrupt institutions and political scaremongering. Two factors have thrust the union of the Emirates into the world consciousness: first, the speed with which the country has emerged from humble beginnings as a modern global citizen and, second, the reliance of that transformation on the strength and vision of a single man, Sheikh Zayed bin Sultan Al Nahyan. On his death in November 2004, big business in the capital ground to a halt, the nation's newspapers hit the shelves without colour and even the awesome tourist machine of Dubai temporarily laid its profitable revelry to rest.

Arguably Sheikh Zayed's greatest gift to the UAE was to inspire unprecedented unity, fashioning an economic powerhouse from a land with little industry bar a dying pearl trade and inhabited by fractious tribes. Where once the country boasted only 200,000 denizens, flung far across a desolate landscape, its population today numbers over three million residents from all walks of life, the majority well-educated city-dwellers. Sheikh Zayed presided over visionary investment too: coming to power in Abu Dhabi in August 1966, he made it his personal mission to finance civic projects such as building roads, new hospitals, schools and water resources through the Trucial States Development Office. It was Sheikh Zayed who realised that only by leveraging the financial might of Abu

Dhabi could the fledgling federation be bound together into a state, safeguarding the future of the United Arab Emirates. Today, the UAE's annual per capita GDP of $20,000 is more comparable to the United States of America than to many of its brothers in the Arab world, including Saudi Arabia.

Before the constitution was signed, Sheikh Zayed set off on a 'Unity Tour' through Dubai, Ajman, Umm Al Quwain, across the Hajar mountains to Fujairah and then into Sharjah. In each sheikhdom he promised to make money available to improve the electricity supply, even setting a low unified price by subsidising costs from his personal funds. The tour, and subsequent flow of electrical power, took on incredible significance, effectively symbolising a new national mindset. This sense of unification would be reinforced by many more national tours in the years of Sheikh Zayed's leadership to come.

Perhaps the key to Sheikh Zayed's ability to draw others to his cause was this capacity for (and demonstration of) understanding. He said that the key to leadership is 'retaining perspective'; no mean feat given the conflicting demands of traditional tribal life and a burgeoning modern state. Even at unprecedented highs in the UAE's growth, Sheikh Zayed maintained a hectic schedule, often meeting state ministers and Bedu tribesmen in the same afternoon. The infallible bond with his people was a trait that British explorer Wilfred Thesiger would identify in his

global economic prosperity. The pearling industry first became a victim of weak international demand for luxury goods, then the Japanese discovery of cultured pearls finished off the fragile trade, throwing thousands of pearl fishermen out of work. In the final years of the trade, financiers were taking up to 36 per cent annual interest on the loans that captains needed to fit out boats and hire staff. As the pearling industry declined, traders redoubled their efforts in black market trade with Persia, where tariffs continued to soar higher than in those ports on the Arabian Peninsula.

As the pearling industry fell into terminal decline, Dubaians with Persian connections built up their illicit cargo trade, making up

for the city's lost revenue. But increasing financial inequality between the traders and the newly unemployed Arab pearl divers amplified societal pressures. Further north in Kuwait, yearning for political reform influenced the setting up of a parliament, giving that emirate the most developed political system in the Gulf. Mirroring growing unease within Dubai society, splits within the royal family also emerged. The ruler's cousin, Mani bin Rashid, led a reform movement that challenged the ruling family's autocratic rule. Domestic slaves pressed for their freedom, not because the British decided to enforce its ban on trading slaves, but because their owners could no longer afford them. Indeed, it wasn't until after World War II that the UK

Sheikh Sultan bin Zayed Al Nahyan, had no expectations of rule, but was called on to assume leadership of the Al Nahyan family in 1922. The devoted family man had four sons, Sheikh Shaikhbut, Sheikh Hazza, Sheikh Khalid and Sheikh Zayed (the latter named after his grandfather, for half a century one of the most influential leaders on the Arabian Peninsula). On the evening of 4 August 1925, Sheikh Sultan climbed the stairs to the roof of his palace – where he would make the sunset prayer – when an assailant leapt from a hiding place, produced a gun and shot the ruler in the back. Sheikh Sultan died almost instantly.

Sheikh Zayed, staying at the family home in Al Ain, never saw his father again. And years later, in August 1966, power was devolved once again, this time to Sheikh Zayed from his reclusive elder brother, Shaikhbut. This development was welcomed as much by the international community as by the adoring people of Abu Dhabi.

Sheikh Zayed had the stature of a true international statesman, stature derived from something beyond the oil rigs and malls, the education system and housing, and the host of benefits felt close to home. Ever an ambassador for Arabic values – and those of Islam – he drew praise from leaders and visionaries the world over. In the words of another famous international futurist, former US President Jimmy Carter: 'A man can only express his admiration for Sheikh Zayed and his leadership. Without his skillful policy, the infrastructure and civil progress of the United Arab Emirates could not have been accomplished in such a brief period.'

book Arabian Sands, having met with Sheikh Zayed during a much earlier tour of the Trucial Coast. Thesiger wrote of Zayed: 'he had a great reputation among the Bedu. They liked him for his easy informal ways and his friendliness, and they respected his force of character, his shrewdness and his physical strength. They said admiringly, "Zayed is a Bedu. He knows about camels, can ride like one of us, can shoot, and knows how to fight." '

Sheikh Zayed's popularity would stand him in good stead when events conspired to thrust him into the echelons of power. Zayed's father,

government started to enforce general manumission, having already called a halt to the trading of slaves in the Gulf states a century earlier.

Against this background of social flux, events turned violent in October 1938. Sheikh Saeed and his followers set up their base in Dubai, while his cousins lined up against the ruler from across the Creek in Deira. After mediation from neighbouring sheikhs and the British political agent, or colonial ambassador, in Bahrain, Sheikh Saeed agreed to the setting up of a consultative council or *majlis* ('place of sitting'), heading up a cohort of 15 members, all of whom were proposed by leading members of the community and theoretically had the power to veto his decisions.

Sheikh Saeed was a reluctant leader and only attended the first few sessions, smarting at a system in which his office was allocated an eighth of the national budget, the remaining earmarked for the *majlis'* projects. He still controlled the treasury and was reluctant to open up the state coffers for the council's projects – such as building state-run schools for the general populace, regulating the customs service and its payroll, adjusting tariffs and setting up a council of merchants to oversee the city-state's expanding commerce.

Six months after the council's foundation, Sheikh Saeed ordered some loyal Bedouin to storm and dissolve it. A strong believer in benign autocratic rule, he suspected that some of his royal rivals were exploiting the *majlis* for their own benefit. Though short-lived, Dubai's six-month flirtation with democracy nonetheless had lasting implications at the highest levels. It sounded the political death-knell for Sheikh Saeed: he devolved most of his authority to his son, Sheikh Rashid, who in time initiated many of the ideas of civic development proposed by the council's members.

POST-WAR DEVELOPMENT

Although spared the horrors that Europe and Asia had to endure during World War II, Dubai still struggled over those six tough years. The city's flourishing trade was brought to a near standstill and short supplies of rice and sugar caused hunger to grip parts of the city. The British government – which continued to land seaplanes in the Creek throughout the course of the conflict – imported food supplies that were to be rationed out among the population. But, never ones to miss a money-spinning trick, Dubai's traders began buying up some of these supplies and smuggling them to Iran's black market, where shortages were even more pressing.

> ### 'Trade was brought to a near standstill and hunger gripped parts of the city.'

Malnutrition was an even more urgent issue in the internal desert countryside, still ruled by autonomous nomadic tribes. Here there was almost constant warfare as the tribes fought for rations, and the leaders of Abu Dhabi and Dubai argued over the boundary between their territories. Open warfare between the two distant relatives, as well as among their allied and rival tribes in the hinterland, continued after the end of World War II until the high number of casualties from Bedouin raids and counter-raids prompted the townsfolk and tribesmen to demand peace in 1948. The British authorities took it on themselves to research the boundary dispute and draw the new frontier – London's first direct intervention in the internal politics of the Trucial States.

BLACK GOLD BOOM

While trade remained at the core of Dubai's development, a revolutionary new prospect came the way of the Trucial States in the early 1950s: oil. For a couple of decades, most petroleum engineers had argued that large deposits would be found somewhere along the Trucial Coast. After all, massive reserves had been found across the Middle East and particularly in the Arabian Peninsula

and Persian Gulf. Oil had first been discovered in Iran in 1908; Bahrain had started significant exports in 1936; and on the eve of World War II, neighbouring Saudi Arabia had found the first of its huge reservoirs. Companies began to explore across the region, frantically searching for more deposits of this black gold. Petroleum Development (Trucial Coast), a British-owned company, won the concession to explore for oil across the Trucial States and Oman.

But the war put a stop to the exploration, condemning the emirates to endure more years of poverty and encouraging thousands of locals to emigrate to neighbouring Kuwait and Saudi Arabia to work on the massive post-war oil development projects there. While a consortium formed by British Petroleum and France's Total found commercially viable oil deposits off the shore of Abu Dhabi in 1958, progress was limited in Dubai's onshore and offshore exploration blocks.

EXPANSION BY AIR AND SEA

Nevertheless, Dubai sought to capitalise on the massive trade opportunities brought by the huge equipment and manpower needs of the oil companies. Mortgaging Dubai with a huge $850,000 loan from oil-rich Saudi Arabia and Kuwait – an amount that far outstripped the city's yearly income – Sheikh Rashid had the Creek dredged by an Australian firm. The ambitious project, which allowed vessels of up to 500 tons to anchor there, greatly increased shipping capacity. The emirate's trade levels jumped by 20 per cent, outpacing the growth in neighbouring Sharjah, which had been snapping at Dubai's heels. Gold smuggling, which peaked in 1970, contributed to the new surge in business. The 3.5 per cent import levies imposed on dhows and steamers docking along its wharfage became the emirate's biggest source of revenue after the war, rising to 4.6 per cent in 1955; yet this was still lower than Dubai's regional rivals.

After seeing off Sharjah's maritime trade competition, Sheikh Rashid also took on his neighbour's airport. Sheikh Sultan of Sharjah had started levying taxes on gold arriving at Sharjah airport, which grew commercially on the back of the UK Royal Air Force base there. In 1960, Sheikh Rashid opened an airport, little more than an airstrip made from the hard sand found in Dubai's salt flats, which he expanded a few years later as demand for weekly flights to the UK grew. An open-skies policy allowed any airline to use the airport at a cheaper cost than other airports in the region, triggering its eventual rise as an international passenger and freight hub.

Sibling rivalry

Questioning the unity of purpose among the country's seven emirates is something of a taboo in the UAE. However, historians privately recount stories of arguments between the leaders of all the emirates, especially the two powerhouses, oil-rich Abu Dhabi and commerce-friendly Dubai. Go back 50 years, and the two emirates were locked in all-out war, with Bedouin allies of the two leaders carrying out raids on their opponents' territory over three bloody years. Rivalries have cooled since the leaders of the seven Trucial States yoked themselves under one flag in the early 1970s. But even in those early days of unity, Dubai's Sheikh Rashid – while committed to the union – fought to give his emirate as much autonomy as possible.

Abu Dhabi's superior size and population translated into greater political power. The discovery of huge oil reserves in Abu Dhabi gave Sheikh Zayed's emirate even more financial clout, as well as military muscle. When the UAE was formed, Abu Dhabi earned ten times more money from its oil revenues than Dubai, whose oil production has fallen to an estimated 150,000 barrels a day. Meanwhile, Abu Dhabi is the world's fourth largest oil exporter – and also earns more than $20 billion a year interest on its huge investments in Western financial markets. The capital controls perhaps 90 per cent of the UAE's national wealth.

The federal government developed around Abu Dhabi's financial largesse. This helped the union's development, but sparked fears in Dubai and other poorer emirates, who were concerned that Abu Dhabi's bureaucrats, keen to control the disbursement of their funds, would whittle away at the emirates' close-knit tribal roots. In 1979, the UAE was in crisis, as Abu Dhabi pushed for more centralised authority than the other emirates would accept. The crisis abated as Sheikh Rashid accepted the role of Prime Minister of the UAE, while securing the rights of individual rulers to continue developing their fiefdoms along their own lines.

The air of international turmoil in the 1980s, as the Iran-Iraq War loomed large over the region, glued the emirates together. With Islamic Revolution boiling in Iran and civil shipping under attack in their own backyard, the seven emirates' petty squabbles paled

into insignificance. Abu Dhabi, as generous as ever, continued to fund welfare systems for the entire country, especially the resource-starved northern emirates. Dubai got on with being Dubai: attracting businesses and allowing its anything-goes attitude to flourish.

Today Abu Dhabi and Dubai are brothers with different characters. Many Abu Dhabians, more restrained and conservative than go-getting Dubaians, are frustrated at the international attention their precocious neighbour receives – but they're also aware that the UAE is all the better for it. Dubai's attitude may not always meet with approval from traditionalists in the capital, but nobody is denying that the city's dynamic economy has also brought regional recognition, as well as offering a blueprint for what Abu Dhabi might achieve as its oil resources dwindle.

Dubai, in turn, has benefited greatly from Abu Dhabi's generosity. The meeting of minds between Sheikhs Zayed and Rashid has been extended to their sons, Mohammed and Khalifa. Abu Dhabi only very recently stopped giving Dubai around 100,000 barrels of oil a day – almost doubling the smaller emirate's production. And if Dubai overextends itself, it can always fall back on its rich cousin: when in 1997 its autonomous armed forces became too much of a financial burden, Sheikh Mohammed just turned them over to the federal government.

Abu Dhabi.

Before then, however, Dubai too struck black gold. In 1966, oil was discovered in an offshore field; exports began three years later. The prospect of imminent oil exports, along with severe overcrowding of the Creek and the commercial centres around it, persuaded the government in 1967 to start building a $40 million seaport. Known as Port Rashid, it eventually opened in 1972 and expanded again in 1978.

Trade and oil combined to give economic growth a massive boost. The petrodollar boom had finally arrived in Dubai, even though its oil reserves and revenue were as minnows in comparison with its oil-rich neighbour Abu Dhabi. The population skyrocketed in response, as migrant labour poured into the city to extract the oil and build and maintain the public services that Sheikh Rashid – remembering the demands of the reform movement when he was being groomed for power – made sure became a high priority for his government. In 1967, as the government planned Sheikh Rashid port, the population stood at 59,000. Five years later, in 1973, the city had doubled in size; by the end of the booming 1970s, 250,000 people lived in Dubai.

FOUNDING OF THE NATION

In 1967, Britain decided that its time in the Middle East was over. London announced its intention to withdraw from colonial outposts east of Suez, giving the Trucial States a departure date of 1971. Unlike in

Go figure

The numbers behind the city...

21.7 million Number of passengers who passed through Dubai Airport in 2004.
40 million Number of passengers expected to pass through in 2010.
2,640 feet (800 metres) Proposed height of the Burj Dubai, the world's tallest building, scheduled to open in 2008.
24°C (75°F) Average January temperature.
41°C (106°F) Average July temperature.
2 Number of presidents of the UAE since its founding in 1971.
690,000 Population of Dubai in 1995.
1,040,000 Population of Dubai in 2004.
1,610,000 Predicted population of Dubai in 2008.
60 Percentage of the population that is Indian, Pakistani and Filipino.
19 Percentage of the population that is Emirati.

Aden, in southern Yemen, where years of insurgency showed a stark desire to see off the imperialists, the leaders of Dubai and the other Trucial States felt almost abandoned by the hastiness of the British retreat. The Conservative opposition of the day also criticised the Labour government's decision to withdraw, arguing that British business exposure across the Gulf amounted to much more than the £16 million annual cost of keeping British forces in the area, and that withdrawal would merely encourage new imperialists, such as the Soviet Union, to extend their influence over a strategic region of vital importance owing to its oil deposits.

Some Trucial leaders hoped that the Conservative government, once it gained power, would reverse the decision to withdraw. But it wasn't to be. Sheikh Zayed of Abu Dhabi and Sheikh Rashid of Dubai met at the frontier between their two sheikhdoms and agreed to form a federation that would jointly decide foreign, defence and social policy. Encouraged by the British, the rulers of the Trucial States – Abu Dhabi, Dubai, Sharjah, Ajman, Umm al-Quwain, Ras al-Khaimah and Fujairah – met in Dubai with the leaders of Bahrain and Qatar in February 1968 to discuss forming a joint federation. The leaders came up with an agreement expressing their intention to form a nine-strong federation, which met with broad regional approval, except from Iran, the Shi'a-led state that had a territorial claim on the majority Shi'a island of Bahrain.

The nine leaders of these islands, city-states and desert regions met on several occasions in the run-up to independence in 1971, discussing models of federation. Differences plagued the meetings, with Bahrain's larger, better-educated population suspicious of a federation in which political power would be spread evenly across the nine emirates, rather than being based on the size of the population of each emirate. Bahrain, having ended border disputes with Iran, told the other prospective federation members that it would retain its independence, yoking its interests to its rich neighbour, Saudi Arabia. Qatar chose the same path.

In July 1971, with the British withdrawal approaching, the seven Trucial leaders met and hammered out a federal document. Six of them, excluding Ras al-Khaimah, signed the provisional constitution, which was used to proclaim a federation in November 1971. Ras al-Khaimah had felt undervalued in the negotiations and wanted to focus on three Gulf islands that Iran had occupied once the British forces left the area. But once the other

Safe harbour: a ship docks at **Jebel Ali**.

emirates agreed to take on the issue of Abu Musa and the Greater and Lesser Tunb islands, it too acceded to the federation in February 1972. The United Arab Emirates was born, led by Abu Dhabi owing to its disproportionate financial contribution to the federal budget, but with significant autonomy for all emirates in local affairs. Sheikh Zayed Al Nahyan became the country's first president; Sheikh Rashid – who through the 1970s pressed for more autonomy for his freewheeling emirate – acted as Zayed's vice president and prime minister (*see p15* **Sibling rivalry**).

THE PETRODOLLAR BOOM
The 1970s were a decade of excess across the Gulf. Petrodollars flowed into the area as the world's seemingly unquenchable appetite for oil lapped up the region's exports. Oil revenues spiralled ever higher during the price shock of 1973 and 1974, triggered by the Arab oil-producing states' boycott of nations supporting Israel in the third Arab-Israeli conflict. Dubai has never had the oil revenues that its rich cousin Abu Dhabi enjoys (Dubai's annual oil income stood at $3 billion by 1980, compared with Abu Dhabi's $15 billion), but these revenues went a long way towards helping Dubai to develop the infrastructure it needed to realise fully the potential of its core economic activities – trade and commerce.

BUILDING FREE ZONES
Maintaining its maritime heritage, Dubai first underwent major expansion beyond the Creek with the completion of Port Rashid in 1973. On completion, the port had 16 berths for ocean-going vessels, rising to 35 after initial success allowed for further development. Port Rashid itself had been regarded as overly ambitious, so when Sheikh Rashid announced

the construction of a new port in Jebel Ali, 40 kilometres (25 miles) along the coast towards Abu Dhabi from the centre of Dubai, the sceptics questioned the ruler's judgement. Not only was the port a speedy success, but the soaring oil prices after the Arab boycott also eased the ruler's repayment schedule.

> **'Petrodollars flowed into the area as the world's seemingly unquenchable appetite for oil lapped up the region's exports.'**

By 1976, flush with petrodollars, Dubai ploughed $2.5 billion into building the 66-berth Jebel Ali Port, the world's largest man-made harbour. Completed in 1983, Jebel Ali Port seemed to be Dubai's first white elephant, the ambitiousness of the project even worrying some of Sheikh Rashid's closest advisers. The massive port, along with Jebel Ali Hotel, stood empty in vast expanses of desert. But by 1985, spurred on by the construction of Jebel Ali Free Zone, business at the port boomed. The free zone was an idea borrowed from Sheikh Rashid's grandfather Sheikh Hasher, who'd lured Persian traders to Dubai at the beginning of the century with similar incentives. The port's fortunes were also helped by the bloody, extended war between Saddam Hussein's Iraq and the Islamic republic of Iran, which disrupted shipping as both sides started to attack tankers and oil facilities. With insurance rates sky-high in the northern Gulf, shippers looked for an alternative in the lower Gulf, turning to Jebel Ali.

DUBAI'S INDUSTRIAL REVOLUTION

Dubai, founded as a trade hub, used growing oil revenues to diversify its economic base, developing heavy industry. With abundant oil and gas resources, the emirates had a competitive advantage in large-scale industrial projects that require vast amounts of energy. Dubai's first great industrial project took the form of Dubai Dry Dock, constructed in 1973 as a ship repair yard, and passed by Sheikh Rashid on to his third son and Dubai's current de facto ruler, Sheikh Mohammed. This venture, too, benefited from the outbreak of maritime war between Iran and Iraq, serving the steady stream of tanker war victims. Two years later, Dubai set up Dubai Aluminium Co, or Dubal, with an initial investment of $1.4 billion, which took advantage of cheap oil to create one of the world's most profitable smelters. As well as industrial projects, the oil wealth of the 1970s brought modern infrastructure. By the end of the decade, a further bridge and a tunnel had been added to the original Maktoum Bridge linking Bur Dubai with Deira.

As Dubai grew from the 1950s on, so did the number of roads, hospitals and schools. The police force, set up in 1956 under the command of British officers, came under local control in 1975. Immigrants started their own schools, complementing the state-run schools that catered for locals and expatriate Arabs.

If the 1970s meant industrial development, the 1980s saw the arrival of big-time commerce. Strong global demand for oil meant that the soaring revenues were enjoyed by oil-producing countries, Dubai continued to diversify. The World Trade Centre, opened in 1979, attracted some of the world's biggest companies to set up local or regional headquarters in Dubai. Once again, cynics whispered that the centre, today dwarfed by the high-rises of Sheikh Zayed Road, was too far from the central commercial district in Deira. But little did it matter, as foreign companies set up shop in a land free of bureaucracy, boasting political stability and liberal social mores; the economy further diversified, and the city kept booming – through the 1980s, Dubai's population doubled to over half a million people.

THE AGE OF TOURISM

In the 1970s, businessmen travelling to Dubai were hard-pushed to find a single decent hotel. Sheikh Rashid even built a personal guesthouse for the trailblazing corporates who visited in the early days. By 1975, the InterContinental (see p45) had opened on the Deira side of the Creek, but was never able to meet the demand created by the growing hordes of travellers touching down at the new airport – it was not unknown for executives to bunk up together in the InterContinental's rooms.

How times change. In the 1990s, after the death of Sheikh Rashid, Dubai busily reinvented itself as a tourist destination. There were 42 hotels in 1985, jumping to 272 by 2002. The establishment in 1985 of Emirates, the Dubai-based international airline, helped the tourism sector flourish, with the airline encouraging passengers to stop over en route to Asia, Africa or Europe. With initial start-up capital of $10 million, the airline – managed by British expats – rapidly expanded, even staying profitable through the global travel slump following 9/11.

With its oil reserves running out, Dubai has turned increasingly to tourism. International events such as the Dubai World Cup horse race and desert rally, as well as golf, tennis and rugby tournaments, fuelled the boom. But Dubai's real love affair is with shopping. Launched in 1996, the Dubai Shopping Festival (see p145) attracted a million or so visitors that year, rising to 2.6 million in 2004, spending a cool $2.5 billion during their visit. A second shopping festival, Dubai Summer Surprises (see p149), was launched in 1998, attracting Gulf visitors who are used to the soaring summer temperatures that put off many Western tourists. Combined with sea, sun and liberal attitudes to entertainment, annual tourist numbers have now reached around five million, five times the city's resident population.

FROM BLACK GOLD TO WHITE COLLAR

Having done trade, commerce and industry, Dubai – punchdrunk on the MBA jargon of its foreign-educated apparatchik hordes – adopted the cluster concept. By zoning similar service-related industries together, say the business gurus, services are sourced from one's neighbours, improving networking potential and reducing costs. Dubai Internet City (DIC), announced in 1999, was the first such attempt to attract more professionals to the emirate. The venture was tailor-made to attract high-tech firms, offering tax-free 100 per cent ownership (outside free zones businesses need a local partner). DIC has since grown rapidly, attracting more than 500 companies by 2003 – although some critics say it's little more than a sales park, with few products actually created on-site. Now Dubai International Financial Centre (DIFC), open for business since early 2005 and set to expand massively, has finally given the city a financial centre that can rival New York and London. The age of pearls and black gold is set to give way to international investment and financial high-flyers.

Dubai Today

No rest for the hungry: Dubai is building leasehold property, iconic landmarks and a financial centre to rival Hong Kong.

Dubai is an enigma, a city that boasts a wealth of contradictions as well as great cultural diversity. It is an emirate where the local population is dwarfed by the number of expatriates from India, Pakistan and other Arab states. The Emiratis are conservative Muslims, and yet the city has adopted a live-and-let-live attitude to all religions and social groups. While lacking deep-rooted public culture or heritage and suffering overpowering heat and humidity for a third of the year, the city has still managed to turn itself into a popular tourist destination. And even though the United Arab Emirates (through Abu Dhabi) is one of the world's most oil-rich states, Dubai – 'blessed' with a lack of natural resources – is hailed as a model of economic development in the Middle East, which ranks bottom in the world, apart from Africa, in terms of wealth and human development.

HEAVYWEIGHT AMBITIONS

Dubai is no more than a small city-state, but its reputation has grown beyond those of the six more parochial neighbouring emirates that make up the United Arab Emirates, thanks largely to its merciless self-promotion. Be it Bill Clinton, the English football team or C-list celebrities from the British entertainment circuit, Dubai has an eye for enticing those who can attract the media's attention to what began life as a sleepy little trading port perched on the edge of a desert backwater.

True, it's got a lot to be proud of. While its neighbours face rising levels of unemployment and economic uncertainty, Dubai continues to grow, attracting foreign workers from all over the world. Throughout the expat explosion, the government has looked after locals by tilting business in their favour, offering them perks such as free land and cheap loans. Underpinning its relentless self-promotion is the city's 'can-do' culture, where projects are realised on time, no matter how ambitious they may be.

Heads of government are never subjected to the trial of re-election by the population. Not that it matters, as there are few rulers in the Middle East that enjoy such widespread support among their own people. Here, the autocratic nature of government – which in the West is regarded as detrimental to economic development – has been central to the UAE's success. Sheikh Zayed, leader of Abu Dhabi and the federation of seven emirates, continues to be idolised by almost every Emirati national, even after his death in November 2004 (*see p8* **Sheikh Zayed, architect of the UAE**). His charitable generosity, and the financial might of his vast oil and investment incomes, effectively bankrolled the foundation of the UAE and much of its development.

> ### 'Dubai, as it has been for a century, is a celebration of moneymaking.'

Alongside the late Sheikh Zayed, Dubai residents have anointed Sheikh Rashid, who over more than 50 years of rule strengthened the foundations on which the city's affluence was built. Today similar reverence is shown to his third son and the de facto leader of Dubai, Sheikh Mohammed (*see below*), who has accelerated Dubai's development over the past decade and enhanced its international standing.

Dubai, as it has been for just over a century, is a celebration of moneymaking. Like a Middle Eastern version of Hong Kong, it has grabbed the position of regional trade, commercial and financial hub. On the outskirts of the troubled Middle East – it boasts Iran and Saudi Arabia as neighbours – Dubai has emerged as an oasis of stability. Free of political torment, it's a place where individuals and businesses feel comfortable to come and profit, either through hard graft in the city's thriving services sector or by exploiting opportunities in this oil- and cash-rich region. Some of Dubai's biggest names in business, such as the Al Futtaim family, were originally Iranian, arriving in the 19th century to set up commercial enterprises. Other families, such as the Jashanmals from India, have become part of local society after creating huge retail empires here. These captains of industry lie second only to the Royal Family in Dubai's social hierarchy.

Sheikh Mohammed, Crown Prince

Equestrian, fighter pilot, poet and, above all, businessman, Sheikh Mohammed (*pictured*) is the leading force behind Dubai's lightning-paced modern-day development. Acting as chief executive of the huge holding company that is the Dubai government, the Crown Prince is behind the strategic and day-to-day running of the emirate. His elder brother Sheikh Maktoum retains the title of ruler but this shy, self-effacing man has, since their father's death in 1990, been happier leading a private life. Conversely, Sheikh Mohammed's boundless energy and unmistakable charisma have propelled him into this definitive role, formalised in 1995 when he was named Crown Prince – or heir apparent – by his brother. Sheikh Mohammed learned the trade of statecraft under the watchful eyes of first his famous grandfather, Sheikh Saeed, and then his much-adored and highly influential father, Sheikh Rashid, who as early as the 1960s was grooming his third son for power.

In his role as UAE defence minister, Sheikh Mohammed had to deal with international crises such as the Arab-Israeli war of 1973 and terrorist hijackings at Dubai airport. Then, as his father's health faltered in the 1980s, he played a greater part in fostering Dubai's businesses and pro-business image. Most notably, this included looking after the oil industry, already in terminal decline, and setting up Dubai's airline, Emirates.

Today, 'Sheikh Mo' (as he's affectionately nicknamed by most expats) continues to develop and update the liberal policies of his Maktoum forefathers. Almost every month he announces a new scheme aimed at raising the emirate's business profile: 'Dubai doesn't need investors, investors need Dubai,' he proclaimed recently. To achieve this goal, he has surrounded himself with the emirate's sharpest minds, drawing on the legions of nationals who have returned with a Western education and business experience.

Yet while they advise, it is Dubai's clear lines of executive power, all of which end with Sheikh Mohammed, that have fostered the emirate's legendarily clear-cut decision-making. A military man, trained in the arts of war by the British Army, Sheikh Mohammed knows the benefits of establishing clear lines of command, and this allows Dubai to follow through its plans with enviable efficiency. Senior employees across the whole spectrum of government say that just one phone call to 'His Highness' can put a plan into action.

EAST MEETS WEST

Tens of thousands of workers come streaming into the city every year, fuelling an ongoing construction boom that has kept Dubai's skyline in a state of constant flux. Many of the arrivals are Western (especially British) professionals who have escaped the prying eyes and greedy hands of the European taxman. Arabs from Lebanon, Syria and Palestine also fill many professional and clerical positions; they come to Dubai seeking work and fleeing the inefficient and corrupt bureaucracies of their homelands. Increasingly, Arabs living in the West are coming to work in Dubai, where they find the professional standards of the West combined with the home comforts of the Arab world. Indian and Pakistani labourers and taxi drivers, although paid peanuts compared to everyone else in Dubai, will often return to their home villages with enough money to set up a business. Filipinas work as maids and shopkeepers, and make the best karaoke and band singers in Dubai. Chinese women are also taking up more and

more positions in the hospitality industry, be it in conditions of five-star opulence or of two-star seediness.

Asian migrant workers make up the vast majority of residents and form the city's backbone. Indian and Pakistani labourers toil day and night, throughout the searing heat of the summer, building, maintaining and cleaning the city. Without their labour, or that of the tens of thousands of east Asians employed in the services and hospitality industries, Dubai wouldn't be what it is today. Workers descend on Dubai every year, eking out a poor wage that goes far in their homelands. The unshrinking stream of labour is used to justify the poor conditions in which they work and live, not to mention their indentured status, with their sponsors or employers often holding their passports and dictating when the worker can spend time back home. International human rights organisations criticise the government about these conditions, but the only charge Dubai has reacted to so far is the use of children as camel jockeys – the practice is now banned.

With so much power vested in a single pair of hands, the cult of personality runs deep. The sheikh's daily schedule receives in-depth, adoring coverage from a fawning press; his presence at public gatherings commands reverence. But Sheikh Mohammed has the common touch too: he drives himself around in a white Mercedes 4x4 (licence plate #1, of course); the Noodle House (*see p87*) in the Emirates Towers is one of the crown prince's frequent lunch spots thanks to its no-nonsense attitude and speedy service; and when Palestinian expats gathered to

protest (illegally) against Israeli abuses in their homeland, the Sheikh arrived to show his support.

Equestrianism is both a hobby and a business for Sheikh Mohammed, who says the love of horses runs through his veins. Raised on a diet of falconry and horse riding, the Crown Prince's personal sporting forte is the marathon of the equestrian world, the punishing discipline of endurance riding, in which he has led UAE teams to many victories in international competition. His fascination with horse racing, sparked as a young student in the UK, almost inevitably mutated into business. Set up in the mid 1990s, the royal family's stable, Godolphin (*see p185* **Colt from the blue**), has quickly emerged as one of the world's top three equine operations, rivalled only by the Aga Khan and Ireland's Coolmore. The company's Dubai stables train their horses through the Gulf's pleasant winter months, before dispersing the steeds across the world for the spring racing season.

The sycophancy surrounding Sheikh Mohammed may seem excessive to Western visitors brought up to regard politicians with deep cynicism, but in a region of under-achieving leaders, the never-ending adulation of Dubai's 'Big Man' is for once well placed.

UAE timeline

1971

Six Trucial States – **Abu Dhabi**, **Dubai**, **Sharjah**, **Umm al-Quwain**, **Ajman** and **Fujairah** – finalise a constitution for the country. The UK ends its treaty with the area and the UAE becomes an independent country. **Sheikh Zayed bin Sultan Al Nahyan** becomes the nation's first president. An early diplomatic incident is sparked when Iran occupies the islands of Greater Tunb, Lesser Tunb and Abu Musa.

1972

Ras al-Khaimah joins the UAE and the 40-member consultative **Federal National Council** is inaugurated.

1981

The UAE becomes a founder member of the **GCC** (Gulf Co-operation Council), holding its first summit in Abu Dhabi.

1980s

The UAE supports Iraq in its war with Iran, all the while maintaining diplomatic relations with both countries.

1990

Sheikh Rashid bin Saeed Al Maktoum dies, and Sheikh Maktoum becomes ruler of Dubai and Vice-President and Prime Minister of the UAE.

1992

Iran sparks outrage in the UAE when it demands that visitors to the disputed **Greater Tunb**, **Lesser Tunb** and **Abu Musa** islands must buy Iranian visas.

1991

The **Bank of Credit and Commerce International** (BCCI), of which Abu Dhabi owns 77.4 per cent, collapses in spectacular fashion. The ruling family of Abu Dhabi is faced with massive claims from investors around the globe. They sue BCCI's executives for billions of dollars worth of damages: an Abu Dhabi court sentences 11 of them to imprisonment. In Kuwait, the UAE's armed forces joined the allies in repulsing Saddam Hussein's invasion force.

1996

Tensions mount yet further when Iran builds a power station and airport on the islands.

1999

In a public show of unity between the two emirates, Dubai's Crown Prince marries a member of Abu Dhabi's royal family. In Dubai the **Burj Al Arab** is opened to great acclaim.

1998

The bottom falls out of the oil market: prices fall 35 per cent in the first quarter of the year, slashing government income. A barge breaks up off the coast, spilling 4,000 tons of oil on to the nation's beaches.

2005

The **Mall of the Emirates** (see p120) opens. Easily the biggest mall in the region, it has the Middle East's first indoor ski slope.

2004

Sheikh Zayed bin Sultan Al Nahyan dies (see p12 **Sheikh Zayed, architect of the UAE**). Sheikh Khalifa, his oldest son, succeeds him.

Still, tree-hugging liberals are rare in Dubai. Generations of subcontinental and Arab expats are more than content to bring up their families here. Many of these long-term residents are taking advantage of the newly offered opportunity to buy property in designated areas, such as the iconic Palm Islands (*see p26* **The silly isles**) or the real-estate developments by local firm Emaar, which is building Burj Dubai, the world's tallest building (*see p31* **Coming attractions**). Furnished with a permanent residency visa, the property buyer cuts out rent, an expat's main living cost. Confusion about the legalities of non-residential purchases hasn't prevented a boom in the property market, with many expats shrugging off issues such as the lack of federal laws and land title. Not only are the new leasehold laws proving popular with expats, but non-resident foreigners are also taking interest in the potential for holiday homes. Indeed, a resale market is now emerging in Dubai, whereby UAE-based speculators snap up waterfront property with the sole intention of selling on the dream to international customers.

A LOCAL TOWN FOR LOCAL PEOPLE

Dubai has arrived on the global map by creating opportunities for foreigners, but it also looks after its own. The government has developed a successful social pact with its people that keeps the emirate safe and stable. Those born in Dubai to Arabs who've lived here for more than a few generations – known as the locals, or nationals – still own this town. Everyone else is a resident. Emirati family businesses form a major part of the economy, having won lucrative agency agreements with importers, such as car and electronics manufacturers. Locals, who until very recently were the only residents who could own property, make oodles of cash by renting it out. Others, for a fee, will 'sponsor' foreigners to stay and work in the emirate; most act as silent business partners, allowing a foreign company to set up shop in a town where, by law, locals have to hold the majority stake in a company. The opening up of land ownership to foreigners is one of the few moves that has prompted local grumbles in recent years. Locals fear that taking away one source of the privileges that have served them so well during Dubai's boom years will erode their status (and income). But landlords fearing tumbling rents will get short shrift from most expats. Despite the explosion in real estate, rents are on the rise in the city, as demand outstrips supply; annual hikes of Dhs10,000 in 2005 have not been uncommon.

These grumbles, the government hopes, will be warded off by political reforms planned over the next few years. In the old days, locals' concerns could be aired at the ruler's *majlis*. After the 2003 war in Iraq, the government decided to form community councils with elected members. The move was similar to reforms now taking place across the largely autocratic Gulf region, amid rising domestic and international calls for a broadening of the decision-making process. But the top-down nature of politics and business in Dubai is not changing particularly quickly, despite a belief in transparency – echoing the clamour for political reform around 70 years ago – that underpins Dubai's continuing bid to become a world city playing by global rules.

CHASING GLOBAL RECOGNITION

Tourism continues to play a major role in Dubai's bid for global domination. In all its hot, sweaty modernity, the emirate may seem a curious tourist destination, but it's even nipping at the heels of established regional attractions like Egypt. The rapid growth of Dubai-based carrier Emirates Airline has certainly helped the town to attract tourists. The award-winning airline has put Dubai on the holiday map by encouraging passengers en route to Asia or Europe to stop over in the emirate. The construction of new iconic tourist traps continues too, the latest being the Madinat Jumeirah complex (*see p120*), an Arabian souk hosting bars, restaurants and retail outlets, flanked by two beautiful hotels and surrounded by meandering waterways. Water parks, beach life and desert safaris combine with the city's ubiquitous shopping and entertainment options to encourage more and more Europeans to make the six-plus hour trip to Dubai.

As Dubai expands its airport, airline and hotel infrastructure, more tourists are expected to descend on the go-getting emirate, before making their return journey clutching stuffed camels and designer apparel. In anticipation of these hordes, the $4 billion project, Dubailand, has begun in earnest. Destined to be the region's largest tourism and leisure destination, the massive development will house 45 separate 'worlds', from a covered eco-tourism zone to indoor ski slopes, the world's largest mall, space-age hotels and dinosaur parks (*see p31* **Coming attractions**). The scale of its vision is matched only by its ambition to attract still more visitors to Dubai: the government wants its current crop of five million tourists to grow to 15 million by the end of this decade.

A MODEL FOR THE 21ST CENTURY

But tourism can only go so far in securing Dubai's future. Sheikh Mohammed, who wants to double the emirate's population by the end of the decade, sees expanding knowledge-based industries as the means of attracting more residents and providing desirable jobs for the local population. The rapid rise of media and internet clusters have encouraged the modern breed of city planners, who help along Sheikh Mohammed's ambitious and somewhat futuristic vision of the city. Such government-sponsored organisations as the curiously named Knowledge Village are working to attract more service-based companies into the rapidly evolving southern end of Dubai, between Umm Suqeim and Jebel Ali port.

> ### 'Dubai's toleration of drinks and parties is enough to make expats forget that they are living under Islam.'

Dubai is also making a serious assault on the world of international finance. The Arab Gulf region has billions of dollars invested in Western and Asian financial markets and Dubai International Financial Centre, the city's latest free-zone initiative, has begun the fight to lure back that capital and keep more from flowing out of the region. By offering asset management to the rich and a stock market in which anyone can invest, DIFC's ambitious aim is to become the region's answer to New York, London and Hong Kong. Battling against Dubai's less-than-perfect reputation in terms of regulating money flows, DIFC has hired senior regulators from around the world to ease investors' concerns about the town's chequered history of financial probity.

Of course, Dubai can plan it all it wants, but it's the combination of location and attitude that will probably secure its ongoing success. The city has made a mint from the troubles that plague the Middle East and the Persian (or, in Dubai, the Arabian) Gulf region – from Persian taxation in the 19th century, via the eight-year Iran–Iraq war in the 1980s and the invasion of Kuwait by Iraq in 1990, to the reconstruction of Iraq following the ousting of Saddam Hussein by the US-led coalition. The headlines about the plight of Iraq may have long since slowed to a trickle, but Dubai still serves as an R&R stop for Western military forces patrolling the Gulf, and local companies are selling their services to the massive reconstruction effort.

Amid this regional turbulence, Dubai offers a pro-business environment, political stability and, perhaps more importantly, hassle-free living. The phones are connected quickly and bills are easy to pay. Theft and crime against the person are rare; indeed, driving is the only dangerous activity in the emirate. And Dubaians' toleration of drinks and parties is more than enough to make expats forget that they are living in the cradle of Islam.

From empty desert, the city's new centre rises at **Dubai Marina**.

The **Emirates Towers**
dominate the Dubai skyline.

Architecture

The city's quest for audacious new buildings continues.

Dubai's hunger for vast architectural landmarks – consider the emirate's affection for the Burj Al Arab and Emirates Towers – is symptomatic of a nascent nation intent on displaying its ambition, and riches, to the rest of the world. It seems today's blueprints for elaborate malls and towering city blocks must scale record-breaking heights or offer unprecedented floorspace to win governmental approval. Gone are the days of the sleepy pearl-diving town. Instead, billboards proclaim the imminent construction of Dubai's next big idea with a mind-boggling sense of self-imposed urgency.

Nostalgics should bear in mind the fact that Dubai's architectural history is extraordinarily compressed: wind tower houses replaced palm-frond shelters in the early 20th century; following the oil boom, these made way for concrete apartment blocks, which in turn were replaced by postmodernist skyscrapers. Only now is a penchant for Arabian chic seeing architects reincorporate wind towers into their designs for 'grand boutique' hotels.

The first exports of oil began to be made from the UAE in the early 1960s and Dubai set about dragging itself into the 20th century

with almost religious zeal. The new mantra was 'out with the old, in with the new' and, coupled with an urgent need for mass housing, this resulted in the razing of most of Dubai's old town and the rapid rise of towers and cheap apartment blocks. It wasn't until the 1990s that the government turned its attention to preserving and restoring what was left of the old town. Even then, for many historians, it was too little, too late. Critics maintain that only Oman offers true examples of traditional Gulf architecture, but there are atmospheric pockets of authenticity left in early 21st-century Dubai.

However, speak of architecture and most Dubaians will think of the contemporary. The audacious Burj Al Arab hotel became an instant icon on its completion in 2000 and started Dubai's passion for breaking height records; the sleek lines of Emirates Towers are widely admired, as are Carlos Ott's National Bank of Dubai and the Hilton Dubai Creek. Meanwhile, the drawing boards of international architects are stacked with plans for future Dubai cities-within-cities: the world's tallest tower and first underwater hotel are scheduled for completion by 2007. Not surprisingly, the debate among local architects still rages as to how to develop a local architectural language that references the past as well as Dubai's high-rise, gleaming future.

EARLY ARCHITECTURE

It was the Bani Yas tribe – ancestors of the Bedouin – who first set up camp in the deserts and mountains of Abu Dhabi and Dubai, splitting their time between animal hair and skin tents, ideal for winter wandering, and *arish* or *barasti* (palm-frond shelters) for summer months spent on date plantations. *Barasti* were also popular among fishermen, pearlers and traders.

Coastal areas featured blocky homes built from bricks of fossilised coral, bonded with *sarooj* (a blend of Iranian red clay and manure, dried and baked in a kiln), or a lime mixture derived from seashells and plastered with chalk and water paste. Large courtyard houses built of *farush* (beach rock) and covered with lime plaster have been excavated in Jumeirah and dated back to the second century of the Islamic era (ninth century AD). When a branch of the Bani Yas – the Maktoums – settled by the Creek in the early 1800s, more permanent homes were built of *guss* (mud blocks) and roofed with palm fronds. These materials were known for keeping their cool, in sharp contrast to the steel and glass widely used today.

Besides ventilation and what is known today as 'intelligent building', the houses prioritised family privacy, as is typical in traditional compounds throughout the Arab world. Most rooms opened on to an airy central courtyard restricted to use only by the family, and male guests were entertained in a separate *majlis* (meeting room). In many new villas the *majlis* is in the main house, but the traditional layout will be familiar nonetheless to those living in 'old' villas built in the 1970s and 1980s.

Public buildings were mostly limited to stone forts, which doubled up as seats of government, and **mosques** (*see p63* **Mosque**

The silly isles

In the marketing-savvy noughties, it seems the odd TV campaign or guerrilla stunt just won't get the job done any more. Instead, when it comes to marketing cities, purpose-built landmarks are the only way to own a slice of the modern tourist's mind. And the bigger, bolder and more bewildering the development, the better. That, at least, is the philosophy in Dubai, whose government will paint upon the blank canvas of the desert such tourist lures as: **Hydropolis**, the world's first underwater hotel; **Dubailand**, a series of theme parks bigger than the city itself; and **The World**, a collection of islands resembling the various nations of the world.

Dubai's earliest offshore icon was **Palm Island** (*pictured*), built off the coast by Al Nakheel Properties, a local construction giant partly owned by the government. While the 'island' increased the city's shoreline by 120km (74 miles), it was only the first of three such creations. Plans to flank the original Palm (duly dubbed Palm Jumeirah) with two more islands were soon proposed: first Palm Jebel Ali and then Palm Deira, announced at the end of 2004. The latter will be built in waters 6m (20ft) deep, with foundations reaching to 22m (72ft) below sea level. The island will measure 14km (nine miles) in length from the landward side to the tip of a crescent that's 8.5km (five miles) wide. At 80 sq km (30 sq miles), the entire development will be as big as Greater London and bigger than Manhattan.

Work on land reclamation continues apace, but the construction of specific buildings has not yet begun. Nevertheless, published plans include provision for luxury homes, spa resorts and boutique hotels. Well-publicised visits by Premiership footballers are doing their bit to fuel the media hype, and the rumour mill regularly reports interest from passing Hollywood and Bollywood celebs.

watching) – check out Bastakia's Grand Mosque, although, unless you're a Muslim, you won't be allowed inside. Bastakia is home to Dubai's oldest building, **Al Fahidi fort** (now home to Dubai Museum), built in 1799 to guard landward approaches to the town, and parts of the old **Dubai wall**, built in 1800.

As Dubai's pearling industry took off in the late 1800s, Bedouin and mountain communities began to gravitate towards the coastal trading villages. The simple, outwardly minimalist homes they built were decorated inside with intricate rugs and wooden latticework on windows, and outside by elaborate carvings on the doors – again, this tradition has continued in the brightly painted metal doors and gates on old villas by the beach, and there are some great antique wooden examples in Bastakia. Historians disagree on whether these decorations were traditionally Arab, based on Islamic designs, or inspired by Indian decorative principles. Homes were built close to each other, with shady *sikkas* (alleys) running down towards the water.

> **'The city's skyline was transformed by sweeping changes that followed the formation of the UAE in 1971.'**

By the late 19th century, spurred on in part by a devastating fire in 1894, Deira's wealthy began to build their homes from coral stone and gypsum, although the poor still lived in *barasti*. Today, *barasti* are constructed to shade farm workers in the desert, picnickers in villa gardens, and cocktail drinkers at hotel beach bars.

Sheikh Saeed Al Maktoum House was built in 1896 on the southern bank of the Creek in Shindagha as a residence for the ruling family, remaining their home until Sheikh Saeed's death in 1958. Probably one of the first houses in the area to sport Iranian-inspired wind towers, it is a traditional coral-block structure built around a large central courtyard. Emirati historian and architect Rashad Bukash, formerly head of the Historical Buildings Section of Dubai Municipality, describes it as 'the best example of traditional architecture, with all the wooden, decorative elements – such as carved latticework, teak doors – that were typical of the times.' The restored house now acts as a museum, displaying old photographs and documents.

By the mid 20th century, a village of around 50 compounds, each with a wind tower or two, was built along the Bur Dubai side of the Creek. It remained more or less intact until the 1980s. A collection of wind tower shops still exists by the abra station; other fine examples open to the public are the **Majlis Gallery** and **XVA**, a restored café, gallery and guesthouse. Former Bastakia residents look back with fondness on these less hurried times. Hafsa Al Ulama, now a senior adviser to Sheikh Mohammed, recalls growing up in Bastakia in the 1960s and 1970s: 'The doors were always open and we used to run between the houses as if they all belonged to us. We never had air-conditioning, so we used to sit under the wind towers to cool off. All the women used to sit on the floor with the children, eat food, take tea, talk and decorate garments with beads. We were self-sufficient: livestock was kept and slaughtered at home in the courtyard and my aunt would make *labneh* from the goat's milk. To go shopping meant a trip on a rowed abra to Deira-side near the gold souk.'

A CITY IS BORN

Dubai's pace of urbanisation – like every facet of life in what were then the Trucial States – was dramatically fast-tracked by the discovery of oil in the early 1960s, first in Abu Dhabi and then in Dubai. The city's skyline was transformed by sweeping changes that followed the formation of the UAE in 1971, notably the explosion in Dubai's population.

The first concrete house was built in Dubai in 1956, but much of the population continued to live in *barasti* until well into the 1960s. Typically, extended families grouped together into compounds separated by thin alleyways; transport was by donkey, camel or abra until the 1960s, when the first roads opened up.

Even before the oil days, Dubai's ambition was evident. Sheikh Rashid, who succeeded his father in 1958, spent his first few years in power setting up a Municipal Council, building and widening roads, constructing the first airport, and bridging the Creek. The arrival of the car created a need for the establishment of a system of land management and ownership – after all, those losing half their compound to a widened road required compensation – and the concept of town planning was introduced. Working out who owned what in the tribal quarters of the city proved tricky but became essential as the value of land rose. Territory that lay outside built-up areas and any reclaimed land (following the dredging of the Creek) belonged to the ruler – a decree that remains in force to this day.

International commentators were sceptical of Sheikh Rashid's grand plans, but there was no shortage of believers: Dubai's population doubled to 120,000 between the late 1960s and early 1970s, and by 1981 had reached well over a quarter of a million. The few apartment blocks that sprung out of the desert around Deira's clock tower roundabout (1963) in the 1960s weren't lonely for long, and by the mid 1970s the Creek was lined with low and high-rise structures. Soaring fortunes, built on increased trade, went stratospheric during the oil crisis of 1973, and the government began construction in earnest. Developing infrastructure took precedence – the **Al Shindagha Tunnel** and **Al Maktoum Bridge** (1969), the dry docks, **Port Rashid**, mosques, hospitals, schools and power stations all date from around this time. Sadly, however, the need for build-'em-quick residential and office accommodation led to some entirely uncharismatic blocks being erected.

One exception is **Dubai Municipality** (1979), on the Deira side of the Creek, a building that's still widely admired for its abstract sensitivity – although the inner glass courtyard and water pools, which create a cool microclimate, weren't added until the 1980s. The **World Trade Centre** hasn't withstood history quite as well. Also built in 1979, it was at the time the signature Dubai landmark and, at 39 storeys, its highest building. Unmistakably 1970s, it is now dwarfed in size and stature by Emirates Towers, and in function by the efficient Ibis and Novotel hotels, built to accommodate delegates to the World Bank and IMF meetings in 2003.

Dubai's ritual building up and tearing down saw many of the smaller structures of the 1960s and 1970s cleared to make way for skyscrapers. But tradition sat cheek by jowl with the shiny and new: timber for interiors and furniture was still imported to the Creek on wooden dhows and, even in the early 1980s, Bur Dubai was still a wind tower village compared to Deira's burgeoning metropolis across the water.

By the end of the decade, Dubai's passion for the shock of the new began to soften slightly, perhaps owing in part to the emergence of the first wave of local architecture graduates. Rumour has it that Prince Charles, the UK's ambassador for architectural conservatism, expressed great enthusiasm for wind towers on a tour of Bastakia, encouraging Dubaians to start conservation projects. Meanwhile, the launch of Emirates Airline in 1985 brought increasing numbers of tourists hungry for a taste of Arabia. The first restoration project – Sheikh Saeed House – was completed in 1986,

and through the 1990s another 70 buildings were saved. Architects began incorporating traditional or Islamic references in their designs. The thoroughly 1980s **Deira Tower** (1984) in Baniyas Square, for example, features a distinctive circular white 'cap', like those worn by Emirati men under their *ghutra* (headdress).

INTO THE NEW MILLENNIUM

On Sheikh Rashid's death in 1990, his sons, notably Sheikh Mohammed (*see p20* **Sheikh Mohammed, CEO, Dubai Inc**), set about furthering their father's plans to create the Hong Kong of the Middle East, with the most notable new buildings dedicated to commerce and tourism. Dubai's macho love affair with the tower became ever more fervent, while foreign architects' efforts to relate their buildings to the local environment ranged from the ultra-literal to the ultra-kitsch. Some managed to be both: visitors heading into the city from the airport can't miss the mock aeroplane hull of **Emirates Training Centre**. **Jumeirah Beach Hotel** (1997) represents a surfer's dream wave, and the unusually low-rise **Dubai Creek Golf & Yacht Club** (1993), the billowing sails of a dhow. Other architects' favourites include Carlos Ott's **National Bank of Dubai** building (1998), known locally as the Pregnant Lady. Supported by two giant columns, the gold, glass and granite sculptural tower references the curved hulls and taut sails of abras and dhows, but in a subtly contextual manner. It's best viewed from an abra on a sunny day, when its curvaceous belly reflects all the nuances of the Creek. Ott is also responsible for the nearby **Hilton Dubai Creek** (2001), a minimalist's dream.

Emirates Towers, currently the place to do business in Dubai, are equally sleek. The Australian design is frowned on by some as 'anywhere architecture', the Emirates Towers remain the city's most spectacular corporate buildings. The office tower reaches 355 metres (1,165 feet) – take a ride in the swooping glass lifts up to Vu's Bar on the 51st floor. **Children's City** in Creek Park has a Duplo-style series of exhibition rooms; it is equally unashamedly modern and unusual in that it provides a spatial as well as a formal experience. The same can be said about ultra-chic **One&Only Royal Mirage** hotel, which uses elements drawn from traditional Islamic architecture. **Madinat Jumeirah**, a massive hotel and souk complex opened in late 2004, also harks back to the days of wind towers and coral block hues.

Of course, it was with Madinat's neighbour, the **Burj Al Arab** hotel, that Dubai really earned its reputation as a record-breaking architect's playground. Tom Wright of WS Atkins aimed to build a 'state-of-the-art, almost futuristic building' that was 'Arabic, extravagant and super-luxurious'. The Burj became an instant icon and on completion, the most recognised landmark in the city. Built 280 metres (900 feet) off shore, it's the world's tallest hotel at 321 metres (1,053 feet), and is supported by 250 columns that descend 45 metres (148 feet) into the seabed. Rumour has it that sand from around the base has to be hoovered out each night to prevent

subsidence, and that the tower sways up to 30 centimetres (12 inches) at the top. Even if you can't afford a night's stay in the hotel, you can check out its 60 floors of pure opulence by visiting one of the several bars and restaurants, probably the best of which is Al Muntaha bar, offering thrilling views from the oval pod that sits at the top of the 'mast'. But be sure to go easy on the cocktails – those with delicate constitutions have been known to find the ostentatious gold decorative features and swirly carpets induce a little seasickness.

A home in Dubai
The ins and outs of the property market.

At first sight, buying property in Dubai looks like a fantastic investment. With projected yields of between seven and ten per cent, it compares favourably with London, which offers returns of three to four per cent. And as Dubai is a virgin market, prices started unnaturally low as an incentive to pioneering investors. Older, wiser European capital cities rarely throw up bargains these days – although, of course, the emirate can hardly compete with them when it comes to heritage and culture.

But the city's building frenzy lies on potentially shaky foundations. Fundamental aspects of land law, freehold and residency are yet to be resolved, and insiders are split on the quality of buildings and the stability of the housing market. Optimists argue that the property boom is about to go supersonic: villas and apartments on the Palms – or, more accurately, bits of paper promising ownership of reclaimed land – are changing hands for the second and third times.

Creating a property market from scratch, particularly when the relationship between emirate and federal laws is uncertain, has led to much confusion over the exact nature of freehold, resale and residency. There is currently no law regarding freehold sales to foreigners, although one is expected. At the moment, developers are promising freehold on transfer of the property, but this is a contractual obligation between seller and buyer, and contracts are drafted in the seller's favour. Sultan bin Sulayem, executive chairman of Nakheel, the company behind the Palms, does not see this as a big problem: 'There is confidence in the UAE leadership,' he says. 'That's why people are buying.' He points out that it was ten years before the wildly successful Jebel Ali free zone received its federal law. 'Dubai never went back on a promise,' he insists.

Regarding residency, you should look carefully at the contract offered by the developer: visas offered with purchases are not always transferable to secondary buyers at the resale stage and this is a contractual matter rather than one enshrined in local or federal law. Some properties are still offered as leasehold, rather than freehold, a surprisingly secure choice. The Green Community near Jebel Ali, for example, offers a 90-year lease which, in value terms, is almost freehold, doesn't infringe on local laws and can include social and domestic controls, such as nuisance controls against noisy neighbours.

While agreeing that freehold is (and will be for some time) a risk, doubters could take heart from the recent endorsement of international banks such as HSBC. HSBC joins existing mortgage lenders Dubai Islamic Bank, Mashreqbank and Emaar subsidiary Amlak, which all offer rates between 5 and 6.5 per cent. These companies tailor mortgages to clients' salary, profession and nationality.

Service charges are a potentially problematic area: most of the apartment blocks charge quite hefty fees for keeping corridors clean and gardens green to Dubai's high standards. As for the small print, estate agents the world over are known for their, ahem, ability to embellish; and given Dubai's penchant for PR, the market does suffer from a little hype. Jumeirah Beach Residence, for example, promises 'your own home on the beach' in 'the last of the beachfront available in Dubai', but getting from living room to sea involves a series of bridges and walkways, and 25 per cent of the properties lack a sea view.

Good companies to contact are **Oryx** (351 5770, www.oryxrealestate.com) and **Better Homes** (344 7714, www.bhomes.com).

By the late 1990s, local architects were muttering about an identity crisis among Dubai's buildings. For some, the attempts by the likes of the Royal Mirage and intimate eco-resort **Al Maha** to reference local or regional history were key to creating a contextual and distinctive Dubai 'look'. For those who question the notion of 'Islamic architecture', these attempts are mere pastiche: such critics say that Dubai's age-old position on the trading crossroads and its new-found identity as a global city necessitate universal buildings.

Dubaians often wryly joke that they go to sleep at night only to wake up next to a skyscraper in the morning. Reflecting the transient and impatient nature of the new Dubai, many of the structures are impressive, but few of them are truly innovative, especially when it comes to environmental concerns. Old-timers question why today's architects have yet to master the integrated use of cool air, shade and natural light perfected in a wind tower house. While European, American and Asian capitals patronise the new breed of superstar architects, Dubai tends to rely on faceless foreign corporations for its construction needs, and the public's imagination has yet to be grabbed by any cultural or public buildings.

But the city evidently has no problem grabbing the headlines with its commercial plans, and the ambition that saw Sheikh Rashid dredging the Creek back in the 1960s is more than evident today. A raft of proposals such as Palm Jumeirah and The World will come to startling fruition by 2008, making the construction of the Burj Al Arab seem like a walk in the park.

Dubai's new role as one massive real-estate project has been facilitated by the launch of freehold property ownership for foreigners, enabling non-Emiratis to buy homes (*see p29* **A home in Dubai**). Despite concerns over a lack of land and mortgage legislation, local and global investors have, so far, proved to be more than willing to partake of the Emirates Dream. And Dubai has yet again displayed its marketing acumen by persuading most of the England national football team to snap up luxury villas on the Palm Jumeirah, thereby securing yet another series of headline-grabbing announcements.

The next decade will see construction of the world's tallest tower and first underwater hotel, plus homes for over a million new people in futuristic cities-within-cities. Exciting? Definitely. Risky? Maybe. Environmentally devastating? Only time will tell.

A new take on traditional architecture at the **Madinat Jumeirah**. *See p28.*

Coming attractions

In its bid to secure urban expansion as hard and as fast as possible, Dubai is pushing for self-contained communities across the city. Success stories like Dubai Internet City (DIC) and Dubai International Financial Centre (DIFC) have encouraged a slew of new plans for vast cities-within-cities, themed developments set to transform the emirate over the next few years. These include **Dubai Festival City**, a 648-hectare (1,600-acre), 20,000-home development with an 18-hole championship golf course that runs up the Creek from Garhoud Bridge, and **Dubai Marina**, at the other end of town, next to the Al Sufouh strip of beach hotels. With six residential towers up and another 200 to go (scheduled for completion between 2008 and 2013), the marina – and the neighbouring **Jumeirah Beach Residences** (36 towers and four hotels) – is likely to move the epicentre of Dubai away from its traditional heart, the Creek.

Besides these new cities, Dubai plans a series of headline projects, destined to break a series of world records. Redefining global architectural and engineering standards, we list the pick of these projects below.

Hydropolis (2006)

Trains will take aquatic tourists from a land station opposite Dubai Marina to the submarine complex of the world's first underwater hotel. Unusually, Hydropolis boasts a philosophy as well as plans for underwater art installations and operas on its 'stage on sea'. Gimmicky? Yes, but the project certainly has a passionate champion in architect-inventor Joachim Hauser. What cynic can deny the appeal of a deep-sea poetry seminar?

Dubai Silicon Oasis (2006)

The UAE's answer to Silicon Valley, DSO will take up 6.5 million sq m (70 million sq ft) of land and bring the global semiconductor industry into the grasp of Dubai industrialists. Tremble at our mighty works, oh California.

Zabeel Park (2006)

A 51-hectare (130-acre) swathe of green, dotted with playgrounds, lagoons, cinemas and an amphitheatre, Zabeel Park will open to the public in 2006. You'll be able to whizz around the gounds in a light train, stopping in at the technology park, before taking a quick dip in the pool.

Tropical Forest (2006)

Covering around two hectares (five acres) of desert, this Dubaian take on the rainforest should open some time in 2006. Details are currently thin on the ground, but it seems the project will be carried out by a Malaysian 'forest-creating' company, and the finished product will be home to 'exotic birds'.

Dubailand (2006)

Billed as the region's premier tourism and leisure attraction, the imaginatively titled Dubailand is a jumble of ideas corralled into one vast, American-style theme park. Located off the Emirates Road, it will incorporate six 'worlds of wonder', ranging from extreme sports zones and car-racing tracks to parks of life-sized dinosaur and medieval castles, along with 'eco-tourism' hotels and, inevitably, the biggest mall in the world, the Mall of Arabia.

Palm Islands (2006-2008)

The world's largest man-made islands, the Palm Jumeirah, Palm Jebel Ali and Palm Deira (*see p26* **The silly isles**) are all expected to have opened by 2008.

Burj Dubai (2007)

Proposed as the tallest tower in the world, the Burj Dubai will dwarf the current flock of skyscrapers along Sheikh Zayed Road. Designed by Chicago-based tower specialists Skidmore, Owings & Merrill, the complex will boast residential, commercial, hotel and leisure outlets, plus parks, a lake and – naturally – a huge shopping mall.

The World (2008)

Just when the world finally managed to absorb the concept of the Palm Islands, Dubai announced The World, a collection of 250 islands to be constructed, you guessed it, in the shape of a global map. Working four kilometres (2.5 miles) off shore, between Port Rashid and the Burj Al Arab, dredgers began reclaiming the islands in 2003. The $1.8 billion project aims to attract the kinds of high-rolling investors who can set their sights on exclusively owning, say, 'France' or 'Australia'. The degree to which the individual countries will be themed in terms of their architecture and landscaping is still open to debate, but let's hope things don't get too realistic, if only for the sake of homeowners in, say, 'Wales'.

WE WERE TRAVELLING

HERE, THERE AND EVERYWHERE.

LUCKILY THEY HAD HOTELS

IN ALL THREE.

There are Hilton hotels at over 400 resorts across the globe,

each providing outstanding service and exceptional facilities.

So wherever you stay, you can stay with us.

Welcome to Certainty.

TAKE ME TO THE HILTON

Culture & Customs

Dubai's marriage of Western lifestyles and Islamic values is sometimes strained, but ultimately successful.

Resident expats often speak of the Dubai 'bubble' when describing the ease with which they navigate life in the forward-thinking emirate. Once the novelty of initial Arabic encounters has worn off, Westerners settle down to a relaxed lifestyle that lacks few home comforts and offers up several benefits – not least of which is a tax-free income. But it is Dubai's basic liberalism (within the limits of Islamic traditions), not cash, that defines the place: tourists with preconceived ideas of Middle Eastern austerity are often surprised by Dubai's overwhelming 'live and let live' philosophy.

All bubbles can burst, however, and Western expats love to peddle urban myths about friends-of-friends rotting away in jail over some minor offence or conspiracy theories about the excesses of the Sheikhs. Cynicism aside, it is easy to misinterpret Dubai's liberalism. A night out guzzling cocktails and dancing on the tables, not to mention dodging kerb-crawlers on the way home, can leave you with the impression that

the city has temporarily relocated somewhere far, far from the Muslim world. But if that's your impression, think again.

Religion is generally a private issue, but the UAE is an Islamic society. You're never far from the muezzin's call to prayer; cleavages and dateline chat numbers are blacked out in foreign newspapers; and, however benign and enlightened the rule, Dubai is a still a Sheikh-dom whose leaders are treated with utmost reverence. Still, if you bear this in mind while soaking up Dubai's laid-back, polite and friendly ambience, you'll negotiate, even come to appreciate, the city's intricacies with ease.

A MELTING POT

Dubai's position at the crossroads of the Gulf, the Indian subcontinent and Africa has always made it home – or at least a port of call – for expats from the region and beyond, but its transformation from pearl-diving town to economic powerhouse over the past 70 years has brought about a dramatic change in the city's ethnic make-up. The population of the UAE stands at around 3.5 million, of whom just over a million live in Dubai. The city is currently growing at around six per cent a year, although this rate is set to rise as Dubai builds up and up, in the reasonable hope of attracting new, foreign homeowners. There are about 2.5 men to every woman, and 80 per cent of the population is made up of foreigners, mostly workers from the Indian subcontinent and the Philippines, plus expats from the Middle East, Europe, Australasia and South Africa.

There is a telling distinction that exists between 'workers' and 'expats' in Dubai. Even fly-by-night tourists can't fail to notice the busloads of labourers who graft all year round, building Dubai's new luxury hotels and homes. Most of them come from India, Bangladesh and Pakistan, live in what are openly called 'labour camps', and work long, round-the-clock shifts. While enthusiastic capitalists argue that the workers are better off earning money for themselves and their families in the Gulf than they would be struggling to find work back home, stories abound of workers arriving in Dubai under false pretences, slaving away in dangerous conditions, and even collapsing in high summer temperatures.

The city's service sector – the lower rungs of the tourist and entertainment industries, plus the maids and cleaners who look after local and expat families – tend to hail from the Philippines, Indonesia and Sri Lanka. Dubai's labouring classes survive for years on end, sending money back via the informal *hawala* system and visiting their families every two or three years. As every other taxi driver will tell you, many plan to come for a couple of years, but find themselves staying much longer; most can name the number of months and days until their next trip home.

Their obvious exploitation contrasts strongly with the city's penchant for brash consumer luxury; for professionals, life in Dubai is a different story. Companies often include annual airline tickets and family memberships to beach clubs in their 'packages' and, while 'things ain't what they used to be', Dubai can still provide a classic expat lifestyle. But change is afoot: today's IT, media, tourist and property industries increasingly attract – in addition to the familiar Brits, sundry other Europeans, South Africans and Australasians – young Arabs, Iranians and Indians, some of whom have an interest in the Middle East beyond its capacity for tax-free sunshine. The motto is still 'work hard, play hard', but a new kind of sophistication is evident – and necessary, given Dubai's pace of development.

GETTING OUT, HAVING FUN

Dubai's glamorous clubbing scene – like its advertising and creative industries – is heavily influenced by the party people of the Arab world, namely the Lebanese. A mix of Muslims and Christians, the Lebanese have always emigrated to far-flung lands, and there are substantial numbers in Dubai. Joining them are Palestinians, Syrians, other Levantine Arabs and Iranians, many of whom have been educated in Europe, the US or other Gulf states.

The local passion for sport, business and shopping is what gets Dubaians together. The Thursday horse-racing nights at Nad Al Sheba attract all levels of society; Arabs and Emiratis often support football teams in the English premier league as well as local teams; and it's easy to tell when a major cricket match is on from the crowds that form outside those Indian and Pakistani cafés that have set up televisions. Besides all things equine (racing, endurance riding, Arab horse racing and beauty contests), Emiratis are committed to their falconry: don't be surprised to see a row of hooded falcons coming through the airport's passport control, or a falconry display in the palace gardens in Jumeirah and Umm Suqeim.

Families bond by hitting the shopping mall every Friday afternoon. There are more than 40 malls in the emirate, with a new one being built every few months. As AA Gill memorably observed, Dubai is the place where malls go on holiday.

But, despite Dubai's generally harmonious and tolerant outlook, and its reputation as the most liberal of the emirates, some professionals do detect a degree of subtle racism – from the patronising attitude of some expats towards the service classes, to club bouncers who sometimes refuse entry to groups of Indian men. At times, compared to cities in Europe, Dubai can seem like a collection of different ethnicities living in parallel, keeping themselves to themselves, rather than a mixed, multicultural society. Certainly, the old order that places Emiratis at the top of the pile, followed by Europeans and then other Arabs, has shown it has staying power. But increasing numbers of professional Indians, the creation of democratically elected local councils, and new laws allowing – even encouraging – foreigners to own property could change this, creating new stakeholders in Dubai society.

While expats, particularly Westerners, might be highly visible, it's the minority of locals who define and rule the city. Many foreigners mistakenly believe that Emirati society is as uniform as its choice of dress, but dig

Urban myths

Clearing up some common misconceptions about Dubai.

You can't drink

There are a huge number of restaurants and bars serving alcohol – the only restriction is that they must be located within the confines of a hotel or sporting stadium. According to the letter of the law, everyone drinking in the bar should be a guest of that hotel, but this is never enforced, which means people are free to drink where they chose. Residents are free to drink in their own homes, providing they own a booze licence issued by the municipality. There are two alcohol distributors, a+e and MMI, who import alcohol and distribute it to bars and sell it through their own shops to licence-holders. Tourists are free to bring limited amounts of alcohol into the country from the duty-free shop at the airport. It is illegal to drink in the streets or in public places.

You can't eat pork

As with alcohol, pork is freely served in restaurants that are located within hotels. Many larger supermarkets have a pork section for use by non-Muslims. You do not need a licence.

Western women have to cover up

While it is still important to respect Islamic culture and dress appropriately, Western women are free to dress as they please. They are not required to wear a veil, nor to cover their shoulders in public.

Women are not allowed drive

Women are subject to the same driving laws as men.

Homosexuality is illegal

All sexual liaisons conducted outside marriage are illegal in the UAE. As gay marriage is not recognised by Islamic law, all homosexual acts are illegal. However, simply being a homosexual person is not illegal.

You are not allowed to enter the country if you are HIV positive

There is no test on entry to check if you are HIV positive. However, if you are found to be HIV positive during your stay, you will face deportation.

Couples need to be married to get a hotel room

Strictly speaking it is illegal for an unmarried couple to share a hotel room. However, very few establishments will actually ask to see a marriage certificate – particularly if you're a Western couple.

You can't display affection in public

It is wise to moderate your behaviour in public. While holding hands and kissing on the cheek is acceptable, more passionate displays of affection can result in fines and even arrests.

---

beneath the surface and you'll find a complex, rapidly changing people. Young professionals, whose grandparents may have lived on camel milk and dates in the desert, deftly straddle Dubai's twin towers of capitalism and tradition. They are likely to combine an arranged marriage, the wearing of the *hijab* and other traditions with business acumen and an international education, as well as absolute respect for the ruling Sheikhs with a deep love of Hollywood. An active programme of 'Emiratisation' aims to get more Emiratis into all areas of employment, but for now they tend to dominate only the public sector.

THAT FRIDAY FEELING

Government and other public offices open from Saturday to Thursday, and employees end the working week with a traditional Thursday family lunch. Many private companies take Friday and Saturday off instead, creating variable and confusing weekends. While Friday remains sacred, business is frenetic on every other day, with most of the population devotedly glued to their mobile phones. When scheduling appointments, however, be aware that you are dealing in 'Dubai time': most commitments, whether to have dinner or sign that multi-million dollar deal, are *Insha'allah* ('God willing'). An expression rather than an absolute, *Insha'allah* reminds us that not everything is in the hands of corporate earth-dwellers. Dubai's hotels may operate to international standards, but take a detour into local life and you should expect very little to happen resolutely on time, or resolutely to happen at all.

THICKER THAN WATER

For Dubai's Emirati population – with only two generations separating modern Dubaians from tribal living – the extended family is of crucial importance, whether in business dealings and traditional gatherings or trips to the mall and races. Names tend to define someone within their immediate family – as *bin* ('son of') or *bint* ('daughter of') – and within their tribe or extended family by the prefix *al*. Protocol dictates that respect and thanks should always be given to the older generations of each family, especially when it comes to official matters. The existence of *wasta*, the 'old boys' network' system of favours given to those with family and friends in high places, still happily resides alongside Dubai's new meritocracy.

KNOW YOUR HOSTS

Emiratis are known for their warm hospitality and politeness. Traditionally, every guest who entered a Bedouin's tent or home had to be unconditionally fed and given shelter for three days. Nowadays, this kind of generosity is not essential for survival, but old habits die hard. If you're lucky enough to meet locals (or other Gulf Arabs) and be invited for tea or coffee, do accept. The ritual of making and presenting coffee – strong, espresso-sized cups – is prized, and you'll be offered refill after refill. If your heart can't quite take it, just gently shake your cup from side to side; your host will know not to offer you any more. If you are doing the entertaining, make sure you press more refreshments on your guest – they may well refuse a few times out of politeness before caving in. If a meal presents itself, expect vast amounts of delicious food, much of which will end up being left – a sign of your host's generosity. Eat only with your right hand – the left hand is used for wiping the backside in the toilet.

Most Emirati men favour the traditional, practical *dishdasha* or *khandura* (a long, white shirt-dress), with *ghutra* (a white headdress) and *agal* (a black rope that holds the *ghutra* in place, traditionally used to hobble camels). When in public, city women tend to wear an *abaya* (long black cloak) over a conservative dress, long skirt or tight designer jeans, with a *hijab* or *sheyla* (a scarf that either wraps around the face and hair, or covers the whole face). Older women sometimes wear a black burkha that just leaves the eyes exposed, or a traditional hardened linen mask that sits on the nose. While obviously influenced by the Islamic tenet for modesty, the clothes are also deeply practical, as anyone who's survived the biting sandy winds of a desert *shamal* (northerly wind) can testify. As for Dubai's population of expats… well, anything goes, but you are advised to dress to suit the occasion. Revealing or tight evening wear is tolerated in clubs, and a bikini is fine on the beach or by the hotel pool, but it's courteous (and advisable if you want to avoid getting stared at) to be more conservative when visiting heritage sites, the souks or anywhere in the city: no shorts is a good rule, and women should wear below-the-knee skirts and cover their shoulders. Be aware that Sharjah has formalised 'decency laws' – be sure to dress conservatively on any day trips there.

> **'The UAE is tolerant and respectful of other religions, and hosts a number of temples and churches.'**

Despite the flagrant exhibitionism of many expats, local police are quick to react to any complaints of harassment by men: should the generally harmless 'starers' at Jumeirah's public beach become anything more disturbing, you can report them to the beach patrols.

KEEPING THE FAITH

The call to prayer is likely to greet you on landing in Dubai; once in the city, you're apparently never more than 500 metres (a quarter of a mile) away from a mosque – expect the melodic intonations of the muezzin to define your day and remind you that you're in Arabia. Most mosques are busy for the Friday 'sermon' – which is also broadcast from the minaret via loudspeakers – but Muslims can perform their five-times-daily prayers anywhere, from the side of the road to an office boardroom, as long as they are facing Mecca, to the west. Avoid walking in front of anyone praying, and don't stare: private yet public praying should be viewed as perfectly normal.

Compared to some other Gulf states, the UAE is tolerant and respectful of other religions – and hosts a number of temples and churches – but active promotion of them is frowned upon. Likewise the consumption of alcohol: while visitors and non-Muslim residents are welcome to buy duty free at the airport, or have big nights out in hotel bars, the hard stuff is tolerated rather than celebrated (*see p178* **Authorised alcohol**). The nights before religious festivals are usually dry; there is pretty much zero tolerance for anyone found drink-driving; and members of the CID tend to keep an eye on raucous parties. The two local importers – MMI and African & Eastern – serve hotels, residents who hold liquor licences and,

Mosques: always within earshot.

In Emirati society, outside the family and private sphere, unmarried men and women generally tend to lead separate lives – although, for young people, the advent of the mobile phone and the popularity of higher education, the cinema and the mall have facilitated a certain level of text message and other long-distance flirting. On public occasions, such as at the racing, it's rare to see Emirati wives accompanying their husbands; at weddings, women, dressed in all their designer finery, usually hold separate celebrations to the men; some areas of life, such as local football matches, are still off limits to women. These traditions, which extend to ladies' days in parks, female-only beaches and women being served first or separately in banks or other queues, sit alongside the rise of the Emirati business-woman and the prominent role taken by some of the Sheikhas.

While Emiratis are always forgiving of blunders, and tend to allow Western and Arab expats to follow different sets of rules, it is advisable to avoid being too informal. For example, wait for a member of the opposite sex to extend their hand before going to shake theirs. Better yet, place your palm on your heart as a sign of your warmth or gratitude. Ask before taking a photo of an Emirati woman and steer clear of snapping any military sites. Chances are that even if you do make a mistake, your Emirati hosts will be understanding – and their warm manner and good sense of humour will keep you blissfully unaware of it.

increasingly, big outdoor entertainment and sporting events, but their outlets are understated and windowless. You may see Gulf Arabs, whether local or visiting from Saudi and other strict states, propping up the bar in quieter establishments, but generally drinking is the preserve of expats.

Other activities that are *haram* (forbidden under Islam) include the consumption of non-halal meat and pork products – which, typically for Dubai, are nonetheless sold to expats from a separate 'pork shop' in supermarkets. Visitors should also resist any public displays of affection between men and women – and be aware that hand signals (beckoning with one finger, pointing directly, as well as the more international rude gestures) can be offensive. Showing the soles of your feet to someone can also be viewed as insulting. Don't be fooled into thinking that the common sight of men holding hands is evidence of a burgeoning gay scene – among Indians, Pakistanis and Arabs this is merely a sign of friendship.

BREAKING THE LANGUAGE BARRIER

Modern Dubai is effectively bilingual: road signs, maps, even several newspapers are in English, and most Emiratis you'll meet will speak the language impeccably. Even if you're an Arabist, many business people will prefer to converse with you in English. However, some public sector workers or those behind the scenes in Emirati businesses don't have the same finesse; at some time during your stay, a public official is bound to bark 'Yanni, give me passport' or 'I want form'. Combined with often unfathomable levels of bureaucracy, requiring bundles of passport photos and forms in triplicate, this can make public offices a bit confusing, but keep your cool (remembering it's much worse in most developing countries) and propriety will win through. Be sure to tune your ear to 'Hinglish' – Indian English, a mix of Hindi or Urdu and English. Many Dubaians from the subcontinent, the 'ethnic majority', also manage their own blend of English with Arabic. Meeting them halfway is the least you can do.

Step into a World of Taste

Experience a wealth of new sensations within our world-class food & beverage venues. Enjoy exotic French Polynesian delights at Trader Vic's, savour the Italian melodies at Prego's or sink your teeth into the best meats at Rodeo Grill. From our German Brauhaus to our Café Columbia, on to the International dining at Rosebuds, for rounding off at The L.A.B and our Global Seafood phenomenon "Finz", you'll find the world at the Beach Rotana Hotel & Towers.

PREGO'S
CUCINA · ENOTECA ITALIANA

RODEO Grill

Rosebuds
International Dining

L.A.B

TRADER VIC'S

Café Columbia
Café & Lounge

Brauhaus
GERMAN RESTAURANT & TERRACE

BENIHANA
STEAK · SEAFOOD · SUSHI

BAY VIEW
RESTAURANT

finz
SEAFOOD RESTAURANT

BEACH ROTANA
HOTEL & TOWERS
ABU DHABI

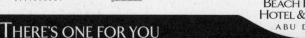

THERE'S ONE FOR YOU

For reservations and more information please call
UAE Toll Free: 800 ROTANA or Tel: +971 2 644 3000

www.rotana.com

Where to Stay

Where to Stay   **40**

Features

Where to Stay

It's still the benchmark for swanky beach resorts, but Dubai is answering skyrocketing demand with a new breed of city cribs and business hotels.

Hotels continue to form the backbone of modern Dubai. Given that only hotels can offer licensed restaurants and bars, these properties are the focus for after-dark social activities for residents and tourists alike. It's also entirely usual for well-heeled visitors to spend more time relaxing in the ostentatious grounds of Dubai's finest resorts than actually exploring the city itself.

Several hotels embody the emirate's taste for architectural showmanship: the **Burj Al Arab** (*see p47*) and **Emirates Towers** (*see p41*), for example, are more than mere sleeping stations: they're revered as iconic symbols of the city. And more is to come; with the first Palm Island project set to house between 30 and 70 five-star properties, the Burj Dubai (the world's tallest tower) renting rooms to visitors, and Hydropolis – the first underwater hotel on the planet – due to open in 2006, it seems that no space, be it land, sea or air, is free from the relentless development of the city. (For all three of these new projects, *see p31* **Coming attractions**.) While there's no need to stretch to such extravagance, getting a room in Dubai is undoubtedly a costly business and you can expect to pay upwards of Dhs700 for a decent bed. Many may baulk at the prices, but your money does go a long way and the level of service and facilities on hand at the top of the Dubai hotel tree are enough to make Europe or America's finest look like fleapits by comparison.

DISTINGUISHING BY DISTRICT

When it comes to hotels, geography largely dictates style, with prices generally dropping the further you get from the shore. **Jumeirah**, with its astonishing beaches, plush malls and sun traps, is currently the most desirable district and where you'll find the really ritzy resorts. The hotels here are far from cheap, but you'll struggle to find one that doesn't send your jaw floorwards with its stunning views, fine facilities and swanky ambience.

Sheikh Zayed Road is home to a shiny new breed of cloud-troubling business hotels, a world away from the rest of the Bur Dubai district (for this reason, we have listed the reviews separately). Prices are as staggering as the architecture, but for location and style

it's hard to beat. Stretching from Creek to coastline, **Bur Dubai** offers some good-value halfway houses between Jumeirah's polish and Deira's urban delights. But beware: while pockets such as Oud Metha, Satwa and Karama are some of the most charming in town, the central area is a heaving mass of squat, tightly packed buildings, swirling exhaust fumes and frustrating taxi commutes.

A colourful mix of souks, skyscrapers and malls, **Deira** is the oldest area of the city, with hotels varying from high-class Creek-huggers such as the Hilton to the cheap and less-than-cheerful establishments that line the red light district of Rigga Road. Some way from the shoreline, Deira – in particular the Garhoud subdistrict, which contains the airport – is mainly geared to business, but contains some great inner-city options.

Those on a truly tight budget may find it hard to locate something suitable, as family-friendly low-end options, while on the increase, are not as prominent as the five-star excess that dominates the Dubai hotel scene. The city is, however, becoming more aware of the economy-minded traveller and offers a few comfortable and cost-effective options. The majority of the budget bunch are clustered around Al Fahidi Street and Bank Street in Bur Dubai, where you can pick up a clean if poky room for a couple of hundred dirhams. Do bear in mind, however, that Bank Street is at the heart of the less salubrious end of Bur Dubai, where it's not unheard of for female tourists to be propositioned while popping into the supermarket in the middle of the day.

Across the Creek the neighbourhood around Al Rigga Road in Deira is another reasonable hunting ground for cheap beds, but again suffers from less-than-squeaky-clean nocturnal activities. Readers looking to stay in this area are advised to go door-to-door, ask to see rooms and make their own judgements; while we realise this isn't ideal, it is the only way of ensuring you find a room that fits.

▶ For full reviews of hotel beach and health clubs, *see pp202-207*.
▶ For reviews of hotel spas, *see pp207-210*.

Al Qasr. *See p44.*

ABOUT THE LISTINGS

Rates are given for high season (October to April). The categories are broken down by the price for a standard double room, with Luxury representing Dhs1,900 and above, Expensive Dhs1,300 to Dhs1,899, Moderate Dhs700 to Dhs1,299, and Cheap below Dhs699. However, this is an inexact science: prices are liable to change and it's worth trying to negotiate when booking. Rates do not include ten per cent municipality tax nor the ten per cent service charge but do generally include breakfast.

Luxury

Sheikh Zayed Road

Emirates Towers

Trade Centre side (330 0000/fax 330 3131/ www.jumeirahinternational.com). **Rates** Dhs2,400 single; Dhs2,600 double; Dhs4,500-Dhs8,000 suite. **Credit** AmEx, DC, MC, V. **Map** p280 H4.

The third Dubaian landmark (although some way behind the Burj and the Jumeirah Beach Hotel in the postcard stakes), Emirates Towers dominates Dubai's skyline. Occupying the taller of the two towers (the other being the most desirable office block in town), the hotel is a big hit with flashy powerbrokers from around the world. A sophisticated lobby lounge and acres of atrium dominate the ground floor, while the glass lifts that shoot up and down the 52 storeys are a vertigo-inducing delight. Rooms are sizeable, with nice dark wood tables, gaudy soft furnishings and panoramas that would blow the socks off the most seasoned of travellers. Despite its business-oriented mentality, the Towers does have many tourist-friendly features, including a large swimming pool and health club, plus complimentary beach shuttle and entry to the Jumeirah Beach Club (*see p43*).

Hotel services *Babysitting. Bars. Beauty salon. Business services. Concierge. Gym. Internet access. Limousine service. No-smoking rooms. Parking. Pools. Restaurants.* **Room services** *Dataport. Minibar. Room service (24hrs). Telephone. Turndown. TV: satellite.*

Fairmont Hotel

Satwa side (332 5555/fax 332 4555/www.fairmont. com). **Rates** Dhs2,500 single/double; Dhs3,000-Dhs4,600 suite. **Credit** AmEx, DC, MC, V. **Map** p285 G9.

An elegant beast of a hotel, the Fairmont juggles the requirements of both business and leisure guests in some style. Catering to the former, the hotel sets high-tech standards in the city, with a wireless internet connection in each room and comprehensive in-house IT support. At the Fairmont's centre is a massive foyer graced with groovy leather sofas and a huge atrium, its walls splashed with every tone of colour to head-spinning effect. Bedrooms are spacious, with large beds, huge windows and well-chosen furnishings – although again they suffer from the 'more is more' approach to colour. The minimalist bathrooms, though large, will seem sterile by comparison.

A keen eye for detail is evident in the two pool areas on either side of the building – the sunset and sunrise decks – decorated with stunning mosaics to reflect their respective themes. There's an impressive health club, plus the pricey

but first-rate Willow Stream Spa (see p210). Because the hotel is situated as close to town as the Sheikh Zayed Road will allow, its lively restaurants pick up a lot of local trade. Set directly across from the Trade Centre, it has four illuminated turrets that change colour throughout the week and have taken on a unique place in Dubai's cityscape. **Hotel services** Babysitting. Bars. Beauty salon. Business services. Concierge. Gym. Internet access. Limousine service. No-smoking rooms. Parking. Pools. Restaurants. **Room services** Dataport. Minibar. Room service (24hrs). Telephone. Turndown. TV: satellite.

Shangri-La

Satwa side (343 8888/fax 343 8886/www.shangri-la.com). **Rates** Dhs2,000 single; Dhs2,200 double; Dhs2,200 executive single; Dhs2,400 executive double; Dhs3,500-Dhs14,000 suite. **Credit** AmEx, DC, MC, V. **Map** p280 H4.

The Shangri-La towers above its more established competitors both literally and figuratively. The elegant and serene foyer is immaculate, visitors can skip between the 41 storeys via the super-speedy lifts and the breathtaking views out over the Jumeirah Beach or the magnificent structures of Sheikh Zayed Road are incomparable. The spacious standard rooms impress with their minimalist chic, and the Aigner-equipped bathrooms feature separate tub, shower and toilet spaces. Business facilities are secluded and state-of-the-art, while the suites dazzle with their luxurious fittings, including Bang & Olufsen entertainment centres. It's not surprising, then, that this is the home to the stars (including Enrique Iglesias and Westlife) when they hit the UAE, although this could also explain why the hotel's prices have almost doubled in the last year or so. **Hotel services** Babysitting. Bars. Beauty salon. Business services. Concierge. Gym. Internet access. Limousine service. No-smoking rooms. Parking. Pools. Restaurants. Spa. **Room services** Dataport. Minibar. Room service (24hrs). Telephone. Turndown. TV: satellite.

Jumeirah

Dar Al Masyaf

Al Sufouh Road (366 8888/fax 366 7788/www. jumeirahinternational.com). **Rates** Dhs2,800-Dhs3,200 single summer house; Dhs2,900-Dhs3,300 double summer house; Dhs7,000-Dhs8,000 Arabian & ocean suites. **Credit** AmEx, DC, MC, V. **Map** p278 A4.

These exclusive summer houses, including seven royal villas named after the seven emirates, offer the best of two worlds: the privacy of secluded surroundings and access to the Madinat's extensive facilities. With one pool to every three villas and 24-hour butler services, the palatial villas are elegance personified. Assuming you can stretch to the hefty price tag, the two-storey quarters with their lush, intimate settings and intricately land-

The best Hotels

For somewhere brand new
Al Qasr (see p44); **Arabian Court Hotel** (see p51).

For sleeping by the beach
Jumeirah Beach Hotel (see p43); Le Meridien Mina Seyahi (see p48).

For celeb-spotting
Shangri-La (see right).

For guaranteed romance
One&Only Royal Mirage (see p48); Ritz-Carlton Dubai (see p44).

For overwhelming opulence
Burj Al Arab (see p47); Grand Hyatt (see p44).

For wheeler dealing
Hilton Dubai Creek (see p55); Emirates Towers (see p41).

For old-school style and service
InterContinental Dubai (see p45); Hyatt Regency (see p55); JW Marriott (see p45).

For bargain beds
Hilton Dubai Jumeirah (see p56); Ibis (see p58); Rydges Plaza (see p57); XVA (see p58).

For oriental class
Dusit Dubai (see p52).

For deluxe desert diversion
Al Maha (see p49 Desert resorts).

For rooms as cheap as chips
Dubai Youth Hostel (see p58).

scaped gardens will excite even the most blasé of holidaymakers. You may find it difficult to leave the comfort of your luxurious haven, but Pierchic (*see p103*), the Madinat's glorious restaurant perched on a jetty jutting far into the sea, is one of the finest dining experiences in Dubai.
Hotel services *Babysitting. Bars. Beach. Beauty salon. Boutiques. Business services. Concierge. Gym. Internet access. Limousine service. No-smoking rooms. Parking. Pools. Restaurants. Spa. Watersports.* **Room services** *Dataport. Minibar. Room service (24hrs). Telephone. Turndown. TV: satellite.*

Jumeirah Beach Club
Beach Road (344 5333/fax 334 6222/www.jumeirah international.com). **Rates** Dhs3,050 junior single suite; Dhs3,200 junior double suite; Dhs8,800 Paradise suite. **Credit** AmEx, DC, MC, V.
Map p286 A15.
This beautiful collection of quality villa accommo-dation and top-notch facilities set around lush gardens, leads to one of the most stunning beach-fronts in town. Guests are put up in one of 50 luxurious suites, each of which has a private garden or balcony and a Jacuzzi. Thick foliage and subtle construction give the place an intense sense of tranquillity that belies its location in the heart of Jumeirah. There's an excellent club where you can offload the kids before heading off for some shore-side bronzing or to make the most of the pools, tennis and squash courts, and limitless access to Wild Wadi (*see p153*), the city's finest

water park. JBC is also home to the Satori Spa (*see p210*), a haven of pampering and plucking from which you can emerge looking a million dollars before tripping over to Prasino's (*see p102*), the mainly Med restaurant. While by no means cheap, a stay at the Beach Club is a guaranteed hit for families looking for some serious downtime.
Hotel services *Babysitting. Bars. Beauty salon. Business services. Concierge. Garden. Gym. Internet access. Limousine service. No-smoking rooms. Parking. Pools. Restaurants. Spa.* **Room services** *Dataport. Minibar. Room service (24hrs). Telephone. Turndown. TV: satellite.*

Jumeirah Beach Hotel
Beach Road (348 0000/fax 348 2273/www. jumeirahinternational.com). **Rates** Dhs2,400 single; Dhs2,500 double; Dhs3,700-10,800 suite; Dhs8,950 villa. **Credit** AmEx, DC, MC, V. **Map** p278 B4.
A Dubaian landmark, the wave-shaped Jumeirah Beach Hotel is the city's best-known piece of architecture after the Burj Al Arab. For all its outer grandeur, however, it's a down-to-earth hotel patronised in the main by young European families in search of a spot of winter sun. In the shadow of its arching blue glass walls there's a decent children's club and a family adventure play-ground; just across the road lies the Wild Wadi flume park (*see p153*), home to aquatic tomfoolery on an epic scale. The hotel's beach hosts Beit Al Bahar, a series of luxury villas that offer an idyllic

Emirates Towers, Dubai's dynamic duo. *See p41.*

Gulfside retreat, overlooked by the lowering hulk of the Burj. Whether you chose to stay in the spacious, colourful rooms of the main hotel or in the refined chic of Beit Al Bahar, you'd be crazy not to tool up at the hotel's dive centre and pay a visit to the man-made coral reef just off shore.
Hotel services *Babysitting. Bars. Beauty salon. Business services. Concierge. Gym. Internet access. Limousine service. No-smoking rooms. Parking. Pools. Restaurants.* **Room services** *Dataport. Minibar. Room service (24hrs). Telephone. Turndown. TV: satellite.*

Mina A' Salam

Al Sufouh Road (366 8888/fax 366 7788/366 7777/ www.jumeirahinternational.com). **Rates** *Dhs1,850 single; Dhs1,950 double; Dhs4,500-Dhs14,000 suite.* **Credit** AmEx, DC, MC, V. **Map** p278 A4.
Built around 3km (two miles) of Venetian-style waterways filled with abras that ferry guests around the resort, the Mina is the first hotel to have been completed in the gobsmackingly ambitious Madinat project that aims to marry Dubai's modern-day opulence with its old-world architecture. The sand-coloured buildings are topped with legions of wind towers and the interior is palatial. Each of the 292 sea-facing rooms are styled in keeping with the Arabian theme: heavy studded doors give way to Moorish arches hung with ornate lanterns, and the beds are piled high with exotic dark blue, red and gold fabrics. The real hook, however, is large terraces jutting towards the water, ideal for sitting and sipping a leisurely G 'n' T as the sun goes down. With walkways along the harbour, alfresco restaurant terraces, the extremely convivial Bahri Bar and a souk full of lavish boutiques, Mina has a distinctly village feel to it – albeit a village full of the deeply affluent.
Hotel services *Babysitting. Bars. Beauty salon. Business services. Concierge. Garden. Gym. Internet access. Limousine service. No-smoking rooms. Parking. Pools. Restaurants.* **Room services** *Dataport. Minibar. Room service (24hrs). Telephone. Turndown. TV: satellite.*

Al Qasr

Al Sufouh Road (366 8888/fax 366 7788/www. jumeirahinternational.com). **Rates** Dhs2,450-Dhs2,840 single; Dhs2,550-Dhs2,940 double; Dhs3,500-Dhs30,000 suite. **Credit** AmEx, DC, MC, V. **Map** p278 A4.
Just when you thought the Madinat Jumeirah with its sprawling Mina A' Salam grand boutique hotel couldn't get any more ostentatious, they introduce 29 villas in the shape of Dar Al Masyaf and the Al Qasr hotel – their newest and priciest additions. Al Qasr was designed to reflect the royal summer residence while providing the 'jewel in the crown' of this resort, and it certainly is grandiose. Erected in September 2004, the huge lobby with Arabian-themed lanterns and plump cushions leads to an opulent cigar lounge, continuing the theme of the Mina A' Salam, although the bedrooms are larger than their original counterparts. What makes

Al Qasr stand out, however, is its 24-hour butler service (not quite the Burj – here you have to share your Jeeves with 11 other rooms) and its proximity to the famous Six Sense Spa (*see p210*), one of the most sensational spas on the Gulf. There are club executive (kid-free) lounges and a kids' club and separate pool, so although Al Qasr is family-friendly, you can also have an adult break without too much intrusion. Transport through the huge resort is by water taxis and golf buggies.
Hotel services *Babysitting. Bars. Beauty salon. Boutiques. Business services. Concierge. Gym. Internet access. Limousine service. No-smoking rooms. Parking. Pools. Restaurants. Spa.* **Room services** *Dataport. Minibar. Room service (24hrs). Telephone. Turndown. TV: satellite.*

Ritz-Carlton Dubai

Al Sufouh Road (399 4000/fax 399 4001/www. ritzcarlton.com). **Rates** Dhs3,560 club; Dhs5,100-Dhs9,250 suite. **Credit** AmEx, DC, MC, V. **Map** p278 A5.
The most classically stylish of Dubai's hotels, the Ritz-Carlton is immaculately presented with a grand marble lobby and gigantic windows offering uninterrupted views of white sands and the lapping Arabian Gulf. Too traditional for those who get off on Arabian chic, the hotel is all about formal European luxury. The wooden-beamed tea lounge could happily host a football match, while the terrace is a delight at sunset. There's a separate adults-only pool offering peace for couples, and even the family dip-pit is large and languid. All the spacious rooms look out to sea and enjoy private balconies and sumptuous soft furnishings; the bathrooms again are an exercise in comfort, with vast, glass-fronted showers and baths deeper than Sartre. For a relaxed stay with some old-world charm, this place is hard to beat.
Hotel services *Babysitting. Bars. Beauty salon. Business services. Concierge. Garden. Gym. Internet access. Limousine service. No-smoking rooms. Parking. Pools. Restaurants. Spa.* **Room services** *Dataport. Minibar. Room service (24hrs). Telephone. Turndown. TV: satellite.*

Expensive

Bur Dubai

Grand Hyatt

Oud Metha Road (317 1234/fax 317 1235/ www.dubai.grand.hyatt.com). **Rates** Dhs1,100-Dhs1,200 single; Dhs1,100-Dhs1,300 double; Dhs2,000-Dhs10,000 suite. **Credit** AmEx, DC, MC, V. **Map** p281 K3.
The largest of Dubai's hotels, with 674 rooms, the Grand Hyatt is impressively bombastic. Housing a running track, three outdoor pools, four tennis courts, a spa, 14 restaurants and bars, and (gulp) its very own indoor rainforest with four-tonne dhows hung overhead, the Hyatt is all about grand gestures. Rooms are light, with contemporary

Jumeirah Beach Hotel.
See p43.

Arabic decor and delightful views of the Creek or the Sheikh Zayed Road. Bathrooms are smallish, although the massaging shower and colossal tub – which could happily house three people plus the family pet – quickly subdue spatial quibbles. Junior suites (Dhs2,500) are titanic, dwarfing most rivals, and can be extended further to create a three-bedroom apartment capable of housing the Waltons. A great deal of planning has gone into separating the business and pleasure areas, with secluded lounges and executive spaces ensuring the money-minded don't have to contend with children playing leapfrog. Big, bold and beautiful, the Hyatt is the only true resort hotel in the centre of the city and comes highly recommended.

Hotel services *Babysitting. Bars. Beauty salon. Business services. Concierge. Gym. Internet access. Limousine service. No-smoking rooms. Parking. Pools. Restaurants.* **Room services** *Dataport. Minibar. Room service (24hrs). Telephone. Turndown. TV: satellite.*

Deira

InterContinental Dubai
Beniyas Road (222 7171/fax 228 4777/www.dubai. intercontinental.com). **Rates** Dhs1,500 single/ double; Dhs3,000-Dhs5,000 suite. **Credit** AmEx, DC, MC, V. **Map** p283 J3.
Almost as old as the United Arab Emirates, this 1970s monolith was Dubai's first five-star and is the granddaddy of the hotel scene. While the

impeccable service, the brilliant restaurants and the interesting decor (reception area aside) still make the InterContinental Dubai a fine place to stay, time has taken its toll: the bathrooms are somewhat small by contemporary standards, and the bedrooms, considered huge when the hotel opened for business, would now be classified as not much more than reasonable. On the plus side, recent renovations have successfully upgraded the place, and the furnishings, although plain, are seriously tasteful. Views are of either the large hotel pool or the majestic Creek, and are stunning regardless of the direction your window faces. The black marble-walled executive club is a little cold but is a popular spot for businessmen to sit and take in the colourful corniche views or listen to the resident jazz band who toot their stuff (every night except Friday). A fair option for travellers who want to experience the city rather than baste themselves on the beach, but in truth, you can get a lot more for your money.

Hotel services *Babysitting. Bars. Beauty salon. Business services. Concierge. Gym. Internet access. Limousine service. No-smoking rooms. Parking. Pools. Restaurants.* **Room services** *Dataport. Minibar. Room service (24hrs). Telephone. Turndown. TV: satellite.*

JW Marriott
Muraqqabat Street (262 4444/fax 262 6264/ www.marriott.com). **Rates** Dhs1550 single; Dhs1,880-Dhs15,000 suite. **Credit** AmEx, DC, MC, V. **Map** p281 K1.

Burj Al Arab

Paris has the Eiffel Tower, London has Big Ben and Dubai has the Burj Al Arab, a landmark that couldn't be more fitting. Rather than remembering a glorious revolution or extolling the virtues of democracy, the Burj stands for the driving forces of Dubai: opulence and ambition. Standing at 321 metres high (1,053 feet), it's the world's tallest hotel and the only one to boast seven stars, even if that is an honour the Burj Al Arab bestows upon itself – official recognition doesn't go beyond five. Set some 280 metres (900 feet) offshore on its own man-made island, the hotel is linked to the mainland by a slender, gently curving causeway. The exterior is a marvellous architectural exercise in sleek white curves, which creates a sail-like canvas lit by an ever-changing sequence of lights come nightfall. Sadly the interior doesn't all live up to this promise and visitors may be overwhelmed by the gold-heavy naffness of it all.

The Burj is owned by Jumeirah, which also counts in its impressive portfolio the equally iconic **Emirates Towers** (see p41), the **Jumeirah Beach Hotel** and the **Jumeirah Beach Club** (for both, see p43), the **Madinat Jumeirah** (see p120) and London's Carlton Tower Hotel. Guests are picked up at the airport in one of a fleet of ten white Rolls-Royces and driven to the door across a bridge from which jets of flame shoot to acknowledge the arrival of a VVVIP. A triumphant waterfall awaits in the lobby, which is flanked by floor-to-ceiling aquariums so vast the staff have to don scuba gear to clean them. Gold leaf covers almost every surface and huge golden pillars reach up into the atrium: greens, reds and blues all vie for prominence in a colourful reminder that style in Dubai is as much a matter of volume as it is of taste. Everything is just as expensive as it looks; lavish decadence to satisfy those who can shell out from Dhs4,000 a night for a duplex suite (the standard room).

Blatant sightseers are frowned upon and, away from the lobby, privacy prevails. No floor houses more than 12 suites, and personal, round-the-clock butlers cater to your every whim. The capacious suites spread across two floors, with a staircase spiralling up to the sleeping quarters. Very much a taste of modern Arabia, expect a printer, fax machine, scanner, internet access, wall-to-wall speakers, a 42-inch plasma screen TV

and, in keeping with the sheer decadence, a remote control allowing you to observe and let your guests in without having to leave the comfort of your armchair.

The hotel that dominates so many photos of Dubai itself offers tremendous views. The best look at Dubai's coastline can be had from the restaurant Al Muntaha (translated as 'the ultimate' or 'the highest'), suspended 200 metres (656 feet) above the Arabian Gulf and reached by an express panoramic lift travelling at six metres (20 feet) per second.

If your budget won't stretch but you want a look around, you'll have to book a table at one of the hotel's exquisite restaurants – **Al Mahara** (see p101), **Majlis Al Bahar** (see p102), **Al Muntaha** (see p102) or **Sahn Eddar** (see p112) – or visit the sumptuous **Assawan Spa & Health Club** (see p207).

Burj Al Arab

Beach Road, Jumeirah (301 7777/fax 301 7000/www.jumeirahinternational.com). **Rates** Dhs4,000-Dhs4,600 deluxe/duplex suite; Dhs4,500-5,100 panoramic corner suite; Dhs38,000 royal suite. **Credit** AmEx, DC, MC, V. **Map** p278 A4. **Hotel services** *Babysitting. Bars. Beauty salon. Business services. Concierge. Gym. Internet access. Limousine service. No-smoking rooms. Parking. Pools. Restaurants. Spa.* **Room services** *Dataport. Minibar. Room service (24hrs). Telephone. Turndown. TV: satellite.*

Keeping in style with Marriotts the world over, this is an elegant and grand hotel attached to the Hamarain shopping centre. Huge sofas and lush cushions all but engulf guests in the lobby, and the enormous staircase is straight out of Cinderella. Strange, then, that the classy ambience is undermined somewhat by an assemblage of plastic palm trees. Rooms are comfortable, offering a breed of old-world formality that's rare in Dubai hotels, with signature Marriott beds ensuring you enjoy a deep slumber. (The JW Royal suite even has its own swimming pool.) As with most downtown hotels, vistas are limited and the neighbouring buildings and busy main road hardly please the eye. The pool and health facilities, aside from the massive gym and training area, are average at best. Where the hotel's attention to detail really comes to the fore is in the daily beach-bound shuttle buses. Before they leave, passengers are presented with a beach bag of towels, iced water and sun lotion and on return iced face towels to calm the sunburn.

Le Meridien Dubai

Airport Road, Garhoud (282 4040/fax 282 4672/ www.lemeridien.com). **Rates** Dhs1,200 single; Dhs1,300 double; Dhs2,000-Dhs9,500 suite. **Credit** AmEx, DC, MC, V. **Map** p281 L2.

A large, low-lying, two-storey hotel, situated near the airport but away from the flight path, the Meridien caters mainly to shotgun visitors in Dubai for a quick shop or a layover. Rooms could be described as 'grandma chic', with dated decor and ageing white sofas. However, peer through the nets and you'll be greeted with some surprisingly pleasant views of the gardens and pool area; add the weighted-up health club, terrace balcony rooms and swim-up bar, and you can understand why this hotel is a popular choice with older American and European tourists and businessmen. The grounds house Le Meridien Village, a culinary tour de force with a throng of eateries set in their own walkwayed gardens. The place comes alive at night, with people eating and drinking alfresco into the early hours. The steep room rates are a turn-off, although you might (depending on the month of your visit) be able to secure yourself a special deal.

Hotel services *Babysitting. Bars. Beauty salon. Business services. Concierge. Garden. Gym. Internet access. Limousine service. No-smoking rooms. Parking. Pools. Restaurants.* **Room services** *Dataport. Minibar. Room service (24hrs). Telephone. Turndown. TV: satellite.*

Jumeirah

Le Meridien Mina Seyahi

Al Sufouh Road (399 3333/fax 399 5505/www.le meridien-minaseyahi.com). **Rates** Dhs1,300 single; Dhs1,400 double; Dhs1,500 Royal Club single; Dhs1,600 Royal Club double; Dhs2,400-Dhs3,900 suite. **Credit** AmEx, DC, MC, V. **Map** p278 A5.

The Mina is a gem of a beach property, ideal for familied-up tan-hunters. It retains a casual ambience that's at odds with its formal big brother, the Royal Meridien *(see p50)*. Rooms may be simple but they are comfortable, with beachside balconies overlooking Palm Island (be sure to specify that you want a room with a view when you book). The bathrooms are standard but include nice little touches like an in-room radio. But it is outside that the Mina really comes into its own. With over 850m (2,800ft) of golden sand, the hotel has more front than any other hotel in Dubai. It utilises every inch of it with a host of water sports, four pool areas, a separate beach party zone and a popular beach bar, Barasti *(see p178)*. The children's facilities, including the Penguin Club and dedicated pools, ensure the sprogs don't interfere with sun-worshipping, while the glass-fronted gym allows you to look out to sea while shedding the pounds. The published room rate is pricey, but check for promotions, which make the possibility of staying here much more realistic.

Hotel services *Babysitting. Bars. Beauty salon. Business services. Concierge. Garden. Gym. Internet access. Limousine service. No-smoking rooms. Parking. Pools. Restaurants.* **Room services** *Dataport. Minibar. Room service (24hrs). Telephone. Turndown. TV: satellite.*

One&Only Royal Mirage

Al Sufouh Road (399 9999/fax 399 9998/www.one andonlyresorts.com). **Rates** *The Palace* Dhs1,875 single/double; Dhs3,615 suite. *Arabian Court* Dhs2,050 single/double; Dhs4,660 suite. *Residence & Spa* Dhs3,035 single/double; Dhs4,430-Dhs17,665 suite. **Credit** AmEx, DC, MC, V. **Map** p278 A5.

One&Only Royal Mirage.

Desert resorts

Al Maha

Opened with the mission statement that 'The United Arab Emirates' rich natural heritage must be protected and conservation made a priority', Al Maha threw up a perimeter fence around 225 square kilometres (86 square miles) of desert, ringing in and protecting the wildlife and shutting out the litter bugs, dune-bashers and building companies. Bordered only by Fossil Rock, Jebel Rawdah and a handful of camel farms, this isolated spot is the country's single largest conservation area.

After being greeted by the enthusiastic desert guide – your personal host during your stay – you'll be golf-buggied over to your chalet, through grassy lanes edged with water features. Hold on to your jaw, because a truly exquisite sight awaits. Through two huge metal-studded doors lies 75 square metres (800 square feet) of suite, an enormous, high-walled octagonal space topped in Bedouin tent style. A vast bed dominates the living area, flanked by a pair of chaises longues and a table laden with bowls of pistachio nuts, almonds and plump dried apricots.

Despite the unfettered luxury, your room is far from being the main draw of the resort. Open the terrace doors to stare out across your personal, heated infinity pool and into the depths of the desert. Stretching away to the horizon, it's punctuated only by a corner of the Hajjar mountain range in the mid-distance: pick up your in-room binoculars and sweep the plain to see bouncing gazelles and frolicking oryxes. This is the true delight of Al Maha – the opportunity to get a personalised experience of Arabian nature, and with only 30 chalets-full of tourists at any one time, your view is never cluttered by fellow guests.

The focus on nature watching is underlined by the bedside reading supplied to all visitors: a checklist of flora and fauna known to live on the site. Truly earnest holidaymakers can wake at 5am for coffee and muffins in the Library, before being driven out into the heart of the dunes as the sun rises to uncover the secrets of the desert. A knowledgeable guide seeks out cat's tail, sodom apple and broombush, making a special detour to find clumps of milkwort and desert dandelions. The tracks of snakes, jerboa and Cheesman's gerbils criss-cross the desert, and sand skinks skitter about unconcernedly as you approach. The sands are surprisingly fertile: patches of dune grass spring up overnight if there's the slightest whiff of water in the air, and the reddish desert's a world apart from the spoilt sands closer to town. The air thrums with birdsong – according to the twitchers' guide, a total of 38 species inhabit the area.

Return to savour a speciality Al Maha breakfast omelette filled with smoked salmon, pecan nuts and artichoke hearts before taking up residence by your private pool or engaging in falconry, archery, horse safaris or sand skiing. Alternatively, the Jamilah Spa is on hand for your pampering needs. Whatever you do, don't forget to book in for the sunset camel ride, a deservedly popular 20-minute trip into the gathering dark. As the sun makes its final dip below the horizon, the group dismount and are served with chilled champagne and strawberries. Relax on the bar terrace and then enjoy a euro-centric dinner, spotted with souped-up versions of classic Emirati dishes. *Al Maha Desert Resort (04 303 4222/4223/ www.al-maha.com). Bedouin Suites from Dhs6,245 (incl tax, full board & 2 activities).*

Alternative out-of-town breaks

Bab Al Shams Desert Resort & Spa

A cheaper but less exciting alternative to Al Maha, Bab Al Shams is a luxury hotel in the middle of the dunes. This grid of low-rise buildings made from pre-scratched, crumbling mock sandstone is filled with hidden corridors and secret stairwells: rooms open directly on to the sands, while a spa and pair of decent restaurants cater to guests' needs. At night the resort is lit up by fires in communal areas, surrounded by visitors puffing on shisha. The range of activities is limited to desert excursions, but there is also a well-equipped children's centre. *Bab Al Shams Desert Resort & Spa (04 832 6699). Double rooms from Dhs1,400/night.*

Mountain Extreme

A sophisticated camping experience awaits, as this company takes groups to remote communities in the Northern Emirates to sample tribal life for a night among the local people who still live there. A trip for groups of two to 12 (maximum) costs Dhs570 for an overnight package, which includes pick-up around 2pm, a hike in the hills to the village, dinner, breakfast and lunch the next day. *Contact: john@mountain-extreme.com/ 050 450 5426.*

Arabian Court Hotel.

Styled on an Arabian fort, the Royal Mirage is a uniquely impressive hotel experience. It's three hotels in one: the Palace, the Arabian Court and the Residence, each offering different levels of plush accommodation. Where many of Dubai's landmarks owe their success to a degree of shock and awe, the Royal Mirage presents an illusion of days gone by with welcome subtlety. Many travellers in the know leave more obvious Jumeirah hotels to the tourists (and their kids) and head instead for this haven of softly lit courtyards, thick with shisha smoke and echoing to the beats of faint Arabic music.

The complex's simple low-rise architecture holds sumptuous interiors of rich fabrics and intricate woodwork. Iron lanterns throw patterned candlelight on to sand-coloured walls, and pockets of rooms are interspersed with Moorish arches and verdant gardens. Add the delicate use of gold and warm tones throughout and the scene is set for the ultimate romantic getaway. The hotel is never more beautiful than at night, when couples emerge to take quiet strolls down past the city's largest swimming pool and on to the beach. Excellent facilities include the clinically named Health & Beauty Institute (*see p209*) and al fresco sipping station the Rooftop (*see p179*). Deluxe rooms are sensibly sized and packed with wonderful examples of attention to detail, from the slippers by the bed to the hand towel artfully folded into the shape of a swan. Every inch of the Royal Mirage seems designed to make you feel good and, as such, it's well worth the expense.

Hotel services *Babysitting. Bars. Beauty salon. Business services. Concierge. Garden. Gym. Internet access. Limousine service. No-smoking rooms.*

Parking. Pools. Restaurants. Spa. **Room services** *Dataport. Minibar. Room service (24hrs). Telephone. Turndown. TV: satellite.*

Le Royal Meridien

Al Sufouh Road (399 5555/fax 399 5999/www. leroyalmeridien-dubai.com). **Rates** Dhs1,500 single; Dhs1,600 double; Dhs3,000-Dhs8,000 suite. **Credit** AmEx, DC, MC, V. **Map** p278 A5.
Roses seem to be quite a big deal at the Royal Meridien. In each room you'll find finger bowls with petals floating in them, rose residue is scattered on the bed, and the bathroom has more blooms than a florist on 13 February. Such in-your-face opulence is typical of Le Meridien's flagship brand and the pools, the gardens and even the hotel's great stretch of sand have been sculpted in a timelessly classic style. Accommodation is offered either in the main hotel or in the stand-alone Tower and Club complexes; whichever you choose, all rooms are sea-facing, large, bright and comfortable, with balconies from which to enjoy the splendid view down the beach or over the Gulf. The 15-storey Tower is the newest and flashiest part of the hotel, with panoramic windows and beds that could happily sleep a hippopotamus. Sexy European clients flit around the upmarket all-beige coffee spaces and bars, and it is doubtful that the pool has seen a full swimsuit in its life. If you should require even more decadence, head to the Caracalla Spa (*see p203*).

Hotel services *Babysitting. Bars. Beauty salon. Business services. Concierge. Garden. Gym. Internet access. Limousine service. No-smoking rooms. Parking. Pools. Restaurants.* **Room services** *Dataport. Minibar. Room service (24hrs). Telephone. Turndown. TV: satellite.*

Moderate

Bur Dubai

Arabian Court Hotel

Al Fahidi Street, opposite Dubai Museum (351 9111/ 351 7744/info@arabiancourt.ae). **Rates** Dhs1,000-Dhs1,100 single; Dhs1,100-Dhs1,300 double; Dhs2,000-Dhs3,500 suite. **Credit** AmEx, DC, MC, V. **Map** p282 H4.

Set in the very heart of Dubai, less than a stone's throw from the Creek and the Souk Al Kabir (Meena Bazaar), this hotel goes such a bundle on the heritage angle that you'll be surprised to discover it's Bur Dubai's newest hotel. A good option for business guests who want to remain central, it is also home to one of the finest Indian restaurants in town. Spacious bedrooms, many of which have Creek views, make this a comfortable stay. Sadly, while its suites command hefty price tags worthy of the luxury category, the hotel lacks sufficient opulence to rival its top-quality competitors. *Hotel services Babysitting. Bars. Beauty salon. Business centre. Concierge. Gym. Laundry. Limousine service. Massage services. Parking. Pools. Restaurants. Sauna.* **Room services** *Dataport. Internet. Minibar. Room service (24hrs). Telephone. Turndown. TV: satellite.*

Jumeirah Rotana

Al Dhiyafa Street, Satwa (345 5888/fax 345 8777/ www.rotana.com). **Rates** Dhs700 single; Dhs800 double; Dhs900-Dhs1,200 suite. **Credit** AmEx, DC, MC, V. **Map** p284 F8.

Cheekily and misleadingly named, the hotel is actually in the shore-free area of Satwa rather than beachy Jumeirah. That said, this busy hotel has a casual atmosphere and a 50/50 mix of business and leisure guests. The spacious and light bedrooms come complete with generously sized beds, plenty of wardrobe space and entertaining views over the back streets. Decor is typical bland Americana: although comfortable, it's nothing to write home about. There's a shuttle service to the Hilton beach club, Mercato and Sahara shopping centres. Guests can enjoy stretching their legs outside on the ever-bustling Al Dhiyafa Street, but if you have a peaceful weekend away or romantic escape in mind, look a little further towards Al Sufouh. *Hotel services Bars. Business services. Concierge. Gym. Internet access. No-smoking rooms. Parking. Pools. Restaurants.* **Room services** *Dataport. Minibar. Room service (24hrs). Telephone. Turndown. TV: satellite.*

Mövenpick Hotel

19th Street (336 6000/fax 336 6626/www. moevenpick-burdubai.com). **Rates** Dhs720 single; Dhs840 double; Dhs1,440-Dhs5,000 suite. **Credit** AmEx, DC, MC, V. **Map** p281 J3.

Modern and still virtually scratch-free, this hotel manages to be comfortable without veering into stuffiness. It offers an inviting ambience, but lacks

the wow factor of the beach hotels, not least because the panorama from the medium-sized rooms is all inner-city Dubai, with the choice limited to apartment blocks, empty stretches of sand or the hotel lobby. That said, the orthopaedic beds are comfy and the furnishings adequate. The suites and executive rooms are a leap up from the standard ones, featuring Jacuzzis in the bathrooms, and health fanatics are well catered for with a gym that includes separate aerobics spaces and massage rooms for either sex. Another of the hotel's attractions is the rooftop, which boasts a large and lovely deck area and a swimming pool, a jogging track and a snack bar. *Hotel services Babysitting. Bars. Beauty salon. Business services. Concierge. Gym. Internet access. Limousine service. No-smoking rooms. Parking. Pools. Restaurants.* **Room services** *Dataport. Minibar. Room service (24hrs). Telephone. Turndown. TV: satellite.*

Ramada Dubai

Opposite Jumbo Electronics, Al Mankhool Road (351 9999/fax 352 7589/www.ramadadubai.com). **Rates** Dhs900 single; Dhs1,000 double. **Credit** AmEx, DC, MC, V. **Map** p282 H5.

Proud owner of the largest stained-glass window in the whole of the Middle East, the Ramada Continental – now in its twenties – is just outside the more hectic heartland of the Golden Sands area. The hotel is frequented both by international guests and by local residents, and its shoreless location means that most of its clients tend to be business folk. Rooms are spacious, though most overlook air-conditioning vents, building sites or the busy streets below. Good service, competitive corporate rates and decent-sized rooms. *Hotel services Babysitting. Bars. Beauty salon. Business services. Concierge. Gym. Internet access. Limousine service. No-smoking rooms. Parking. Pools. Restaurants.* **Room services** *Minibar. Room service (24hrs). Telephone. Turndown. TV: satellite.*

Sheikh Zayed Road

Crowne Plaza Dubai

Satwa side (331 1111/fax 331 5555/www.ichotels. com). **Rates** Dhs1,080 single/double; Dhs2,400-Dhs9,000 suite. **Credit** AmEx, DC, MC, V. **Map** p285 G10.

This comfortable city-centre business hotel does a nice sideline in the tourist trade. The prime location at the Creek end of Sheikh Zayed Road means that guests are a short drive from the beach or indeed from anywhere in the city. The grand lobby area, which is reached via steep and skinny escalators, has aged well on the whole, although the once-swish decor is no longer up to speed, as the 1950s-style display cases and the carpet testify. Both the health club and pool are spacious and casual, and the club floor features an executive lounge allowing VIP visitors to eat away from the chattering masses. Standard rooms are pretty small and crowded, while the itsy-bitsy bathrooms are dated even in the suites. The views, however, are as good as any in Dubai.

Hotel services *Babysitting. Bars. Beauty salon. Business services. Concierge. Gym. Internet access. Limousine service. No-smoking rooms. Parking. Pools. Restaurants.* **Room services** *Dataport. Minibar. Room service (24hrs). Telephone. Turndown. TV: satellite.*

Dusit Dubai

Trade Centre side (343 3333/fax 343 4222/http:// dubai.dusit.com). **Rates** Dhs1,200 single/double; Dhs2,300 executive single; Dhs2,400 executive double; Dhs2,600-Dhs2,900 suite. **Credit** AmEx, DC, MC, V. **Map** p280 H4.

One of the most striking buildings on the street, the Dusit is a shiny marriage of glass and steel. Its Thai-style theming is evident throughout, from the Asian-chic decor of the rooms to the smart sarong-wearing staff. Rooms are lovely, with rich browns and sweeping views. Guests can work out in the well-stocked gym with its bird's-eye city views or laze in the 36th-floor open-air pool, before heading to the mini spa where they can get themselves primed for a night out. This used to be the closest you'd get to a high-class bargain on Sheikh Zayed Road, but prices now increase annually.

Hotel services *Babysitting. Bars. Beauty salon. Business services. Concierge. Gym. Internet access. Limousine service. No-smoking rooms. Parking. Pools. Restaurants.* **Room services** *Dataport. Minibar. Room service (24hrs). Telephone. Turndown. TV: satellite.*

Bow-legged beauty: **Dusit Dubai**.

Millennium Airport Hotel

Casablanca Road, Garhoud (282 3464/fax 282 0627/www.millenniumhotels.com). **Rates** Dhs720 single/double; Dhs2,000 suites. **Credit** AmEx, DC, MC, V. **Map** p281 K2.

As you'd expect from the name, this comfortable crash pad is within spitting distance of Dubai's main airport terminal and attracts a great deal of fleeting business from European suits and crew. Kenny G-style Muzak aside, the marble-heavy hotel foyer is elegant and inviting, while the large swimming pool and banks of green grass make it a low-key family favourite. Rooms are large (a shared twin could easily sleep four cosy adults), airy and have pleasant garden views. Wardrobe space and beds are both ample, and a subtle Arabic touch runs throughout the decor and furnishings. The hourly airport bus service makes it an obvious choice for business travellers, but leisure visitors will also find the place a perfectly comfortable place to stay – although it's a long way from the beach.

Hotel services *Babysitting. Bars. Beauty salon. Business services. Concierge. Internet access. Limousine service. No-smoking rooms. Parking. Pool. Restaurants.* **Room services** *Dataport. Minibar. Room service (24hrs). Telephone. Turndown. TV: satellite.*

Novotel

Behind World Trade Centre (318 7000/fax 318 7100/www.novotel.com). **Rates** Dhs850 single/double; Dhs1,375-Dhs1,700 suite. **Credit** AmEx, DC, MC, V. **Map** p285 G10.

Built to house the World Bank and IMF meetings held in Dubai back in 2003, the Novotel boasts much higher standards in the lower price bracket than the city is accustomed to. The lobby – all dark wood, open space and ordered sophistication – is a stylish reminder that this purpose-built cheapish hotel was nonetheless designed to impress some of the world's most important travellers. Its rooms are small, but they're not cramped and the facilities more than satisfy. The hotel holds little appeal for sun-seekers, offering only a small pool and gym, but it will score highly with business types operating along Sheikh Zayed Road.

Hotel services *Bars. Business services. Concierge. Gym. Internet access. No-smoking rooms. Parking. Pools. Restaurants.* **Room services** *Dataport. Minibar. Room service (24hrs). Telephone. Turndown. TV: satellite.*

Towers Rotana Hotel

Satwa side (343 8000/fax 343 8901/www.rotana.com). **Rates** Dhs850 single; Dhs950 double; Dhs1,500 suites. **Credit** AmEx, DC, MC, V. **Map** p280 H4.

Surrounded by grander and considerably more expensive five-star properties, the Towers Rotana has a minimal design style and a younger clientele than its neighbours. Rooms are of average to cosy size but are very comfortable and the views over Jumeirah will wobble the knees of most tourists. Decor is light and airy in the bedrooms, and there's a large pool space and gym situated in a

Al Bustan Rotana.

separate wing of the building. While pitched predominantly at business travellers, the Rotana is seconds away from the nightlife of the Sheikh Zayed strip; not a bad option for holidaymakers who can't afford the lavishness of the Jumeirah strip yet want to avoid the drudgery of Deira.
Hotel services *Babysitting. Bars. Beauty salon. Business services. Concierge. Gym. Internet access. Limousine. No-smoking rooms. Parking. Pools. Restaurants.* **Room services** *Room service (24hrs).*

Deira

Al Bustan Rotana

Casablanca Road, Garhoud (282 0000/fax 282 8100/ www.rotana.com). **Rates** Dhs925-Dhs975 single/ double; Dhs1,200 Club Rotana single; Dhs1,300 Club Rotana double; Dhs2,000-Dhs7,500 suites. **Credit** AmEx, DC, MC, V. **Map** p281 K2.
Located within striking distance of Dubai's airport, this Rotana has earned a reputation as a convenient business hotel. Not that it's all work and no play – the hotel has a vast amount of leisure facilities too, including a spacious swimming pool, a popular nightclub and a well-equipped, if poorly attended, gym. Standard bedrooms are reasonably sized, with huge beds, but wardrobe space is limited and the bathrooms are dated. A handful of rooms come with their own private terraces, which face the pool deck, raising their appeal considerably. Executive club levels are a distinct improvement with larger rooms, a dedicated check in/out area, TV lounge, breakfast area and net access.
Hotel services *Babysitting. Bars. Beauty salon. Business services. Concierge. Gym. Internet access. Limousine service. No-smoking rooms. Parking. Pools. Restaurants.* **Room services** *Dataport. Minibar. Room service (24hrs). Telephone. Turndown. TV: satellite.*

Coral Deira

Muraqqabat Street (224 8587/fax 221 7033/ www.coral-deira.com). **Rates** Dhs1,000 standard; Dhs1,200 Club select; Dhs1,500 Club suites. **Credit** MC, V. **Map** p283 L3.
Amid Deira's bustle lies a welcome haven of extravagance in the shape of the Coral Deira. A short drive from the airport, it dominates Muraqqabat Street in the commercial heart of the city. The second dry five-star hotel in Dubai, the Coral is popular with visitors from Gulf countries, particularly businessmen from Saudi Arabia. Get past the unconvincing exterior purple lights and the hotel is stylish in look and warm in atmosphere. Modern-day comforts include Villeroy & Boch bathrooms with elongated baths, while excellent business facilities include two conference rooms and a well-equipped business centre. There's even a florist on site. Three restaurants provide a decent range of food, of which the all-you-can-eat buffet at Nafoora is the answer to your cravings for Middle Eastern cuisine. The courtesy coach service and travel reservations are handy if you're pressed for time, while free access and transport to Coral Beach Resort's pool and beach area are a major attraction.
Hotel services *Babysitting. Business centre. Concierge. Gym. Hairdressing salon. Internet. No-smoking rooms. Parking. Pool.* **Room services** *Dataport. Minibar. Telephone. TV: satellite.*

Immersed in you

The Coral difference goes deeper than you'd imagine

CORAL SUITES
AJMAN

CORAL DEIRA
DUBAI

CORAL ORIENTAL
DUBAI

CORAL BOUTIQUE
HOTEL APARTMENTS
DUBAI

CORAL BEACH RESORT
SHARJAH

CORAL AL NAHDA
RESORT & SPA
MUSCAT

Member of

Boutique Hotels

Just when you thought all hotels are alike, comes a refreshing new approach to the business of making people feel at home. A philosophy called Coral. Based on the belief that the word, "guest" is not just another way to say, "customer", but means someone who has come to spend a precious part of their lives with you - be it a couple of hours over a meal or a few days on vacation. That's why "Coral" will be a hallmark of hospitality properties where you can look forward to be with people who are passionate about understanding what our guests are really looking for. We look forward to having you over.

CORAL INTERNATIONAL LLC
Muraqqabat Street, Deira Mezzanine Level
P.O.Box 66232, Dubai, U.A.E.,
Tel: +971-4-22 33 448 Fax: +971-4-22 77 449

CORAL INTERNATIONAL
HOTELS · RESORTS · SPAS

e-mail: info@coral-international.com www.coral-international.com

Hilton Dubai Creek

Beniyas Road (227 1111/fax 227 1131/www.hilton.com). **Rates** Dhs775-Dhs850 single; Dhs825-Dhs1,000 double; Dhs1,750 suite. **Credit** AmEx, DC, MC, V. **Map** p283 L4.

The classiest and most stylish city-centre hotel in Dubai, the Hilton Dubai Creek was designed by Carlos Ott (the brains behind the Opéra de la Bastille in Paris) and has cuisine by world-renowned culinary master Gordon Ramsay at Verre (*see p96*). Glide into the zen-like foyer, where peaceful water features lap against glass and gleaming chrome, and you enter a world of designer purity. For some, this exercise in modernism is just too cool, but if you want stylish urban chic, this is the place for you. The large rooms are statements in contemporary luxury, and the huge comfortable beds and ultra-cool black and white bathrooms prove there is substance beyond the style. The Hilton Dubai Creek comes highly recommended, though prices have escalated significantly since opening.
Hotel services *Babysitting. Bars. Beauty salon. Business services. Concierge. Gym. Internet access. Limousine service. No-smoking rooms. Parking. Pools. Restaurants.* **Room services** *Dataport. Minibar. Room service (24hrs). Telephone. Turndown. TV: satellite.*

Hyatt Regency

Deira Corniche (209 1234/fax 209 1000/www.dubai.regency.hyatt.com). **Rates** Dhs900 single; Dhs1,000 double; Dhs2,500-Dhs9,400 suite. **Credit** AmEx, DC, MC, V. **Map** p283 J1.

Built in 1980, this vast 400-room stalwart sits close to the mouth of the Creek in downtown Deira. Tried and tested, the Regency is an unashamed courter of business guests, and a successful one at that. Wheeler-dealers, in particular those from East Asia, are wooed in their droves by the hotel's reputation, professionalism and plush suites. The out-of-the-way location – around 7km (four miles) from the city and out of easy reach of Jumeirah's beaches – has created something of a siege mentality, and the hotel has every leisure facility going, including a revolving restaurant, nightclub, cinema, ice-skating rink, mini golf course and its very own shopping centre. The rooms are dominated by large glass windows offering fine views of Dubai, the Corniche and Sharjah, with fresh flowers and plants to spruce up the slightly dated furniture. One floor has recently been entirely renovated and re-opened, and the first floor boasts a plush new waterhole, simply named The Bar. An excellent hotel, but its location proves off-putting to many.
Hotel services *Babysitting. Bars. Beauty salon. Business services. Concierge. Gym. Internet access. Limousine service. No-smoking rooms. Parking. Pools. Restaurants.* **Room services** *Dataport. Minibar. Room service (24hrs). Telephone. Turndown. TV: satellite.*

Sheraton Dubai Creek

Beniyas Road (228 1111/fax 221 3468/www.sheraton.com/dubai). **Rates** Dhs850 single; Dhs900 double; Dhs1,800-Dhs6,500 suite. **Credit** AmEx, DC, MC, V. **Map** p283 K4.

Stunning from the outside, with its tower and thrusting waterfront extension, the Sheraton is slick but straightforwardly business-like within. A huge escalator leads the way up to the dimly lit foyer, where suited executives sink cappuccinos and munch fresh-baked muffins. The tower rooms offer some of the most elevated views over the city, a panoramic snapshot of the Bur Dubaian shoreline framed by heavy curtains. The rooms are comfortable, and while they don't exactly ooze character you can cheer yourself with the fact that they're excellent value for money. The key advantage for tourists is the location – though the Sheraton is far from the beach, it is a short skip from the likes of the abra station and gold souk, and within walking distance of a string of other hotels' restaurants and bars. If that sounds like too much effort, Vivaldi (*see p97* **The brunch bunch**) is one of the best Italian restaurants in town.
Hotel services *Babysitting. Bars. Beauty salon. Business services. Concierge. Gym. Internet access. Limousine service. No-smoking rooms. Parking. Pools. Restaurants.* **Room services** *Dataport. Minibar. Room service (24hrs). Telephone. Turndown. TV: satellite.*

Al Sondos Suites

Opposite City Centre (294 9797). **Rates** Dhs750-Dhs1,200 single/double. **Credit** AmEx, DC, MC, V. **Map** p281 K2.

These luxurious suites combine the convenience of self-catering with five-star service, making it ideal for long-staying guests. Handily located opposite the City Centre mall and a short hop from the Creek, Al Sondos will satisfy both businessmen and avid shoppers. There's an impressive burnt-orange lobby and the tiled rooms are spacious, clean and stylishly comfortable. Special touches include daily shoe-shining, turndown services and high-speed internet facilities.
Hotel services *Beauty salon. Business centre. Gym. Internet access. Laundry. Pool. Restaurant.* **Room services** *Room service (24hrs). Telephone. Turndown. TV: satellite.*

Jumeirah

Dubai Marine Beach Resort & Spa

Beach Road (346 1111/fax 346 0234/www.dxbmarine.com). **Rates** Dhs900 single; Dhs984 double; Dhs1,320-Dhs10,800 suite. **Credit** AmEx, DC, MC, V. **Map** p284 D8.

At the beginning of Beach Road in Jumeirah, this is the only beachfront hotel in the city proper – the others start on the Al Sufouh Road, some 15km (nine miles) up. The property's great location, small but attractive beach, lush gardens and two swimming pools make it an ideal leisure venue, while its proximity to the city gives it the edge for beach-loving business travellers. Accommodation is scattered in 33 low-rise villa-style buildings that are spread throughout the resort, with each villa containing only six suites. Its quiet, green gardens and sun-drenched stretch of sand make Dubai Marine a perfect chill-out spot. The rooms themselves could do with a facelift, but the complex as a whole is a great place to relax.

Hotel services *Babysitting. Bars. Beauty salon. Business services. Concierge. Garden. Gym. Internet access. Limousine service. No-smoking rooms. Parking. Pools. Restaurants. Spa.* **Room services** *Dataport. Minibar. Room service (24hrs). Telephone. Turndown. TV: satellite.*

Hilton Dubai Jumeirah

Al Sufouh Road (399 1111/fax 399 1112/www. hilton.com). **Rates** Dhs875-Dhs1,250 single; Dhs925-Dhs1,300 double; Dhs1,700-Dhs4,000 suite. **Credit** AmEx, DC, MC, V. **Map** p278 A5.

Sun worship at **Oasis Beach**.

A classic resort hotel, the Hilton Jumeirah is more package than out-and-out luxury: the decent-sized rooms are comfortable and functional rather than decadent, with cute little balconies affording views of the Gulf. The hotel's large pool has a swim-up bar with underwater stools on which to sit and slurp your cocktail. Pleasant terraced gardens lead down to the white sandy beach where a number of water sports are available, and a decent health club and gym add to the list of facilities on offer. Although it's family-friendly, the hotel is also a great spot for couples, with sophisticated bars and one of the best restaurants in Dubai, Bice (*see p101*). If you can get a room for the advertised rate or below then bite their arm off to do so: this is a true bargain for the beachfront.

Hotel services *Babysitting. Bars. Beauty salon. Business services. Concierge. Gym. Internet access. Limousine service. No-smoking rooms. Parking. Pools. Restaurants.* **Room services** *Dataport. Minibar. Room service (24hrs). Telephone. Turndown. TV: satellite.*

Oasis Beach

Al Sufouh Road (399 4444/fax 399 4200/www. jebelali-international.com). **Rates** Dhs950-Dhs1,595 single/double; Dhs1,685 Executive seaview; Dhs1740 Club seaview. **Credit** AmEx, DC, MC, V. **Map** p278 A5.

The Oasis is the only four-star hotel on the beach (all the others are five or above) but it has two cards up its sleeve: reasonably affordable prices and one of the best beach clubs in town. These elements are enough to make it fiendishly popular with package holidaymakers looking for a day on the sand. While the public areas are a touch rough and ready, the rooms are surprisingly attractive, decked out with a touch of oriental style. When booking, be sure to ask for a shoreside room; the others overlook a vast and ever-expanding building site. Private balconies offer tropical views over the palms and the pools, with the occasional jet-skier cutting up the waves in the middle distance. Look out for regular price promotions.

Hotel services *Babysitting. Bars. Beauty salon. Business services. Concierge. Gym. Internet access. Limousine service. No-smoking rooms. Parking. Pools. Restaurants.* **Room services** *Dataport. Minibar. Room service (24hrs). Telephone. Turndown. TV: satellite.*

Sheraton Jumeirah Beach Resort

Al Sufouh Road (399 5533/fax 399 5577/www. starwoodhotels.com). **Rates** Dhs770-Dhs915 single; Dhs810-Dhs950 double; Dhs1,170 Tower single; Dhs1,175 Tower double; Dhs1,245-Dhs4,000 suite. **Credit** AmEx, DC, MC, V. **Map** p278 A5.

Currently the furthest beach property from the city (although this is likely to change with Dubai's constant expansion), the Sheraton is a stylish resort property with a good stretch of sand, decent beach club, spacious gardens and a fine swimming pool. Popular with European package tourists, the hotel blurs the five-star lines with the overall feel more comfortable than lavish; indeed, it's hard to believe it belongs in the same class as the Mirage. Rooms are large and overlook either the sea and resort area or the rather less pleasing building sites of the developing Dubai Marina and Jumeirah Beach Residence. Still, it's a great-value place for those looking to escape the trappings of inner-city vacations, which is just as well as a taxi ride into town will set you back over Dhs40. Along with the Oasis and Hilton Dubai Jumeirah, this is the best-value spot on Al Sufouh Road.

Hotel services *Babysitting. Bars. Beauty salon. Business services. Concierge. Garden. Gym. Internet access. Limousine service. No-smoking rooms. Parking. Pools. Restaurants.* **Room services** *Dataport. Minibar. Room service (24hrs). Telephone. Turndown. TV: satellite.*

Cheap

Bur Dubai

Capitol Hotel

Mankhool Road, Satwa (346 0111/fax 346 0333/ www.capitol-hotel.com). **Rates** Dhs475-Dhs550 single; Dhs660 double; Dhs1,250-Dhs1,750 suite. **Credit** AmEx, DC, MC, V. **Map** p284 E7.

A good alternative to Dubai's garish glitz, the Capitol's room rates have stabilised over the last year. Though a tad prosaic, the standard rooms are a decent size, with huge beds but banal views of built-up Bur Dubai. Suites are large and welcoming, with a well-decorated living space, and can be extended through the use of an adjoining twin room. The hotel's rooftop is, however, home to a forlorn swimming pool, sadly departed fountains and a lonely café. The gym is poky but holds a good selection of equipment. Should the mood take you, you can request one of three masseuses to carry out treatments in your room. Situated close to both Satwa's shopping streets and the beach, this remains a popular choice for leisure travellers from Eastern Europe, the Gulf States and India, as well as more regular business guests.

Hotel services *Babysitting. Bars. Beauty salon. Business services. Concierge. Gym. Internet access. No-smoking rooms. Parking. Pools. Restaurants.* **Room services** *Dataport. Minibar. Room service (24hrs). Telephone. TV: satellite.*

Al Faris Apartments

Al Fahidi Street, opposite Lamcy Plaza (336 6566/ 335 5626). **Rates** Dhs550 studio apartments; Dhs880 single. **Credit** AmEx, MC, V. **Map** p281 J3.

Practical if uninspirational, these well-maintained lodgings used to be a top money-saving option, but prices have soared since 2004. Nonetheless, they are still a viable no-frills option.

Hotel services *Housekeeping. Mini gyms. Pool.* **Room services** *Room service. Telephone. TV: satellite.*

Golden Sands Hotel Apartments

Off Bank Street (355 5553/fax 352 6903). **Rates** Dhs550 studio; Dhs750 1-bedroom; Dhs1,300 3-bedroom. **Credit** AmEx, MC, V. **Map** p283 J5.

Comprising a large number of sizeable and fully serviced self-catering flats, these range from one-bedroom studios to three- and four-bedroom apartments, with additional services such as a gym, sauna and squash courts. Long-term visitors can extend their stay to a year, which costs up to Dhs60,000 for a studio and Dhs90,000 for a two-bedroom apartment.

Hotel services *Gym. Housekeeping. Pool. Sauna. Squash courts.* **Room services** *Room service (24hrs). Telephone. TV.*

President Hotel

Trade Centre Road, Karama (334 6565/fax 336 8915). **Rates** Dhs300 single; Dhs350 double. **Credit** AmEx, MC, V. **Map** p285 H7.

Sat on one edge of the bargain-heavy Karama markets, this 50-room, two-star hotel seems as happy to offer knockdown prices as the traders who have set up shop behind it. The dark and dimly lit hallways lead into similarly gloomy rooms, with views of surrounding buildings and the busy road out front. The beds themselves are quite small, and the tiny bathrooms with their shampoo sachets are just enough to get by on. Staff are very friendly and helpful, although given there are so few of them, efficiency is notable by its absence and the guests, mainly Indian and Gulf Coast families, keep them teetering on the brink of a collective nervous breakdown. Dirt-cheap and central, the President is a fair choice, but you're better off splashing out that bit more for the Jumeirah Rotana or, if you can live without a pool, the Ibis.

Hotel services *Bars. No-smoking rooms. Parking. Pools. Restaurants.* **Room services** *Minibar. Room service (24hrs). Telephone. TV: satellite.*

Rush Inn

Bank Street (352 2235/fax 352 2244). **Rates** Dhs250 single; Dhs350 double/standard suite. **Credit** AmEx, MC, V. **Map** p282 H4.

A well-priced hostelry, the Rush Inn has a foyer hung with slightly dismal snapshots of karaoke stars working the plethora of themed in-house bars (one Pakistani, one Filipino and one African), but the rooms are modestly comfortable. But if you're looking for a tranquil getaway, this place is probably not for you – the hotel's line-up of nightspots means it can be noisy until the wee small hours.

Hotel services *Laundry.* **Room services** *Room service (24hrs). Telephone. TV.*

Rydges Plaza

Satwa roundabout, Satwa (398 2222/fax 398 3700/ www.rydges.com/dubai). **Rates** Dhs600 single/ double; Dhs1,400 suite. **Credit** AmEx, DC, MC, V. **Map** p285 F8.

Occupying a city-centre location next to Satwa roundabout, this nine-storey hotel delivers far more in terms of comfort, style and facilities than its mundane exterior promises. The good position, attentive staff and faux classical pool area attract repeat clientele of business travellers and elderly tourists. Bedrooms are spacious and comfortable but the furnishings, although unchipped and clean, match the somewhat dated style of the hotel. Most rooms have a clear view of the bustling streets below, and the suites come complete with 120-year-old stand-alone iron tubs that each weigh over a tonne. Rydges is undoubtedly the best hotel in this price bracket.

Hotel services *Babysitting. Bars. Business services. Concierge. Gym. Internet access. Limousine service. No-smoking rooms. Parking. Pools. Restaurants.* **Room services** *Dataport. Minibar. Room service (24hrs). Telephone. Turndown. TV: satellite.*

XVA

Al Fahidi Roundabout, Bastakia, behind Basta Art Café (353 5383/fax 353 5988/xva@xvagallery.com). **Rates** Dhs450-Dhs660 single/double. **Credit** AmEx, MC, V. **Map** p282 H4.

This stunningly attractive property is unique in Dubai: built more than 70 years ago from coral and clay, it has been faithfully restored and reopened as a gallery, restaurant and boutique guesthouse. Nestled in the pocket of old Dubai known as Bastakia, an ornate, if often overlooked area alongside the Creek, this is one of a handful of wind tower-topped buildings holding out against the lightning modernisation of the city. There's currently a new surge of interest in looking after the last vestiges of pre-oil Dubai, and Bastakia is at the crest of the preservation wave; the care lavished on the building and the sense of time having slowed to a crawl within its walls makes XVA (named after the number of the street it lies in) one of the most interesting places to stay in town. The guesthouse's facilities are minimalist but include a living room and café. There's also a gallery that regularly exhibits work by local artists. Enjoy the rooftop terrace, where you can swing in suspended rocking chairs looking out over the skyline of old buildings and mosques to the bright lights of Bur Dubai proper. XVA houses just a few guests at any one time, so book early. The unique atmosphere here is only heightened by the incredibly competitive rates, which, refreshingly, haven't changed since 2004. Just round the corner are the Majlis Gallery (*see p162*) and the excellent Basta Art Café (*see p107*).

Hotel services *Concierge. Restaurant.* **Room services** *Minibar. Stereo.*

Deira

Dubai Youth Hostel

Ousais Road, nr Al Mulla Plaza (298 8161/fax 298 8141). **Rates** Dhs80 dormitories; Dhs150 single; Dhs160 double. **No credit cards. Map** p281 L1.
More of an upmarket boarding house than a hostel, 'dormitories' contain a maximum of two beds and

there are spruce, well-maintained family rooms for travellers with kids.

Hotel services *Gym. Housekeeping. Laundry. Pool. Restaurant. Telephone. TV.*

Al Mamzar Apartments

Al Waheeda Road (297 2921/fax 269 1305). **Rates** Dhs300 1-bedroom; Dhs475 2-bedroom. **Credit** AmEx, MC, V. **Map** p279 D1.

This complex boasts modest but fully furnished apartments with a swimming pool and gym, which can be used for a small surplus charge. Although a little distance from the town centre (near Dubai Library), the apartments are blessed with being in easy reach of the delightfully peaceful Al Mamzar beaches; unlike the calm Jumeirah waters, these have waves that are perfectly suited to bodysurfing. They also attract far fewer tourists.

Hotel services *Gym. Housekeeping. Pool.* **Room services** *Room service (24hrs). Telephone. TV.*

Sheikh Zayed Road

Ibis

Behind World Trade Centre (318 7000/fax 318 7100/www.ibishotel.com). **Rates** Dhs295-Dhs395 single/double. **Credit** AmEx, DC, MC, V. **Map** p285 G9.

A rarity in the Dubai hotel trade, the Ibis is a fuss-free affair that caters to tourists seeking to spend their time in the city, rather than in their hotel rooms. Accommodation is cheap and without extras, breakfast is a flat Dhs35 and there's no pool. But by not trying to do it all, the hotel has been able to invest its time and energy in the fundamentals, developing a high-class feel for a three-star property. The lobby is elegant, simple and dotted with Phillippe Starck furniture. Rooms are comfortable – though at 20sq m (215sq ft) quite small – and offer pretty drab glimpses of the Dubai World Trade Centre apartments. A sound choice for shoestring travellers with no particular desire for fancy extras.

Hotel services *Bars. Internet access. No-smoking rooms. Parking. Restaurants.* **Room services** *Dataport. Telephone. TV: satellite.*

Golden Sands Hotel Apartments. *See p57.*

Sightseeing

Introduction

What to see and where to go in the City of Gold.

Sightseeing

Postcards from Dubai tell similar tales of landmark hotels perched on the coastal stretch of Jumeirah Beach and, further inland, camel rides led by weathered locals in national dress. The clichés are in part due to European visitors who, exploring the Middle East for the first time, want to experience precisely this sun-drenched if sanitised taste of Arabia. But the issue is also due to the overwhelming newness of Dubai; impressive and various, the skyscrapers that line the city's main artery, Sheikh Zayed Road, were nonetheless all built within the past 20 years. Almost all of the most striking buildings here are just a few years old.

The fact that Dubai is perpetually under construction means that it can be both unattractive and tiresome to navigate. Visitors in search of history and tradition will have to search far harder than those wishing to enjoy the city's glitz and glamour. But while Dubai is not rich in historic or cultural sights, there are a scattering of worthwhile and rewarding excursions – if you know where to look.

GATEWAY TO THE GULF

Dubai sits on the Arabian Gulf, which is key to the city's tourism success today and has been a source of both food and trade for centuries.

Historically Dubai was two settlements built on either side of the Creek, a 15-kilometre (9.5-mile) inlet around which the city's trade developed. Deira is a catch-all term for the area to the north of the Creek, and Bur Dubai refers to the south. The terms 'Deira side' and 'Bur Dubai side' are still used to differentiate between the areas north and south of the Creek. A little further along the coast, Bur Dubai merges with Jumeirah, where residential, retail and tourist development stretches for some 15 kilometres (9.5 miles) southwards. The recommended sights mentioned in these pages are categorised by these three areas.

When petrodollars began to flow into the emirate in the 1960s, Deira and Bur Dubai developed rapidly, the former becoming the trade centre and the latter the residential area. Today, however, all the major developments in the city are taking place on the Bur Dubai side, with projects such as Knowledge Village and Media City springing up alongside Sheikh Zayed Road. This thoroughfare runs from Abu Dhabi, the UAE's capital, to Bur Dubai and feeds Deira with traffic via two bridges, dubbed Garhoud, after a district, and Al Maktoum, after the ruling family. When

Taking a seat at the **Heritage & Diving Village**. *See p66.*

travelling from one end of the city to another, Sheikh Zayed Road is a faster if less scenic option than the Beach Road.

GETTING AROUND

Dubai is not well served by public transport. There are plans for a rail system, and a bus service called 'Mass Rapid Transport' has evolved. However, the best way to get around the city is by car and, as a result, traffic problems are increasing. Dubai's road network is mostly new and, for the most part, easy to navigate, but many additions to the network are under construction, which frequently causes traffic chaos. *See also p247* **Navigation**.

In your quest for Dubai's more rewarding sights, taxis are the best way of getting around. The government recently introduced competition into this previously state-run service, and the effect has been a dramatic improvement in quality. Drivers are generally courteous and knowledgeable, and all cars have meters. A growing number of taxis accept credit cards. The exceptions to the rule are cabs that hail from the neighbouring emirate of Sharjah, who'll happily pull over for tourists as part of an opportunistic foray into Dubai even though the government frowns upon them. Despite the plush interiors, these often odorous cars are private vehicles and lack meters. If you'd rather face the hassle of an independent operator than wait for Dubai's finest to show, negotiate a price with the driver and make sure that he knows how to reach your desired destination before pulling away. Generally speaking, taxis loiter outside any building that will provide a steady stream of customers, or can be hailed on almost any street corner, day or night. *See also p247* **Taxis**.

Choosing to drive yourself means dealing with all other road users. Drivers from other Middle Eastern or subcontinental countries will find driving a breeze, but those arriving from the West will be alarmed by the weaving motorists who drive too fast then too slow, too close to each other, and never with the use of indicators. *See also p248* **Driving**.

Dubai's lack of effective street addresses will also become painfully obvious. Residents offer and receive directions according to landmarks such as parks, banks and, predominantly, hotels. It pays to have a well-known point of reference if you're looking for somewhere off the beaten track. *See also p250* **Addresses**.

SEE HERE

What Dubai lacks in ancient architecture it makes up for in character and ambition; in the shadow of proud, uncompromising hotels and office structures nestle heaving souks and

The best Sights

For Dubai's earliest settlement

The oasis town of **Hatta** (*see p73*), which slumbers in the foothills of the Hajar mountains, has glorious Arabic architecture and crystal-clear rock pools.

For Islamic understanding

Go beyond the beach with an eye-opening tour of **Jumeirah Mosque** (*see p71*) conducted by the Sheikh Mohammed Centre for Cultural Understanding.

For ancient crafts

Witness a day in the life of early weavers and pearl divers at the **Heritage & Diving Village** (*see p66*).

For cutting-edge architecture

Stop for coffee at the **Burj Al Arab** (*see p47*). Try not to gawp.

For a blast from the past

Wander unhurried around **Bastakia** and stop by the **Dubai Museum** (for both, *see p64*).

For souk heaven (or hell)

Get your bearings, plunge into **Deira** (*see p66 and p122* **Golden opportunities**) and bedeck yourself with gold.

For off-road thrills

Have a qualified driver take you on a **desert tour** (*see p79*) into the dunes for a barbecue and belly dance.

For bird watching

Great white egrets, spoonbills and greater flamingos are just some of the thousands of species that can be seen at **Al Khor Dubai Wildlife Sanctuary** (*see p72*).

forlorn shipyards, the briefest glimpse of the small fishing village swallowed up by the big city forever. While it may be tempting to cling to the beached splendour of Jumeirah, a trip down town to the Creek is unmissable.

Further afield are unspoiled beaches, wadis and water holes easily explored in a day. While dune bashing requires a masterful hand, those not yet skilled can turn to nearly any local tour operator for a 4x4 safari with barbecue and belly dancing thrown in for good measure. For weekend excursions Dubai's sister emirates (*see pp226-244*) are sleepier, but prettier, with opportunities to walk along deserted shores or laze at the feet of cool mountains.

Sightseeing

Urban Dubai

Where modern metropolis meets traditional fishing village.

Among the thousands of international tourists wooed into visiting Dubai for the first time each year are many intrepid souls who came to the emirate on business long before its marketing machine kicked into overdrive. Most do not recognise the booming Arabian metropolis, now defined by high-rise towers and austere glass structures, where once there was little to witness but fledgling enterprises among miles of sand. The past decades have been an exciting whirlwind of urbanisation, and yet much of the city's admittedly limited traditional architecture has become lost or renovated in the process.

The result is not, therefore, a city for sightseeing in the classic sense. There are few museums of note here, and no galleries aside from commercial ventures showcasing work from contemporary Arabic artists. For those in search of history, it is far better to view Dubai as a living museum, a place founded on strong Arabic values but where the world's cultures are woven together and change unfolds at a blistering pace.

Dubai Museum. *See p64.*

The resulting city offers tourists a wealth of rich experiences and goes some way to explaining Dubai's stellar rise to prominence as a travel destination of choice; not bad for a village once viewed as a mere stop-off point for traders, sailors and pilots.

Bur Dubai

As Dubai was settled, a residential area developed along the sandy southern banks of the Creek and became known as Bur Dubai. It is here that the emirate's rulers made their home in sea-facing fortifications, and the district remains the seat of the Diwan (the Ruler's Office), which is Dubai's senior administrative body. As the city grew, the area became home to embassies and consulates, creating an atmosphere of diplomatic calm, with commercial activity centred on the mouth of the Creek. Today the situation is changing fast, and while the banks of the Creek are still free from development, Bur Dubai has sprawled inland, with tower blocks springing up on practically every available inch of sand.

As the residential community has grown, so commerce has developed to support local residents. The once tiny souk has expanded dramatically, supermarkets and shopping malls have opened, and several highways traverse the area.

Dubai Museum (*see p64*) makes a good starting point for exploration of Bur Dubai, and visitors with cars can park in the adjacent space. From the museum, make your way northwards towards the Creek and enjoy **Bur Dubai souk** (Map p282 H4) on foot. A curious mixture of old and new, it lacks the traditional charm of Deira's **old souk** (*see p66*) but does boast a vast array of goods. At worst this lesser-known area could be described as tacky and cheap; at best it would be fair to say it's a haphazard market-style collection of shops.

Be sure to pass through the **textile souk** (*see p123*). This is a great place to buy traditional Arab clothing, Pakistani and Indian saris, and *salwar kameez*, the traditional baggy shirt and trouser outfits worn by women in Pakistan, Afghanistan and to a lesser degree in India. These can be tailored from the fabric of your choice in a matter of hours.

Mosque watching

Mosque building in the UAE reached a peak in the 1970s and 1980s as the population and the wealth of the emirate grew, but it does have a few examples of older structures. The UAE's oldest mosque – the '**Ottoman Mosque**' – is in Badiyah village, Fujairah, along the road between Khor Fakkan and Dibba. A recent study dates the simple, pleasing structure to around the end of the 15th century; some say that it was built by a fisherman grateful for the discovery of an oversized pearl. Other notable mosques include the modestly designed **Grand Mosque** in Bastakia (the oldest in the city), the more elaborate **Ali Ibn Ali Taleb Mosque** (also in Bastakia), the intricately tiled **Iranian Mosque** in Satwa, and – for modern aesthetics – **Bin Madiya Mosque** near Al Nasser Square, Deira, built in the 1970s by Greek architects. If taking a trip to Abu Dhabi, you can't miss its **Grand Mosque**, just outside the city. Currently under construction, when finished it'll be one of the grandest in the world and possibly the largest built in modern times. At the other end of the scale are tiny, prefab, roadside mosques that closely resemble the kitschy alarm clock versions you can snap up for Dhs10 in Karama.

Most mosques in the UAE feature a simple, open space for praying, generally roofed over, that includes a *mihrab*, from which the *imam* leads prayer, and a *minbar*, a kind of pulpit that often features a minaret. The floor is covered in mats, and worshippers leave their shoes at the door. There is sometimes a separate area for women to pray in.

The UAE does not allow non-Muslims to enter mosques – with the exception of the **Jumeirah Mosque** on Jumeirah Beach Road (*pictured*). While nothing like the spectacular examples to be found in Syria or Iran, the

Jumeirah Mosque is grand, reflecting Egyptian Fatimid design and modelled – as are most mosques in the UAE – on an Anatolian structure, with a massive central dome. The **Sheikh Mohammed Centre for Cultural Understanding** conducts interesting and informative tours of the mosque on Thursdays and Sundays at 10am.

Young guides from the non-profit-making centre, set up to bridge the gap between the different cultures in the UAE, are on hand to explain the mosque's layout, describe the five pillars of Islam, and take questions. Visitors should dress conservatively (no shorts) and women bring a headscarf; children under five are not usually admitted.

Streets filled with fabric and tailoring shops soon lead you to the covered area of the **Bastakia souk**, which is filled with Arabic curios and souvenirs. The best prices and bargains are to be found in the less attractive streets beyond the renovated centre. A walk through the covered area ends at the abra crossing point, where a left turn will lead you to the collection of shops known as the **watch souk**. Hefty doses of caution and scepticism are advised, but some of the watches on display are genuine and prices are hard to beat. If you head

west from this point you will reach the electrical souk (also known as **Electrical Street**; *see p125*), a great place to buy camera and video equipment or white goods. As with most souks, the boundaries are hazy, but those in search of computers, software or games would do well to explore its southern streets.

Bur Dubai sprawls southwards to merge with the coastal development of **Jumeirah** and westwards to **Port Rashid** on the coast, but the most rewarding sights are to be found where it all began – along the Creek.

Bastakia

Between Al Fahidi Street & the southern bank of the Creek. **Map** p282 H3.

One of Dubai's most picturesque heritage sights, Bastakia is being carefully renovated and turned into a pedestrianised conservation area. By the end of 2005 some 50-plus houses will have been completed; a museum, more restaurants and a cultural centre are also planned. The name Bastakia comes from the first people to settle the area, who were traders from Bastak in southern Iran. The ruler of Dubai encouraged such immigration in the early 1900s by granting favourable tax concessions. Many came and most stayed, which explains why so many Emiratis are of southern Iranian descent.

Stepping into the narrow alleyways of Bastakia is to walk into Dubai's past. Many buildings sport traditional wind towers, a surprisingly efficient form of natural air-conditioning that was designed to capture the breeze and funnel the cooler air into the rooms below. Many older Emirati nationals tell of summers spent in Bastakia when entire families would gather to sleep outside on raised platforms to escape the heat of indoor rooms.

Dubai Museum

Al Fahidi Fort, Bastakia (353 1862/www.dubai tourism.co.ae). **Open** 8.30am-8.30pm Sat-Thur; 2.30-8.30pm Fri. **Admission** Dhs3; Dhs1 concessions; free under-5s. **No credit cards.** **Map** p282 H4.

Considered by many residents to be a must for visitors, the museum is undoubtedly one of Dubai's best efforts and is well worth a visit. The Al Fahidi Fort was built in 1787 as Dubai's primary sea defence and also served as the ruler's residence. In 1970 it was renovated so the museum could be housed within its walls. Inside, the displays are creative and imaginative, allowing you to peek into an Islamic school, walk through a 1950s souk,

Customs and exercise
A walking tour of old Dubai.

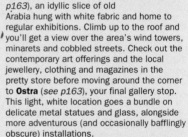

One of the few walkable districts in this otherwise car-centric town, the Creekside neighbourhood of Bastakia has enjoyed a true renaissance in the last two years. It's the oldest part of Dubai, settled at the turn of the 20th century by Iranian traders who built houses from coral and topped them with windtowers, an early form of air-conditioning. Until recently the houses were in decay, encroached upon by the bustling modern district of Bur Dubai. Happily, thanks to a new drive for cultural preservation, they are now being restored to their former glory, and relaunched as cafés, galleries and guesthouses.

Start your walk at the **Majlis Gallery** (*see p162*) on Al Fahidi Road, which houses a wonderful collection of local art, including paintings, illustrations, sculpture, silverwork and Arabian trinkets. You can comfortably browse the entire collection in half an hour, and leave anything you buy with the friendly owners for picking up later. Step out of the Majlis, turn right and 30 metres (100 feet) down you'll see the **Basta Art Café** (*see p107*), a beautiful courtyard eaterie. After checking out their limited range of local crafts, snag a table in the shade of the central tree and order some super-healthy, super-tasty pitta wraps or salads, washed down with lime and mint juice.

Once you're feeling fully refreshed, continue the heritage stroll by turning down the narrow alleyway that separates the Majlis and the Basta. At the end of the alley you'll see the back side of **XVA** (*see p163*), an idyllic slice of old Arabia hung with white fabric and home to regular exhibitions. Climb up to the roof and you'll get a view over the area's wind towers, minarets and cobbled streets. Check out the contemporary art offerings and the local jewellery, clothing and magazines in the pretty store before moving around the corner to **Ostra** (*see p163*), your final gallery stop. This light, white location goes a bundle on delicate metal statues and glass, alongside more adventurous (and occasionally bafflingly obscure) installations.

Leaving Ostra, head out of the windtower quarter and down towards the Creek. You'll emerge next to the **Bastakia mosque**, near a clutch of abras for hire. Turn left along the waterfront and stroll along the boulevard until you hit the **textile souk** (*see p123*). Weave through this network of cloth-pushing salesmen and you'll rejoin the Creek. From here it's a ten-minute saunter to **Shindagha**, the other remaining pocket of Old Dubai, where you can take a trip around **Sheikh Saeed's childhood home** (*see p66*), the **Heritage Village** (*see p66*) and end up on the terrace at **Al Bandar** restaurant for a leisurely shisha and lashings of mint tea.

Bastakia. *See p64.*

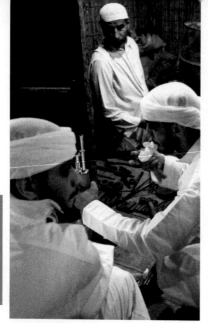

Craftsmen at work in the **Heritage Village**.

watch traditional craftsmen at work and even to (almost) experience the tranquil beauty of a night spent out in the desert.

Heritage & Diving Village

Al Shindagha (393 7151/www.dubaitourism.co.ae).
Open 10am-midnight Sat-Thur; 4pm-midnight Fri.
Admission free. **Map** p282 G3.
This pleasant 'living' museum by the Creek, staffed by guides, potters, weavers and other craftspeople, focuses on Dubai's maritime past and depicts the living conditions of original seafarers, who harvested the Arabian Gulf for pearls and fish to trade. Static but entertaining displays chart the history of Dubai's pearling industry, and a tented village gives a glimpse of the Bedouin way of life that remained unchanged until well into the 20th century. During religious holidays, such as Eid Al Fitr (late Oct/early Nov) and Eid Al Hadha (Jan), and throughout the Dubai Shopping Festival (mid Jan-mid Feb), traditional ceremonies are laid on, including sword dancing and wedding celebrations. At these times old pearl divers are often on hand to recount tales of adventure and hardship.

Sheikh Saeed Al Maktoum House

Al Shindagha (393 7139/www.dubaitourism. co.ae). **Open** 8am-10pm Sat-Thur; 3-10pm Fri. **Admission** Dhs2; Dhs1 concessions; free under-8s. **No credit cards. Map** p282 G3.
Built in 1896 out of coral covered in lime and sand plaster, this traditional house was the home of Dubai's former ruler until his death in 1958 – hence its strategic position at the mouth of the

Creek. Now fully restored and converted into a museum, it displays small exhibitions of historic documents, stamps, currencies and a collection of old photographs of Dubai and its ruling family. Guided tours are available.

Deira

Deira is a bustling, chaotic, dusty commercial hub where plate-glass office blocks tower over the single-storey buildings of the old souks. It is an area best explored on foot. Broadly speaking, the term 'Deira' is used to describe everything north of the Creek that, in reality, is an amalgam of sub-districts. The most exciting part for the visitor, however, is the original Deira on the Creek – the heart and soul of Old Dubai.

The best way to start discovering Deira is to walk along the Creek where old meets new with full force. Five-star hotels such as the Sheraton and InterContinental are situated just yards away from wharfs that haven't changed in the past 60 years. On the roads, limousines and 4x4s jostle for space with pick-up trucks, while sharp-suited businessmen and women wait at zebra crossings alongside sarong-clad workers from the subcontinent pushing handcarts, and fishermen in work-stained kandouras. Traditional dhows still line the Creek wharf and, day and night, seamen unload goods destined for the many tiny shops that make up Dubai's oldest trading area.

It's here that you'll find **Deira old souk**, sprawling around the mouth of the Creek on the north shore, where the waterway widens at the entrance to the Gulf (Map p282 H3). The area is best explored during late afternoon or evening, when temperatures are lowest and the traders are at their busiest. The entrance to the old souk stands under renovated buildings with traditional wind towers. Like most markets, it has evolved into sections defined by the goods sold in each and criss-crossed by alleyways. In this case the areas are known individually as the **spice souk**, **antique souk** and **textile souk** (*see p123*).

Step into the spice souk and you instantly breathe in the scents of Arabia and the East. Chillies, cardamom and saffron are piled high outside spice shops; ornately decorated glass-stoppered bottles line shelves in traditional perfume shops; and the sweet aroma of frankincense fills the air. At one time more valuable than gold, frankincense (a gum resin obtained from trees of the genus *Boswellia*) remains one of Arabia's most prized perfumes and is the base for some of the world's most expensive scents. Traditionally, crystals are

Abra rides

One of the best ways to view the Dubai Creek is by abra – traditional wooden water taxis that cross the Creek day and night. These seemingly rickety but watertight boats have been ferrying residents and traders across the Creek since Dubai was first settled; originally they were rowing boats, but are today powered by smelly diesel engines. Even now, almost 15,000 people still cross the Creek by abra every day.

To take a ride on an abra, look for the clearly marked boarding points on both sides of the Creek: in Deira by the dhow wharfage near the entrance to the old souk, and in Bur Dubai at the end of Al Seef Road by the entrance to the renovated part of the Bastakia souk. The crossing takes a few minutes and costs 50fils per person. The abras are commuter vehicles

for manual and low-paid workers, and boarding can be chaotic at peak times when hundreds of workers jostle for space on the stone steps where the boats pull up. You are likely to find yourself pulled across the decks of several boats by helpful abra captains, who are quick to extend welcoming but rather soiled hands to anyone hesitating or uncertainly looking for a space on the bench seating.

The basic crossing allows you to take in the atmosphere of the Creek and gives a great insight into how the city operated in the past. For a more comprehensive tour of the Creek it's well worth hiring your own abra; simply ask a boat captain and agree a price and the length of the tour before you set out. A journey up and down the Creek should cost no more than Dhs50.

Sightseeing

placed in a frankincense burner and heated over a flame, allowing the resulting aromatic smoke to waft through clothes and rooms alike. Shopkeepers are happy to demonstrate the custom and both frankincense crystals and the burners can be bought at very reasonable prices throughout the souk.

The original coral-stone shops have been renovated and, sadly, much of the dusty charm of the souk has been lost, but it is now a far cleaner place to visit. Take the time to make your way through the myriad alleyways to explore the many shops selling Arabic curios and antiques. Once you reach the antique shops you know that you are approaching the renowned **gold souk** (*see p122* **Golden opportunities**). Its centre is a wide alley covered by a roof and supported by carved wooden pillars, but the souk extends into the adjoining streets. It's worth venturing beyond the main plaza-like area to explore the outer alleys where many specialist shops trade in silver, pearls and semi-precious stones. Bargaining or haggling is expected in all souks; don't be afraid to leave a shop to try next door if you cannot reach a price that you consider reasonable. Most shopkeepers will offer tea or cold drinks while a deal is struck – a sign of traditional hospitality and an indication that negotiations are progressing well.

The view from above

Due to its extreme youth, Dubai is almost entirely lacking in traditional landmarks. However, when viewed from above this modern metropolis can be a breathtaking sight, a steel and concrete oasis springing from the desolate desert. To get your bird's-eye view, call **Lama Tours** (273 2240, www.lama dubai.com), who offer a ten-minute helicopter ride over the city every Saturday for Dhs350 per person for groups of four or more. The hover takes in Emirates Towers and the Burj Al Arab (*pictured*) before zipping across to the Palms project to witness the birth of the huge new islands. For an equally spectacular but more sedate trip skywards **Amigos Balloons** (390 3505) offer a one-hour ride for Dhs780 per person, which also includes transportation and breakfast.

A cheaper option is the cable car at **Creekside Park** (336 7633), offering charming views over the water. OK, it's a bit creaky – and there's inevitably a point when you're convinced you're about to plummet to earth and crush a tribe of merry picnickers – but once you've quelled your fears you'll have a ball. Entry to the park is Dhs5 and it's a further Dhs25 (Dhs15 for concessions) to ride the wire.

Dubai's skyscrapers also offer opportunities to check out the city from above. VU's bar on the 51st floor of **Emirates Towers** (330 0000, www.emiratestowershotel.com) offers the best views in the classiest location. There is a strict dress code in force – those wishing to drink in the clouds must be wearing a collar and shoes. The increasingly fierce lift operator is also sniffy about allowing visitors to use the glass lifts that take you to the 40th floor, insisting that those not staying in the hotel use the conventional elevator. Of course, should you take this lift or the stairs to the first floor before switching to the transparent beauty he'd be none the wiser – but of course we would never suggest such a thing...

Sightseeing

Deira's skyline is best viewed across **Dubai Creek**.

What Deira lacks in refinement it makes up for in atmosphere and character. And to experience it first hand all you have to do is to walk along the corniche that borders the Creek. Note that Deira is by no means pristine: despite the Dubai Municipality's efforts, litter abounds and spitting in the street is commonplace.

Al Ahmadiya School & Heritage House

Near Gold House building, Al Khor Street, Al Ras (226 0286/www.dubaitourism.co.ae). **Open** 8am-8pm Sat-Thur; 2.30-8pm Fri. **Admission** free. **Map** p282 G3.

Established in 1912, this was the first school in Dubai and was renovated as a museum in 1995. Next door is the Heritage House, a traditional house with interiors from 1890. Guides and touch screens take you through the tour of these two small – and ever so slightly dull – museums.

Jumeirah

Just half a century ago, Jumeirah was a fishing village several kilometres outside Dubai. Today it is one of the most high-profile areas of the city and residents often refer to it, with tongue placed firmly in cheek, as the Beverly Hills of Dubai. A few original villas survive and are much sought after by expatriate residents as (almost) affordable beachside homes. The area commonly referred to as Jumeirah – Jumeirah forms only a part of it – stretches along Dubai's southern coast for some 16 kilometres (ten miles), incorporating the

suburb of Umm Suqeim. It is serviced by two main roads: the Beach Road that runs along the coast and the Al Wasl Road that runs parallel a few blocks inland. A haphazard network of streets lined with luxury villas links the two thoroughfares.

Jumeirah developed southwards from Satwa's borders and the oldest part, known as Jumeirah 1, remains one of the most desirable addresses in Dubai. It is here that the first chic malls and coffee shops grew up, and it is still a popular choice today for residents in search of a latte or manicure. At this end of the Beach Road the **Jumeirah Mosque** (*see p71*) is one of the city's most picturesque and the only one to welcome non-Muslims to participate in a guided tour.

Along the Beach Road are various shopping malls (of which Mercato Mall can boast the most fashionable clientele), the shameful **Dubai Zoo** (*see below*) and several public beaches. The shoreline runs from Jumeirah 1 to the far end of Umm Suqeim, where the **Jumeirah Beach Hotel** (*see p43*) and **Burj Al Arab** (*see p47*), next to **Wild Wadi** water park (*see p153*), mark the beginning of the resort strip. If you're heading to the beach, chances are you're heading to Jumeirah.

Dubai Zoo

Beach Road, Jumeirah 1 (349 6444). **Open** 10am-6.30pm Sat-Mon, Wed-Fri. **Admission** Dhs3. **No credit cards. Map** p280 G3.

The animals at the Dubai Zoo are the survivors, and progeny, of a private collection now owned by the Dubai Municipality. The zoo has been heavily

Animal tragic: the much-criticised **Dubai Zoo** is best avoided. *See p69.*

criticised for being old-fashioned, with the animals caged and able to enjoy little by way of freedom of movement. There are allegedly plans to move the zoo to a more spacious site somewhere out of town but, despite many promises, there has been little sign of action. The range of species is surprisingly wide and includes lions, tigers, giraffes, bears, reptiles and birds, but it's up to your conscience as to whether you would enjoy a visit.

Gold & Diamond Park Museum

Gold & Diamond Park, Interchange 4, Sheikh Zayed Road (347 7788/www.goldanddiamondpark.com). **Open** 10am-10pm Sat-Thur; 4-10pm Fri. **Admission** free. **Map** p278 B4.

The Gold & Diamond Park features examples of Arabian, Italian and Indian jewellery, and conducts guided tours to the manufacturing plant, showing visitors how diamonds are cut and how gold is produced. There are plenty of opportunities to purchase, although you may get a better deal in the souks.

Jumeirah Mosque

Beach Road, Jumeirah 1. **Map** p284 D9.

Arguably the most beautiful mosque in Dubai, the Jumeirah Mosque stands at the northern end of the Beach Road. Non-Muslim visitors are not normally allowed inside mosques, but the Sheikh Mohammed Centre for Cultural Understanding (344 7755, smccu@emirates.net.ae) organises visits to the Jumeirah Mosque at 10am on Sundays and Thursdays. You'll get a chance to walk through the mosque with a small group of fellow sightseers before putting questions to your guide about the mosque and the Islamic faith. You must wear modest clothing (no shorts) and women should put on a headscarf (*see p63* **Mosque watching**). Both men and women will be asked to remove their shoes before entering. A worthy destination in its own right, this also makes a good starting point from which to explore Jumeirah.

Majlis Ghorfat Um Al Sheef

Beach Road, Jumeirah 4; look for the brown heritage signposts (394 6343). **Open** 8.30am-1.30pm, 3.30-8.30pm Sat-Thur; 3.30-8.30pm Fri. **Admission** Dhs2. **No credit cards. Map** p278 B4.

Built in simple traditional style from coral and stone, the two-storey majlis was used by the late ruler of the city, Sheikh Rashid bin Saeed Al Maktoum, the founder of modern Dubai. Majlis means 'meeting place' in Arabic and is a building where matters of business or other importance are discussed. This particular one has been carefully preserved by the Dubai Municipality. The ground floor consists of an open veranda and a first-floor majlis room, furnished with cushions and Arabic antiques. The open-air rooftop terrace was used for sleeping, as the height ensures the platform enjoys a stiff sea breeze. The fact that many of the visionary plans for modern Dubai were probably hatched in such a simple structure, by a man who had known nothing of 20th-century luxury for most of his life, is remarkable. A visit to the majlis highlights the dramatic development and the extent of the changes that Dubai has undergone in just a matter of decades, particularly as you can see the Burj Al Arab hotel (*see p47*) from the rooftop. That said, the majlis only really merits a short visit: it's fascinating as a contrast between old and new Dubai, but does not necessarily rate as a significant cultural experience.

Further Afield

Get out of town for desert dunes, remote beaches and crystal-clear pools.

Sightseeing

Top hotels and a burgeoning restaurant scene help Dubai hold its own against modern tourist destinations the world over. But there is life beyond the glittering city – albeit at a greatly slowed pace. Quieter times but no less stirring sights await the more adventurous traveller: hit the road and you'll find towering desert dunes and chill mountain pools are yours for the savouring.

These next few pages cover recommended sights beyond the city boundaries, all of which are an easy ride away. Unfortunately, Dubai's lack of public transport makes driving the only viable option. Taxis are not cost-effective over longer journeys (across to Hatta, for example), not to mention the impracticality of hailing a cab for the return journey. Hiring wheels – preferably a four-wheel drive – for excursions during your stay is a much better idea (for details, *see p248*).

Miscellaneous sights

Jebel Ali Beach

Sheikh Zayed Road, between Jebel Ali Hotel & Ghantoot.

Dubai's most remote and unspoiled beach lies some 40 minutes' drive south of the city towards Abu Dhabi and stretches, unencumbered by development, for some 15 km (9.5 miles) to the Abu Dhabi/Dubai border. This expanse of unbroken sand represents Dubai's only remaining 'natural' beach, yet there are strong rumours that, despite the fact that it is a nature reserve, development plans are underway. The area will most certainly be affected by the Jebel Ali Palm (*see p26* **The silly isles**) and there are fears that this valued area will soon be damaged or lost forever. A favourite with beach-loving residents and kite surfers, who relish the freedom of the emirate's longest free stretch of coastline, the beach is open to all, but those who wish to spend some time camping on the beach, which comes highly recommended, must apply for a permit from Dubai Municipality.

Take the exit signposted for the Jebel Ali Hotel off the Sheikh Zayed Road. Turn left at the round-about before the hotel and follow the tarmac road that runs along the coast behind the dunes. Pick your spot and turn right towards the sea – the beach is straight ahead. A 4x4 is essential to get on to the beach itself, although hard-packed sand tracks enable two-wheel-drive vehicles to reach the northern edge. There are showers (not all of which work) and *barasti* (palm-leaf) sunshades, but no other amenities; this is not a beach for those who enjoy luxury or need facilities to be close at hand.

Al Khor Dubai Wildlife Sanctuary

Ras Al Khor industrial area (223 2323). **Open** 9am-4pm Sat-Thur. **Admission** Free. **Map** p281 J4.

Managed by the World Wide Fund for Nature and the Emirates Wildlife Society, Al Khor Wildlife Sanctuary is the only urban protected area in Dubai and one of only a handful in the country. Located at the beginning of the Creek, the marshy ground is home to thousands of flamingos, waders and other birds, many of which migrate to Dubai seasonally. The area was previously closed to the public, but the WWF – with the help of the National Bank of Dubai – has recently opened three hides, affording twitchers spectacular views of the birds against a backdrop of the Dubai skyline. The first viewing area, aptly dubbed 'Flamingo', is located opposite the Emarat garage on the Oud Metha road and offers spectacular views of the pink birds in all their glory. From here it is just a short walk to the Lagoon sanctuary, a quieter hide that looks back across the marshes. If you return to the Oud Metha Road and travel in the direction away from the city, before taking the left turn to Ras Al Khor you'll find the Mangrove Hide – located behind the Exiles Rugby Club. Although further from the wildlife this wooden shack boasts superb views back across the wetlands towards the city and shows the sanctuary's startlingly close vicinity to the skyscrapers. Admission to the hides is free, but there's only a maximum of ten people permitted in a hide at one time and groups larger than four must apply for an entry permit from the Municipality (206 4240). Forms can be downloaded direct from their website, www.environment.dm.gov.ae.

Mushrif Park

On the airport road towards Al Khawaneej, nr Mirdif (288 3624). **Open** 8am-11.30pm daily. **Admission** Dhs3; Dhs10 per car. *Swimming pool* Dhs10; Dhs5 concessions. *Train* Dhs2. **Map** p279 F3.

The park is approximately ten minutes drive out of town, close to the residential suburb of Mirdif. It is so huge that you can drive around it or take the miniature train that tours every afternoon. The variety of themed displays include miniature houses from around the world; camel and pony rides are available in the afternoons. Wildlife such

Sightseeing

The pink pound: flamingos at the **Al Khor Dubai Wildlife Sanctuary**. *See p72.*

as deer and gazelles roam the farthest corners of the park, where landscaped gardens give way to sand dunes covered with indigenous vegetation. Dogs are not allowed.

Hatta

Snugly tucked between Dubai and Oman, the oasis town of Hatta is a welcome change of pace from Dubai's fast-lane living and is a popular day trip for tourists with wheels. An excursion to Hatta offers plenty of off-road action and just a dash of heritage, making for a varied day out.

From Sheikh Zayed Road, Dubai, take either the Trade Centre roundabout, or Interchange 1 or 2, and turn inland. From here you will see signs to Hatta. As you continue along the highway, you will notice the landscape change colour slowly, from a washed-out pale yellow to a rich red ochre. It's the iron oxide present in the sand that gives it this unusual warm glow; in the right light it can be spectacular.

Shortly after the village of Madam (expect a large roundabout and little else) you will pass through a small patch of Oman. Be aware that most hire-car insurance will not cover trips outside of the UAE and you will be uninsured for this section of road should you have an accident, even though there are no official border posts to notify you.

The views are inspiring, and the layers of jagged peaks fading off into the distance across the gravel plains and the acacia trees give the area something of an African air.

At last you will reach the town of **Hatta**, considered to be the oldest village in the emirate of Dubai. The town is overlooked by two defensive towers built in the 1880s and boasts a real old-world, country charm. Its tranquil setting in the foothills of the Hajar Mountains, the rocky range that spans the eastern flank of the UAE, is compelling, and the location offers numerous routes to explore on foot, by mountain bike or 4x4, plus wonderful natural rock pools.

Pool position

Getting to Hatta Pools from Dubai

- From Dubai take route 44 until you reach Hatta
- At the Fort Roundabout go right (first exit) and head through the town
- Take the turning to the left signed Hatta Heritage Village
- At the next junction turn left
- Take the next right and travel over the multiple speed bumps
- Continue straight for approximately 4km (2.5 miles) travelling through a small village where the tarmac will end
- Take the gravel track towards Buraimi
- After the Al Bon sign take the well-used track off to the left. This will take you towards the Wadi and a makeshift car park where you can leave your vehicle and make the rest of the way by foot

Sightseeing

Hatta Fort Hotel

Hatta (852 3211/www.hattaforthotel.com). **Rates** from Dhs495; Dhs1,440 suites. **Credit** AmEx, DC, MC, V.

One of the country's oldest hotels, this is the only place to stay in Hatta and well worth a stop-off for a sundowner even if you're not planning to stay the night. The building houses two food options, Café Gazebo, whose terrace has great views over the mountains, and the more formal Jeema Restaurant.

The 50 individual chalet-style rooms offer uncovered stone walls as well as rustic, high A-frame wooden ceilings, and all look out over the rolling green lawns of the 80-acre (30ha) property. The grounds are home to a teeming wealth of birdlife: keep a particular eye out for the brilliant turquoise flash of the elusive Indian roller. The facilities include a swimming pool, nine-hole golf course, jogging track, tennis court and archery, and experienced guides are happy to conduct 4x4 mountain and desert excursions.

Breakfast is included in the basic rate and there are excellent offers during summer, with rates as low as Dhs300 per room for weeknights throughout the low season. But be warned: while the mountains escape the humidity endured by coastal areas, temperatures can still rise well above 50°C.

Hatta Rock Pools

The major draw to this corner of the emirates for tourists is Hatta's natural pools, a 45-minute drive from Hatta Fort Hotel (*see above*). No matter how hot the weather, there is always cold, clear water flowing here. Deep gorges have been eroded by the rushing river over countless centuries, and if you walk downstream you'll reach an area where the wadi widens and you can loll in the shallows or swim over to a waterfall. Visiting the pools for a picnic or swim is an inspirational experience, but it can get very busy at weekends. It also suffers from the same problem as other beauty spots in the UAE – the unwelcome attention of litter louts and vandals.

Heritage Village

Hatta (852 1374). **Admission** free. **Open** 8am-5pm daily.

A subdued slice of culture, the Heritage Village was established to commemorate a traditional mountain village set in an oasis, and it makes for a nice morning expedition. The village, almost always eerily quiet, is bordered by two round towers built to protect the town from attacks during the rule of Sheikh Hasher bin Maktoum bin Butti in the late 1880s. It consists of various Omani-styled fortified and public buildings (these include a 200-year-old mosque), and holds about 30 houses fully restored to their original architectural style, with primary materials including mud and *barasti* (dried palm leaves tied together) used for authenticity. The village strives to educate visitors in the multiple uses of palm-tree products and dates – date honey, anyone? To find the Village, turn right at the Fort roundabout and follow the brown signboards.

Nad Al Sheba

The Nad Al Sheba area, a ten-minute drive inland from Dubai, is home to two of the sports at the heart of Arab heritage – horse- and camel-racing – and one beloved of Western expats – golf. By taking in both the Nad Al Sheba golf and racing clubs, and the camel souk and racetrack, it's possible to experience the extremes of modern-day luxury and traditional Arabia in one visit, as well as watching sports at polar ends of the financial spectrum.

Nad Al Sheba Camel Souk & Racetrack

Map p278 C4.

Opposite the splendour of the horse racecourse you'll find a less glamorous, but no less spectacular activity going on: camel racing. Also known as the 'ships of the desert' and prized by locals, camels might have earned a reputation for trudging miles without water in the harshest of environments but there's nothing plodding about a racing camel. They can reach surprisingly high speeds at full gallop, and some fine specimens are even worth as much as their equine counterparts. The schedule of camel races is frustratingly erratic but the area

Hatta Rock Pools. *See p74.*

is worth a visit anyway, since camel training takes place throughout the day and well into the night. The entrance to the track is adjacent to the camel souk, a small cluster of shops selling everything that the camel owner could need. Don't be put off if you are *sans* dromedary – traditional camel blankets make fantastic throws for sofas and racing ropes double as superb dog leads. Trainers follow their charges in 4x4s shouting instructions in guttural Arabic to the young jockeys, most of whom are happy to pose for photographs. Always ask first, however, to avoid causing offence.

Across the road from the camel racetrack you will find the camel farms. The sand is soft and deep here, so a 4x4 is essential if you wish to venture into this so-called 'Camel Farm Alley' but, if you're properly equipped, it's certainly worth making the effort. Simply follow the camel trains as they cross the road from the racetrack to see where they live. If you're desperate to see them in full stride, your best chance to watch a race will be when the major meetings take place in the early morning during the Eid holidays (falling in late October/early November and January) – again, you'll need to be driving a 4x4 to follow all the action. The Dubai Government has made recent efforts to clean up the sport, which has in the past been frequently accused of employing underage children as jockeys; now all riders are required by law to be over 15 years of age.

Nad Al Sheba Club & Racecourse

336 3666/3031. **Map** p278 C4.

Home of the world's richest horse race, namely the Dubai World Cup (*see p144*), Nad Al Sheba Club incorporates both a racecourse and a flood-lit 18-hole golf course. The club is surrounded by racing stables that house some of the world's most valuable bloodstock: for just the price of a drink, it's possible to catch a glimpse of the finest fillies being put through their paces every morning from the vantage point of the Spike Bar. Between November and March the club hosts race meetings on Thursdays and Saturdays, the most prestigious of which are the Dubai Racing Festival meets, held over nine weeks, starting in January (*see p146*).

Nad Al Sheba Racing Tour & Godolphin Gallery

336 3666/www.nadalshebaclub.com. **Open** *Sept-June* from 7am Mon, Wed, Sat. **Tour admission** Dhs130; Dhs60 concessions. **Credit** AmEx, DC, MC, V. **Map** p278 C4.

This unique four-hour tour (you must phone in advance) gives an intimate peek into the world of horse-racing. Having watched the noble beasts train, you head to the clubhouse for full cooked breakfast. After questions, it's time for a behind-the-scenes look at grandstands, jockeys' and steward's enquiry rooms, and the Godolphin Gallery – trophy-laden shrine to Sheikh Mohammed bin Rashid Al Maktoum's phenomenally successful international racing operation (*see p185* **Colt from the blue**).

Big Red

About half an hour outside Dubai, in the direction of Hatta, you will come to a huge sand dune on your righthand side. Affectionately known to expats as Big Red, it's a majestic, looming sight, a fiery orange-red mass set against a brilliant blue sky. But if you've made it this far, don't sit lovingly by the roadside in your 4x4. Big Red is a playground for big kids with big engines: by far the best way to enjoy this stretch of desert is to get stuck right in.

Nearby is a popular quad-biking centre, which is great fun but somewhat chaotic, meaning accidents can happen. You have a choice of 50cc, 80cc and 200cc bikes. Prices range from Dhs15 for 15 minutes on a 50cc to Dhs200 for an hour on the 200cc bike. You can even hire a Land Cruiser for Dhs50 per 30 minutes for a shot at getting to the summit of Big Red itself. Rentals operate from 8am to sunset each day and, should you be in need of something to eat, there are a supermarket and restaurant (as well as toilets) on hand.

Most tour operators run trips to Hatta via Big Red, but you can always set your own schedule and hire a 4x4. One of the best places to do so is Budget (285 8550), which offers Toyota Land Cruisers fully kitted out and complete with steel bumpers and roll bar for Dhs550-Dhs600 per day, including insurance. If you choose to drive yourself, remember that it's not safe to venture off-road with just one vehicle; get someone to hire another vehicle and accompany you. You're likely to be out of contact with civilisation, as mobile phone coverage is extremely poor in the mountains, so be sure to carry at least one full cool-box of water (10-12 litres) for every two people, ample food, first aid kit, some tow rope and a shovel.

Sightseeing

Guided Tours

Escort services for the curious tourist.

There is a certain egotistical rush to be enjoyed when taking the wheel of a 4x4 – family and friends safely belted into their respective seats – and masterly navigating the off-road challenges posed by the UAE's toughest dunes. Unfortunately, heading off the beaten track without a clue is a surefire ticket to disaster. No one will thank you for getting stuck fast in sand if a partner vehicle isn't on hand to tow you out. And so, if you don't know where to start or are ill-equipped to strike out on your own, it's a good (and affordable) idea to experience the emirate of Dubai by taking a tour.

Numerous operators run an array of organised tours that range from guided city trips to overnight camping adventures in the desert. While we've recommended some reliable tour operators (*see p79* **Tour operators at a glance**), be warned: many unscrupulous companies in the UAE seem to employ drivers with little local knowledge who are hardly fit to act as tour guides.

City tours

For a summarised (and air-conditioned) account of the sights of the city, and to ensure that you don't get lost, it's a good idea to take an organised trip. Tour operators run a variety of forays into Dubai, with the general themes being either heritage or shopping. Heritage tours will provide a time-efficient overview of new and old Dubai, taking in the souks, the mosques, Bastakia wind tower houses and the Creek. A shopping tour will combine visits to Dubai's ultra-modern shopping malls with starkly contrasting stops at traditional souks. Shopping tours normally last for half a day and run during the daytime and in the evening.

Few tour operators specialise in any given trip, instead running various tours of the city, as well as more adventurous outbound adventures.

BUS TOURS
The arrival of the **Big Bus Company** (324 4187, www.bigbustours.com) in Dubai in 2002 gave the city double-deckers straight from London. As with all the company's tours worldwide, you get to hop off to explore in your own time (at no fewer than 22 specified

Wonder Bus.

points), before catching a subsequent bus to continue your journey. There is live and informative commentary in English on every bus, and two routes are offered: the red route (city tour) starts outside Biella restaurant at Wafi city; the blue one (beach tour) at City Centre. Both cost Dhs120 for adults, Dhs75 for children and Dhs315 for a family (two adults, two children); this includes entrance to **Dubai Museum** (*see p64*) and **Sheikh Saeed Al Maktoum House** (*see p66*), a Wafi City Advantage card, and a walking tour (Oct-Apr). The four-hour tours run daily from 9am to 5pm, with frequent departures.

For a slightly more surreal look at the city the amphibious **Wonder Bus** (359 5656, www.wonderbusdubai.com) offers a road trip around Dubai's landmarks before splashing headlong into the Creek by Garhoud Bridge. The two-hour trip (Dhs115; Dhs75 concessions; Dhs350 family, 2+2) leaves from the **BurJuman Centre** (*see p116*) and takes in Wafi City, the Grand Hyatt and Creekside Park. Gimmicky, yes, but plenty of fun.

Desert tours

The 'absolute must' for all visitors is a trip to the desert. For UAE nationals and resident expatriates the desert is a big playground, a practically unrestricted adventure park in which all are free to frolic. Dune driving and overnight camping trips are popular with those who live in the emirate – and for good reason. The desert can be breathtakingly beautiful and there is tremendous fun to be had in the rolling dunes. The high number of 4x4s on UAE roads testify to the fact that most residents spend at least some of their leisure time in the sands. Of course, there is a downside to the freedom that all enjoy in Dubai's dunes: there is no doubt that desert driving is damaging the region's eco-structure. Much of what should be pristine wilderness is heavily littered and, as yet, nothing effective has been done to clean up the mess.

Most tour operators run a selection of desert safaris, comprising half-day and full-day trips or overnight stays. Experienced desert drivers (some tour companies run their own desert driving schools) will collect you from your hotel in an immaculate 4x4 and whisk you 45 minutes inland. Here, the gold of coastal sands gives way to deep red, originating in the rock of the Hajar mountains that run from north to south across the country.

A desert adventure typically begins close to an outcrop known as **Fossil Rock** that rises above the desert some 30 kilometres (20 miles) from the Dubai–Hatta road. A brief stop allows the driver to deflate the vehicle's tyres (think 'high heels on grass' – fully inflated tyres sink into soft sand, whereas partially deflated ones pass over all but the softest surfaces). Your journey will then take you past ramshackle camel and goat farms, over small scrub-covered dunes and into the red desert.

After a rollercoaster ride up and down more demanding dunes, and with heart firmly in mouth, you will visit a purpose-built Arab campsite for lunch or dinner and, depending on the length of your tour, a range of entertainment. This is likely to include belly dancing and the chance to ride a camel – if only for 20 metres or so. It's all good fun, but staged purely for the tourists, with the displays bearing little resemblance to traditional Emirati life. In fact, the camel handlers are normally Sudanese, while the belly shaking so energetically in front of you is invariably Russian or Lebanese in origin.

Tour operators normally require a minimum of four people to embark on a trip, and will often group couples and individuals together with others in order to make up the numbers. Typically (with the exception of full-day tours), safaris begin in the afternoon as temperatures drop towards the end of the day. Many

Tour operators at a glance

Arabian Adventures *303 4888/www.arabian-adventures.com. (Part of the Emirates group.)* Tours include: dune dinner safari (Dhs295, Sept-May; Dhs270, June-Aug), overnight safari (Dhs440) and stable tours (Dhs205; Dhs143.50 concs).
Arabian Desert Tours *268 2880.* Tours include: desert safari (Dhs150; Dhs100 concs), dhow dinner cruise (Dhs120; Dhs90 concs) and city tour (Dhs80; Dhs50 concs).
Desert Rangers
340 2408/www.desertrangers.com. Tours include: dune buggy safari (Dhs375), dune dinner safari (Dhs260) and canoe rental at Khor Kalba (Dhs150).
East Adventure Tours
355 5677/www.holidayindubai.com. Tours include: desert safari (Dhs240; Dhs110 concs), camel safari (Dhs355; Dhs155 concs) and city tour (Dhs155; Dhs110 concs).

Lama Tours *273 2240/www.lamadubai.com.* Tours include: desert safari (Dhs220; Dhs150 concs), east coast tour (Dhs180; Dhs100 concs) and guided city tours of Dubai, Abu Dhabi and Al Ain (Dhs90-Dhs170; Dhs60-Dhs100 concs).
Net Tours *266 6655/www.netgroupdubai.com.* Tours include: desert safari (Dhs260; Dhs180 concs), dhow dinner cruise (Dhs200; Dhs150 concs) and Hatta trek (Dhs310; Dhs250 concs).
Off-Road Adventures
343 2288/www.arabiantours.com. Tours include: desert safari (Dhs270; Dhs175 concs) and Hatta trip (Dhs200; Dhs130 concs).
Voyagers Xtreme
345 4504/www.turnertraveldubai.com. Tours include: desert safari (Dhs200; Dhs180 concs), Hatta safari (Dhs260; Dhs185 concs) and city tours (Dhs110-Dhs175; Dhs55-Dhs85 concs).

Wadis: the UAE's best natural attraction.

overnight safaris will combine a desert tour with a wadi-bashing mountain trip the next morning. Wadis are river beds that are dry for the majority of the year and form wonderfully rugged tracks to follow in your 4x4 – an act known to expats as 'bashing'. In some places pools of water remain all year round and it may even be possible to swim in them.

Expect to pay in the region of Dhs350 for an overnight desert safari. Normally all food and beverages are included, but check before you set out. In the UAE you are never far from a main road and mobile phone coverage extends everywhere but the most mountainous areas. Tour groups rarely travel without back-up vehicles too, but it is still wise to take a few precautions. Carry at least a small bottle of water with you and a few basics such as plasters and sunscreen. Long, loose clothing is recommended (long shorts are acceptable for both men and women) and you should take a hat. The most practical headgear is the traditional Arab headdress (*ghutra*), which both protects from the sun and can be wrapped Bedouin-style around your face to keep off blowing sand. If you are staying overnight it's wise to take a sweater, as the desert can cool rapidly after dark. To tackle the hot desert sand, opt for boots over flip-flops or sandals.

MOUNTAIN AND WADI TOURS
Towards Dubai's eastern border with Oman lie the Hajar mountains. Frequently referred to as the 'backbone of the Arabian peninsula', this

spectacular mountain range runs from the Empty Quarter in Oman across the length of the UAE before rising to its zenith in the north in the Musandam, above the Straits of Hormuz. Traditionally, Dubai's ruling Al Maktoum family would escape the coastal humidity of the summer in the oasis mountain village of **Hatta** (*see p73*), close to the Omani border.

Today a small and slumbering town, Hatta still boasts some of the most dramatic scenery in the emirate. Storms can lash the mountains at any time of year, creating flash floods that turn wadis into raging torrents. Over the centuries, water has carved paths into the limestone and Hatta is perhaps best known for its crystal-clear freshwater pools (*see p74*). Mountain and wadi tours explore this charming, desolate region over a full day, with lunch either eaten picnic-style in the mountains or at **Hatta Fort Hotel** (*see p74*) during the sticky summer months. As with the desert, boots should be worn, not beach footwear; sunscreen and a hat are essential. Expect to pay up to Dhs350 for a mountain and wadi tour, including lunch.

ACTIVITY TOURS
Most tour firms also offer supervised activities that allow you to experience the thrill of the desert first-hand. No firm specialises solely in activity tours, but contact our recommended companies (*see p79* **Tour operators at a glance**) to try the bizarre sport of sand-skiing (effectively snowboarding in the desert) or the adrenaline rush of dune buggying.

Eat, Drink, Shop

**YOU KNOW
WHO YOU ARE.**

DUBAI
INTERCHANGE # 5
SHEIKH ZAYED RD.
+971-4-399-2888

Restaurants

Dubai is rapidly evolving into a culinary powerhouse.

Since alcohol can only be sold in hotel restaurants, most visitors to Dubai (along with resident Western expats) tend to find themselves swanning through lobbies whenever they go out for dinner. With 36 five-star hotels already in operation in 2005, each of which has between five and 15 restaurants, competition is fierce. Top international chefs have been lured to the city and – given the region's terminal dryness – quality ingredients are imported daily.

This dependence on hotels means that many restaurants feel a little formulaic, having been programmed in corporate boardrooms. However, furious competition does force many outlets to strive for originality and results in great deals for customers – you'll find that you can afford to eat in incredibly luxurious settings and not feel the pinch too much.

A world away from the glamour, there's another side to Dubai's dining scene: despite the lack of alcohol, independent restaurants flourish. Avoid affluent Jumeirah and head to downtown Bur Dubai and Deira, where you can eat yourself silly for a pittance. Indian and Pakistani curry houses abound, serving delightful street food in spartan settings, and you can pick up a freshly sliced shoarma (a spicy chicken doner kebab) for mere peanuts at any roadside grill. Many other nationalities are represented by the city's independent restaurants, with authentic cuisine from the Philippines, Iran, Russia, Mexico, Morocco, Korea and Ethiopia serving the city's multicultural expatriate population. European-style cafés are also mushrooming, especially among the towers, bright lights and fast-food joints of the Sheikh Zayed Road.

Dubaians are a carnivorous bunch and vegetarian visitors may be disappointed. Although there are hundreds of meat-free Indian restaurants, there isn't a single dedicated veggie outlet where you can have a glass of wine. The other gaping deficiency is in local food: Emirati cuisine is not widely available outside the homes of UAE nationals (*see p89* **Emirati eats**). The national dish is whole baked lamb or camel, but Lebanese moutabal and Pakistani biryanis are far more widely consumed.

For in-depth coverage of dining, buy the *Time Out Guide to Eating & Drinking in Dubai* (Dhs20) from bookshops across the city.

Eat, Drink, Shop

The essentials

The restaurants in this chapter have been grouped by area (Bur Dubai, Deira, and Jumeirah, which covers Jumeirah Beach Road and the so-called 'golden mile' of beach hotels starting at the Burj Al Arab). We've also subdivided them by broad cuisine categories (for a more detailed breakdown, *see p105* **Restaurants by cuisine**) and have included the **average** price of a meal. This is the typical price of a three-course dinner for two with drinks: a glass of house wine per person if the restaurant is licensed, a glass of juice if it isn't. You'll find that all restaurants have air-conditioning, and that in fine-dining restaurants dress codes are less stringent than in many Arab and Western countries. While you won't be welcome in top-end restaurants in shorts and a T-shirt, only the Burj Al Arab insists on jackets and no jeans for dinner. Reservations are essential when eating in hotels, both because popular restaurants get incredibly oversubscribed and because they have an annoying habit of changing their opening hours on a near-weekly basis. During Ramadan (currently falling in late October/early November; *see p144*), you'll find that restaurants aren't open for lunch and many have different opening times in the evenings. You will, however, be able to indulge in the pleasures of Iftar, the fast-breaking tents where expats and locals congregate to eat meze, nibble dates, slug back coffee and puff on shishas over a game or two of backgammon. Wherever and whenever you eat in Dubai, don't forget to tip good service: 10-15 per cent is standard, although most hotel restaurants simply add a charge of 10 per cent to your bill.

Arabic

Awtar

Grand Hyatt Dubai, Oud Metha Road (317 1234).
Open 12.30-3pm, 7.30pm-2am Sun-Fri. **Average**
Dhs250. **Credit** AmEx, DC, MC, V. **Map** p281 K3.
Barbecued meat is the house aroma at Awtar. The
scent of smoking wood and flame-grilled lamb hits
you the moment you enter and works your hunger
to fever pitch in seconds. The decor is reminiscent
of an ultra-lavish Bedouin tent: opulence and
Arabic style spiral out from the swathes of lush
fabric to the vibrantly coloured glass lanterns.
Plough through fresh meze: hot chicken livers in
sassy lemon-infused sauce, deep-fried cheese, white
bean salad and spicy sausages are all impeccable.

Bastakiah Nights

Bastakiah (353 7772). **Open** 12.30-11.30pm
daily. **Average** Dhs280. **Credit** AmEx, DC,
MC, V. **Map** p282 H3.
Bastakiah Nights is a quite beautiful and unique
eaterie, whose only real fault is its superhuman
expectations of how much the average person can
consume. It perches atop a traditional open-roofed
building in the heart of Old Dubai, and its diners are
seated at low tables overlooking the atmospheric
torch-lit courtyard below. Choose the set menu and
you'll receive Herculean piles of excellent meze,
presented with near-geometric precision.

Bastakiah Nights.

Fatafeet

Al Seef Road (397 9222). **Open** 11am-1.30am
daily. **Average** Dhs100. **Credit** AmEx, DC,
MC, V. **Map** p283 J3.
This open-air eaterie beside the Creek lays on a
huge number of Egyptian classics. Try the delicious
fish tagine stew and the 'tarb', a plate of delicately
spiced lamb sausages. A round of thick manakish
unleavened bread topped with melted cheese and
some fatafeet foul (a garlicky, beany mix) should
also be mandatory. Round off with flaky fiteer
mishaltit bread, filled with cream and covered in
bitter-sweet honey. Wash it all down with mugs of
sahlab, a sweet custard-like drink with nuts, and
puff on shisha as the dhows float by. Bliss.

Al Mallah

Al Dhiyafah Street, Satwa (398 4723). **Open** 6am-
4am daily. **Average** Dhs100. **Credit** AmEx, DC,
MC, V. **Map** p285 F8.
The boldest and brightest of Arabic eateries, Al
Mallah has cheese bread and banana milkshakes to
die for. The sun-shaded street seating is packed
around the clock during the cooler months with
locals and tourists elbow-deep in kibbeh, falafel and
manakish. Enjoy the prime people-watching point
on the strip while sipping on huge cream-topped
layered fruit cocktails.

Marrakech

Shangri-La Hotel, Sheikh Zayed Road (343 8888).
Open 1-3pm, 8pm-12.30am daily. **Average** Dhs380.
Credit AmEx, DC, MC, V. **Map** p287 F12.
From the low armchairs, booths and fountain to
the crockery and beaten-metal serving dishes,
Marrakech is elegantly themed around white, blue
and silver, and the food is generally prepared with
an impressively light touch. Try the tagine kofta,
which comes in a rich, tangy sauce that bubbles
and spits like something from the cauldrons of
Mordor, or the bastilla al bahra – easily big enough
for two – which is packed with a rustic, citrus
flavour. Dishes of carrot, roasted aubergine with
preserved lemon, and melt-in-the-mouth lentils
all have a garlicky, tangy tone that give the taste
buds a wake-up call.

Al Nafoorah

*Emirates Towers Shopping Boulevard, Sheikh
Zayed Road (330 0000).* **Open** noon-3pm, 7.30pm-
midnight daily. **Average** Dhs250. **Credit** AmEx,
DC, MC, V. **Map** p280 H4.
This is unquestionably one of the best Lebanese
restaurants in the emirate. After nibbling on
pistachios, iced almonds and deliciously acidulated
carrot, get stuck into some unstoppably good meze:
a purée of roasted garlic potatoes, houmous with
warm pine kernels, tangy labneh yoghurt and
chicken livers with pomegranate sauce. The
desserts – you'll be offered green dates and
honey, fresh fruit and Arabic sweets – are all
impeccable, complimentary and arrive in quite
unreasonably large quantities.

Eat, Drink, Shop

Olive House
Tower No.1, Sheikh Zayed Road, opposite Emirates Towers (343 3110). **Average** Dhs80. **No credit cards. Map** p287 F12.
A glass-fronted café with a small delicatessen and bakery counter, Olive House is a cosmopolitan hangout combining low prices with sophisticated Leb-Med food. The menu is a well-planned mix of salads, pizzas and grills; before any orders arrive, hot pouches of bread turn up with helpings of soft cheese, oily black tapenade and sun-dried tomato paste. Avoid wasting your appetite on the freebies: it would be a travesty to miss out on the chicken and beef kebabs, dunked in houmous, moutabel and lashings of chilli sauce.

Al Tannour
Crowne Plaza Hotel, Sheikh Zayed Road (331 1111). **Open** 8.30pm-3am daily. **Average** Dhs250 before 11pm; Dhs220 minimum per person (incl set menu & entertainment) after 11pm. **Credit** AmEx, MC, V. **Map** p285 G10.
This is the kind of place where eight is company and there's no such thing as a crowd. You'll need a large group to get through the huge quantities of food served. Enjoy fresh bread cooked over the saj, tabouleh full of crunchy ground wheat and lemon, rounds of halloumi cheese and lightly fried lamb's brain. Finish with a fresh fruit platter that wouldn't look out of place at a medieval banquet, and cream-filled sweets with rose syrup. The live music kicks off demurely at 11pm to a mostly empty restaurant but, by midnight, every seat is taken and the atmosphere – fuelled by a fantastic belly dancer – reaches intoxicating heights.

European

Bateau Dubai
Dubai Creek, near British Embassy (399 4994). **Cruise departs** 8.30pm daily (boarding at 8pm). **Average** Dhs450. **Credit** AmEx, DC, MC, V. **Map** p283 J4.
Sleekly shaped, glass-encased and blessed with a chic contemporary interior, this boat is not for those craving a traditional Arabian experience. But for luxury cruising – complete with red-carpeted welcomes, tinkling classical piano and Manhattan-style sophistication – there's no competition on the Creek. The food is good without being excellent, but the waiter service marks a welcome change from the usual cruise buffet fare.

The Exchange
Fairmont Hotel, Sheikh Zayed Road (332 5555). **Open** 7pm-1am daily. **Average** Dhs500. **Credit** AmEx, DC, MC, V. **Map** p285 G9.
The design is a little frosty and the refined atmosphere perhaps more conducive to a form of genteel muttering than to convivial chat, but the Exchange has established itself as a home of fine steak. The chateaubriand is grilled to meltingly tender and reassuringly pink perfection. As an alternative, the

The best Restaurants

For Dubai's very best food
Gordon Ramsay's exquisite dishes at **Verre** (*see p96*); Michel Rostang's superb French cuisine at **Café Chic** (*see p93*); and the city's best Lebanese food at **Al Nafoorah** (*see p84*).

For the best views
Majlis Al Bahar (*see p101*) for close-up views of Burj Al Arab; **Shoo Fee Ma Fee** (*see p100*) to admire the full majesty of the Madinat Jumeirah from the upstairs terrace; and **Vu's** (*see p86*) on the 50th floor of the Emirates Towers.

For visiting with children
Johnny Rockets (*see p91*) for 1950s-style diner fun and fantastic burgers, and **Maria Bonita's** (*see p102*), the only place in town where kids can get away with ordering main courses smothered in gooey chocolate.

For that all-important first date
Pierchic (*see p103*) for the most glamorous setting in the city; the modern Arabian chic of **Eau Zone** (*see p102*); and the hyper-expensive but undeniably romantic **Al Mahara** (*see p101*) at the Burj Al Arab.

For eating well without spending too much
Al Mallah (*see p84*) in Satwa for fantastic shoarma and fruit juices; **India House** (*see p91*) for budget thalis; and **Ravi's** (*see p91*) for Pakistani food, all night long.

For drinking copious amounts
The drink-inclusive buffets at **Market Place** (*see p95*) and **Spice Island** (*see p96*).

regular sampling menus always offer extremely good value. Scheduled for late summer 2005, a complete refurbishment should hopefully warm the atmosphere up a bit.

Links
Nad Al Sheba Club, off the Dubai–Al Ain road (336 3666). **Open** 6pm-2am daily. **Average** Dhs270. **Credit** AmEx, DC, MC, V. **Map** p278 C4.
An outdoor restaurant at the world-famous Nad Al Sheba Club (*see p77*), where on race nights world-class horses thunder past as you dine. The salad buffet is the only starter on offer, and although choice is limited, the ingredients are just fabulous: pipirade salad of roasted vegetables with whole cloves of divinely smooth garlic, a self-assembly Caesar salad with bags of parmesan, Waldorf salad

with massive chunks of apple, and not a limp leaf in sight. You can then move on to the main focus of the restaurant: juicy and tender fillet steaks and Hokubee tenderloins that melt in the mouth. After closing for summer renovations, the restaurant will reopen in October 2005 at the beginning of another Dubai racing season.

Medzo
Wafi Pyramids at Wafi City mall, off Oud Metha Road (324 0000). **Open** 12.30-3pm, 7.30-11.30pm daily. **Average** Dhs250. **Credit** AmEx, DC, MC, V. **Map** p281 J3.
Dining on the terrace of Medzo is a decidedly postmodern experience. Thanks to globalisation, you can enjoy Italian haute cuisine served by a French-speaking Filipino waiter at a table that is surrounded by faux Egyptian artefacts. In contrast to the hotchpotch surroundings, the food is an exercise in subtle harmony. Pasta is Medzo's forte, and though it doesn't always get it 100 per cent right, it packs in enough jaw-to-the-floor dishes (check out the chilli linguine with sautéed garlic prawns and lime) to make it a lasting favourite.

Il Rustico
Rydges Plaza Hotel, Satwa roundabout, Satwa (398 2222). **Open** noon-3pm, 6pm-midnight daily. **Average** Dhs200. **Credit** AmEx, DC, MC, V. **Map** p285 F8.

Il Rustico: exemplary Italian cuisine.

This snug, low-lit place, with a wood-burning pizza oven, offers hearty soul food at prices that are extremely reasonable. Cheese-packed tortellini and carbonara are guaranteed to put you in a good mood, and the comfy setting is conducive to long-drawn-out chats over espressos and grappa shots. The weekday lunch deal is particularly good value: Dhs35 will get you any pizza, pasta or appetiser and a glass of wine – a dining bargain at one of the best-value Italian restaurants in the city.

Vu's
Emirates Towers Hotel, Sheikh Zayed Road (330 0000). **Open** 12.30-2.45pm, 7.30-11.30pm daily. **Average** Dhs500. **Credit** AmEx, DC, MC, V. **Map** p280 H4.
The view from the 50th floor of Emirates Towers is staggering. Out towards the ocean Dubai seems monumentally flat – taking the (absurdly speedy) lift up the Emirates Towers is like scaling a pop-up birthday card. The impressive menu and relaxed atmosphere do justice to the location. Try the fillet of beef Rossini – wonderfully tender with a generous portion of delicate pan-fried foie gras, and crispy potato hidden in the juices. Round off your evening at Vu's Bar *(see p174)* on the floor above.

Far Eastern

Benjarong
Dusit Hotel, Sheikh Zayed Road (343 3333). **Open** 7pm-midnight daily. **Average** Dhs300. **Credit** MC, V. **Map** p280 H4.
Serenity rules at Benjarong: all the rage of Sheikh Zayed Road is left at the door and any remaining personal stress dissolves as you enter the dark, temple-like interior. Pretty wooden pillars inlaid with mother-of-pearl frame a small stage where traditional dancers perform. By the time your cocktail-filled pineapples and melons have arrived, a state of Thai tranquillity is pretty much guaranteed. Staples like tom yam goong and beef green curry are flawless, and the crispy crayfish salad, dressed and mixed with green mango at the table, teases with exquisite flavours, scents and textures.

ET Sushi
Emirates Towers Hotel, Sheikh Zayed Road (319 8088). **Open** 12.30-3pm, 7.30pm-midnight daily. **Average** Dhs200. **Credit** AmEx, DC, MC, V. **Map** p280 H4.
At 12.30pm on the dot a sushi carousel fires into life, trundling round dispensing its colour-coded wares, from yellow plates of crab stick through to black platters of freshwater eel. Slurp on icy fruit drinks such as pineapple shakes while you swipe plastic-hatted saucers filled with maki and sushi from the rolling display. Giant seaweed-lined rounds of sweet omelette, slabs of succulent reddish-pink tuna and wonderful spicy salmon and avocado wraps all score highly. For those in need of less fishy fare, a la carte offerings include a mean chicken teriyaki and super-refreshing soba noodles.

Ginseng
Wafi Pyramids at Wafi City mall, off Oud Metha Road (324 4777). **Open** 7pm-1am daily. **Average** Dhs250. **Credit** AmEx, DC, MC, V. **Map** p281 J3.
Hip and contemporary, Ginseng is lounge, bar (*see p169*) and restaurant in one. The space is small and the decor has that minimal look that you know must have cost a fortune. Exotic fusion cocktails and Asian tapas are the name of the game: try thick wedges of aloo tikki potato cake dunked in cooling yoghurt, barbecue beef quesadillas with Korean kimchee, sticks of shrimp roll zipped through spice-studded dip, and wonderfully tangy goat's cheese samosas.

Hoi An
Shangri-La Hotel, Sheikh Zayed Road (343 8888). **Open** 7.30pm-1am daily. **Average** Dhs400. **Credit** AmEx, DC, MC, V. **Map** p287 F12.
Hoi An's menu is a wily combination of Vietnamese and classic French styles. Barring major seafood allergies, you should get some Dungeness crab, an exotically flavoured mixture served in green bamboo tubes. When it comes to picking mains, the smart money's on an order of wok-cooked beef tournedos. Served in a rustic French casserole pot, the cognac-marinaded meat is tear-jerkingly good and layered with sweet onions, watercress and spice to deliver a sophisticated thump to the palate. Round off with an orange filled with kaffir lime mousse. Exquisite.

Indochine
Grand Hyatt Hotel, Oud Metha Road (317 1234). **Open** 7pm-midnight Sat, Sun, Tue-Fri. **Average** Dhs350. **Credit** MC, V. **Map** p281 K3.
Trip down the curving slate steps of the Grand Hyatt foyer, through a vast crop of lanky trees and outlandish shrubbery, and you'll hit Indochine, a beautifully decorated Vietnamese joint filled with light lacquered wood and Asian knick-knacks. Nibble on rice crackers slathered in soy, hot sauce and unfeasibly moreish chicken dip before hitting the intriguing menu, which bulges with wonderful dishes and exotic ingredients, from lotus root to cotton fish and papaya to banana flower.

Lemongrass
Next to Lamcy Plaza mall, Oud Metha (334 2325). **Open** noon-3pm, 7-11pm daily. **Average** Dhs200. **Credit** MC, V. **Map** p281 J3.
This beautiful and bright contemporary Thai restaurant has some attitude – it's an independent establishment, and it shows. The all-Thai staff are more attentive than elsewhere, and the decor is that bit quirkier than many hotel-based joints. On the menu special highlights include the tod man talay fish cakes, the whole deep-fried hammour, and the lemongrass juice, which is a clear, sweet, orchid-topped drink that drinks like the liquid equivalent of Turkish delight. Lemongrass is one of the best Thai restaurants in town.

Noodle House
Emirates Towers Boulevard mall, Sheikh Zayed Road (330 0000). **Open** noon-12.30am daily. **Average** Dhs150. **Credit** AmEx, DC, MC, V. **Map** p280 H4.
Noodle House is a slice of cosmopolitan chic in the slickest building in town. It's perfect for a lunch date: the noise, bustle and super-fast service will minimise those embarrassing gaps in conversation and the communal tables lend the place an easy, ice-breaking kind of atmosphere. Whizz through the tick 'n' mix pad and order some moreish Thai chicken with cashew nuts, a portion of Shanghai beef noodles and a sturdy helping of Cantonese duck with all the hoisin trimmings.

Buying booze

The purchase of alcoholic drinks from off-licences in Dubai is restricted to non-Muslims and controlled by the issue of a licence, costing Dhs150, by the Dubai police. You cannot buy alcohol from a+e or MMI shops without a valid licence, and if the police catch you carrying alcohol without a licence you're liable to a fine or worse. The application process is a little tedious: happily, MMI remove all the hassle by doing it for you. All their shops carry application forms and can explain the requirements. To kickstart the process, visit one of these MMI stores:

Sheikh Zayed Road
321 1223.
Driving out of Dubai, and past the Fairmont, take the turn-off on to the service road before Crowne Plaza. The store is behind Pizza Hut, about half way down.

Deira
294 0390.
Located on the ground-floor level of the Emirates office block. From Garhoud Bridge, follow the signs for Al Garhoud and turn left at City Centre mall. Turn left at the second set of lights and then right into the service road immediately after the bus stop.

Ibn Battuta Mall
368 5626.
Located in the Andalusia Court of Dubai's newest mall. You'll find it between junction 5 and junction 6 of Sheikh Zayed Road, after the Dubai Marina complex.

Peppercrab

Grand Hyatt Hotel, Oud Metha Road (317 1234).
Open 7-11.30pm Sat, Mon-Fri. **Average** Dhs500.
Credit AmEx, DC, MC, V. **Map** p281 K3.
Fish-heads rejoice: Peppercrab is a place of inspired piscine creation where you can soothe your meat-weary soul. Notionally a Singaporean joint, it offers not only fantastic, innovative food, but also a charming setting both inside and out. The menu is an exhilarating read all round, with main courses of crustaceans and fish plucked directly from the tank. Start off with a light, fluffy omelette, stuffed with cooked oysters, and move straight on to the house speciality, 1.5kg (3lb) of mud crab in hot sauce: get your hands messy digging out the soft white meat before tucking into a whole spiced hammour.

Sakura

Crowne Plaza Hotel, Sheikh Zayed Road (331 1111).
Open 7-11pm daily. **Average** Dhs300. **Credit**
AmEx, DC, MC, V. **Map** p285 G10.
The sushi at Sakura is merely a sideshow. With all the clanging knives, twirling rice bowls and egg juggling, the preparation of food is like Cirque du Soleil with cutlery, or perhaps a kitchen in a Kurosawa film. On most nights, this theatre of the teppanyaki results in some fantastic grilled lobster and prawns dipped in apple-tinged soy sauce. Traditional Japanese flute music occasionally gives

way to dissonant clanging, somewhat distracting from the symmetry of the meal, but all is forgiven when proceedings end with a scoops of green-tea ice-cream, cool and leafy fresh.

Shang Palace

Shangri-La Hotel, Sheikh Zayed Road (405 2703). **Open** 12.30-3pm, 8pm-midnight daily.
Credit AmEx, DC, MC, V. **Average** Dhs400.
Map p287 F12.
Diners choose between an inner sanctum of tables, shielded by a wall of antiques and a tornado of gold roses, or an open balcony which overlooks the foyer below. The chef, who hails from Hong Kong, lays on echt Chinese food that's regularly impressive: hits include beancurd with spring onion and crunchy nuggets of fried shrimp, strips of honey-sweet smoked fish and on-the-bone wedges of tender roast pigeon. Shang has settled firmly into its stride and is now one of the best Chinese joints in town.

Teatro

Towers Rotana Hotel, Sheikh Zayed Road (343 8000). **Open** 11.30am-3pm, 6pm-2am daily. **Average** Dhs300. **Credit** AmEx, DC, MC, V. **Map** p280 H4.
One of Dubai's favourite fusion restaurants, Teatro is reliably excellent if you're looking for some intriguing flavour combinations. The kitchen, sushi

Emirati eats

Emirati cuisine is an elusive beast, and even the most integrated, right-on Dubai expats could be forgiven for going their whole time in the UAE without trying any national dishes.

In truth, Emirati food is not highly flavoured. Starters tend to be very straightforward: bowls of dango chickpeas and bajilla broad beans, eaten raw with a smattering of melted butter, a squeeze of lemon and a sprinkle of cumin. To dig into dango, head to **Kan Zaman** at the Heritage Village (393 9913), a terrace restaurant inches from the Creek which offers beautiful night-time views of the lantern-lit wind towers of the village. Kan has a couple of other local treats on offer: along with your salty chickpeas, you can indulge in thick puffs of chobab bread, eaten with dark honey, and musallah filled with cheese and egg.

Another classic Emirati starter is gerger: green leaves reminiscent of a particularly bitter form of rocket, whose high iron content has earned it a reputation as the natural Viagra. They serve it daily at **Khalid Horiya Kitchen** (06 538 0555), a 25-minute whizz out of Dubai on the main road from Sharjah to Ajman. Nip to Sharjah, take the Sharjah

Airport Road (Al Dhaid Road) and at the first interchange (Waseed Square), turn towards Ajman. The café is a few hundred metres down on your right, just before the Eppco station. Head to the two upstairs rooms (one for men and one for women) and prepare yourself for a proper Emirati feast. Seating is on the floor – having washed your hands (cutlery is strictly for the tourists), tuck one leg under yourself, shove the other one out and get stuck in to some harees. This is the best-known local dish, a bland blend of meat and barley. The ingredients are cooked together for hours, then mashed to the consistency of porridge.

The most common form of harees is made with veal, and can be enjoyed nightly at **Al Areesh** in the Al Boom Tourist Village (324 3000), on the Bur Dubai side of Garhoud Bridge. Other delights that appear at this bamboo-lined buffet restaurant include ouzi – a goat baked with rice, onions and eggs and then topped with rigag, a traditional Emirati bread – and tharid – an ancient dish made with vegetables, meat and bread, slow-cooked into a tasty stew.

Eat, Drink, Shop

bar, bar and well-stocked wine cellar are each carefully integrated into the dining area. The chef takes his position at centre stage, conducting a culinary orchestra made up of a Western kitchen to his left and an Eastern kitchen to his right. The food is an unusual but exciting mix, as might expected given the variety of preparation methods: clay tandoor, wok, wood-burning pizza oven, lavastone grill, rotisserie and Chinese smoke oven.

Thai Chi

Wafi Pyramids at Wafi City mall, off Oud Metha Road (324 4100). **Open** 12.30-3pm, 7.30pm-midnight daily. **Average** Dhs280. **Credit** AmEx, DC, MC, V. **Map** p281 J3.

Two restaurants – Thai and Chinese – have come together under one roof at Thai Chi. Each has its own distinct interior: bamboo decoration for the casual Chinese area and a more formal, traditional setting for the Thai dining room. The glass noodle salad with raw chilli spice and zesty lime juice is an artful creation, and the stir-fried crab, roughly chopped in a sweet and spicy curry with (believe it or not) scrambled eggs, satisfies at ten different levels. The sticky coconut rice pudding is another lick-the-plate-clean winner.

Yo! Sushi

BurJuman Centre, Trade Centre Road (359 5479). **Open** noon-11pm Sat-Thur; 2pm-midnight Fri. **Average** Dhs130. **Credit** AmEx, DC, MC, V. **Map** p281 J2.

Despite a less than edifying location – backing on to the BurJuman car park, with lines of 4x4s clearly visible through the glass – this turquoise-beamed

Conveyor belt dining at **Yo! Sushi**.

space is pretty, and filled with hustling waiters in branded caps and aprons. The warming and tasty miso soup and green tea are bottomless, and all the food is fresh-tasting and well-presented. The California roll with avocado, crabstick and tiny orange fish eggs has a smooth fishy taste, and the seared hammour is excellent, with a thick meaty texture and chilli-coated spicy edge.

Indian

Asha's

Wafi Pyramids at Wafi City mall, off Oud Metha Road (324 0000). **Open** 12.30-3.30pm, 7.30pm-2am daily. **Average** Dhs300. **Credit** AmEx, DC, MC, V. **Map** p281 J3.

This extremely successful Indian restaurant is the brainchild of singer Asha Bhosle. There are three distinct cuisines on offer: traditional, contemporary fusion and a selection of Ms Bhosle's personal favourites. The food is excellent: try the murg biryani awadh, stuffed with dried fruit and nuts and cooked with basmati rice, or perhaps the seared red snapper with garam masala. During the winter, the terrace is idyllic, and the cocktail list is one of the finest in the city.

Coconut Grove

Rydges Plaza Hotel, Satwa roundabout, Satwa (398 3800). **Open** noon-3pm, 7pm-midnight daily. **Average** Dhs60. **Credit** AmEx, DC, MC, V. **Map** p285 F8.

If you crave comfort, quiet and Keralite food then Coconut Grove is your place. Load up on freshly cooked appam pancakes, thick-gravied meen made with tamarind, coconut-milk fish moilee, and dosa rolls stuffed with spicy vegetable sambar. Wash it down with a kurumba punch of lime, mint and honey, and your bill will still be laughably petite. The Dhs35 Friday brunch offers exceptionally good value and the views of a sun-dappled Dubai are marvellous in the middle of the day.

Delhi Darbar

Opposite Karama post office (273 3444). **Open** 8am-1am Sat-Thur; 7.30-11.30am, 1.30-3.30pm Fri. **Average** Dhs40. **No credit cards. Map** p281 J2.

Delhi Darbar is a classic Indian cheap eat. It's a step upmarket from other local curry houses, and boy do the prices reflect this: delicious vegetable dishes such as palak paneer and malai kofta come in at a whacking Dhs7.50, and mutton kadai at Dhs9.50. Even with naan and rice, you're unlikely to hit the Dhs20 mark. The chicken tikka masala (Dhs13.50) rivals those served in five-star hotel restaurants at four times the price. The dal is intriguing, packed with all sorts of beans and lentils, including a tiny black variety that pops in your mouth.

Gazebo

Gazebo, Trade Centre Road, Karama (397 9930). **Open** noon-3pm, 7-11.45pm. **Average** Dhs100. **Credit** AmEx, DC, MC, V. **Map** p283 J5.

Asha's. *See p90.*

Gazebo has a well-deserved reputation among Dubai's curry fanatics for being one of the best independent Indian restaurants in the city. It's the complexity of the spicing (usually enough to get tongues purring) that sets Gazebo apart from the competition. The biryani selection is one of the best in the city – try the version with spinach-stuffed mushrooms – and the naan breads are immensely flavourful and perfectly light. A meal for two people shouldn't cost more than Dhs100 – a real bargain, in anybody's terms.

India House
Al Fahidi Street (352 6006). **Open** 7am-12.30am Sat-Thur; 7.30-11.30am, 1.30pm-12.30am Fri. **Average** Dhs50. **No credit cards. Map** p282 H4.
One of the few restaurants on Al Fahidi Street in the Bur Dubai electronics souk (halfway down, next to Choitram Supermarket and just opposite Sheeba Electronics), India House is one of the finest and cheapest Indian restaurants in the city. In among the extraordinary range of dosas, puris and individual Punjabi dishes, it is the thali that's king. Efficient waiters repeatedly fill your seven or eleven small stainless steel dishes with gorgeous curries, piping hot puri, rice and sweets until you can eat no more. Accept no substitute.

Ravi's
Satwa High Street (331 5353). **Open** 5am-3am daily. **Average** Dhs60. **No credit cards.** Map p285 F8.
Craig David's favourite Dubaian curry house is one of the cheapest in the city and well-loved by expats in search of a discount spice-fest. Regulars get stuck into flavoursome lentil dal and chunks of grilled boneless chicken, freshly made to order in the tiny open kitchen. Sit on garden furniture outside or in the super-spartan interior and eat until you waddle, for next to nothing.

International

Johnny Rockets
Jumeirah Beach Road, opposite Jumeirah Centre (344 7859). **Open** noon-midnight daily. **Average** Dhs80. **Credit** AmEx, DC, MC, V. **Map** p284 D9.
The hamburgers at Johnny Rockets are eminently photogenic specimens, with thick juicy patties, crispy lettuce, crunchy onions and solid, unsoggy, tastefully burnt-round-the-edges buns. The 'number 12' burger is a densely packed wedge of beef with Tillamook cheese and patented 'red, red sauce', which is probably just standard tomato ketchup. Avoid the sloppy chilli and the straight-forward sandwiches and head straight for the main, meaty attraction.

Manhattan Grill
Grand Hyatt Hotel, Oud Metha Road (317 1234). **Open** 7.30-11.30pm Sun-Fri. **Average** Dhs680. **Credit** AmEx, DC, MC, V. **Map** p281 K3.
Manhattan Grill lands a killer blow when it comes to hunks of sizzling Nebraska cow. The interior nods towards the downtown 1950s diner, with red leather banquettes filling one wall, but otherwise the Grill's style is totally uptown – all aluminium shelving, open kitchens, wine-filled glass cabinets and stiff white tablecloths. For sheer indulgence, order the monolithic tenderloin, with sides of sautéed mushrooms, creamed spinach, garlic mash and roasted root vegetables.

Accept no imitations: **Johnny Rockets** serves the best burgers in town. *See p91.*

Spectrum on One

Fairmont Hotel (332 5555). **Open** 7pm-1am daily.
Average Dhs600. **Credit** AmEx, DC, MC, V.
Map p285 G9.

Ascend from the contemporary opulence of the Fairmont Hotel foyer into a chic New York-style eaterie. You'll find a walk-in cellar, a cigar room and a stylish bar with a city view, all luxuriating in their buzzy decadence. No less than eight open kitchens create authentic food from eight different countries. We recommend the divine dim sum and excellent Thai curries, to be followed up with one of the accurately named 'Compilation of Spectrum desserts', which will be enough to make you want to carve your name in the table and never leave.

Trader Vic's

Crowne Plaza Hotel, Sheikh Zayed Road (331 1111).
Open 7-11pm daily. **Average** Dhs300. **Credit**
AmEx, DC, MC, V. **Map** p285 G10.

Trader Vic's is a wood-lined Polynesian haunt adorned with voodoo statues and model boats. While the food can be variable, the cocktails and mocktails remain outstanding at any time – don't miss the trademark Mai Tai. Try the medium-rare beef with a sprig of rosemary, expertly matched by green beans and topped with a pebbly plateau of macadamia nuts. Finish with the tropical fruit soup, bolstered by scoops of thick and chunky sorbet.

Deira

Arabic

Al Dawaar

Hyatt Regency Hotel, Deira Corniche (209 1100).
Open 12.30-3pm, 7-11.30pm daily. **Average**
Dhs320. **Credit** AmEx, MC, V. **Map** p283 J1.

Dubai's only revolving restaurant may be getting a little old (the Hyatt Regency was built back in 1980) but it remains impressive: a full revolution takes a little under two hours and it provides a spectacular view of Dubai, from 25 storeys above the Creek. A different Dhs160 deal is served every night, and the international mix (Mediterranean, Arabic, Japanese) is a cut above most buffets.

Al Mansour Dhow

InterContinental Hotel, Baniyas Road (222 7171).
Cruise departs 8.30pm daily. **Average** Dhs330.
Credit AmEx, DC, MC, V. **Map** p283 J3.

This big, pretty, happily licensed boat cruises off on regular dinner voyages, sculling down as far as the gold souk before turning back to Al Maktoum Bridge. At night-time, the river is utterly beautiful, and would justify the fare on its own: just as well, given the run-of-the-mill international buffet on offer. After dinner, soak up the stunning views over a post-prandial shisha, while a fez-headed oud doodler strums. Be

Eat, Drink, Shop

warned, though: don't even think of booking a cruise in the summer months, unless you like the idea of nibbling in a waterborne sauna.

Al Mawal

Al Bustan Rotana Hotel, Casablanca Road, Garhoud (282 6530). **Open** 12.30-3.30pm, 8pm-12.30am daily. **Average** Dhs300. **Credit** AmEx, DC, MC, V. **Map** p281 K2.
Alive with evocative music, gyrating bellies and masses of revellers clouded in a sweet shisha haze, Al Mawal has a deservedly great reputation. The waiters love a bit of showmanship, the tabouleh is vibrant and piquant, and the mixed grill impressive. In fact, the food is excellent all round: flavours are fresh and linger in the mind for days. The pricing is very reasonable for food of this calibre, and the entertainment certainly draws in the crowds.

Al Mijana

Le Meridien Dubai, Airport Road, Garhoud (282 4040). **Open** 12.30-3pm, 8pm-midnight daily. **Average** Dhs300. **Credit** AmEx, DC, MC, V. **Map** p281 L2.
A high-end home to the best of Lebanese cuisine. Al Mijana's menu is split into three set sections, each of which houses more food than your local supermarket. Service is uniformly superb, with a barrage of helpful and amusing waiting staff more than happy to guide you through the maze of meze on offer. The highlight of the cold dishes is the kibbeh nayee, an emulsified paste of the freshest raw lamb and burghul wheat – the meat dissolves beautifully on the tongue, leaving a satisfying tang.

Shabestan

InterContinental Hotel, Baniyas Road (222 7171). **Open** 12.30-3.15pm, 7.30pm-1am daily. **Average** Dhs350. **Credit** AmEx, DC, MC, V. **Map** p283 J3.
The gentle sound of a spouting fountain permeates Shabestan, and the scent of flat breads, baked in an on-site clay oven, wafts through the air. A host of Persian classics compete for your attention – try the chicken soup, a gorgeously flavoured dish full of thick noodles; the shrimp kebab infused with a highly concentrated saffron marinade; and delicious lamb, two enormous slabs of tenderly grilled meat served with a helping of delicately-flavoured rice. Shabestan makes a convincing case for itself as the best Persian restaurant in the city.

Shahrzad

Hyatt Regency Hotel, Deira Corniche (209 1200). **Open** 12.30-3.30pm, 7.30-11pm Sat-Thur. **Average** Dhs300. **Credit** AmEx, DC, MC, V. **Map** p283 J1.
A Persian restaurant, beautifully decked out with carved wooden screens, patterned walls, Iranian rugs and stunning copper lamps. The open-plan kitchen, with its traditional tandoor oven and a charcoal grill under a beaten copper canopy, adds extra ambience and fabulous smells to the restaurant. Top meze, bread cooked fresh and delivered to the table by the in-house baker, beautiful stews and kebabs all hit the spot.

European

The Aquarium

Dubai Creek Golf & Yacht Club, Garhoud Road (295 6000). **Open** 12.30-3pm, 7pm-midnight daily. **Average** Dhs500. **Credit** AmEx, DC, MC, V. **Map** p281 K3.
The Aquarium has the feel of an elaborately decorated watchtower. This thick-carpeted glass-house of leaning metal columns looks out at the Creek and down over the heads and shoulders of diners at the Boardwalk (*see below*). The major attraction here is the vast tube of gleaming blue water, in which schools of yellow-finned tiddlers scull their way round. As you'd expect, seafood rules here and you're sure to be won over by the dazzling à la carte selection of fish.

The Boardwalk

Dubai Creek Golf & Yacht Club, Garhoud Road (295 6000). **Open** 8am-midnight daily. **Average** Dhs200. **Credit** AmEx, DC, MC, V. **Map** p281 K3.
A triumph of style over substance, the Boardwalk's stunning Creekside views more than compensate for the mediocre menu. Avoid the harsh lighting and uncomfy chairs at the bar and head over to the terrace, warmed by Parisian café-style heaters on cool evenings. The setting is romantic, the surroundings interesting, and the water only half a footstep away. The menu doesn't offer anything very exciting, though you could opt for the seafood platter, stuffed to the gills with fried hammour, tiger prawns and sea bass, lifted by a light saffrony sauce. If you're in the mood for something lighter, there's the couscous salad, a super-healthy but rather unadventurous palate-cleanser.

Café Chic

Le Meridien Dubai, Airport Road, Garhoud (282 4040). **Open** 12.30-2.45pm, 8-11.45pm daily. **Average** Dhs340. **Credit** AmEx, DC, MC, V. **Map** p281 L2.
Offering an authentic range of French cuisine, this restaurant is indeed très chic. Intimate yet airy, the bar and lounge areas offer a quiet venue for an aperitif or late-night coffee and cigar. Michel Rostang, possessor of two Michelin stars, has assembled a catalogue of authentic French ensembles, which are presented with flair. Munch your way through a perfect asparagus salad, followed by striking tuna and scallop carpaccio, but be sure to leave enough room for the killer chocolate soufflé. Consider a lunchtime visit, when you can pick up a three-course set meal for well under Dhs100.

Casa Mia

Le Meridien Dubai, Airport Road, Garhoud (282 4040). **Open** 12.30-3pm, 8-11.30pm daily. **Average** Dhs300. **Credit** AmEx, DC, MC, V. **Map** p281 L2.
A warm, inviting womb of a restaurant, Casa Mia manages to rise above the staggering spectacle of waiters exchanging 'buon appetito' with customers who don't speak Italian either. The dishes are

Eat, Drink, Shop

positive eating + positive living

fast and fresh noodle & rice dishes and freshly squeezed juices

wagamama dubai
crowne plaza dubai sheikh zayed road
telephone + 971 4 305 6060

opening hours:
monday - sunday : 7.30am - midnight

for menu visit: **www.wagamama.com**
uk ı ireland ı amsterdam ı australia ı dubai ı antwerp ı auckland

Casa Mia. *See p93.*

served with skill and dedication, but without devastating flair. Try the gnocchi with Parma ham to start with and the well-executed tiramisu for a sweet denouement. The rabbit leg stuffed with Italian sausage is another guaranteed crowd-pleaser.

Focaccia
Hyatt Regency Hotel, Deira Corniche (209 1600).
Open 12.30-3.30pm, 7-11.30pm daily. **Average** Dhs320. **Credit** AmEx, DC, MC, V. **Map** p283 J1.
Focaccia is a light, airy, spacious place, with huge plush chairs and a beautiful view of the ocean, framed by precisely separated palm trees. The eponymous bread is fluffy, permeable and delicious enjoyed with roasted cloves of garlic, and starters are excellent, especially the squid salad, stacked tall with cubes of potato, cherry tomatoes, olives and green beans. One of Dubai's classiest Italians.

JW's Steakhouse
JW Marriott Hotel, Al Siddique Road (262 4444).
Open 12.30-3pm, 7-11pm daily. **Average** Dhs400. **Credit** AmEx, DC, MC, V. **Map** p281 K1.
JW's is restlessly inventive with meat, turning out complex dishes that regulars rave about; we're amazed the place is still not besieged by ravenous carnivores. Seating is in super-comfy armchairs and the steaks cut like butter. Savour the filet mignon, complete with a beautiful béarnaise sauce, one of the finest couples since Fred first twirled Ginger. Accompaniments of baked potatoes with soured cream and crisp vegetables satisfy the breaks between meaty mouthfuls, but leave little doubt as to the star of the show.

Legends Steakhouse
Dubai Creek Golf & Yacht Club, Garhoud Road (295 6000). **Open** 7.30-11pm daily. **Average** Dhs340. **Credit** AmEx, DC, MC, V. **Map** p281 K3.
In a break from the dark, leatherbound steakhouse norm, Legends is a high-ceilinged, pastel-coloured space with wide-open views over the golf club, the perfect setting for a serious meatathon. The menu covers a belly-pleasing spread of damn-the-calories fare, heavy on the cream. The pick of the mains is the peppercorn tenderloin steak, flambéed in brandy and red wine before your very eyes.

Market Place
JW Marriott Hotel, Al Siddique Road (607 7977).
Open 12.30-3pm, 7.30-11.30pm daily. **Average** Dhs280. **Credit** AmEx, DC, MC, V. **Map** p281 K1.
The Market Place is is a cut above many of the all-you-can-eat deals offered in Dubai. Floppy-hatted chefs cook up fresh pasta, chicken and curry to order, and there's plenty of good-quality sushi, antipasti and oysters on offer. A wall of fresh bread and an array of salads pad things out nicely. Load up on flame-grilled mini steaks, gratin potatoes and osso bucco, and by the time you hit the enormous dessert colony, you'll be too full to be disappointed at the synthetic sponginess of it all.

M's Beef Bistro
Le Meridien Dubai, Airport Road, Garhoud (282 4040). **Open** 12.30-3.30pm, 8pm-12.30am Sat-Thur. **Average** Dhs300. **Credit** AmEx, DC, MC, V. **Map** p281 L2.
M's makes you feel so at home you'll think you could turn up in pyjamas and no one would bat an eyelid. Dining takes place outside on the attractive terrace, inside by candlelight or up at the bar, and minimal tables make for an intimate atmosphere and attentive service. The menu itself holds few surprises: cow is the top dog, though soups and seafood are also on hand to whet the appetite.

Oxygen
Al Bustan Rotana Hotel, Casablanca Road, Garhoud (282 0000). **Open** 6pm-3am daily. **Average** Dhs120. **Credit** AmEx, DC, MC, V. **Map** p281 K2.
In the bowels of the Al Bustan Rotana hotel lies the wonderfully stylish yet refreshingly unpretentious Oxygen restaurant. The ritzy decor takes its cue from a more decadent era: the place is stuffed with mouldings, candelabras and candles the size of the Burj. You'd be forgiven for thinking it would cost the earth to dine here, but Oxygen offers exceptional value for money. It also lays on some quirky treats: try, for example, the shrimp cakes and the barbecue chicken.

Seafood Market
Le Meridien Dubai, Airport Road, Garhoud (282 4040). **Open** 12.30-3pm, 7-11.30pm daily. **Average** Dhs300. **Credit** AmEx, DC, MC, V. **Map** p281 L2.
One of the best of the pick-your-own restaurants in Dubai: trot over to the ice-packed shelves, which heave with fresh fish, pick your favourite and have

Eat, Drink, Shop

Fine dining at Gordon Ramsay's **Verre**.

it cooked and sauced to your specifications. Bottles of white and rosé are set to chill alongside the fish, so it's easy to choose drinks as you pick your food.

Spice Island

Renaissance Dubai Hotel, Salahuddin Road, near the JW Marriott Hotel (262 5555). **Open** 7-11.30pm daily. **Average** Dhs260. **Credit** AmEx, DC, MC, V. **Map** p281 K1.

Pulling in the punters with regular all-you-can-eat-and-drink gorge-athons, Spice Island is noisy and chaotic, more like a bustling market than a remote and exotic isle. You have to be assertive among the determined hordes of grazers, but the choice is vast, with every corner of the culinary world covered at the feasting stations. However, it is undoubtedly the 'all you can drink' aspect that draws the crowds.

Verre

Hilton Dubai Creek, Baniyas Road (227 1111). **Open** 7-11pm Sun-Fri. **Average** Dhs500. **Credit** AmEx, DC, MC, V. **Map** p283 L4.

Gordon Ramsay's Middle Eastern outpost, Verre is a serious contender for finest restaurant in Dubai. The restaurant manager charms his way around the tables, making each of the guests feel like the evening has been laid on for them alone, and the sommelier is permanently on hand to recommend the perfect bottle. An evening here doesn't come cheap, but the contemporary cuisine served is immaculate, convincing your mouth it's died and gone to taste-bud heaven.

Far Eastern

Blue Elephant

Al Bustan Rotana Hotel, Casablanca Road, Garhoud (282 0000). **Open** 11am-3pm, 7-11.30pm daily. **Average** Dhs290. **Credit** AmEx, DC, MC, V. **Map** p281 K2.

The Elephant's decor has something of an alfresco feel to it: the sloping roofs, ponds, bridges and a cascading waterfall all give the illusion of the place having been turned outside-in. Although it's by no means innovative, the food is fine: try the herby muak lek corn cakes followed by an explosive dish of himmapan vegetables with stir-fried tofu and a sturdy helping of Bangkok fish, which comes as a slab of hammour smothered in a pungent chilli mix. Expect a delicate but delicious selection of fresh exotic fruit with coconut ice-cream for dessert. Only the steep mark-up on wine blots an otherwise enchanting dining experience.

China Club

InterContinental Hotel, Baniyas Road (222 7171). **Open** 12.30-3pm, 7.30-11pm daily. **Average** Dhs300. **Credit** AmEx, DC, MC, V. **Map** p283 J3.

A high-design establishment with elegant service, intimate atmosphere and ambitions to fine-dining status. Sliding into a side booth you'll notice the musical backdrop eschews the lobe-wrenching misery of panpipes in favour of Sinatra's sultry croonings, interwoven with some jazz wizardry

The brunch bunch

With Dubai's Western expat community letting its collective hair down every Thursday night, the start of the Dubaian weekend, many breakfasts are missed on a Friday morning. Which is why almost every hotel and many of the independents lay on special buffet brunches. These are some of our favourites.

The Alamo
Dubai Marine Beach Resort (346 1111). **Brunch served** 11am-3pm. **Price** Dhs60; Dhs30 children.
Popular international and Tex-Mex brunch.

Aquarium
Creek Golf & Yacht Club (295 6000). **Brunch served** 11.30am-3pm. **Price** Dhs75; Dhs35 children.
All sorts of seafood and salads.

Boston Bar
Jumeirah Rotana (345 5888). **Brunch served** noon-4pm. **Price** Dhs40; Dhs20 children.
Plenty of salads and a few US-style mains.

The Brunch
Dusit Dubai (343 3333). **Brunch served** 12.30-3pm. **Price** Dhs95.
Buffet fare spread over several restaurants.

Carter's
Wafi Pyramids (324 0000). **Brunch served** 11.30am-3pm. **Price** Dhs65; Dhs30 children.
Boozy brunches with global fare.

The Cellar
Aviation Club (282 4122). **Brunch served** 11.30am-4pm. **Price** Dhs60.
Unlimited food from the à la carte menu.

The Colonnade
Jumeirah Beach Hotel (348 0000). **Brunch served** noon-3.30pm. **Price** Dhs130; Dhs65 children.
Prettily presented Arabic and European fare.

Long's Bar
Towers Rotana Hotel (343 8000). **Brunch served** noon-4pm. **Price** Dhs49; Dhs25 children.
A relaxed and nicely priced brunch.

More
Nr Welcare Hospital (283 0224). **Brunch served** 11am-4pm. **Price** Dhs65; Dhs35 children.
Calm and comfortable café-style brunch.

Al Muntaha
Burj Al Arab (301 7777). **Brunch served** 11am-3.30pm. **Price** Dhs240; Dhs120 children.
One of the priciest brunches in town.

Prasino's
Jumeirah Beach Resort (344 5333). **Brunch served** 12.30-3pm. **Price** Dhs130; Dhs65 children.
A classy brunch option.

Scarlett's
Emirates Palace (319 8768). **Brunch served** 11.30am-4pm. **Price** Dhs70.
A favourite with the hangover crowd.

Spectrum on One
Fairmont Hotel (332 5555). **Brunch served** noon-3pm. **Price** Dhs288; Dhs108 children.
Excellent brunch, with unlimited bubbly.

Splendido
Ritz-Carlton (399 4000). **Brunch served** 12.30-3.30pm. **Price** Dhs140; Dhs70 children.
Classy, relaxed, sun-speckled brunch.

Vivaldi
Sheraton Dubai Creek (207 1717). **Brunch served** 12.30-3.30pm. **Price** Dhs70; Dhs35 children.
Piles of sumptuous Mediterranean fare.

Waxy O'Conner's
Ascot Hotel (352 0900). **Brunch served** noon-6pm. **Price** Dhs50; Dhs15 children.
Dubai's most notoriously boozy brunch.

Waxy O'Conner's.

THE WORLD'S YOUR OYSTER

from Ella Fitzgerald. The food doesn't hit the mark every time, but it is inventive and some dishes excel: try the jin ling duck soldiers or Szechuan prawns.

Kiku
Le Meridien Dubai, Airport Road, Garhoud (282 4040). **Open** 12.30-3pm, 7-11pm daily. **Average** Dhs250. **Credit** AmEx, DC, MC, V. **Map** p281 L2.
Kiku has two sections: the sushi bar, facing an open kitchen, and a main restaurant with private dining rooms and teppanyaki tables. The best deals on an eclectic menu are the set menus and bento boxes. Try the sushi gozen bento, with sushi, crab salad, grilled fish and a fantastic array of other niceties.

Long Yin
Le Meridien Dubai, Airport Road, Garhoud (282 4040). **Open** 12.30-3.30pm, 7pm-1am daily. **Average** Dhs300. **Credit** AmEx, DC, MC, V. **Map** p281 L2.
This is a haven of Cantonese kitsch, complete with Chinese bridges, ponds of goldfish and tanks full of doomed lobsters. The menu is, thankfully, more refined. The spare ribs are a chin-wiping,

The sushi bar at **Miyako**.

finger-sucking success, and the crispy duck is probably the best in Dubai. Long Yin is by no means cheap, with starters at around Dhs45 and mains at Dhs60, but it is an excellent choice for a sophisticated Chinese feed.

Minato
InterContinental Hotel, Baniyas Road (205 7333). **Open** 12.30-3pm, 7-11pm daily. **Average** Dhs300. **Credit** AmEx, DC, MC, V. **Map** p283 J3.
Minato serves some of the most imaginative Japanese dishes in town, so it's a smart choice if you want to experiment with something other than run-of-the-mill sushi and yakitori. Star of the menu is the sukiyaki hotpot, a huge cauldron, brimful of goodness, housing beef sirloin cut in bacon-like strips, baby mushrooms, noodles, seared cabbage, onion (both spring and regular) and huge hunks of tofu. A top choice for a foray into the exotic.

Miyako
Hyatt Regency Hotel, Deira Corniche (209 1234). **Open** 12.30-3pm, 7-11pm daily. **Average** Dhs400. **Credit** AmEx, MC, V. **Map** p283 J1.
Miyako is a calm and intimate restaurant, with a pretty sushi bar. The menu is extensive, but short on English-language explanation, so those unfamiliar with the cuisine will appreciate the fact that the waitresses are well-versed in the particulars of every dish. Teppanyaki is clearly the real joy at Miyako, and they've got it down to a fine art: the freshest possible ingredients, the best cuts of meat and priceless live-cooking entertainment.

Sukhothai
Le Meridien Dubai, Airport Road, Garhoud (282 4040). **Open** 12.30-3.30pm, 7.30pm-12.30am daily. **Average** Dhs300. **Credit** AmEx, DC, MC, V. **Map** p281 L2.
Duck and fruit is universally recognised as a wonderful combination, but the lychee variation at Sukhothai is without doubt the best thing happening to game in a two-mile radius: tasty pieces of bird come simmered in spicy red curry sauce with nuggets of soft fruit. The carved wood and Kim-music provide the perfect backdrop to some of the best Thai food in town.

Jumeirah

Arabic

The Chalet
Beach Road, just after Al Manara Road (348 7557). **Open** 11.30am-1.30am daily. **Average** Dhs40. **No credit cards. Map** p278 B4.
The Chalet seems to have been interior-designed by pixies: toadstool tables topped with strawberries, indoor trees and enormous blue sunflowers abound. The same woodland folk have produced a menu of budget Lebanese grills and seafood, most of which romps in firmly under the Dhs20 mark. Follow up your friendly welcome with a huge Arabic biryani,

Eat, Drink, Shop

Beach Bar & Grill.

a vast bed of rice with four marinated mutton chops and three bowls of sauce – salsa, raita and chicken broth. Very filling, and a bargain at Dhs14.

Chandelier
Marina Walk, Dubai Marina (04 366 3606). **Open** 8.30am-3pm, 6pm-2.30am daily. **Average** Dhs200. **Credit** AmEx, DC, MC, V. **Map** p278 A5.
Chandelier has colonised large swathes of prime terrain at Dubai Marina, with the whole area around the dancing fountain packed on cool nights. The meze is among the best in the city, featuring brisk lemony tabouleh, spicy basterma and, for the adventurous, fried sparrows in pomegranate syrup.

Al Khaima
Le Royal Meridien Beach Resort & Spa, Al Sufouh Road (399 5555). **Open** 10am-6pm, 7pm-midnight daily. **Average** Dhs400. **Credit** AmEx, DC, MC, V. **Map** p278 A5.
A large wooden deck extends out towards the sea from this idyllic beachside restaurant, with a stretch of lawn leading onwards to the sand. The menu comprises classic hot and cold Lebanese meze, with a good range of meat dishes, a sprinkling of seafood and some authentic specialities such as delicious baby marrows stuffed with minced lamb. The grilled hammour with garlic is also excellent. After dinner, enjoy a lazy shisha while listening to the live traditional music.

Shoo Fee Ma Fee
Souk Madinat Jumeirah (366 8888). **Open** 6pm-1am daily. **Average** Dhs400. **Credit** AmEx, DC, MC, V. **Map** p278 A4.
The modern Moorish enclave of Shoo Fee Ma Fee is crammed with ornate Eastern lanterns, elaborate timber screens and heavily embroidered rugs. The

food is mostly excellent, with mellifluously sweet baba ganoush, noisily crunchy aubergine chips and crumbly pigeon pastilla. You'll find shisha being chugged and cocktails being slurped on the spacious upstairs roof terrace.

Tagine
One&Only Royal Mirage Hotel, Al Sufouh Road (399 9999). **Open** 7-11.30pm Sat, Sun, Tue-Fri. **Average** Dhs600. **Credit** AmEx, DC, MC, V. **Map** p278 A5.
A fine Moroccan experience awaits at Tagine. The interior is candlelit, the music is live and the waiters are all done up in traditional dress. The menu is full of classic dishes, with the emphasis, unsurprisingly, on tagines and couscous. Visitors would do well to start with harira soup and fresh bread, perked up by a dollop or two of red-hot harissa. You can't go wrong with the main courses: the chicken tagine, tinged with rosewater and loaded with almonds and apricots, is particularly good.

European

La Baie
Ritz-Carlton Hotel, Al Sufouh Road (399 4000). **Open** 7-11pm Sat, Mon-Fri. **Average** Dhs350. **Credit** AmEx, DC, MC, V. **Map** p278 A5.
La Baie offers formal dining in a stylish setting, cheered up by rampant candles and bowers of fresh blooms. Waiters insinuate their way round the room, a pianist tinkles elegantly in the corner and the menu heaves with hearty meat dishes served with indulgent sauces and creamy mash. Try the beef tenderloin with onion reduction, but make sure you save room for the masterly baked cheesecake.

Barasti

*Le Meridien Mina Seyahi Hotel, Al Sufouh Road
(399 3333).* **Open** 11am-2am daily. **Average**
Dhs200. **Credit** AmEx, DC, MC, V. **Map** p278 A5.
Better known for its beach parties and poolside
barbecue, Barasti is also first-class for an elegant
meal in laid-back surroundings: on the outside terrace, you sit mere metres away from the lapping
Gulf. The clientele ranges from smartly dressed to
the Bermuda-shorted, and the atmosphere's relaxed,
lending itself equally well to early evening drinks or
a full three-course meal. The menu covers innovative
comfort food like seafood spaghetti in bouillabaisse
cream or Cajun fried calamari with minted mayo.

Beach Bar & Grill

*One&Only Royal Mirage Hotel, Al Sufouh Road
(399 9999).* **Open** 7-11pm daily. **Average** Dhs300.
Credit AmEx, DC, MC, V. **Map** p278 A5.
The name is instantly forgettable, but the setting
is among the most romantic in the city. Take a table
on this dining platform, from which vantage point
you can admire the broad sweep of the moonlit
beach and hear the waves lapping at the shore a
stone's throw from your plates of fresh warm
bread. The food is good rather than outstanding –
lots of reasonably executed grill classics like seared
freshwater prawns and lamb loin with fennel – but
the location makes it perfect for dating, doting or
even popping the big one.

Bice

Hilton Dubai Jumeirah, Al Sufouh Road (399 1111).
Open noon-midnight daily. **Average** Dhs300.
Credit AmEx, DC, MC, V. **Map** p278 A5.
Run by a Riminian restaurant manager who keeps
it real by importing top-class ingredients from Italy,
Bice is a sophisticated and authentic joint. Start
with pots of grissini and focaccia loaded with a
pungent black tapenade, then order at will – you
can't put a foot wrong. From ruffles of bresaola with
crumbling aged parmesan to tender pieces of veal
and beef ragù draped on own-made spaghetti, from
rich risottos positively humming with truffle oil to
the teak-brown chocolate soufflé, everything is
magnificently well done.

Boudoir

Dubai Marine Beach Resort, Beach Road (345 5995).
Open 7.30-11pm daily. **Average** Dhs500. **Credit**
AmEx, DC, MC, V. **Map** p284 D8.
If Toulouse-Lautrec met Colonel Gaddafi in a black
forest gateau, the scene might have approached the
outrageously opulent decor of Boudoir. By evening,
it's an elaborate yet warmly inviting restaurant;
come midnight, the central tables are all cleared
away to allow the beautiful people to boogie away,
champagne glasses in hand. After starting with
warm sun-dried tomato and olive bread, pick your
dishes carefully: the lobster main is a good bet, but
the lamb shank is rather bland. The desserts are
uniformly excellent, though, with a divine crème
brûlée and a magically light raspberry soufflé.

Celebrities

*One&Only Royal Mirage Hotel, Al Sufouh Road
(399 9999).* **Open** 7-11.30pm Sun-Fri. **Average**
Dhs600. **Credit** AmEx, DC, MC, V. **Map** p278 A5.
Stunning views down a palm-lined avenue towards
a gazebo and the beach beyond leave you in no
doubt you're luxuriating in a marvellous corner of
the Arabian Peninsula. The restaurant is home to
Freddie Foster, one of the big names in Dubai's
eat-out scene. It serves up some of the best fine-
dining food in the city, but at great expense and to
the accompaniment of over-loud and often quite
dreadful musicians.

Al Hambra

Al Qasr, Madinat Jumeirah (366 8888). **Open**
noon-3pm, 7-11.30pm daily. **Average** Dhs450.
Credit AmEx, DC, MC, V. **Map** p278 A4
Nestled in the heart of a labyrinthine spectacle of
wind towers and waterways, Al Hambra rejoices
in its Moroccan-themed decor and a menu of fine
Andalusian tapas. These bite-sized treats are
simply the best in town: try the cod brandada, slices
of salted fish each as smooth as the finest pâté. It's
also worth trying the chef's excellent paella – a
splendid stew of cheesy excellence. The classiest
Spanish food in Dubai, and by some distance.

Al Mahara

Burj Al Arab Hotel, Beach Road (301 7600). **Open**
12.30-3pm, 7pm-midnight daily. **Average** Dhs600.
Credit AmEx, DC, MC, V. **Map** p278 A4.
This is the only restaurant in Dubai that is entered
by means of a submarine. Guests enter a padded
capsule with all-round video screens that are filled
with pixelated fish, and steered down to the main
room, a stylish corridor encircling an enormous
illuminated aquarium. The beauty of the place,
combined with the subtle service and the gentle
music, guarantees an atmosphere of serenity and
romance, and the fish-centric menu pushes the
experience towards heavenly. Beware, though: the
price tag is pretty substantial too.

Majlis Al Bahar

*Opposite Wild Wadi & the Burj Al Arab, Beach Road
(301 7777).* **Open** 10am-midnight daily. **Average**
Dhs400. **Credit** AmEx, DC, MC, V. **Map** p278 A4.
Flickering candles and uplit palm trees surround
the seating area at Majlis al Bahar, which is but
inches from the immaculate beach and the lapping
Gulf. The restaurant's large tables are ready laid
with bistro cutlery and pots of fragrant rosemary
on arrival, and soon filled further by appetising
cushions of fresh bread with an assortment of
flavoured feta, labneh and olives. You'll pay through
the nose to eat here, but the exquisite service
makes it worthwhile. Book in advance or security
may get shirty at the gate.

Al Muntaha

Burj Al Arab Hotel, Beach Road (301 7777). **Open**
12.30-3pm, 7pm-12.30am daily. **Average** Dhs800.
Credit AmEx, DC, MC, V. **Map** p278 A4.

Eat, Drink, Shop

On entering beneath the arch of stuttering lights you'd be forgiven for thinking you'd stumbled on a surreal TV set lying inelegantly between 1970s sci-fi and some gaudy 1980s game show. Thankfully, the food is excellent, although you may need a bank loan to pay off any self-indulgences, especially if you make an extravagant foray into the wine list. Try the melt-in-the-mouth veal with sweet potato purée and crunchy al dente asparagus spears.

Prasino's

Jumeirah Beach Club, Beach Road (344 5333). **Open** 12.30-3pm, 7.30-11pm daily. **Average** Dhs400. **Credit** AmEx, DC, MC, V. **Map** p286 A15.
Prasino's is a classy joint with a parade of quirky twists: one corner hosts a mad voodoo wardrobe, a hundreds-and-thousands chandelier hangs from the roof, and a big stone sits in the corner looking inscrutable and holy. The international menu often changes, but is always crammed with enticing, well-prepared dishes, like slow-cooked swordfish in goose fat and prosciutto-wrapped pork with smoked apple chutney.

Retro

Le Meridien Mina Seyahi Hotel, Al Sufouh Road (399 3333). **Open** 7-11pm daily. **Average** Dhs700. **Credit** AmEx, DC, MC, V. **Map** p278 A5.
With such relaxed atmosphere and unostentatious decor, Retro is perhaps best described as informal fine dining. The tables have great views towards the sea and while at night you can't see the waves, they still beckon diners for a romantic after-dinner stroll along the beach. Prices are high, but you may just be treated to a flash of culinary genius – the liquorice lamb dish, for example, is joyously tender.

Signatures

Jebel Ali Hotel, off Exit 13 on Sheikh Zayed Road (883 6000). **Open** 7-11pm Sat, Sun, Thur, Fri. **Average** Dhs300. **Credit** AmEx, DC, MC, V. **Map** p278 A5.
This neo-rustic eaterie is filled with candles and floored with slate, backed with a show kitchen where chefs are visible beavering away over their pots. The menu is modern French, offering both à la carte and five-course gourmet selections, and the wine list consists of an intelligent mix of Old and New World bottles. The terrace is ideal for a pre-dinner sharpener and the food is the best of fine dining: try the lobster salad with lightly sautéed foie gras or the seared sea bass on a bed of braised red cabbage. Drawbacks? The restaurant is a fair old bop out of the centre of town.

The Wharf

Mina A' Salam, Madinat Jumeirah, Al Sufouh Road (366 8888). **Open** noon-3pm, 7-11pm daily. **Average** Dhs400. **Credit** AmEx, DC, MC, V. **Map** p278 A4.
The Wharf occupies one of the most attractive locations in town, a hotel that combines a beach-side spot with Arabian decoration and Venetian waterways. The restaurant's Gothic chandelier, exposed brickwork and barrel-filled interior are unexciting, but the canalside terrace is simply blissful in winter. The Wharf's seafood is quite excellent: consider trying the perfectly cooked scallops in a creamy spinach and mushroom sauce.

Far Eastern

Eau Zone

Arabian Court, at One&Only Royal Mirage Hotel, Al Sufouh Road (399 9999). **Open** 12.30-3.30pm, 7-11.30pm daily. **Average** Dhs450. **Credit** AmEx, DC, MC, V. **Map** p278 A5.
Eau Zone is without a doubt one of Dubai's most dreamily romantic restaurant settings: head down one of the boardwalks that spider out from the main restaurant and take a table in the middle of a lagoon-like pool. Dim lights make reading the menu a tad tricky, but the decor is superb and the ambience spot on. The food could be described as contemporary with an Asian twist – perhaps king-fish teriyaki with spring radish and black olive cream.

Zheng He's

Mina A' Salam Hotel, Al Sufouh Road (366 8888). **Open** noon-3pm, 7-11.30pm daily. **Average** Dhs400. **Credit** AmEx, DC, MC, V. **Map** p278 A4.
Sitting above Mina A' Salam's ludicrously pretty man-made harbour, with its gliding electric dhows and views out over the Arabian Gulf, Zheng's offers some of the finest Chinese food this side of Shanghai. Try the authentic dim sum – melt-in-the-mouth scallop numbers packed with fresh flavour, fabulous crystal shrimp dumplings, and juicy pork and pak choi dumplings – and follow with Zheng's excellent half Beijing duck with all the trimmings. You'll shell out for the experience (expect to pay big if you want fresh seafood or multiple main courses), but it's worth every last fil.

International

Maria Bonita's

Al Sheif Road (395 4454). **Open** 12.30-11.30pm daily. **Average** Dhs140. **Credit** AmEx, DC, MC, V. **Map** p278 B4.
Maria Bonita's is the only restaurant in the city to offer authentic Mexican food, and the difference in quality between Tex-Mex and bona fide South of the Border grub is evident as soon as you crunch on your first salsa-dunked tortilla chip or mole-smothered taco. Their fantastic burritos are your best bet, made with tantalisingly spiced chunks of chicken, meat or shrimp.

Napa

Al Qasr, Madinat Jumeirah (366 8888). **Open** noon-3pm, 7-11.30pm daily. **Average** Dhs600. **Credit** AmEx, DC, MC, V. **Map** p278 A4.
In stark contrast to Al Qasr's lavish main hall, Napa is a tastefully understated venue. The colours of northern California's wine country are mirrored in

The Wharf – the Mina A' Salam's flagship seafood restaurant. *See p102.*

the decor – a calming blend of ocean blue and earthy brown. Dishes are prepared the modern Californian way, with meticulous attention to detail and stress placed on retaining the individual tastes of each ingredient. One highlight is the duo of rabbit dish, which comes as a tender 'Wellington' fillet and a crumbly, savoury sausage, along with delicious and unfathomably velvety lentils.

Nina

Arabian Court, at One&Only Royal Mirage Hotel, Al Sufouh Road (399 9999). **Open** 8pm-midnight Sat-Thur. **Average** Dhs300. **Credit** AmEx, DC, MC, V. **Map** p278 A5.

Decorated in deep red and purple tones, Nina draws diners down the stairs with the twinkle of diwali candles: once you're inside, it's all subtle lighting, showers of delicate silver beads and velvety curtains. As befits its clientele of seniors, families, trendies and skinny Bollywood starlets, Nina offers a wide choice, from tasty morsels to hefty meals; main courses range from small vegetarian stir-fries and curries to lobster wrapped in banana leaf. The head chef is Australian, but his team are Indian: the delicate use of fresh herbs in Thai cooking, so beloved down under, has been applied here to high Indian cuisine with maximum effect.

Pachanga

Hilton Jumeirah, Al Sufouh Road (399 1111). **Open** 7pm-midnight daily. **Average** Dhs350. **Credit** AmEx, DC, MC, V. **Map** p278 A5.

Settle in at the bar and try a couple of mango Mojitos before your dinner. You may well be sat next to the band, an authentic Latino group who perform their winning brand of enthusiastic South American ballads throughout the night. The menu draws on Argentina, Brazil and Mexico, and while not overly authentic, it all works pretty well. Try the wonderful hanks of wagyu steak, backed up with appropriately indulgent mash.

La Parrila

Jumeirah Beach Hotel, Beach Road (406 8181). **Open** 7pm-1am daily. **Average** Dhs400. **Credit** AmEx, DC, MC, V. **Map** p278 B4.

The starters are uninspired, the prices high and the atmosphere irritatingly gung-ho. However, this Argentinian grill room does have one major redeeming factor – the steaks. Unutterably brilliant slabs of prime South American meat turn up flame-grilled, thick as a brick and a thousand times tastier. Finish with caramelised strawberries and sit back to watch some of the vigorous Latino rope-dancing, which is either flamboyant or laughable depending on your perspective.

Pierchic

Madinat Jumeirah (366 8888). **Open** 7-11.30pm daily. **Average** Dhs700. **Credit** AmEx, DC, MC, V. **Map** p278 A4.

Situated at the end of an ocean walkway, Pierchic is a contemporary fairytale of a restaurant, as directed by Baz Luhrmann. After taking in all the decorative fine details, tuck into the wonderful gourmet salad, a delicately dressed assortment of crisp leaves, slow-roasted plum tomatoes, broad beans and artichokes. Move on to the sea bream, pan-fried to perfection and topped with asparagus tempura, before finishing it all off with a sinfully creamy crème brûlée.

Who am I getting all dressed up for?

Myself.

ISSIMO
MARTINI BAR

At the Hilton Dubai Creek 04 2271111

Restaurants by cuisine

Chinese
China Club (*see p96*), Long Yin (*see p99*), Shang Palace (*see p89*), Thai Chi (*see p90*), Zheng He's (*see p102*).

Egyptian
Fatafeet (*see p84*).

French
La Baie (*see p100*), Boudoir (*see p101*), Café Chic (*see p93*), Verre (*see p96*), Vu's (*see p86*).

Fusion
Eau Zone (*see p102*), Ginseng (*see p87*), Nina (*see p103*), Oxygen (*see p95*), Teatro (*see p89*), Spectrum on One (*see p92*).

Indian
For Indian restaurants, *see pp90-91*.

Iranian
Shabestan (*see p93*), Shahrzad (*see p93*).

Italian
Bice (*see p101*), Casa Mia (*see p93*), Focaccia (*see p95*), Medzo (*see p86*), Il Rustico (*see p86*).

Japanese
ET Sushi (*see p86*), Kiku (*see p99*), Minato (*see p99*), Miyako (*see p99*), Sakura (*see p89*), Yo! Sushi (*see p90*).

Lebanese
Awtar (*see p84*), Bastakiah Nights (*see p84*), The Chalet (*see p99*), Chandelier (*see p100*), Al Dawaar (*see p92*), Al Khaima (*see p100*), Al Mallah (*see p84*), Al Mansour Dhow (*see p92*), Al Mawal (*see p93*), Al Mijana (*see p93*), Al Nafoorah (*see p84*), Olive House (*see p85*), Al Tannour (*see p85*).

Mediterranean
Bateau Dubai (*see p85*), Beach Bar & Grill (*see p101*), The Boardwalk (*see p93*), Celebrities (*see p101*), Majlis Al Bahar (*see p101*), Market Place (*see p95*), Al Muntaha (*see p101*), Prasino's (*see p102*), Retro (*see p102*), Signatures (*see p102*).

Mexican
Maria Bonita's (*see p102*).

Moroccan
Marrakech (*see p84*), Shoo Fee Ma Fee (*see p100*), Tagine (*see p100*).

Noodle bars
Noodle House (*see p87*).

North American
Johnny Rockets (*see p91*), Napa (*see p102*).

Polynesian
Spice Island (*see p96*), Trader Vic's (*see p92*).

Seafood
The Aquarium (*see p93*), Barasti (*see p101*), Al Mahara (*see p101*), Pierchic (*see p103*), The Seafood Market (*see p95*), The Wharf (*see p102*).

Singaporean
Peppercrab (*see p89*).

South American
Pachanga (*see p103*).

Spanish
Al Hambra (*see p101*).

Steakhouses
The Exchange (*see p85*), JW's Steakhouse (*see p95*), Legends Steakhouse (*see p95*), Links (*see p85*), Manhattan Grill (*see p91*), M's Beef Bistro (*see p95*), La Parrila (*see p103*).

Thai
Benjarong (*see p86*), Blue Elephant (*see p96*), Lemongrass (*see p87*), Sukhothai (*see p99*), Thai Chi (*see p90*).

Vietnamese
Hoi An (*see p87*), Indochine (*see p87*).

China Club. *See p96.*

Cafés & Bars

Cosmopolitan coffee shops, chic snack bars and Arabian shisha spots.

Much like everything with a consumerist bent in this town, Dubai's café culture is booming. Traditional Arabic hospitality – sitting and chatting over endless coffees, dates and the occasional shisha – has mixed with Western traditions to give birth to a scene that values both the old and the contemporary. While Arabic cafés humming with conversation and the occasional click from a backgammon board still dominate, an increasing number of calorie-conscious outlets and high-class caffeine pushers have also opened, adding some much-needed diversity.

The bar food scene is not as advanced, with places tending to concentrate on beer fodder rather than fine dining. Notable exceptions are **Vintage**, **Carters** and **Lotus One**, which all flirt with gastro-pubbery. We've recommended the better food-minded bars in the following pages, but if you're after the full lowdown on the drinking scene turn to the **Nightlife** chapter (*see pp166-181*).

Along with contact details and opening times, we've included the average price of a meal. This is the typical price of a one-course meal for two people, with drinks: a glass of house wine per person if the bar or café is licensed, a glass of juice if it isn't. It's customary to leave a ten per cent tip when eating in cafés and the posher bars – this is particularly important in a city where waiting staff's wages can be incredibly low.

Enjoy salads and wraps in a traditional setting at the **Basta Art Café**. *See p107.*

Eat, Drink, Shop

Bur Dubai

Aroma Garden Caffé

Oud Metha Road, next to Dubai TV (336 8999). **Open** 10am-2am Sat-Thur; noon-1.30am Fri. **Average** Dhs100. **Credit** AmEx, MC, V. **Map** p281 J2.

On one side of this vast café there's a greenhouse-like territory full of lush plantation, a vegetative quantum leap away from the world outside. AGC's central district is less exciting, with a gloomy purple ceiling that evokes the moments before a thunderstorm, and a rim that creates an electric-blue horizon. The chairs are incredibly comfortable, reclining at such an angle that hours vanish like pennies lost down the back of a sofa. The food is sadly rather nondescript, but portion sizes are very generous. The shisha menu is far better, taking in every flavour under the sun.

Basta Art Café

Al Fahidi roundabout, next to the Majlis Gallery (353 5071). **Open** 10am-7pm daily. **Average** Dhs80. **No credit cards. Map** p282 H4.

This wonderful courtyard café offers cool respite from the Bur Dubaian hurly-burly outside. It's set up perfectly for spending a long afternoon on your own, flicking idly through a paperback as you sip at an icy mocktail (try the zing-filled lime and mint juice). The salads and wraps are unfeasibly good: check out the souk salad, with crunchy cashews, wedges of tomato, chicken strips and couscous, or the 'wind tower' sandwiches, lavished with cheddar cheese, apple and sweetcorn, beefed up with thick chunks of turkey bacon. There's a dinky *majlis*, beautifully furnished and stuffed with cosy cushions, but the real draw is the courtyard, which makes Basta a wonderful place for those in search of a bit of Dubai character.

Cosmo

The Tower, Sheikh Zayed Road (332 6569). **Open** 7am-1.30am daily. **Average** Dhs120. **Credit** AmEx, MC, V. **Map** p280 H4.

Cosmo is a place of modern chic. Built in concrete and wood, its walls are splashed with stylish art and trendy blue spots, sunk into the floor, guide your legs to the sink-in sofas. The clientele is as elegant as the interior, featuring well-to-do Lebanese expats in Italian suits, who munch on high-piled greenery from the salad bar. Unlike the decor, the menu doesn't seem to hang together very well, stretching from antipasti to yakitori: an appealing but worryingly wide-ranging blend. Expecting the food to be presented as smartly as the interior, you may be surprised at the massive portions. Cosmo is a deeply popular caff that's worth popping into for a snack just to soak up the buzzing atmosphere.

Dôme

BurJuman Centre, Trade Centre Road (355 6004). **Open** 7.30am-1.30am daily. **Average** Dhs100. **Credit** MC, V. **Map** p283 J5.

Against the odds, this Australian chain manages to bring a slice of laid-back charm to the BurJuman mall. With its parquet walls, waiters in cute black berets, faux-marble tables and an odd montage of fruit and coffee tins behind the long counter, it pleases a surprising variety of Dubaians. Above all, this is a coffee shop, but it serves a decent choice of wholesome and highly substantial snacks – although weight-watchers may want to disable their calorie counters. Temperature permitting, it is nice to sit at the outdoor tables, which face away from the shopping centre and allow patrons to enjoy the constant movement (and almost uninterrupted tooting) of one of the city's busiest junctions. **Other locations:** Jumeirah Plaza mall (349 0383); Al Reef mall (222 7820); Souk Madinat (368 6550).

Eat, Drink, Shop

Shisha story

The primitive version of shisha (otherwise known as hookah, nargileh and hubbly-bubbly) was a makeshift contraption invented by some entrepreneurial Indians using a coconut shell. The modern version of the shisha has been used since the early 16th century, when the Turks decided that their smoke wasn't sweet enough. They first added fruit molasses and honey to the tobacco, and over time were able to develop a variety of other flavours.

There's nothing particularly complicated about the mechanics of shisha smoking. There's a bendy tube with a mouthpiece at one end and a glass container of water at the other. Above this container is a tall silver pipe, on top of which live the tobacco and molasses (and sometimes also honey and fresh fruit).

This mix isn't directly lit; it's covered in silver foil, on which small lumps of charcoal are burned. When you inhale, the smoke cools as it passes through the water, resulting in a smooth and refreshing taste.

Shisha are less harmful and addictive than cigarettes (the tar and nicotine content is far lower), although smoking them can still become a compelling habit.

Pretty much every café with an Arabic bent and many hotel-based eateries deal out shisha of varying quality. The best smokes in town can be found at Egyptian restaurant, **Fatafeet** (*see p84*), the jungle-themed and curiously misspelled **Aroma Garden Caffé** (*see above*) and, for a beach-side bubble, **Barasti Bar** (*see p113*).

In the company of greatness: **Shakespeare & Co.** *See p109.*

Elements

Wafi City mall, Oud Metha Road (324 4252). **Open**
10am-1am Sat-Thur; noon-1am Fri. **Average**
Dhs200. **Credit** AmEx, MC, V. **Map** p281 J3.
Everything at Elements is a bit off-kilter, a touch
eccentric, belying its role as a straightforward café
in a shopping mall. You can, for example, sit outdoors under a Rennie Mackintosh-style lantern
and treat yourself to a great view of recently
scrawled hieroglyphics on a pretend pillar, as well
as the Wafi car park. Trying to make sense of the
menu is a task in itself, given that it both esoteric
and haphazardly arranged. With dim sum and Thai
soups at the top, followed by main courses, sandwiches and desserts in the middle, and then the
selection of tapas and sushi at the bottom, it could
do with a users' manual. Still, Elements provides a
fantastic one-size-fits-all eating, drinking and
shisha-smoking solution.

French Connection

Al Wafa Tower, Sheikh Zayed Road (343 8311).
Open 7am-midnight daily. **Average** Dhs70.
Credit MC, V. **Map** p287 F12.
The ambience at French Connection is informal,
and the decor fresh and relaxing – done in shades
of beige and baby blue, there are pale wood floor-
boards and fittings, all complemented by plenty of
natural light. The selection of snacks, including
freshly baked croissants, panini, strawberry tartlets
and hot chocolate with marshmallows, does good
service all round.

Goodies

Wafi City mall, Oud Metha Road (324 4433).
Open 9.30am-midnight daily. **Average** Dhs150.
Credit AmEx, DC, MC, V. **Map** p281 J3.
Make your way through racks of gold-wrapped
chocolates, tanks full of fresh goat's cheese, mountains of truffle-dashed black olives and intricately
shaped marzipan sweets to place an order at the
long chilled counter. Goodies' daily specials are
universally excellent, but staff are particularly
gifted at chickpea and pine nut baked fish and
cheese-capped moussakas and lasagnas. The mall-
based eatery also has an entire corner devoted to
the making and grilling of gourmet kebabs: pick
your stick from a platoon of multicoloured meats
and match it with some delicious raisin-filled rice.

Hakaya Café

*Near the York International Hotel, Bank Street
(355 6100).* **Open** noon-3am daily. **Average**
Dhs120. **Credit** AmEx, DC, MC, V. **Map** p282 J4.
We adore this eccentric and illiterate little place.
Its idiosyncrasies are entirely endearing, the food,
drinks and shisha are superb, and it provides a
comfortable and engaging environment. The live
Arabic music is great fun, and if the fake tree in
the centre gets in the way of your view of the oud
players (it almost certainly will), you can watch
the action on screens dotted around the walls. The
Lebanese meze platter offers enough food for
three to share, and the stuffed vine leaves are
among the finest we've ever tasted.

Al Reef Lebanese Bakery
Zaabeel Road, next to Karama post office (396 1980).
Open 24hrs daily. **Average** Dhs40. **No credit cards. Map** p281 J2.
Open round the clock, the Al Reef bakery is an excellent place to eat breakfast, lunch or an after-hours snack. Whenever you visit, it always seems to be busy, with punters queuing up for the fine and filling sandwiches on offer. From the extensive list of combinations, the sausage and egg option (Dhs5) comes highly recommended. The sheer weight of customer numbers can make Al Reef a confusing place: remember that you must order at the counter first, then pay at the till. While you wait, sneak a look through the serving hole to watch zataar bread inflating in the saj oven.

Shakespeare & Co
Kendah House, Sheikh Zayed Road (331 1757).
Open 7am-1am daily. **Average** Dhs100. **Credit** AmEx, DC, MC, V. **Map** p287 F12.
Shakespeare is battling a world of hotel-created uniformity with quirkiness and flair. The decor is somewhat old lady's living room: there are a host of battered old sofas draped with doilies in which to loll, plus plenty of aimlessly scattered books and magazines to browse. Outside there's a charming area built around a large cage filled with brightly plumed birds. It's the sort of place you could eat at every day for a week and not get bored. Particular favourites on the menu are the gnocchi with a nutty

cheese sauce, the magically creamy mushroom soup and the super-light rice and tuna salad.
Other locations: Safa Centre (394 1121); The Village (344 6228); Gulf Towers (335 3335).

Tché Tché
Near BurJuman Centre, Bank Street (355 7575).
Open 10am-2am Sat-Thur; 3pm-2am Fri. **Average** Dhs80. **No credit cards. Map** p283 J5.
The perfect antidote to Dubai's hotel lifestyle is on offer at Tché Tché. Here mixed crowds of young Emiratis, Jordanians and Westerners can be found chuffing on hubbly bubblies, sipping at mud-thick Turkish coffee and chewing on brick-sized slabs of cheesecake, all soundtracked by Arabic fusion musica and the occasional session of football commentary from the overhead TVs.

XVA Café
XVA Gallery, Bastakia (353 5383). **Open** 9am-8pm Sat-Thur. **Average** Dhs125. **Credit** AmEx, MC, V. **Map** p282 H4.
An interesting hybrid of café, gallery, guesthouse and shop, XVA is one of the prettiest places in the wind tower district – and one of the hardest to find. The lantern-clad walls of the courtyard open on to an inside cabin decked with Arabic seating and stripy bolsters. The whole tranquil, pretty-as-sin space is hung with billowing sails of cloth and, somewhat incongruously, a raft of polka-dotted bark shavings. Sadly the talented Jordanian chef who opened the café has since departed, leaving

Eat, Drink, Shop

Cafés and bars
The best

For interior delights
Gallery meets gastronomy at the arty **XVA** (*see above*); **More** (*see p111*) revels in its own quirkiness; and the ridiculously opulent **Sahn Eddar** (*see p112*), in the lobby of the Burj, has to be seen to be believed.

For a light lunch
Lime Tree Café (*see p112*) boasts inventive and generously proportioned sandwiches and salads, plus some terrific cakes, while **Basta Art Café** (*see p107*) serves healthy wraps and zingy lemon juices in the courtyard of one of Dubai's few historic buildings.

For a break from shopping
Dôme (*see p107*) feeds the masses with aplomb in one of Dubai's busiest shopping centres; **The One Café** (*see p112*) is even classier than its furniture; **Elements** (*see p108*) is a funky Wafi option; and the hearty sandwiches and own-made quiche at **Paul** (*see p112*) will tempt even hardened mall-dodgers into Mercato.

For something different
Café Céramique (*see p111*) allows you to paint pots while enjoying great bagels; **Aroma Garden Caffé** (*see p107*) comes with its own rainforest; and low-rent but highly bonkers **Hakaya Café** (*see p108*) offers live oud playing nightly under an enormous plastic tree.

For alfresco eating
Try **Shakespeare & Co** (*see above*) to eat cakes beside a giant birdcage, **Creek View** (*see p111*) for average Arabic food but great watery vistas, or **Japengo Café** (*see p112*) to witness the madness of Dubaian driving from the safety of a roadside terrace.

For drinks and nibbles
The Creek views, cocktails and fresh pizzas at **QD's** (*see p111*) are irresistible; **Barasti Bar** (*see p113*) is the best option on the beaches; **Vintage** (*see p110*) has a great wine and cheese list; and **The Irish Village** (*see p111*) is simply the best pub in town.

the place in slightly shaky hands. Nonetheless, the sandwiches are still great and the place remains one of the loveliest settings in Dubai to enjoy a light bite.

Zyara
Al Salam Tower, Sheikh Zayed Road (343 5454).
Open 9am-1.30am daily. **Average** Dhs100.
Credit AmEx, MC, V. **Map** p280 H4.
Zyara is part of a clutch of young upstarts striving to inject some Franco-Lebanese bohemia into the unforgiving, angular avenue of skyscrapers that makes up Sheikh Zayed Road. The decor is charm itself: beaten-up wooden chairs and tables compete for your attention with welcoming sofas covered in flowery fabric; the wooden floors are covered in Iranian kilims and the walls are used to display regular exhibitions of work by local artists. The sandwich-and-snacks menu is original (look out for the gloo gloo salad), but the quality's reasonable rather than outstanding.
Other locations: Dubai Media City (391 8031).

Bars

The Agency
Emirates Towers Hotel, Sheikh Zayed Road (330 0000). **Open** 12.30pm-1am Sat-Thur; 3pm-1am Fri. **Average** Dhs100. **Credit** AmEx, DC, MC, V. **Map** p280 H4.
The Agency is an upmarket London/New York style wine bar, with a low-lit and chilled-out interior that's made for conversation. Match your bottle of chilled white with fondues, charcuterie and booze-snacks ranging from bruschetta to chilli prawns. More sophisticated tapas are constantly being added: try Italian Roma tomatoes infused with basil oil and stuffed with gorgonzola, a round of creamy French goat's cheese topped with chopped olives and walnuts, and a tasty citrus seafood cocktail of uncertain origin. Dishes more loyal to the tapas tradition include crispy chorizo served on a bed of spicy tomatoes or the deliciously fresh, brackish rolls of marinated anchovies and prawns, properly soaked in a deep orange chilli oil that'll have you reaching for gulps of chilled Pinot Grigio. *See also p171.*

Carters
Wafi Pyramids at Wafi City mall, off Oud Metha Road (324 0000). **Open** 12.30pm-midnight daily. **Average** Dhs300. **Credit** AmEx, DC, MC, V. **Map** p281 J3.
An excellent restaurant posing as a mediocre bar, Carters is as close as Dubai gets to a gastropub. Imaginative, immaculate and inspired dishes such as leek and mustard crumble with stilton mash, pan-roasted pork tenderloin with black pudding, and braised beef in Guinness pie tumble from the menu, each one capable of inspiring moans of satisfaction. The outside terrace is pleasant and offers blessed relief from the in-house band, who are so middle-of-the-road they should sport cat's eyes.

Zyara.

Lotus One
Dubai International Convention Centre, next to Novotel (329 3200). **Open** noon-2pm, 7pm-2am daily. **Average** Dhs300. **Credit** AmEx, DC, MC, V. **Map** 285 G10.
Having recently been granted a booze licence, Lotus One is flying. The decor is seriously stylish, with low lighting, glass floors, miles of chrome and the funkiest suspended chairs this side of Vegas. Lotus One also has a fabulous cocktail menu, which has helped to bring Dubai's beautiful people flocking here to listen to chilled tunes courtesy of the resident DJ. The menu is described as 'Far Eastern with a Western twist', which means you can get dishes as diverse as betel leaf shark fillet and a classic roast lamb stack.

Vintage
Wafi Pyramids at Wafi City mall, off Oud Metha Road (324 0000). **Open** 6pm-1am daily. **Average** Dhs180. **Credit** AmEx, DC, MC, V. **Map** p281 J3.
Through the imposing, sphinxy doors at Wafi Pyramids lies Vintage, a cosmopolitan wine bar with a legendary list of bottles, printed in a book-sized menu. As well as having more drink on offer than you could comfortably work through in three lifetimes, Vintage also supplies perfect tippling food: ham, fondue, gourmet pies and a beautiful assortment of cheeses. The sort of place you could happily settle in for the evening. *See also p174.*

Deira

Creek View
Near InterContinental Hotel, Baniyas Road (223 3223).
Open 10am-2am daily. **Average** Dhs100. **No credit cards. Map** p282 J3.
You can't miss Creek View: a large, illuminated, fake gold palm tree outside the venue serves as a beacon to thirsty strollers, and this idyllic café is unlikely to disappoint those thus enticed. Despite its proximity to bustling Baniyas Road, the sound of traffic can't be heard within, replaced instead by Arabic music and the phut-phut of abras in the distance. There's a large outdoor seating area, which is decorated with thousands of twinkling fairy lights and lush green trees, where many an hour can be whiled away, puffing on tasty shisha and watching the Creek traffic chug happily along. Hungry guests can expect standard Arabic fare, nicely presented and satisfyingly fresh.

More
Next to Welcare Hospital, behind Lifco supermarket, Garhoud (283 0224). **Open** 8am-10pm daily. **Average** Dhs150. **Credit** AmEx, DC, MC, V. **Map** p281 K3.
A wonderful place to come for relaxed meals with friends, or for a long-drawn-out coffee and cake on your own, More is the lunch venue of choice for many Garhoud office workers. The main room is a warehouse of kookiness: under a purple ceiling, you'll find a room filled with melons on pedestals and sofas studded with ball bearings. Clients sit on comfy leather seats and eat at huge mahogany tables scattered with papers and magazines. Main courses range around the world, from Canadian salmon to Australian beef and Dutch pannekoeken. The complimentary Wi-Fi internet access is shaky, but a bonus when it is up and working.

Bars

The Cellar
The Aviation Club, Garhoud Road (282 4122). **Open** noon-4pm, 7pm-midnight daily. **Average** Dhs150. **Credit** AmEx, MC, V. **Map** p281 K3.
Dubaians love the Cellar for its range of wines and bar snacks, but it's increasingly making a name for itself as a European eaterie to be reckoned with. The fondues are outstanding, and the Dutch meat balls, smoked salmon ruffles and other upmarket nibbles are all more than welcome after a hard evening's drinking.

The Irish Village
Dubai Tennis Stadium, Garhoud Road (282 4750). **Open** 11am-1.30am daily. **Average** Dhs120. **Credit** AmEx, DC, MC, V. **Map** p281 L3.
One of Dubai's most popular watering holes, the Irish Village is probably your best bet for proper pub fodder: toasted BLTs, light and fluffy cheese omelettes, and a daily roast. Boasting a massive

outdoor area and regular live music, the IV is the ideal venue for alfresco boozing during the winter months. *See also p175.*

QD's
Dubai Creek Golf & Yacht Club, Garhoud Road (295 6000). **Open** 6pm-2am daily. **Average** Dhs130. **Credit** AmEx, DC, MC, V. **Map** p281 K3.
Nestled in the grounds of the spruced-up Dubai Creek Golf & Yacht Club, QD's has jaw-dropping views over the water and an ambience that verges on perfection. The full cocktail list invites you into a world of inebriation; wood-burning pizza ovens pull you back from the brink. *See also p174.*

Jumeirah

A'Rukn
Souk Madinat (366 8888). **Open** 10am-8pm daily. **Average** Dhs150. **Credit** AmEx, MC, V. **Map** p278 A4.
If A'Rukn – the Madinat's perfectly average Arabic café – were any more workman-like it would require signs bearing little men wielding shovels. Every offering involves fine, if rather uninspired, clippings from Arabia's culinary tree, with the regular array of houmous, salads and kebabs all present and correct. The smattering of Emirati dishes, and the fact that the place is licensed, does set the place apart from the barrage of Arabic cafés you'll find on the streets. But the lack of Lebanese wine is a major omission and, unless you happen to be hankering for Arabic food while in the souk or need a beer while you eat, you'd be better off seeking a kebab station downtown.

Café Céramique
Town Centre mall, Beach Road (344 7331). **Open** 8am-midnight Sat-Thur; 10am-midnight Fri. **Average** Dhs100. **Credit** AmEx, MC, V. **Map** p286 C12.
Café Céramique's USP is providing clay figures to decorate – a brutally effective way to keep the kids occupied for a few hours, but a source of tiresome noise for sprog-free diners. Thankfully for such people, a terrace looking beyond the Beach Road to the sea offers asylum: here the reasonably priced menu can be enjoyed in peace. The food is fairly average – a selection of middle-of-the-road hits such as chicken quesadillas and salads – but can be rounded off with excellent tiramisu and carrot cake. Nippers will be too busy unleashing their creativity to care too much about what they eat, but the straightforward execution of junior favourites such as chicken nuggets does the trick.

Gerard's
Magrudy Centre, Beach Road (344 3327). **Open** 7am-midnight daily. **Average** Dhs80. **Credit** AmEx, DC, MC, V. **Map** p284 D9.
A Dubai institution, Gerard's lies in a small but cunningly constructed mall that has an open-air courtyard at its heart. Inside, the feel is upmarket,

with soothing classical background music setting the scene. It's a popular venue for people trying to finish reading that novel or simply wanting to meet Jumeirah-based friends for a mid-morning gossip. The snacks, cakes and sandwiches are nothing to write home about, but the mint tea, iced coffee and cappuccinos all hit the spot.
Other locations: Deira City Centre (295 7744).

Japengo Café
Palm Strip Mall, Beach Road (345 4979).
Open 10am-1am Sat-Wed, Fri; 10am-2am Thur. **Average** Dhs150. **Credit** AmEx, DC, MC, V. **Map** p284 D9.
The people behind this immensely popular local chain are clearly doing something right, because all four branches get packed to the rafters. If you visit their Beach Road branch on any evening of the week, you'll have to fight for a table on the outdoor terrace. Japengo's menu is worryingly diverse – covering Italy, Lebanon, Japan, China and south-east Asia – but it's been hard to find fault with their cooking. Prices are a little steep, the service is somewhat brisk, and if you don't get one of those terrace tables it's easy to feel like you're missing out; but for a group of people who can't decide what to eat, Japengo is a very solid bet.
Other locations: Oasis Tower, Sheikh Zayed Road (343 5028); Souk Madinat (368 6574); Wafi City (324 5411).

Lime Tree Café
Beach Road (349 8498). **Open** 7.30am-8pm daily.
Average Dhs70. **Credit** AmEx, MC, V. **Map** p284 D9.
Lime Tree's biggest draw is its stylish but cosy courtyard, with lush green plants, trickling water and shady trees. Walled off from the road, it feels like a haven from the heat and noise, and it makes an ideal post-beach refuelling spot. The menu changes all the time, but whatever you order you can be certain that it will be fresh, imaginatively crafted and wonderfully tasty. You can't go wrong with any of the sandwiches or salads, and the coffees are always flawlessly brewed. Best of all is their legendary carrot cake – it's lip-smackingly moist and fluffy. The only downside to Lime Tree is that it's only open until 8pm, but in a city so consumed by corporate culture, early closing can seem like a defiant assertion of independence.

Lobby lounge (Ritz-Carlton)
Ritz-Carlton Hotel, Al Sufouh Road (399 4000).
Open 9am-2am daily. **Average** Dhs120.
Credit AmEx, DC, MC, V. **Map** p278 A5.
Teatime at the Ritz (served 2pm to 6pm daily) sees fresh-baked scones served to customers so deeply entrenched in their sofas that they may well never leave. On the ocean side of the lounge, the furniture is less well sprung, but any decrease in comfort is made up for by the glorious sea views, complete with waving palm trees. During winter, an outdoor terrace provides a perfect place for sipping and watching the waves lap the shore.

Lobby lounge (Royal Mirage)
One&Only Royal Mirage Hotel, Al Sufouh Road (399 9999). **Open** 7am-midnight daily. **Average** Dhs150. **Credit** AmEx, DC, MC, V. **Map** p278 A5.
The lobby lounge of the Royal Mirage is breathtaking in itself, but the veranda that overlooks the sea really takes the biscuit. Head over for a waistexpanding afternoon tea (from 3pm to 6.30pm daily) and enjoy watching the sun sinking into the sea over the rim of a fine teacup.

The One Café
The One (shop), Beach Road, next to Jumeirah Mosque (345 6687). **Open** 9am-9.30pm Sat-Thur; 2-9.30pm Fri. **Average** Dhs120. **Credit** AmEx, MC, V. **Map** p284 D9.
Trawling for furnishings while famished is no fun at all. This shopping truism is well understood by Dubai's home-grown lifestyle sages The One, and their chic café – decked out with mahogany tables and low-slung, cream-coloured lampshades (all for sale, naturally) – offers relaxing respite from the mayhem of the shopping floor. The sophistication of the café is reflected in a well-planned menu, chock-a-block with delightfully unusual sounding titbits, just perfect for mid-morning munchies (try the pecan nut and sun-dried cranberry soufflé), a lunchtime hiatus (orange-scented ravioli) or a teatime treat (cream tea with finger sandwiches). The desserts are devilishly addictive, so make sure you leave room – perhaps for a heavenly spoonful or two of the balsamic and black pepper cheesecake.

Paul
Mercato Mall, Beach Road (344 3505). **Open** 9am-11pm daily. **Average** Dhs120. **Credit** MC, V. **Map** p286 C12.
To recreate the higgledy-piggledy charm of a Parisian boulangerie-cum-bistrot in the sterility of a shopping mall is no easy task, but Paul, which is part of an upmarket French chain, makes a valiant effort. The restaurant plays chirpy Gallic retro-pop and there's a scattering of nostalgic photos of bread-making in the Paris of yesteryear on the wood-panelled walls. Freshly baked pastries, breads and quiche are the keynotes here, and they are all outstandingly good. Cheesy, hypercalorific tourtes, creamy gratins and ham-topped tartines all come with dressed salad and just-baked olive and sesame rolls. Service is as slow as a tortoise, but Paul is still ideal for a relaxed lunch to punctuate a day's shopping.

Sahn Eddar
Burj Al Arab Hotel, Beach Road (301 7777).
Open 7am-2am daily. **Average** Dhs360. **Credit** AmEx, DC, MC, V. **Map** p278 A4.
The decor at the Burj's lobby area tearoom is opulent to the point of sickliness, and the food is average and immensely pricey: you'll pay Dhs180 for a carousel of mediocre finger sandwiches and a stack of cakes. Despite these crazy prices, Eddar remains the cheapest eating option in the visitor-

Paul: one of the best mall-based cafés in the city. *See p112.*

impressing opulence of the Burj, thus rendering itself almost immune to criticism, and people will continue to visit the tearoom just to say they've seen what seven-star luxury looks like.

Bars

Barasti Bar

Le Meridien Mina Seyahi Hotel, Al Sufouh Road (399 3333). **Open** noon-2am daily. **Average** Dhs250. **Credit** AmEx, DC, MC, V. **Map** p278 A5.
Perched just above the beach, with a perfect view of the sea one way and the sci-fi skyline of Dubai Media City the other, there is no arguing with Barasti's location. During the week it has a gentle buzz, as groups of suited workers stop by for sundowners. At weekends, though, things liven up considerably. Arrive early if you want a seat and be aware that on a Friday night – even at the far end of the terrace – you'll have to raise your voice to be heard over the live rock-pop classics, happy house and DJ patter. As the crowds increase, the service also becomes pretty sporadic, but that's all fine if you're wanting to join the dancers by the bar rather than engage in intimate conversation over some excellent Mojitos. *See also p101 and p178.*

Dhow & Anchor

Jumeirah Beach Hotel, Beach Road (348 0000). **Open** 12.30-11.30pm daily. **Average** Dhs120. **Credit** AmEx, DC, MC, V. **Map** p278 B4.
Apparently the interior designer behind the JBH's Brit-themed pub, chose not to base his boozer on any of the UK's multitude of quaint country inns, cosy dens or otherwise charming pint stations.

Instead the deranged stylist must have walked into one of London's most depressing chain pubs, complete with giant screens and can't-swing-a-cat banality, and thought 'yes!'. This place is just a thin sliver of a drinking cranny, packed out with beleaguered expats and clogged with smoke and the permanent drone of the television. But do not despair. If you manage to break through to the patio, you're in for a treat: this gorgeous, expansive terrace more than makes up for the sins of the inner sanctum. The food here is a triumph too. Try the gloriously authentic steak and mushroom pie, which consists of healthy hunks of beef in a rich peppery gravy, encased in crisp puff pastry. The inside may be hackneyed, but outside it's heaven.

Trader Vic's

Souk Madinat Jumeirah (366 5646). **Open** 7-11.15pm daily. **Average** Dhs200. **Credit** AmEx, DC, MC, V. **Map** p278 A4.
Situated in the heart of the Madinat – whose palm trees and waterways are in keeping with the global brand's playful notion of tropical paradise – Trader Vic's is a fine, if expensive, Polynesian bar. Buoyed up by punch-packing but pricey cocktails and succulent finger food, Trader Vic's is the perfect springboard on to the Madinat's multitude of nightspots, including JamBase (*see p177*), Bar Zar (*see p178*) and club de jour Trilogy (*see p175*). Although it's difficult to determine the single theme uniting a profusion of bamboo objects, black-and-white naval images and the house band's flute-driven hotchpotch of percussive sounds, it's all undeniably good fun. *See also p92 and p181.*
Other locations: Crowne Plaza Dubai (331 1111).

Le Royal Méridien Abu Dhabi

Royal Dining at Its Very Best

Le Royal Méridien Abu Dhabi i
unrivaled choice for exquisite d
at its very best. Guests will
exceptional service, exclusive cor
and sophisticated dining option
suit all tastes.

Enjoy a dining with a taste of Ita
Amalfi, or try sushi and noodle
Soba. Diners can experience a
selection of traditional Indian cu
at Zari-Zardozi. When eating
L'Opéra Brasserie guests can enjo
exclusive menu of internati
cuisine.

Unwind at the Palm Lounge
traditional English afternoon tea
experience an all-Irish night a
O'Reilly's. Meet and greet friends
dance the night away at the Illus
nightclub. Savour intimate dining
modern European cuisine at Al Fa
the only revolving restaurant in
capital with breathtaking views of
city and sweeping views of
Arabian Gulf.

Host that very special occasion
party when you cruise and dine
board Shuja yacht. Relish the fres
of seafood delights at Oceans. An
the jazziest tunes of the live b
transform your evenings at the Sa

Le Royal Méridien Abu Dhabi ens
an authentic dining experie
heightened by renowned hospital

For reservations call:
+971 2 6950539/583

or e-mail us at:
restaurants@leroyalmeridien-abudhabi.c

EGYPT • INDIA • INDONESIA • KUWAIT • RUSSIA
SAUDI ARABIA • UNITED ARAB EMIRATES • UNITED KINGDOM

Le ROYAL MERIDIE
ABU D

www.lemeridien.
In Partnership with Nikko Ho

Shops & Services

With malls, markets and an entire festival dedicated to shopping, Dubai is the place to indulge your consuming passions.

Much has been made of Dubai's mall culture: the rate at which the city builds new shopping centres continues to astonish even the most avaricious expat. The pressure is now on to distinguish one mall from another, such that new announcements come ready with a unique sell, whether that's the sheer size of the development (the **Mall of the Emirates** has opened as the largest mall in the region – but for how long?) or sheer novelty value (the bonkers **Ibn Battuta** mall is named after a renowned local explorer and features some amazing ersatz multicultural architecture).

Despite the city's tax-free status, prices in the malls aren't generally cheaper than you might find in other major cities in other parts of the world. Bargains galore are promised during the month-long **Dubai Shopping Festival** (*see p145*), when posters declaring discounts of anything up to 75 per cent are the norm. In truth, however, these deals are hard to find and some retailers actually raise their prices in line with the increasing number of tourists. Nonetheless, the festival does boast a fine array of promotions and raffles, with everything from bars of solid gold to brand-new cars up for grabs. To enter, all you usually have to do is hand over your till receipt.

Dubai does offer the customer a great deal of choice: the main shopping malls are full of international brands, designer labels and speciality stores, and equipped with adequate parking and fierce air-conditioning. Malls don't follow Western opening hours – most open Saturday to Thursday from 10am to 10pm, and on Friday they open at 4pm and close at 11pm. During the holy month of Ramadan, shop hours vary: most open 9am-1pm and 7-10pm Saturday to Thursday; on Friday they only open in the evening, from 7-11pm.

For all this fancy shop talk, don't forget the independent stores and bustling souks: **Karama** (*see p136* **Market values**) is the place for searching out fake designer goods, the gold souk (*see p122* **Golden opportunities**) is a must for jewellery, and the **textile souk** (*see p123*) has plenty of fabrics, which one of the city's many tailors can transform into a top-notch suit. Exect to find shops in these areas closed at lunchtime (between 1pm and 4pm) and on Friday until 4pm.

Wafi City, home to high-end designer labels and upmarket jewellery stores. *See p117.*

In the malls, all major retailers accept credit cards and many also have foreign currency exchange centres and ATM machines. Small traders, souks and local convenience stores will, however, only accept cash. American dollars are widely accepted, but the best bargains are to be had using local currency. Being equipped with dirhams will make shopping a whole lot easier, quicker and, if you haggle hard, cheaper.

Thursday is the busiest shopping day, since for many people it's the start of the weekend. Unless you enjoy the competition, you may find the inevitable crowds unbearable.

BARGAINING

Haggling is a tradition in Dubai's souks and it really is rare to pay the full price on the tag – if there is one. Most shopkeepers will quote you a figure saying that it is the price 'before discount'. Even 'best price' isn't necessarily as low as you can go. The trick to haggling is to take your time, be polite and to decide what you are happy to pay for the item. A common rule is to offer half the quoted price at first. If you can't get the price down, simply walk away; many shop assistants will literally chase you out into the street to secure a purchase. Bargaining is not common practice in malls, although it doesn't hurt to ask for a discount, especially if you're paying cash.

SHIPPING

To export goods home contact a cargo or shipping agency directly (*see p251* **Courier companies**) or consult the Yellow Pages under 'Shipping'. A good agency will give you a quote for shipping bulk items home and most operate globally. The price of exporting things varies depending on the item (electronic goods can be more expensive) and quantity. In the end visitors may find it isn't worth the money to ship items home, as export tax makes the process very expensive. During the **Dubai Shopping Festival** (*see p145*) and **Dubai Summer Surprises** (*see p144 and p149*) a few courier companies offer special rates.

REFUNDS

There are no laws, codes or regulations in Dubai to protect customers, which means that it is up to the store whether they offer refunds or an exchange for faulty goods. Faulty goods are more easily exchanged than refunded, especially if you have kept the receipt. If you are returning an unwanted gift you'll have more luck if the item has not been worn or used and is still in its original packaging. To be on the safe side, always check the refund and exchange policy before making a purchase.

The best | Malls

BurJuman Centre
The new extension is the final word in upmarket appeal, awash with designer clothes and high-end jewellery. *See right.*

Deira City Centre
Easily the most popular mall in Dubai, with everything from handbags and jewellery to cosmetics and trendy clothes. Brace yourself for the crowds. *See p119.*

Mercato
The best mall in Dubai for hip, young fashion. Funky independent clothes shops and the trendiest high-street labels dominate. *See p120.*

Souk Madinat Jumeirah
Within sight of the Burj Al Arab and built to resemble an Arabian marketplace, this labyrinthine mall is shopping heaven by day and home to the city's hottest new clubs by night. *See p120.*

Wafi City
Eclectic in look, with a stained-glass ceiling and Egyptian features, Wafi City boasts a vast range of designer clothes outlets and unique home-furnishing shops. *See p117.*

Malls

Bur Dubai

BurJuman Centre
Trade Centre Road (352 0222/www.burjuman. com). **Open** 10am-10pm Sat-Thur; 4-10pm Fri. **Map** p283 J5.
The BurJuman is a classy affair, with plenty of exclusive outlets selling designer brands: Donna Karan, Christian Lacroix, Calvin Klein, Cartier, Tiffany and Louis Vuitton. With the recent completion of a Dhs1.4 million extension, the BurJuman has expanded to four times its former size. New shops to look out for include Saks Fifth Avenue, Prada and Chanel. Electronics, perfume, cosmetics and home furnishings can also be found.

Emirates Towers Boulevard
Sheikh Zayed Road (330 0000). **Open** 10am-10pm Sat-Thur; 4-10pm Fri. **Map** p280 H4.
The Shopping Boulevard, mapped out over two floors, links the Emirates Hotel and Office towers. As befits the location, this is a place for serious, smart shopping. The ground floor is dominated by designer-label boutiques – superstars Giorgio

BurJuman Centre, now four times bigger. *See p116.*

Armani, Gucci, Yves Saint Laurent and leather accessory store Bottega Veneta. Upstairs there's anchor shop Villa Moda, housing top-notch designs from the likes of Prada, Alexander McQueen and Stella McCartney. For glamorous shoes and bags to accessorise, head to Jimmy Choo, then round off your spree with some seriously sexy lingerie from Janet Reger just next door.

Holiday Centre

Next to Crowne Plaza Hotel, Sheikh Zayed Road (331 7755). **Open** 5pm-10pm Sat; 10am-10pm Sun-Fri. **Map** p285 G10.

Guests at the Crowne Plaza Hotel need merely travel down a few steps to reach two floors of shops and boutiques. Within this mall are designer outlets such as Rodeo Drive, a wonderful instrument retailer named the Music Chamber, Middle Eastern food and gift stores, sports shops, hair salons and an internet café. There's a surprisingly big branch of the Choitrams supermarket on the first floor, which is open all day every day from 8am to 10pm. A spacious exhibition area hosts regular events.

Lamcy Plaza

Oud Metha (335 9999). **Open** 10am-10pm Sat-Wed; 10am-10.30pm Thur. **Map** p281 J3.

Lamcy is not an especially good-looking mall: the decor is dated, the layout confusing, and the huge waterfall and replica Tower Bridge rather tacky. Escalators connect the levels, but they're carefully hidden, so finding your way round can be tricky. However, if you're looking for cheap 'n' cheerful goods, from footwear to home accessories, Lamcy is the place. High-street fashion outlets include Dorothy Perkins, Tammy and Jeffrey Rogers, while cut-price outlets encompass Shoemart, Fashion Factory and Mr Price. The feng shui shop on the ground floor, with its oriental knick-knacks,

candles, wall hangings and Buddha statues, is also worth a visit. Lamcy is always full of shoppers taking advantage of the constant promotions, so be prepared for bustling crowds.

Oasis Centre

Between Interchanges 2 & 3, Sheikh Zayed Road (339 5459). **Open** 10am-10pm Sat-Thur; 2-10pm Fri. **Map** p278 B4.

This glass-fronted, elongated mall is often overlooked because it's located away from the hub of Dubai action, a ten-minute drive along Sheikh Zayed Road, heading towards Jumeirah. Shops are spread over two floors and focused around the Home Centre, which stocks quality furniture and furnishings at affordable prices. The Lifestyles store is also good for bargain-priced brand-name cosmetics, bath accessories and gift items, while other cheap outlets include fashion store Splash and sensible footwear shop Shoemart. There's also a jungle-themed food court and free play area for children, plus Cyborg, a noisy, neon venue with a ten-pin bowling alley.

Wafi City

Oud Metha Road (324 4555). **Open** 10am-10pm Sat-Thur; 4-10pm Fri. **Map** p281 J3.

Wafi is easy to spot, thanks to three glass pyramids that surround it. A quiet, upmarket mall that extends over four floors, it is modern and elegant in design, and competes with BurJuman on the chic label front. Chanel, Givenchy and Jaeger are just some of the international names that share floor space with regional designer labels. On the first floor are shops with more affordable price tags, such as Miss Sixty, Jumbo Electronics and shoe store Connexion. There's a good range of coffee shops and restaurants, ranging from much-loved Indian eaterie Asha's (*see p90*) to laid-back

One destination
Twelve fabulous cuisines

SPHINX - STYLISH DINING & COCKTAIL LOUNGE • **GINSENG** - THE LOUNG
SEVILLE'S - THE SPANISH TAPAS BAR • **THAI CHI** - TWO RESTAURANTS UNDER 1 ROO
MEDZO - ITALIAN WITH A MEDITERRANEAN TWIST • **THE SQUARE** - INTERNATIONAL CAF
CARTER'S - LOUNGE, BAR & BISTRO • **VINTAGE** - THE CHEESE & WINE BA
CHAMELEON & VICE - THE GLOBAL BAR, RESTAURANT & LATE NIGHT VENU
ASHA'S - CONTEMPORARY INDIAN CUISINE • **PLANET HOLLYWOOD** - A STA
STUDDED DINING EXPERIENCE • **BIELLA** - CAFFÉ PIZZERIA RISTORANT

Present this ad to your server and receive 20% discount on your total food and beverage bill
www.waficityrestaurants.com

Call us on 04 324 4100 / 324 4777.
Email:rachel.matthews@wafi.com / marizel.salvador@wafi.com

Not valid in conjunction with any other discount or promotion

Duty Free calls

For all of the city's architectural landmarks, few can boast as much tourist draw as the **Dubai Duty Free** shopping haven. Scooping international industry awards on an annual basis, the airport's tax-free paradise offers a impressively vast array of cosmetics, perfumes, electronics, music, tobacco and alcohol. Only its range of clothes is limited – we advise you make time in the malls for any serious thread-browsing. Each shopper is allowed to bring up to four items of alcohol (whether bottled spirits, wine or a case of beer) and two cartons of cigarettes into the UAE (*see p252* **Customs**). There's even good news for those who like a flutter: promotions to win instant fortunes are held daily.

café Elements (*see p108*). There's also the Lebanese delicatessen Goodies (*see p135*), which dishes out Arabic and continental cuisine to take away or enjoy on the terrace. A children's entertainment centre, Encounter Zone, is on the third floor, and there are pizzas and burgers in the food court next door.

Deira

Deira City Centre

Garhoud (295 1010). **Open** 10am-10pm Sat-Thur; 2-10pm Fri. **Map** p281 K2.
The most popular mall in Dubai, Deira City Centre has more than 280 shops, an entertainment centre, two food courts and cinema multiplex spread over three floors. Chain stores include Debenhams, IKEA and high-street fashion names Top Shop and River Island, while giant hypermarket Carrefour dominates the first floor. But the mall also contains plenty of independent outlets selling local artefacts, knick-knacks and cut-price jewellery; try the Jewellery Court, Textile Court and themed mini souk Arabian Treasures, which sells antiques, carpets and sundry other gifts. Among the 30-plus eateries are Burger King, McDonald's, Starbucks and Costa Coffee. You'll even find an eight-lane bowling alley. Children can go wild in the sprawling amusement centre, Magic Planet. Parking here can become ridiculously congested at peak times, though, even with 4,000 spaces available.

Al Ghurair City

Al Rigga Road (223 2333). **Open** 10am-10pm Sat-Thur; 2-10pm Fri. **Map** p283 K3.
This 20-year-old mall (the oldest in Dubai) combines Arabian decor with modern design. Popular outlets include Guess, French Connection, Nine West, Virgin Cosmetics and Book Corner. The mall is

a bit of a maze, covering only two floors but with corridors branching out at all angles. Still, it's worth persevering with the place: tucked into the alleyways are excellent speciality stores selling everything from Arabic jewellery and rugs to South African beauty products and children's dresses from Italy. There is also an eight-screen cineplex, as well as numerous food and coffee outlets.

Hamarain Centre

Abu Bakr Road, beside Marriot Hotel, Deira (262 1110). **Open** 10am-10pm Sat-Thur; 4.30-10pm Fri. **Map** p281 K1.
This large mall near the clock tower in Deira is missed by most people out on a shopping binge, but there's plenty here to prise your hard-earned dirhams from your pocket. It's a mix of traditional and cutting edge: retailers selling abayas sit next to chic fashion boutiques offering modern designer creations. Elsewhere, the furniture shops offer mock antique chests, embroidered wall hangings and imported Asian knick-knacks, while excitable stall owners try to offload the latest mobile phones and other consumer technology. Add the large selection of cheap eateries and you have one of the best malls in the area.

Al Mulla Plaza

Sharjah Road (298 8999). **Open** 10am-10pm Sat-Thur; 5-11pm Fri. **Map** p281 L1.
Al Mulla Plaza is a bit of a Dubai landmark, since you can see it from miles away. It's one of the city's older malls and houses dozens of local independent shops and stalls. Located on the Sharjah Road heading out of the city, in front of the Rashid Stadium, it's home to a host of women's fashion shops and jewellery stores. But by far the pick of the bunch is the 'antique' furniture shop Peshawar Furniture, which has a huge selection of odd and very old-looking furniture.

Twin Towers

Baniyas Road, near Hotel InterContinental Deira (224 9222). **Open** 10am-10pm Sat-Thur; 5-10pm Fri. **Map** p283 J3.
Aka the Mall on the Creek, the Twin Towers is an ideal refuge from chaotic Deira traffic (assuming you can find a parking space). Luxury shopping is the flavour, with predominantly men's designer fashion labels on the ground floor. Other shops offer upmarket shoes, carpets and jewellery. There is a fabulous view of the Creek and its bustling wharf from the open-air terrace of the Apple Café & Restaurant, located among third-floor food outlets.

Jumeirah

Dune Centre

Al Diyafah Street, Satwa (324 4213). **Open** 10am-10pm Sat-Thur; 4-10pm Fri. **Map** p284 F8.
Dune Centre is the pink building that sits opposite Al Diyafah Street's many restaurants and pavement cafés. Shops are on the ground floor only, with offices

Eat, Drink, Shop

and a hospital above. It isn't all that glam as far as Dubai shopping centres go, but there are some interesting and varied shops, including rent-a-frock Formal Wear and petrolhead favourite Motorcycle 3000. Saad Flowers, located in the forecourt, sells a refreshing array of fresh flowers and bouquets.

Ibn Battuta (Gardens Mall)

Between Interchanges 5 & 6, Sheikh Zayed Road (882 1414). **Open** 10am-9pm Sat-Thur; 5-9pm Fri. **Map** p278 A5.
Ibn Battuta is a fair distance out of town, but it is probably Dubai's most exotic mall: it boasts five themed shopping zones with influences from Egypt, Morocco, Persia, India and China. Outlets include Next, Top Shop, Evisu and Fidel, while French hypermarket Géant provides groceries, textiles, fashion, electronics and household items.

Jumeirah Centre

Beach Road (349 9702). **Open** 10am-9pm Sat-Thur; 5-9pm Fri. **Map** p284 D9.
This small, attractive mall is very popular with Jumeirah residents. Benetton, Emirates Sport and Body Shop are located downstairs, while upstairs discounted designer fashions can be found at Blue Cactus and local handicrafts at Sunny Days. The range of textiles and Persian rugs is a further highlight. You can also just sit back with a coffee at La Brioche and soak up the quiet, calm surroundings.

Jumeirah Plaza

Beach Road (349 7111). **Open** 10am-10pm Sat-Thur; 5-10pm Fri. **Map** p284 D9.
The Plaza is a small shopping centre with an eye-catching pink front. Stores include gift shop Susan Walpole and the excellent second-hand bookshop House of Prose. There are also a few craft and rug shops upstairs, plus a safe play area for children.

Mall of the Emirates

By Interchange 4, Sheikh Zayed Road (409 9000). **Open** 10am-10pm daily. **Map** p278 B4.
In the very last throes of construction as we went to press, the Mall of the Emirates is set, once completed, to be easily the biggest shopping centre in the region. Thousands of top-name brands have taken retail space here, from Harvey Nichols and Debenhams to Carrefour. Among the plethora of leisure facilities, the pick of the crop must be the first indoor ski-slope in the UAE.

Mazaya Centre

Sheikh Zayed Road (343 8333/www.mazaya centre.com). **Open** 10am-10pm Sat-Thur; 4.30-10pm Fri. **Map** p287 E14.
The massed foliage and a mildly alarming water sculpture go some way to cheering up the rather dark and gloomy interior of this mall. It's popular with Western expats because of the Homes R Us furnishings store and a convenient Spinneys supermarket. Among the smaller outlets located here are Gulf Greetings, selling gifts and greetings cards; Intelligent Homes, a purveyor of projector

clocks and more toys to the high-tech and house proud; and Crafters' Home, a creative arts centre for adults and children alike. Covered parking to the rear of the mall is a bonus.

Mercato

Beach Road (344 4161). **Open** 10am-10pm Sat-Thur; 2-10pm Fri. **Map** p286 C12.
When it comes to looks, this brave new mall takes top prize, with its richly coloured walls, Venetian murals and numerous meandering passageways. While Spinneys supermarket caters for foodies and Home Centre offers a range of furnishings, the mall has also developed a reputation for innovative clothes stores. Make sure you check out the funky swimwear at Moda Brazil, *Sex and the City*-style dresses at Fleurt and cute, affordable shoes at PrettyFIT. You'll also find Top Shop and Mango for mainstream trends, and Massimo Dutti and Hugo Boss for the more mature shopper. Other stores worth visiting are funky home interiors shops Kas Australia and Living Zone, the cosmetic outlets Areej and MAC, and a Virgin Megastore for all your music and DVD needs.

Palm Strip

Beach Road (346 1462). **Open** 10am-10pm Sat-Thur; 5-10pm Fri. **Map** p284 D9.
This small whitewashed mall is the only open-air shopping centre in Dubai. The downstairs is dominated by a monolithic Mango clothes store, a Starbucks coffee shop and the Japengo Café (*see* p112), while upstairs you'll find CD shop Music Master and the N-Bar (a nail bar). Other fashionable outlets include Karen Millen, Escada Sport and Young Designers Emporium. Because it's alfresco, the mall has no dire piped music, but there's also no air-conditioning, making it quite uncomfortable during the summer months.

Souk Madinat Jumeirah

Al Sufouh Road (366 6546/www.madinat jumeirah.com). **Open** 10am-11pm daily. **Map** p278 A4.
This is the city's most opulent mall. A massive site just past the Burj Al Arab at the end of Jumeirah Road, Madinat Jumeirah has been built to resemble a traditional Arabian marketplace. Fans of jewellery, antiques and art will all find their appetites sated by the high-quality stores on offer, but tourists are plentiful and their prices are high. The place really comes into its own with a massive selection of excellent bars and restaurants: Left Bank (*see* p179) and Bar Zar (*see* p178) are both already firm favourites with the city's barflies.

The Village

Jumeirah Beach Road, opposite Jumeirah Plaza (344 7714). **Open** 10am-10pm Sat-Thur; 4-10pm Fri. **Map** p284 D9.
The Village is an avant-garde shopaholic's dream. The shops here are exclusive, international and unusual – particularly given Dubai's penchant for

Souk Madinat Jumeirah. *See p120.*

Golden opportunities

Every city in the world boasts a jeweller's shop, and every jewellery shop in the world boasts a window full of shiny trinkets. There, however, any similarity with Dubai stops. Head for the gold souk, near Baladiya Street in Deira, and you'll find enough bracelets, rings, pendants and necklaces to leave stars in your eyes for weeks. The windows are full of all manner of exotic, mind-boggling pieces; designs are modern and traditional, heavy and delicate; and shops line the streets as far as the eye can see. The gold sold in Dubai is crafted in India and comes in several shades: the most popular jewellery is 24-carat and orangey in colour, but you can also get 18-, 21- and 22-carat. Some of the antique shops also sell genuine Omani Bedouin silver, which is not only beautiful but increasingly rare (and thus valuable) with demand outstripping supply.

There are very strict laws involving the authenticity of gold, so if a shop attendant tells you a piece of jewellery is 24-carat, it probably is. Prices fluctuate depending on whether the piece was made by a craftsman or a machine, and on the price of gold on that day. Most items are sold by weight, but you should always bargain hard.

In the unlikely event that you can't find a design you like, take in a photo or drawing of what you want and a craftsman will make it up for you. You can even ask for money clips, touristy knick-knacks and gold tiaras. For something more unusual, have your name cut on to a necklace in English or Arabic.

There are also plenty of alleyways leading off to little shops where you can haggle over a shisha, a backgammon set or even a voluminous black abaya (the best of these are listed below), so allow plenty of time to explore. Benches in the covered walkway are perfect for resting on mid-browse, but sit for more than a second and you'll get jumped on by traders attempting to flog everything from bottles of juice to counterfeit watches.

Aries Trading

Old Gold Market, opposite gold souk main entrance (225 9891). **Open** 9am-1.30pm, 4-10pm Sat-Thur; 9-11.30am, 4.30-10pm Fri. **No credit cards. Map** p282 H3.
Expect bargains galore at this silver jewellery store. Heavy chokers, chunky chain bracelets and tarnished Indian toe rings are all stocked, alongside more unusual pieces.

AST

Next to Aries Trading, Old Gold Market, gold souk (225 5727). **Open** 9.30am-2pm, 4-10pm Sat-Thur; 4-10pm Fri. **Credit** AmEx, MC, V. **Map** p282 H3.
AST is good for cheap pashminas that look far more expensive than they are – prices start at Dhs15. There's no shortage of variety either, from plain to printed, beaded and embroidered. If you do want to splash out, the store offers beautiful examples that cost up to Dhs2,500.

Gulf Novelties

Turn right at main entrance to gold souk, then left down an alleyway (226 4720). **Open** 9am-1pm, 4-9.30pm Sat-Thur; 4-9pm Fri. **Credit** AmEx, MC, V. **Map** p282 H3.
This crammed shop is a great place for gifts and curiosities, including wooden camels, dishdashes (men's ankle-length shirts) and tacky Burj Al Arab miniatures.

Al Jaber Gallery

Turn right at main entrance to gold souk, at far end of alley (226 8092). **Open** 9am-1pm, 4-10pm Sat-Thur; 4-10pm Fri. **Credit** AmEx, MC, V. **Map** p282 H3.
A good source of shisha (Dhs45-Dhs100, depending on your haggling skills), wooden backgammon sets (Dhs50) and heavy, silver Arabic bracelets.

Eat, Drink, Shop

the international chain store. Just as refreshing is the centre's style: archways over water, plants, mosaics and fountains arranged in a higgledy-piggledy Mediterranean fashion. Highlights include the gift-wrapping masterpieces of Cadorim, the bread sculptures at Shakespeare & Co (see p109) and the South Pacific wonders at Irony. Hidden on the ground floor is a very practical post office.

Souks

Dubai is awash with local markets, with the Creekside souks a remnant of the 19th century, when the city was a thriving as a port for smugglers and traders. Much has changed since those days, but the Deira and Bur Dubai souks still have plenty that's worth haggling over.

Food

Food souk
Near gold souk, Deira. **Open** 9am-1pm, 4-10pm Sat-Thur; 4-10pm Fri. **Map** p282 H2.
This bustling fruit and veg market shares a huge, hangar-like space with the fish market. A quick tour of the more pungent parts will get you stocked up with fish in seconds, as salesmen force their wares on you – sometimes to the extent of slipping fish into your basket and then demanding cash. Having haggled over hammour (the local version of cod) and bartered for some barracuda, head to the much less frantic fruit and vegetable arena, where huge piles of melons, guava and onions are yours for the taking, at very reasonable prices.

Spices

Spice souk
Between Al Nasr Square & the Creek area at gold souk, Deira. **Open** 9am-1pm, 4-10pm Sat-Thur; 4-10pm Fri. **Map** p282 H3.
Buying food at the markets and souks of Dubai isn't necessarily cheaper than supermarket shopping, but it's a million times more fun. Entering the spice souk by the main abra station on the Deira side of the Creek, you plunge into a cobweb of thin alleyways, filled with mainly Iranian shops piled high with fragrant goods. Spend some time wandering around, absorbing the atmosphere, and be prepared to haggle when you find something that you want. Big barrels of cumin, dried lemons and coriander seed surround you on all sides, vying for space with baskets of star anise, stacks of cinnamon sticks and oodles of frankincense.

Textiles

Textile souk
Al Fahidi Street, Bur Dubai. **Open** 9am-1pm, 4-10pm Sat-Thur; 4-10pm Fri. **Map** p282 H4.

With so many textile shops in Dubai, it makes financial sense to buy material here and have it made up into the style of your favourite trousers or shirt. Tailors (see p133) can copy an original item or a pattern, with simple designs costing about Dhs30 and taking only a day or two to complete. A good tailor will advise on how much cloth you need (buy a little extra to be on the safe side) and should offer at least one fitting. If you're not completely happy with the way your finished garment looks, don't be shy to ask them to make alterations.
For the best range of textile shops within a single area, head to Al Fahidi Street in Bur Dubai; we especially recommend the two listed below. It's a good place to pick up material for your suit, shirt or skirt. Most of the shops close around lunchtime, so get there early in the morning or late afternoon, and avoid taking a car, as parking is a nightmare and the one-way street certain to be congested with taxis, pedestrians and cyclists. If you get caught short of cash, there are ATM machines and a Thomas Cook exchange bureau.

Meena Bazar
Meena Bazar Lane, off Al Fahidi Street, Bur Dubai (352 1374). **Open** 9.30am-1pm, 4.30-10pm Sat-Thur; 4.30-10pm Fri. **Credit** AmEx, MC, V. **Map** p282 H4.
The best-known textile shop in the area, Meena Bazar is the place all the taxi drivers will take you to if you ask for the 'textile souk'. The store stocks raw and Burberry silk, chiffon, metallic net and plain cotton, as well as plenty of more expensive embroidered material. Prices vary and, as ever, you should be prepared to haggle.

Rivoli
Al Fahidi Street, Bur Dubai (353 5448). **Open** 9.30am-1pm, 4.30-10pm Sat-Thur; 4.30-10pm Fri. **Credit** AmEx, MC, V. **Map** p282 H4.
A smart textile shop, with men's fabrics downstairs and ladies' materials upstairs. The shop assistants are keen to offer 'best discount' on Swiss cotton, French chiffon and silk, and textiles purchased here can be made up into clothes at the Rivoli tailor's shop in Karama at a discount.

Antiques & curios

Creative Art Centre
Behind Choithram supermarket, Beach Road, Jumeirah (344 4394). **Open** 8am-6pm Sat-Thur. **Credit** MC, V. **Map** p286 C12.
A quirky gallery, run for the well-heeled denizens of Jumeirah and their souvenir-hungry visitors, the Centre is set in two spacious villas that are full of antiques, gifts and pieces of local fine art. In the array of Arabic knick-knacks and tourist treasures are heavy wooden chests and old Omani doors, refashioned into talking-point coffee tables. Those who are after a more portable keepsake can explore the trove of Bedouin silver and a range of curios designed around freshwater pearls.

Lucky's

Industrial Area No.11, Sharjah (06 534 1937).
Open 9am-1pm, 4-8.30pm Sat-Thur; 9am-noon,
4-8.30pm Fri. **Credit** MC, V. **Map** p279 F1.
Lucky's three enormous warehouses are piled high
with all manner of delightful pieces, ranging from
coffee tables and cabinets to candlesticks and
bizarre figurines. You'll find bargain prices unheard
of when buying wooden furniture in Europe, but
bring your imagination with you: the proprietors
stack goods to the ceiling, leaving you to navigate
narrow winding spaces among furniture mountains
thick with dust. All items are cleaned and stained
to your requirements before delivery.

Marina Gulf Trading

*Al Barsha, Interchange 4, Sheikh Zayed Road, Bur
Dubai (347 8940).* **Open** 9.30am-8.30pm Sat-Thur;
3-8.30pm Fri. **Credit** AmEx, MC, V. **Map** p278 B5.
Dubai's reputation for cheap but chunky items of
quality wooden furniture is built on the supply of
dealerships like Marina, which is a warehouse-
cum-showroom jam-packed with Indian and
Indonesian furniture. Expect coffee tables, chests
and desks, punctuated by brass figurines and
handmade silk throws. Marina isn't quite the haven
for antiques it purports to be, but it does offer a few
original items alongside the attractive imitations.

Petals

Wafi City mall, Oud Metha Road (324 6266). **Open**
10am-10pm Sat-Thur; 4-10pm Fri. **Credit** AmEx,
MC, V. **Map** p281 J3.
Shopping at Petals is a unique experience to say
the least. You might be forgiven for thinking that
you had stumbled into Elton John's dressing room,
the place is so full of chic leopard-print chaises
longues and lavish, coloured chandeliers. There's
one major difference, of course: everything here is
for sale. Intricate chairs covered in crushed-velvet
go for close on Dhs9,000, and are displayed here
alongside Victorian mirrors and mahogany dressing
tables with a Dhs7,000 price tag.

Port of Call

*4th floor, Kendah House, Sheikh Zayed Road, Bur
Dubai (332 6006).* **Open** 4.30-7.30pm Sat-Thur.
Credit AmEx, MC, V. **Map** p287 F12.
The atmosphere at petite Port of Call is friendly
towards browsers, who are welcome to wander
into this showcase of antiques, furniture, pieces of
contemporary art and accessories. It's a small operation, with limited opening hours, but a good place
nonetheless for digging out the occasional gem.

Showcase Antiques, Art & Frames

*Beach Road, off Interchange 3, Sheikh Zayed Road,
Umm Suqeim (348 8797).* **Open** 10am-1pm, 4-8pm
Sat-Thur; 4-8pm Fri. **Credit** AmEx, MC, V. **Map**
p278 B4.
The wonderful display of antiques, collectibles and
art at this shop includes local dowry chests, silver
Bedouin jewellery (such as fabulous chunky rings),
silver *khanjars* (daggers), and antique coffee pots

and coffee tables. There is also furniture from
Europe for sale, including a selection of British
antiques which is housed upstairs.

Books

Censorship laws in Dubai mean that all books
coming into the country are checked, and
anything too controversial regarding politics
or Islam is likely to be banned, as are any art
(or other) books containing pictures of nudes.
You can buy most international magazines,
but any revealing photos will have been
blacked out by a thick, black marker pen.

Book Corner

*Al Ghurair City mall, Al Rigga Road, Deira (228
2835).* **Open** 10am-10pm Sat-Thur; 2-10pm Fri.
Credit AmEx, MC, V. **Map** p283 K3.
This is the largest bookshop in the Middle East and
it shows: the stock includes titles on everything
imaginable, from architecture to zoology. Book
Corner is also usually quick to get in the latest
releases, and often offers good discounts.
Other locations: Dune Centre, Satwa (345 5490).

Books Plus

Lamcy Plaza mall, Oud Metha (336 6362).
Open 10am-10pm Sat-Thur. **Credit** AmEx,
MC, V. **Map** p281 J3.
Books Plus sells a wide selection of fiction, non-
fiction and children's books. You're more likely to
find biographies or the latest John Grisham than
Booker Prize longlist novels here, but magazine
fanatics are spoiled for choice, with a good range
of international newspapers and magazines in both
English and Arabic.

BookWorld

Al Hudaiba Street, Satwa (349 1914). **Open** 10am-
1pm, 5-9pm Sat-Thur; 5-9pm Fri. **Credit** AmEx,
MC, V. **Map** p284 E9.
The biggest and best range of second-hand books
in Dubai, all in good condition and arranged in
alphabetical order on sliding bookshelves. Buy,
read, then return to get a percentage of your
money back. There's also a selection of old international and local magazines.

Book Worm

*Near Park'n'Shop, Al Safa Complex, Jumeirah (394
5770).* **Open** *Summer* 10am-1pm, 4-7pm Sat-Thur.
Winter 10am-8pm Sat-Thur. **Credit** AmEx, MC, V.
Map p280 F5.
The only bookshop in Dubai dedicated to children's
books, selling them in English, French and Arabic.

House of Prose

*Jumeirah Plaza mall, Beach Road, Jumeirah
(344 9021).* **Open** 10am-10pm Sat-Thur;
5.30-8pm Fri. **No credit cards**. **Map** p284 D9.
This second-hand bookshop may not be as big as
BookWorld (*see above*), but its selection is excellent
and the tomes well kept. You'll find kids' books,

Magrudy's, the UAE's leading bookstore.

classics, contemporary fiction and travel guides, all neatly arranged in alphabetical order. The shop will also buy used books.

Magrudy's

Deira City Centre mall, Garhoud (295 7744).
Open 10am-10pm Thur-Sat; 2-10pm Fri.
Credit AmEx, MC, V. **Map** p281 K2.
Magrudy's is the best bookshop in the Emirates: if you can't find it here, you're unlikely to find it anywhere else. Browse through the hundreds of shelves, covering everything from biographies to blockbusters. There's also a small stationery section and a coffee shop.
Other locations: Magrudy Centre, Beach Road, Jumeirah (344 4192).

Virgin Megastore

Mercato mall, Beach Road, Jumeirah (344 6971). **Open** 10am-10pm Sat-Thur; 2-10pm Fri. **Credit** AmEx, MC, V. **Map** p286 C12.
The pounding beat from the vast music section makes it almost impossible to stand around and gently browse. If you're here for books, you're best off with the impressive range of glossy coffee-table reading matter. *See also p140.*

Computing & electricals

For a real bargain, head to **Computer Street**, where past and present collide headlong in a flurry of shops selling electronics in a modern twist on the souks of yesteryear. Found along Bur Dubai's **Khalid Bin Al Waleed Road** (Bank Street; Map p282 G4), it's more of a concept than a physical street, but provides a colourful, neon experience. Start where the road intersects with Mankhool Road and you'll soon see the large **Computer Depot** (355 1515), an open-plan showroom that stocks PCs and peripherals from all the big brands. From here you'll discover about a mile of shops squeezed along one side of the road, with their small, glass fronts stacked with the latest computers, printers, scanners and almost every other conceivable networking toy.

Just a blip away on your GPS system lies **Electrical Street**, which shares space with the textile souk (*see p123*) on Al Fahidi Street. At night its shopfronts blaze with fluorescent and flashing lights, proudly proclaiming such manufacturers as Sharp, Sony, Panasonic and Philips. There's a vast range of electrical goods to choose from, and over-eager shop assistants will do their best to entice you in. Take your time looking out the best deal. On the whole prices are competitive, owing to the number of places offering the same or similar products, so you should be able to pick up a bargain DVD player, digital camera or stereo if you haggle hard. It's always worth plugging in your purchase in the shop to make sure it works properly. Most shops close for prayers between 1pm and 4pm, opening again in from late afternoon until 11pm.

It pays to do a little research before heading out on the hunt for electrical goods, as shop attendants are not always knowledgeable about their stock. And if you are planning to take your item back home with you, check that

MEXX
set the style

mexx.com

Bahrain • Cyprus • Jordan • Kingdom of Saudi Arabia • Kuwait • Lebanon • Morocco • Qatar • UAE

the model you buy will work in your home country (TVs are set to operate at different frequencies in different parts of the world, and DVD players are restricted to play discs from a certain region, so what works in Dubai won't necessarily work in London or Lahore).

Carrefour
Deira City Centre mall, Garhoud (295 1600).
Open 10am-10pm Sat-Thur; 2-10pm Fri.
Credit AmEx, MC, V. **Map** p281 K2.
At the best of times Carrefour is a bit of a scrum, but this vast hypermarket can't be beaten for its wide range of bargain electronics. Alongside the cameras and music systems are plenty of cheap, high-quality household items: you can pick up a microwave for as little as Dhs169 or a small fridge for just Dhs285.

CompuMe
Near Aviation Club, Zalfa Building, Garhoud Road, Garhoud (282 8555). **Open** 10am-10pm Sat-Thur; 4-10pm Fri. **Credit** AmEx, MC, V. **Map** p281 K3.
This giant cubic greenhouse rising out of Garhoud is home to one of the city's few dedicated IT stores. The broad range of hardware features laptops, PCs, PDAs and printers, including big-name brands like HP, IBM, Dell and Toshiba. The self-titled 'megastore' sells specialist computing magazines, books and software, and has a PC clinic, where repairs can be carried out while you wait.

Dubai Audio Centre
Sheikh Zayed Road, after Defence Roundabout (343 1441). **Open** 10am-10pm Sat-Thur; 4-10pm Fri. **Credit** AmEx, MC, V. **Map** p287 E14.
Arguably the most clued-up audio pushers in the city, the folks at DAC have seriously raised the bar in Dubai by stocking many of the world's premium audiophile brands, such as Brit legends Linn and Naim – brilliant, provided you can afford it. Even the cables in this place are gold-plated, for optimal signal transfer. The two-storey, six-room building also provides the best attempt yet to demonstrate authentic home cinema in a Dubaian showroom.

Emirates Computers
Deira City Centre mall, Garhoud (294 0564). **Open** 10am-10pm Sat-Thur; 4-10pm Fri. **Credit** AmEx, MC, V. **Map** p281 K2.
Known for year-round sales promotions and raffles, multi-brand EC typically has a deal or two on products from its primary ranges – Nokia and Dell – but the UAE-wide distributor also stocks Proxima, Lexmark and Apple, and complements its IT stock with high-tech toys like joysticks and mobile phone accessories. Look out for particularly generous discounts during the annual shopping festival (*see p145* **Dubai Shopping Festival**).

Jacky's Electronics
Airport Road, Garhoud (282 1822). **Open** 9am-1pm, 4-9pm Sat-Thur; 4-9pm Fri. **Credit** AmEx, MC, V. **Map** p281 K2.

Jacky's Electronics stocks a good range of electrical equipment and white goods at better-than-average prices. Its audio-visual choice is pretty restricted, running mainly to popular Japanese brands, but it does also include the odd unit assembled on an Asian production line for less than you'd expect. There's a useful camera department too, with many digital camcorders and snap-shooters.
Other locations: Deira City Centre mall, Garhoud (294 9480).

Jumbo Electronics
Opposite Ramada Hotel, Al Mankhool Road, Bur Dubai (352 3555). **Open** 10am-1pm, 4.30-10pm Sat-Thur; 4-10pm Fri. **Credit** AmEx, MC, V. **Map** p282 H5.
Jumbo Electronics enjoys a massive presence in Dubai, and is popular for its exhaustive range of Sony and Panasonic kit. It's particularly reliable for entry-level home theatres, games consoles, DVD players and simple but effective hi-fi systems.
Other locations: Wafi City mall, Oud Metha Road (324 2077).

Plug-Ins
Deira City Centre mall, Garhoud (295 0404). **Open** 10am-10pm Sat-Thur; 2-10pm Fri. **Credit** AmEx, MC, V. **Map** p281 K2.
This store picks up a lot of passing trade from its prime spot in City Centre mall, but many shoppers single out Plug-Ins for its broad range of kit, including household consumer giants such as Toshiba and JVC, as well as more specialist brands – diminutive Bose speakers and enormous Denon amplifiers, for example. You'll find everything from printers to laptops and digital cameras to plasma screens.

Sharaf Enterprises
Opposite Astoria Hotel, Al Fahidi Street, Bur Dubai (353 4978). **Open** 9am-1pm, 4.30-10pm Thur-Sat; 9am-noon Fri. **Credit** AmEx, MC, V. **Map** p282 H4.
Filling the niche between bargain basement and reputable store, this place has every type of home appliance and electrical equipment you could wish for, from Sony CD Walkmans to Kenwood car radios, via Olympus cameras and Panasonic stereo systems. It even has an area selling gold and silver watches.

VV & Sons
Al Fahidi Street, Bur Dubai (353 2444). **Open** 9am-1pm, 4.30-9.30pm Sat-Thur. **Credit** AmEx, MC, V. **Map** p282 H4.
If you want to create some serious sound, this is the place to go. There's a vast range of speakers displayed at the back of the shop, while the upstairs holds a selection of high-quality DVD players and amplifiers for heavy-duty home-theatre systems. In terms of brands, the lesser-known names such as Jamo and Sherwood sit next to international favourites like JBL. Turntables and professional DJ sound equipment are not stocked in the shop, but staff can order them in for you.

Eat, Drink, Shop

Department stores

Bhs

Al Ghurair City mall, Al Rigga Road, Deira (352 5150). **Open** 10am-10pm Sat-Thur; 2-10pm Fri. **Credit** AmEx, MC, V. **Map** p283 K3.

Most British expats will pinch themselves on discovering a branch of Bhs thriving in Dubai. But thrive it does, with quality ranges at affordable prices. In practice, it's more of a children's clothing retailer than a full-blown department store, with the womenswear, home furnishing and lighting departments that have transformed the brand elsewhere in the world yet to be launched in the UAE. **Other locations:** BurJuman Centre (351 5551).

Debenhams

Deira City Centre mall, Garhoud (294 0011). **Open** 10am-10pm Sat-Thur; 2-10pm Fri. **Credit** AmEx, DC, MC, V. **Map** p281 K2.

The Dubai branch of Britain's biggest department store stocks all the things you would expect from this comprehensive retailer. As well as housing a perfumery and own-brand clothing, Debenhams provides a home for collections by such designers as John Rocha, Jasper Conran and Pearce Fionda. Also on sale here is the entire Debenhams home line, including all their soft furnishings, fashion accessories and kitchen appliances.

Jashanmal

Wafi City mall, Oud Metha Road (324 4800). **Open** 10am-10pm Sat-Thur; 4-10pm Fri. **Credit** AmEx, DC, MC, V. **Map** p281 J3.

Jashanmal is the leading home-grown retailer in the Gulf. Both of the Dubai branches contain home furnishings, electrical appliances and a range of home accessories. The Wafi City branch also contains clothing collections by Thomas Burberry, Mexx and Clarks.
Other locations: Al Ghurair City mall (227 7780).

Marks & Spencer

Salahudin Road, Deira (222 2000). **Open** 10am-10.30pm daily. **Credit** AmEx, DC, MC, V. **Map** p281 K1.

This is one of only eight M&S stores outside the UK to have launched 'per una', the women's fashion brand and brainchild of design guru George Davies. The Dubai branches also deliver with the kind of quality underwear, clothing and fashion accessories you'd expect from this brand.
Other locations: Wafi City mall, Oud Metha Road (324 4555).

Saks Fifth Avenue

BurJuman Centre, Trade Centre Road (351 5551). **Open** 10am-10pm Sat-Thur; 2-10pm Fri. **Credit** AmEx, DC, MC, V. **Map** p283 J5.

Since its inception in 1924, Saks Fifth Avenue has evolved into a global icon of excellence. Here in Dubai, the discerning shopper's paradise spans two levels, making it the second-largest Saks outside the USA. On the first level, you'll find life's not-so-necessary niceties – cosmetics and fragrances, designer sunglasses, contemporary collections, the D&G Boutique – but Level Two is where shopping gets serious. Here you'll find individual designer boutiques and collections: Tiffany, Scavia, Prada, Alberta Ferretti, Philosophy, Jean Paul Gaultier and Christian Dior. There's also a fine jewellery department, handbags and accessories, a bridal salon and lingerie. The posh Fifth Avenue Club provides personalised shopping services, and the store runs a complimentary delivery service.

Five Green. *See p129.*

Fashion

Beachwear

Heatwaves

Town Centre mall, Beach Road, Jumeirah (342 0445). **Open** 10am-10pm Sat-Thur; 5-10pm Fri. **Credit** AmEx, MC, V. **Map** p286 C12.
Heatwaves is reliable for basic, simple bikinis and swimsuits in a range of plain colours. Styles tend towards the conservative, but some designs with high-cut bikini bottoms and strapless bikini tops have usually been added to the mix.

Moda Brazil

Mercato mall, Beach Road, Jumeirah (344 3074). **Open** 10am-10pm Sat-Thur; 3-10pm Fri. **Credit** AmEx, MC, V. **Map** p286 C12.
This boutique stocks the widest selection of fashionable bikinis in town, covering everything from racy swimsuits to tropical-coloured bikinis. Sizes are generally on the small side, but the designs are straight off the catwalk.

Women'secret

Deira City Centre mall, Garhoud (295 9665). **Open** 10am-10pm Sat-Thur; 2-10pm Fri. **Credit** AmEx, MC, V. **Map** p281 K2.
Women'secret stocks a decent range of patterned swimsuits, pretty halternecks and string bikinis, in a variety of colours.

Boutiques

Abiti

Dana Centre, Al Maktoum Street, Deira (222 3383). **Open** 9am-1pm, 4-9pm Sat-Thur. **Credit** AmEx, MC, V. **Map** p283 K3.
This super-glamorous boutique is the place to come if you're looking for dramatic evening dresses or hand-embroidered jeans. The emphasis is squarely on feathers and sequins.

Blue Cactus

Jumeirah Centre mall, Beach Road, Jumeirah (344 7734). **Open** 10am-9pm Sat-Thur; 6-9pm Fri. **Credit** AmEx, MC, V. **Map** p284 D9.
The selection at Blue Cactus is small but covers a mix of top-quality chain-store labels and designer womenswear. Kay Unger dresses, Prada short-sleeve shirts and DKNY outfits are all offered at a fraction of their usual retail price.

Eve Michelle

Magrudy Centre, Beach Road, Jumeirah (342 9574). **Open** 9.30am-8pm Sat-Thur. **Credit** AmEx, MC, V. **Map** p284 D9.
A boutique selling costume jewellery, fashionable and glamorous tops, and a variety of casual clothes. Many items are imported straight from London, and deliveries are regular, so you've a good chance of happening on some hip and up-to-the-minute clobber. Hats and shoes are a further attraction.

Five Green

Behind Aroma Garden Café, Oud Metha (336 4100). **Open** 10am-10pm Sat-Thur; 4-10pm Fri. **Credit** AmEx, MC, V. **Map** p281 J2.
Five Green is, quite simply, the best independent clothes shop in the city. It will take you a couple of attempts to find them, but when you push through the huge metal door that separates the shop from the outside world you're in for a treat. Inside, the white, minimalist interior is adorned with printed tees, trainers, shirts and jeans from street labels such as Gesus, Paul Frank, Evisu and 57Seven. Their clobber is a little on the expensive side but, as you are unlikely to find any of it elsewhere, it's a premium worth paying.

Fleurt

Mercato mall, Beach Road, Jumeirah (342 0906). **Open** 10am-10pm Sat-Thur; 2-10pm Fri. **Credit** AmEx, MC, V. **Map** p286 C12.
This sassy store has a small but desirable range of sexy Betsey Johnson dresses, glam Kosiuko outfits, colourful leather handbags and stylish, modern jewellery. A great one-stop shop.

Childrenswear

Armani Junior

Mercato mall, Beach Road, Jumeirah (342 0111). **Open** 10am-10pm Sat-Thur; 2-10pm Fri. **Credit** AmEx, MC, V. **Map** p286 C12.
Deck your little darling out in some seriously cool casuals: a broad range of Armani jeans, T-shirts and hats is arranged neatly along the shelves.

Barbie Shop

Mercato mall, Beach Road, Jumeirah (349 3490). **Open** 10am-10pm Sat-Thur; 2-11pm Fri. **Credit** AmEx, MC, V. **Map** p286 C12.
An ultra-girlie, pink store, dedicated to the plastic fantastic one. Barbie dolls and accessories are stocked on one side, children's roller skates, pink sunglasses, sweatshirts, beach shoes and beauty sets on the other.

Little Bunnies

BurJuman Centre mall, Trade Centre Road, Bur Dubai (3517955). **Open** 10am-10pm Sat-Thur; 4-10pm Fri. **Credit** AmEx, MC, V. **Map** p283 J5.
Little Bunnies is home to pretty pinafore dresses, romper suits, practical hooded tops, tracksuits and jeans for girls and boys up to the age of 14. The highlight, though, has to be the fabulous range of silk and linen party dresses from Dhs1,250.

Little Castle

Wafi City mall, Oud Metha Road (324 6525). **Open** 10am-10pm Sat-Thur; 5-10pm Fri. **Credit** AmEx, MC, V. **Map** p281 J3.
Cute designer dresses, trendy T-shirts and smart suits for kids can all be found here. The shop stocks Italian labels only – Young Versace, Moschino, Diesel and Mona Lisa among them – and caters for

three-month-old babies up to eight-year-olds. To complete the stylish look, there are belts, dinky rucksacks, and both casual and party shoes.

Lugean

Al Ghurair City mall, Al Rigga Road, Deira (228 4317). **Open** 10am-10pm Sat-Thur; 2-10pm Fri. **Credit** AmEx, MC, V. **Map** p283 K3.
The place to go for lovely girlie party dresses and handsome tiny-tot suits. Items aren't cheap (frocks cost from Dhs200), but they're so cute you'll want to keep them forever.

Tom Tailor

Wafi City mall, Oud Metha Road (324 1170). **Open** 10am-10pm Sat-Thur; 4-10pm Fri. **Credit** AmEx, MC, V. **Map** p281 J3.
Tom Tailor is a no-nonsense, affordable fashion store for pre-teen girls. You won't find any glittery tops, just lots of casual clobber, ranging from trendy jeans to hip body jackets. There's also a smaller collection for early teens.

Designer

Bugatti

Falcon Tower, behind Hilton Dubai Creek (Baniyas Road), Deira (228 5109/5118). **Open** 10am-10pm Sat-Thur; 5-10pm Fri. **Credit** AmEx, MC, V. **Map** p283 L4.
Tucked away in downtown Deira, this sparkling white boutique is a label-lover's dream, a glittering paean to all things modish. Shoes, bags and daywear are downstairs, evening gowns, corsets and grown-up glamour upstairs, with many items exclusive to Bugatti. Also hanging gracefully from the rails are clothes from other designers, including Dolce & Gabbana, Jean Paul Gaultier and Ben de Lisi.

Chanel

Wafi City mall, Oud Metha Road (324 0464). **Open** 10am-10pm Sat-Thur; 5-10pm Fri. **Credit** AmEx, MC, V. **Map** p281 J3.
Fans of the classic French design house won't be disappointed, as there are two large boutiques in town. The biggest and best can be found in Wafi City, where Chanel's latest collection arrives only weeks after leaving the Paris catwalk. Accessories like bags and jewellery feature heavily here, as does their expanding range of make-up, but they also have a select array of tweed suits and classic dresses to tempt you to part with the big bucks.
Other locations: BurJuman Centre (351 5551).

Gianni Versace

Al Maktoum Street, Deira (227 3741). **Open** 9.30am-1pm, 5-9.30pm Sat-Thur. **Credit** AmEx, MC, V. **Map** p283 K3.
This spacious, quiet store has sharp suits for men downstairs and daywear for women upstairs, with Moschino shirts and skirts sitting among Versace offerings. There are also plenty of bags, shoes, belts and bikinis, and a small selection of killer dresses for those red-carpet occasions.

Giorgio Armani

Emirates Towers Boulevard mall, Sheikh Zayed Road, Bur Dubai (330 0447). **Open** 10am-10pm Sat-Thur; 4-10pm Fri. **Credit** AmEx, MC, V. **Map** p280 H4.
This vast shop is full of all the latest Armani designs: suits and shoes for men, lots of well-cut skirts and smart jackets for women. If you have cash to splash, check out the hugely expensive gowns.

Gucci

Al Maktoum Street, Deira (221 5444). **Open** 10am-1pm, 5-9.30pm Sat-Thur; 5-9.30pm Fri. **Credit** AmEx, MC, V. **Map** p283 K3.
Stretching over two floors, this boutique is much larger than the other outlet in Emirates Towers Boulevard. Women get a large range of ladieswear and accessories, while gents can browse through the collection of smart suits, shoes and briefcases.
Other locations: Emirates Towers Boulevard mall, Sheikh Zayed Road (330 3313).

Hugo Boss

Mercato mall, Beach Road, Jumeirah (342 2021). **Open** 10am-10pm Sat-Thur; 4-10pm Fri. **Credit** MC, V. **Map** p286 C12.
For no immediately apparent reason, the Hugo Boss store in Mercato mall has been hidden away in a corner of the ground floor. Once you've found it, though, you will be treated to a host of Germanic tailored delights. Offering both their sporty Orange range and the more classic formal menswear line, Hugo Boss is ideal whether you're looking for an off-the-peg suit to make you look dapper in the office or something a little more comfortable to relax in. To complete your outfit (and further squeeze your wallet), they also have a fantastic range of unisex eyewear.

Paul Smith

BurJuman Centre mall, Trade Centre Road, Bur Dubai (359 0099). **Open** 10am-10pm Sat-Thur; 4-10pm Fri. **Credit** AmEx, MC, V. **Map** p283 J5.
'Classic with a twist' has always been the Paul Smith mantra, and this simple design philosophy has kept the designer at the very top of the British menswear pile for 15 years. Tony Blair famously wears Paul Smith shirts with a saucy lady motif inside the cuff but, despite this, the clothes have retained their cachet. This remains the young rake-about-town's outfitter of choice.

Villa Moda

Emirates Towers Boulevard mall, Sheikh Zayed Road, Bur Dubai (330 4555). **Open** 10am-10pm Sat-Thur; 4-10pm Fri. **Credit** AmEx, MC, V. **Map** p280 H4.
Nicknamed the Harvey Nicks of the Middle East, Villa Moda is a favourite one-stop shop for designer fashion. All the latest designs from luminaries like Prada, Marni, Alexander McQueen and Stella McCartney hang beside Lulu Guinness bags and Gina shoes. The selection for men is much more restricted than that for women.

Eat, Drink, Shop

Lingerie

There are plenty of shops selling luxury
lingerie in Dubai, but the majority are rather
underwhelming, with their frilly numbers put
together with little erotic flair. No-nonsense,
everyday underwear is also difficult to come
by, and prices are often marked up heavily.
Nonetheless, the following stores fight the
good fight against mediocrity.

Agent Provocateur

*Level 2, Saks Fifth Avenue, BurJuman Centre
(351 5551).* **Open** 10am-10pm Sat-Thur; 4-10pm
Fri. **Credit** AmEx, MC, V. **Map** p283 J5.
In a conservative city like Dubai, lingerie retailer
Agent Provocateur really could have lived up to its
name. But rather than churning out a load of sleazy
bedwear, the brand has opted for a saucy range of
retro lingerie inspired by undergarments from the
1930s, 1940s and 1950s. If you're looking for an X-
rated hedonistic haven you'll be disappointed, then,
but Agent Provocateur is still classy, understated
and by far the best lingerie shop in the city.

Inner Lines

Deira City Centre mall, Garhoud (295 0627). **Open**
10am-10pm Sat-Thur; 2-10pm Fri. **Credit** AmEx,
MC, V. **Map** p281 K2.
You can't really go wrong with Calvin Klein underwear, and at Inner Lines you'll find a small but
rather attractive selection, encompassing sexy, lacy
knickers and bras in every colour. Other brands
stocked here include BodySlimmers, which give
quick-fix solutions to sagging bums and tums; and
the Princess Tam Tam range, designed to offer
support for the fuller chest.

Janet Reger

*Emirates Towers Boulevard mall, Sheikh Zayed
Road, Bur Dubai (330 0660).* **Open** 10am-10pm
Sat-Thur; 4-10pm Fri. **Credit** AmEx, MC, V.
Map p280 H4.
This store offers camisole tops, French knickers,
silk nightwear and beautiful corsets and suspenders.
Sophisticated, sexy, top-quality stuff.

Nayomi

Mercato mall, Beach Road, Jumeirah (344 9120).
Open 10am-10pm Sat-Thur; 4-10pm Fri. **Credit**
MC, V. **Map** p286 C12.
Nayomi is the leading Middle Eastern retailer of
quality lingerie, stocking lacy dressing gowns from
Dhs845 and rather less sexy neck-to-ankle night-
dresses from Dhs325.

La Perla

*BurJuman Centre mall, Trade Centre Road, Bur
Dubai (355 1251).* **Open** 10am-10pm Sat-Thur;
4-10pm Fri. **Credit** AmEx, MC, V. **Map** p283 J5.
Every woman deserves her little bit of La Perla,
the ultimate in luxury lingerie. This small store has
lacy Italian bras, satin, silk and cotton bodywear,
and sexy corsets, all at top-end prices.

Paul Smith: still a cut above. *See p130.*

Mid-range

Diesel

Mercato mall, Beach Road, Jumeirah (349 9985).
Open 10am-10pm Sat-Thur; 2-10pm Fri. **Credit**
AmEx, MC, V. **Map** p286 C12.
This well-known store sells trendy beachwear
dresses, denim jeans and casual clobber for
demanding teenagers and dressed-down folk in
their twenties. It's very hip, but not exactly cheap.
Other locations: Deira City Centre mall, Garhoud
(295 0792).

Karen Millen

Palm Strip mall, Beach Road, Jumeirah (346 1106).
Open 10am-10pm Sat-Thur; 5-9.30pm Fri. **Credit**
AmEx, MC, V. **Map** p284 D9.
This English chain stocks a fine selection of ultra-
sexy, strappy dresses and beaded, halter-neck and
strapless tops.
Other locations: Deira City Centre mall, Garhoud
(295 5007).

Mango

Palm Strip mall, Beach Road, Jumeirah (346 1826).
Open 10am-10pm Sat-Thur; 5-10pm Fri. **Credit**
AmEx, MC, V. **Map** p284 D9.
Mango is strong on trendy casual pieces that are
easy to mix and match. Expect smart trouser suits
and grown-up summery dresses.
Other locations: Deira City Centre mall, Garhoud
(295 0182).

Massimo Dutti

Deira City Centre mall, Garhoud (295 4788). **Open**
10am-10pm Sat-Thur; 2-10pm Fri. **Credit** AmEx,
MC, V. **Map** p281 K2.

Scissor sisters love **Dream Girl Tailors**. See p133.

Popular with the mature shopper, Massimo Dutti is reliable for well-cut leather and suede jackets, glamorous eveningwear and sophisticated suits in fabrics such as corduroy and linen.
Other locations: Mercato mall, Beach Road, Jumeirah (344 7158).

Miss Sixty

Wafi City mall, Oud Metha Road (324 1998). **Open** 10am-10pm Sat-Thur; 4.30-10pm Fri. **Credit** AmEx, MC, V. **Map** p281 J3.
Plenty of sassy clothes are up for grabs here, from funky fitted jeans to sexy micro minis. There's also a small selection of trendy trainers and thigh-high boots, designed to be worn with attitude.

Sixty Men

Wafi City mall, Oud Metha Road (324 6161). **Open** 10am-10pm Sat-Thur; 4.30-10pm Fri. **Credit** AmEx, MC, V. **Map** p281 J3.
The masculine version of the Miss Sixty brand, Sixty Men is chock-full of fashion gems.

Top Shop

Mercato mall, Beach Road, Jumeirah (344 2677). **Open** 10am-10pm Sat-Thur; 2-10pm Fri. **Credit** AmEx, MC, V. **Map** p286 C12.
Popular with both sexes for catwalk fashion. Priced for the high street, the range runs from hipster jeans to vintage-style shirts. The collection changes regularly, but always includes cheeky underwear.
Other locations: Deira City Centre mall, Garhoud (295 1010).

Zara

Deira City Centre mall, Garhoud (295 3377). **Open** 10am-10pm Sat-Thur; 2-10pm Fri. **Credit** AmEx, MC, V. **Map** p281 K2.
Part of the well-known Spanish chain, this is the largest fashion store in Dubai and probably the most popular. The back of the shop houses funky retro garments and kids' clothes, while the front has the latest in fashionable tops and bottoms for

men and women. There's also an appealingly bijou selection of shoes and belts. Great value for money.
Other locations: BurJuman Centre mall, Trade Centre Road, Bur Dubai (351 3332).

Sportswear

Adidas

BurJuman Centre mall, Trade Centre Road, Bur Dubai (359 0995). **Open** 10am-10pm Sat-Thur; 4-10pm Fri. **Credit** MC, V. **Map** p283 J5.
All the latest Adidas trainers, tracksuits, shorts and T-shirts for men, with a smaller range of gymwear and footwear for women. Adidas watches round out the collection.
Other locations: Adidas Factory Shop, Airport Road, Garhoud (282 5868).

Golf House

BurJuman Centre mall, Trade Centre Road, Bur Dubai (351 9012). **Open** 10am-10pm Sat-Thur; 4-10pm Fri. **Credit** AmEx, MC, V. **Map** p283 J5.
Among the golfing equipment you'll find a good selection of irons, while the men's and women's fairway fashion includes a popular line of Burberry hats, shirts, trousers and shorts.

Intermilan

Near Lal's supermarket, Al Hudaiba Street, Satwa (349 7765). **Open** 9am-11pm Sat-Thur; 9-11.30am, 3-11.30pm Fri. **No credit cards.**
Map p284 E9.
This is the best place in town for cheap football shirts, tracksuit bottoms and men's trainers. Check the Dhs10 rail at the front of the shop for Oakley shorts and Fox T-shirts.

Sports Market

Opposite Jumeirah Centre mall, Beach Road, Jumeirah (344 3799). **Open** 10am-1pm, 4-10pm Sat-Thur; 2-10pm Fri. **Credit** AmEx, MC, V. **Map** p284 D9.

Here you'll find sports equipment including golf clubs, tennis racquets, bikes and in-line skates. There's also sporty clothing for men and women from brands such as Nike, Dunlop and Slazenger.

Sun&Sand Sports

Khalid Bin Al Waleed Road (Bank Street), Bur Dubai (351 6222). **Open** 10am-10pm Sat-Thur; 2-10pm Fri. **Credit** AmEx, MC, V. **Map** p283 J5.
Sun&Sand Sports is the biggest sports shop in Dubai, stocking everything from gym equipment to tennis gear, including a section dedicated to Nike clothing and kit. Trainer addicts might not find the very latest styles, but prices are reasonable and Adidas and Puma are among the brands on offer. **Other locations:** Deira City Centre mall, Garhoud (295 5551).

Tailors

For buying fabrics, *see p123* **Textile souk.**

Century Tailoring

Shop No.25, Block C, Karama (337 6610). **Open** 9am-10.30pm Sat-Thur; 9am-11am, 4-10.30pm Fri. **No credit cards. Map** p285 J7.
These tailors, based in the Karama market area, specialise in men's suits, trousers and shirts. It takes two days to make up the clothes, with one fitting included. Prices start at Dhs30.

Coventry Tailoring

Next to Deepaks material shop, Al Hudaiba Road, Satwa (344 7563). **Open** 9.30am-1pm, 4-9.30pm Sat-Thur. **No credit cards. Map** p284 E9.
These Satwa tailors have built up a fine reputation in an area already swamped with cloth-cutters. Their workmanship is second to none and they're pretty quick, usually being able to knock out a well-crafted copy of a pair of trousers in a week.

Dream Girl Tailors

Opposite Emirate Bank International, across from Satwa roundabout, Satwa (349 5445). **Open** 9.30am-1.30pm, 3.30-10pm Thur-Sat; 6-8pm Fri. **No credit cards. Map** p285 F8.
This popular place is always busy, so you may have to wait a couple of weeks for a garment to be made up. Bring in a pair of, say, your favourite trousers and Dream Girl will copy them exactly; evening dresses (which start from about Dhs200) come out particularly well.

Gents Tailors

Near the Astoria Hotel, Al Fahidi Street, Bur Dubai (353 1460). **Open** 9.30am-2pm, 4.30-10pm Sat-Thur; 4-10pm Fri. **Credit** AmEx, MC, V. **Map** p282 H4.
At Gents Tailors, stick figures scrawled on scraps of paper are swiftly transformed into beautifully fitted, good-value clothes. Staff can also carbon copy anything you bring along. The suits, dresses and shawls hanging from the shop's lofty steel racks reflect their tremendous talent.

Fashion accessories

Hats

Blue Cactus

Jumeirah Centre mall, Beach Road, Jumeirah (344 7734). **Open** 10am-9pm Sat-Thur; 5-9pm Fri. **Credit** AmEx, MC, V. **Map** p284 D9.
If you visit between January and March, you'll find a small selection of hats here. Among the lampshade headwear, the odd show-stopping design turns up – and it shouldn't cost a fortune.

Designers' Club at St John

Wafi City mall, Oud Metha Road (324 0028). **Open** 10am-10pm Sat-Thur; 4.30-10pm Fri. **Credit** AmEx, MC, V. **Map** p281 J3.
A good range of expensive, stylish, dressy and sophisticated headwear. Prices start from Dhs990 and rise to Dhs1,500.

Oasis Fashion

Wafi City mall, Oud Metha Road (324 9074). **Open** 10am-10pm Sat-Thur; 4.30-10pm Fri. **Credit** AmEx, MC, V. **Map** p281 J3.
Not a place for shrinking violets, Oasis excels at producing hats with feathery, frilly and flowery appendages, all at affordable prices.

Sunny Days

Jumeirah Centre mall, Beach Road, Jumeirah (349 5275). **Open** 10am-9pm Sat-Thur; 5-9pm Fri. **Credit** MC, V. **Map** p284 D9.
Local milliner Lynn Holyoak can often be found selling her colourful creations here in the run-up to the Dubai World Cup, when demand, naturally, skyrockets. The prices are reasonable, though – expect to pay around Dhs400.

Jewellery

The best place in Dubai for jewellery is the gold souk (*see p122* **Golden opportunities**), which offers designs to suit all tastes and budgets, but for designer jewellery and international brands like Graff and Cartier, head to the major shopping malls. All the latest pieces arrive in Dubai as soon as they become available elsewhere in the world, so collections are always up to date.

Cartier

Emirates Towers Boulevard mall, Sheikh Zayed Road, Bur Dubai (330 0034). **Open** 10am-10pm Sat-Thur; 5-10pm Fri. **Credit** AmEx, DC, MC, V. **Map** p280 H4.
Gorgeous gems, from opal to sapphire, delicately set in rings, bracelets and necklaces.

Damas

Deira City Centre mall, Garhoud (295 3848). **Open** 10am-10pm Sat-Thur; 2-10pm Fri. **Credit** AmEx, DC, MC, V. **Map** p281 K2.

Eat, Drink, Shop

Riches from the comfort zone

Dubai's glittering stockpiles of precious metals and jewels are no secret: tourists have been battling through Deira's bustling souks for some time, determined to emerge with enough bling to make Mr T green with envy. What isn't so well known, however, is that the frantic and often smelly souk experience is no longer your only option. A dedicated jewellery mall has opened in Dubai, a pristine gathering of no fewer than 37 outlets, all vying gently for your attention in eerily quiet air-conditioned comfort. You'll find yellow, white and even purple gold, as well as pearls and platinum. Most stores encourage you to commission your own designs, and many a newly wed Dubaian can be seen sporting a unique creation from the Gold & Diamond Park on their finger. Just in case you need a bit of further persuasion before you open your wallet, guided tours of the local factories are available too.

Gold & Diamond Park

By Interchange 4, Sheikh Zayed Road (347 7574). **Open** 10am-10pm Sat-Thur; 4-10pm Fri. **Credit** AmEx, MC, V. **Map** p278 B4.

Damas has outlets in nearly every major shopping mall. The jewellery is predominantly chunky and gold. New collections arrive regularly, but the emphasis is always on big diamonds and heavy rings, with a definite Arabic flavour.

Graff

Wafi City mall, Oud Metha Road (324 4221). **Open** 10am-10pm Sat-Thur; 4.30-10pm Fri. **Credit** AmEx, DC, MC, V. **Map** p281 J3.

Graff is the only company in town that produces, manufactures and retails its own gems, which means their dazzling range changes every day rather than, as at other jewellers' shops, with the seasons. The necklaces, earrings and rings are classically beautifully rather than garish.

Tiffany & Co

Deira City Centre mall, Garhoud (295 3884). **Open** 10am-10pm Sat-Thur; 2-10pm Fri. **Credit** AmEx, DC, MC, V. **Map** p281 K2.

The outlet may be small, but the selection of classy jewellery and chic accessories is jaw-dropping. **Other locations:** BurJuman Centre mall, Trade Centre Road, Bur Dubai (359 0101).

Shoes

Al-Fareed Shoes

Al Musallah Road, opposite Special Ostadi Restaurant, Bur Dubai (359 2862). **Open** 8.30am-2pm, 4-11pm Sat-Thur; 3-11pm Fri. **No credit cards. Map** p282 H4.

Khalid Javed, owner of Al-Fareed Shoes, is famed as a master shoe-maker. Nowadays, his tiny shop is more concerned with repairs, but hanging in the windows are exquisite, soft leather, gold or silver embroidered slipper-shoes. Each pair is uniquely decorated and if your size isn't available, he'll be happy to make up a bespoke pair within 24 hours. Best of all, it will only set you back Dhs30.

Jimmy Choo

Emirates Towers Boulevard mall, Sheikh Zayed Road (330 0404). **Open** 10am-10pm Sat-Thur; 4-10pm Fri. **Credit** AmEx, MC, V. **Map** p280 H4.

Fabulously chic heels, for those who can flex the plastic. Load up on ornate sandals, strappy kittens, sheer leather boots, ankle shoes and bridal slippers.

Milano

Mercato mall, Beach Road, Jumeirah (344 9517). **Open** 10am-10pm Sat-Thur; 2-10pm Fri. **Credit** AmEx, MC, V. **Map** p286 C12.

Milano boasts something to suit every woman's footwear mood, occasion and price range, with everything from vampish heels to everyday flats. There's also a selection of men's leather shoes, which are a little more conservative. **Other locations:** Deira City Centre mall, Garhoud (295 0792).

Nine West

Deira City Centre mall, Garhoud (295 6887). **Open** 10am-10pm Thur-Sat; 2-10pm Fri. **Credit** AmEx, MC, V. **Map** p281 K2.

This familiar chain is great for day-to-day basics as well as sparkly sandals. It's also one of the few shops in Dubai that offers shoes in large sizes. **Other locations:** Town Centre mall, Beach Road, Jumeirah (344 4038).

PrettyFIT

Mercato mall, Beach Road, Jumeirah (344 0015). **Open** 10am-10pm Sat-Thur; 2-10pm Fri. **Credit** AmEx, MC, V. **Map** p286 C12.

Shoes here are neither glam nor staid, but a workable average somewhere in between. Flats and heels, strappies and slip-ons come in a variety of colours, usually decorated with stripes, polka dots, checks or flowers. Prices start at around Dhs80.

Stuart Weitzman/Moreschi

BurJuman Centre mall, Trade Centre Road, Bur Dubai (359 0568). **Open** 10am-10pm Sat-Thur; 4-10pm Fri. **Credit** AmEx, MC, V. **Map** p283 J5.

Celebrity designer Stuart Weitzman offers shoppers seriously sexy shoes, with every foot size well catered for. In the same shop sits a smaller line of high-quality Moreschi leather footwear.

Florists

Blooms
Beach Road, Jumeirah (344 0912). **Open** 9am-1pm, 4-9pm Sat-Thur. **Credit** AmEx, MC, V. **Map** p286 C11.
As well as indoor plants and dried flowers, Blooms has carved out a niche for silk flower craft, offering unique flower arrangements and frilly matching decorative items for the home. The store also stocks a small selection of fresh flowers.

Desert Flowers
Near the Iranian Hospital, Al Hudaiba Road, Satwa (349 7318). **Open** 8am-1.30pm, 4-10pm Sat-Thur; 4-10pm Fri. **Credit** AmEx, MC, V. **Map** p284 E9.
There are lots of flower shops on Al Hudaiba Road, but Desert Flowers is the best. From the outside it looks like a market stall, with potted plants laid out on the pavement, but there are plenty of fresh, artificial and dried flower arrangements and stems tucked away inside.

Oleander
Century Plaza mall, Beach Road, Jumeirah (344 0560). **Open** 8am-9pm Sat-Thur; 4-9pm Fri. **Credit** AmEx, MC, V. **Map** p284 D9.
Oleander is more of a garden accessory shop than a dedicated florist, but go to the back of the store and you'll find some beautiful, perfumed bunches of flowers hidden behind the huge green plants and outdoor furniture.

Food shops

Dolce Antico
Mercato mall, Beach Road, Jumeirah (344 0028). **Open** 10am-10pm Sat-Thur; 5-10pm Fri. **Credit** AmEx, MC, V. **Map** p286 C12.
This small but elegant Italian food shop caters mainly to the sweet of tooth: head over there to stock up on handmade chocolates and preserved fruit in beautiful, heavy glass jars.

Goodies
Wafi City mall, Oud Metha Road (324 4433). **Open** 10am-10pm Sat-Thur; 4-10pm Fri. **Credit** AmEx, DC, MC, V. **Map** p281 J3.
Goodies is stocked to the rafters with Arabian cheeses and sweets, and shoppers are ringed by baskets of fat olives, truffles and dates. The home-made ice-cream is simply delicious, and the luxury chocolates worth every fil. No wonder it's Dubai's favourite gourmet goods shop.

Pronto
Fairmont Hotel, Sheikh Zayed Road, Bur Dubai (332 5555). **Open** 7am-11pm daily. **Credit** AmEx, MC, V. **Map** p285 G9.
A reasonable mini deli, selling nice-looking mustards and jams, cold meats and cheeses. The Parma ham and smoked salmon are worth queuing up for, as are the own-made muffins, gourmet salads and freshly baked loaves.

Sweety Sweets
Al Musallah Road, Bur Dubai (397 1380). **Open** 9am-1.30pm, 4.30-10.30pm Sat-Thur; 9.30-11.30am Fri. **No credit cards. Map** p282 H4.
A snack-lover's paradise. Saunter round inhaling the chilli-laced air and lose yourself in the rows of *papads* (mini poppadoms), pickles, puri, *vada pav* (spicy fried potato) and Bombay mix. Pick up half a kilo of *methi chakli* for Dhs15 – the crispy, fenugreek-flavoured fried rice-flour is about the most addictive snack you can imagine.

Health & beauty

Cosmetics & perfume
Every major mall has at least one perfume or cosmetics shop. New fragrances are available as soon as they are launched in their country of origin, but prices can be high here, so you're better off stocking up at the airport duty free.

Ajmal Perfumes
Deira City Centre mall, Garhoud (295 3580). **Open** 10am-10pm Sat-Thur; 3-10pm Fri. **Credit** AmEx, MC, V. **Map** p281 K2.
Ajmal specialises in Arabic perfumes, which are stronger and spicier than Western scents. There is a large selection of ready-mades, but you can also have fun blending your own perfume with the help of the in-store perfumer.

Areej
Mercato mall, Beach Road, Jumeirah (344 6894). **Open** 10am-10pm Sat-Thur; 2-10pm Fri. **Credit** AmEx, MC, V. **Map** p286 C12.
All the international perfumes, cosmetics, lotions and potions are stocked at this huge store, among them Lancôme, Estée Lauder and Calvin Klein.

MAC
Deira City Centre mall, Garhoud (295 7704). **Open** 10am-10pm Sat-Thur; 2-10pm Fri. **Credit** AmEx, MC, V. **Map** p281 K2.
As the city's largest MAC branch, this store has a superb range of foundations and nail, eye and lip colours. Disco divas will love the sassy glitter eye-liner, which comes in a rainbow of colours, and the tinted lipgloss. Also recommended is the Shimmer Soufflé, a water-based formula that provides a glitter-rich shimmery effect on the skin.
Other locations: Mercato mall, Beach Road, Jumeirah (344 9536).

Mikyajy
Deira City Centre mall, Garhoud (295 7844). **Open** 10am-10pm Sat-Thur; 2-10pm Fri. **Credit** AmEx, MC, V. **Map** p281 K2.
Mikyajy's range of international fragrances and quirky cosmetic brands isn't huge, but the shop is worth checking out for its own-brand make-up boxes and cosmetic palettes, which are cheaper than most other high-street brands.

Eat, Drink, Shop

Paris Gallery

Deira City Centre mall, Garhoud (294 1111).
Open 10am-10pm Thur-Sat; 3-10pm Fri.
Credit AmEx, MC, V. **Map** p281 K2.
With two locations in Deira City Centre (the Level
Two store is the bigger and better one), Paris
Gallery stocks an array of international perfumes
and cosmetics, as well as a good range of designer
sunglasses and watches.

Red Earth

Deira City Centre mall, Garhoud (295 1887).
Open 10am-10pm Sat-Thur; 2-10pm Fri.
Credit AmEx, MC, V. **Map** p281 K2.
This trendy brand of make-up covers everything
from shimmery foundation and luscious lip-gloss
to canary-yellow eyeshadow. You'll also find an
especially big choice of lip and nail colours.

Rituals

Deira City Centre mall, Garhoud (294 1432).
Open 10am-10pm Sat-Thur; 2-10pm Fri.
Credit AmEx, MC, V. **Map** p281 K2.
The range of bodycare products at this Dutch store
may be small, but it has the advantage of covering
items for both men and women. Body scrubs,
shower gels and slimming tea are all available to
complete your healthy lifestyle.

Villa Moda

*Emirates Towers Boulevard mall, Sheikh Zayed
Road (330 4555).* **Open** 10am-10pm Sat-Thur;
4-10pm Fri. **Credit** AmEx, MC, V. **Map** p280 H4.
Villa Moda is a clutch of pricey boutiques dotted
around the Emirates Towers Shopping Boulevard.
It's home to strangely named Three Custom Color
Specialists, a company with a long list of celebrity

Market values

You might dine out every evening at the
finest restaurants along the Creek, you
may rest your head on the softest pillows
that Jumeirah's hotels can muster, but a trip
to Dubai isn't complete without at least one
dip into the strange world of **Karama**. The
market area is awash with fake designer T-
shirts, handbags and shoes – you can barely
move through the kooky network of streets
and courtyards without banging into racks of
cheap tracksuits and trendy skatewear.

Shopkeepers compete with each other to
attract passers-by into their stores, offering
'best price' for fake Rolex watches, Gucci
handbags and pirate DVDs. You'll see plenty
of bargain-hunting tourists clutching grey
plastic bags, evidence that they've been
busy spending, their new purchases virtually

indistinguishable from the real designer
goodies toted by rich locals.

If you're not just here for the experience,
make sure you ask to see the rest of the stock
before making your purchase. Many places have
'secret' back doors or attic rooms crammed with
products they are not allowed, by law, to show
off. There are plenty of good copies of Christian
Dior, Bulgari and Louis Vuitton to be had,
as well as souvenirs such as fluffy camels,
backgammon boards and shisha.

Many of the outlets follow traditional shop
opening hours, so your best bet is to arrive
early in the morning or late in the afternoon.
Allow plenty of time to wander around, and
remember to bring your bargaining skills:
polite but firm haggling is very much the
order of the day.

clients that is on a mission to create custom-made cosmetics to match whatever magazine photo or stub of old lipstick you care to produce.

Salons

Curve
BurJuman Centre, Trade Centre Road, Bur Dubai (355 3788). **Open** 10am-10pm Sat-Thur; 4-10pm Fri. **Credit** AmEx, DC, MC, V. **Map** p283 J5.
Every girl in Curve seems to be called Nadia but, whether you get Nadia No.1 or No.4, the chances are you're going to get a great haircut or treatment at a bargain price (the typical cost of a haircut is a mere Dhs100). This is a no-nonsense operation, with staff who forgo the holiday chit-chat to work wonders quickly on head and body.

1847
Emirates Towers Boulevard mall, Sheikh Zayed Road (330 1847). **Open** 10am-10pm daily. **Credit** AmEx, MC, V. **Map** p280 H4.
A trip to this gents' salon is now a must for any male visitor to Dubai. The host of therapies of offer include hour-long facials, sports pedicures and foot-waxing. Be sure to try the '1847' shave, a 35-minute bliss out that comprises a massage with oil, double shave with a genuine badger brush, pore-closing with alum, and an aftershave mask. You'll feel a million dollars and only have to pay Dhs75.

Nail Station
Town Centre Mall, Beach Road, Jumeirah (349 0123). **Open** 9am-9pm Sat, Thur; 2-9pm Sun-Wed. **Credit** AmEx, DC, MC, V. **Map** p286 C12.
Although the all-white, almost futuristic interior looks a little cold at first, the smiling staff soon make up for it. The technicians here are quick and competent at all manner of manicures, and with the comfy armchairs facing a huge plasma screen that shows feel-good movies, even impatient customers should be happy to sit still for a while.

Reflections
Villa 3, past Spinneys Centre, Al Wasl Road, Jumeirah (394 4595). **Open** 9am-6pm Sat, Thur; 9am-8pm Sun-Wed. **Credit** MC, V. **Map** p280 F5.
Based in a house on Al Wasl Road, Reflections provides a convivial welcome. The salon, which is split over two levels, offers a good range of beauty treatments (including facials and tanning) on the first floor, while down below a small but intimate hair salon sees mops chopped with no little style. More interested in a healthy chinwag than the high (lights) fashion, the staff are warm and friendly.

Le Salon
Dubai Marine Beach Resort & Spa, Jumeirah (346 2266). **Open** 10.30am-8.30pm Sat-Thur; 4-8.30pm Fri. **Credit** AmEx, MC, V. **Map** p284 D8.
This friendly Jordanian-run salon is the perfect place to get your barnet whipped into shape. Despite the upmarket surroundings, prices are competitive:

men pay Dhs100 for a cut and blow-dry, women pay Dhs185 for the same, and highlights will cost you upwards of Dhs200. And one tip: if they tell you that you need to go short, trust them.

Toni & Guy
Emirates Towers Boulevard mall, Sheikh Zayed Road (330 3345). **Open** 10am-10pm Sat-Thur; 4-8pm Fri. **Credit** MC, V. **Map** p280 H4.
If you only trust one salon with your crowning glory, it has to be T&G. Don't expect to find mere hairdressers or, god forbid, barbers here – these people are self-appointed hair technicians. So don't expect a visit here to be cheap (a wash, cut and blow-dry costs up to Dhs250), but you can be sure your hair is in safe hands.

Home furnishings

Bayti
Deira City Centre mall, Garhoud (294 9292). **Open** 10am-10pm Sat-Thur; 2-10pm Fri. **Credit** AmEx, MC, V. **Map** p281 K2.
Nestled above Woolworths on the second floor of Deira City Centre, Bayti adds a touch of flair to the mall's homeware offerings. Its reasonably priced collections boast seasonal colours, with an oriental flavour: you'll find fake flora, pungent candles, dark wooden trays and cute glazed vases, all of them coming in at under Dhs100 apiece.

Home Centre
Mercato mall, Beach Road, Jumeirah (344 2266). **Open** 10am-10pm Sat-Thur; 2-10pm Fri. **Credit** AmEx, MC, V. **Map** p286 C12.
The kitchenware and other home furnishings here are cheaper and plainer than at IKEA, with the bonus that they're pre-assembled, so you don't have the hassle of doing it yourself. You'll find an expansive floor of artificial flower displays, weird and wonderful lampshades, curtains, cutlery and more.
Other locations: Oasis Centre mall, between Interchanges 2 & 3, Sheikh Zayed Road (339 5217).

IKEA
Deira City Centre mall, Garhoud (295 0434). **Open** 10am-10pm Sat-Thur; 2-10pm Fri. **Credit** AmEx, MC, V. **Map** p281 K2.
Home to every conceivable type of houseware, this is the place nest-builders newly arrived in the city swing by to pick up all the basics. Expect an abundance of self-assembly kitchen, bedroom and bathroom accessories. Clean minimalist lines, comforting wooden frames, and cute but curious Swedish names are the order of the day.

Kas Australia
Mercato mall, Beach Road, Jumeirah (344 1179). **Open** 10am-10pm Sat-Thur; 2-10pm Fri. **Credit** MC, V. **Map** p286 C12.
Kas Australia has an excellent collection of citrus-coloured pillows, plumped up against extravagantly textured throws and brightly coloured fabrics. Don't get overexcited, though: a little of it goes a long way.

Eat, Drink, Shop

It's all about good living.

MARKS & SPENCER

DUBAI • ABU DHABI • SHARJAH • OMAN • KUWAIT • QATAR • BAHRAIN

The One.

Afghan, Iraqi and tribal designs at low prices.
Deira Tower on Al Nasr Square is also worth
a look, with around 40 shops offering a wide
variety of rugs from all over the region.

Al Madaen
*Near Iranian Hospital, Pagoda House, Satwa (345
4488).* **Open** 10am-1.30pm, 5-10pm Sat-Thur;
5-10pm Fri. **Credit** AmEx, MC, V. **Map** p284 E9.
Al Madaen is a small shop that sells Iranian carpets
in all sizes. Prices start at Dhs1,500, but can go up
to Dhs100,000 for antique rugs (which come with
gold frames – they are collector's pieces to be hung
on the wall, not something you walk on).

Pride of Kashmir
Deira City Centre mall, Garhoud (295 0655).
Open 10am-10pm Sat-Thur; 2-10pm Fri.
Credit AmEx, MC, V. **Map** p281 K2.
This shop is part of the covered 'mock souk' in Deira
City Centre. There's a wide selection of rugs from
Iran, Kashmir and Turkey, antique and modern,
which start from around Dhs200 and go up to maybe
Dhs60,000. You can even order a reproduction of the
world's oldest surviving rug, the Pazyryck rug.

Toshkhana Trading
*Behind Al Anwar Jewellery, gold souk, Deira (225
4440).* **Open** 9.30am-10pm Sat-Thur; 4-10pm Fri.
Credit AmEx, MC, V. **Map** p282 H3.
Located down one of the alleyways in the gold
souk, Toshkhana has plenty of expensive carpets.
Handmade silk and cotton rugs cost between
Dhs1,500 and Dhs15,000, while wool carpets are
from Dhs800 to Dhs1,500. For something more
unusual, there are bejewelled velvet-trimmed
rugs for around Dhs2,500.

Total Arts
*The Courtyard, between Interchanges 3 & 4 of Sheikh
Zayed Road, Al Quoz (228 2888).* **Open** 10am-1pm,
4-8pm Sat-Thur. **Credit** AmEx, MC, V. **Map** p278 B4.
Total Arts is a gallery rather than a shop, but it
holds regular exhibitions of tribal weavings and
rugs from Iran that are available to buy. Each piece
is clearly labelled with details of its age and origin,
and the knowledgeable staff are on hand to answer
any queries you might have.

Music

Ohm Records
*Opposite BurJuman Centre mall, Trade Centre Road,
Bur Dubai (397 3728).* **Open** 2-10pm daily. **Credit**
DC, MC, V. **Map** p283 J5.
Ohm Records is the first record shop in the Middle
East to sell vinyl shipped in from London, New
York, France and Belgium. All the records come
from independent labels, with not a mainstream
tune in sight. Professional and bedroom DJs gather
at the weekends to play on the decks for free. For
the complete look, the shop also sells record bags
and a small line of streetwear.

The Living Zone
Mercato mall, Beach Road, Jumeriah (344 5994).
Open 10am-10pm Sat-Thur; 2-10pm Fri. **Credit**
MC, V. **Map** p286 C12.
Three outlets here are rolled into one: American-
owned Bombay is the place for luxurious bedroom
accessories, expensive feathered lampshades and
crushed-velvet cushions; Danish outlet the Zone
has attractive stainless steel and chrome kitchen
utensils; and Swiss store Bodum, although tiny in
comparison, has enough cafetières and colourful
coffee mugs to kit out your entire street.

The One
Beach Road, Jumeirah (345 6687). **Open** 9am-10pm
Sat-Thur; 2-10pm Fri. **Credit** AmEx, DC, MC, V.
Map p284 D9.
When even tourists arrive in Dubai with mystical
instructions to seek out 'The One', somebody somewhere has hit the jackpot. Established in 1995, this
local company is the most popular home accessories
shop in Dubai, thanks to a design-led product range,
neatly marrying ethnic accessories (think incense
burners, Buddha heads and textured photo frames)
with bold, contemporary items of furniture.

Rugs

If it's rugs and carpets you're after, Dubai
can offer a vast range, from contemporary
to traditional, antique to new, and cheap
to expensive. They come from a number of
countries, including Iran, Turkey, Pakistan and
Central Asia. If you're planning on purchasing
an antique rug, the best way to spot a good one
is to check its reverse side. The more knots
there are on the underside, the better the rug's
quality and the longer it's likely to last. On the
whole, silk is more expensive than wool, and
rugs from Iran are generally more valuable
than the equivalent from Turkey or Kashmir.

Be sure to visit Global Village during the
Dubai Shopping Festival (*see p145*) for

Eat, Drink, Shop

Virgin Megastore

Mercato mall, Beach Road, Jumeirah (344 6971).
Open 10am-10am Sat-Thur; 2-10pm Fri. **Credit**
AmEx, MC, V. **Map** p286 C12.

All musical tastes are catered for at Virgin, from international bands to Arabic music and Bollywood soundtracks. Despite the wide range of DVDs, CDs and videos, everything will have been screened and, if required, censored. So you may not find the latest Hollywood flick or must-have CD.
Other locations: BurJuman Centre mall, Trade Centre Road, Bur Dubai (351 3444); Deira City Centre mall, Garhoud (295 8599).

Opticians

Most malls have an optician; eye tests are often free if you buy glasses or contacts.

Bahrain Opticians

Wafi City mall, Oud Metha Road (324 2455). **Open**
10am-10pm Sat-Thur; 4-10pm Fri. **Credit** AmEx,
MC, V. **Map** p281 J3.

A slick operation offering upmarket frames from Police, Carrera and Emporio Armani. You can go from eye test to fitting in only a couple of days, and there's a raft of lens options available, from tinted to scratch-resistant.

Al Jaber Optical Centre

Deira City Centre mall, Garhoud (295 4400).
Open 10am-10pm Sat-Thur; 2-10pm Fri.
Credit AmEx, MC, V. **Map** p281 K2.

Al Jaber stocks plenty of branded frames, making it a good place to pick up a pair of Chanel or Ray

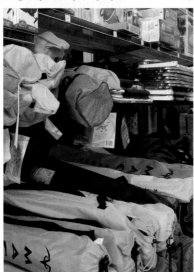

Camp as you like: outdoor kit at **Picnico**.

Ban sunglasses. You'll also find super-light frames: check out offerings from Strip Titanium and Spirit, so dainty you'll forget you're wearing them.

Outdoor equipment

Ace Hardware

Near Oasis Centre mall, between Interchanges 2 & 3, Sheikh Zayed Road, Bur Dubai (338 1416). **Open**
9am-9pm daily. **Credit** AmEx, MC, V. **Map** p278 B4.

The largest hardware store in Dubai, Ace has everything from DIY gear to outdoor accessories. It also has Dubai's best selection of barbecues, tents, sleeping bags and camping equipment.

Carrefour

Deira City Centre mall, Garhoud (295 1600).
Open 10am-10pm Sat-Thur; 2-10pm Fri.
Credit AmEx, MC, V. **Map** p281 K2.

The place to go for cheap outdoor kit. A three-person Sundome tent costs Dhs199, an adult snorkelling kit will set you back Dhs99, and disposable barbecues cost Dhs10. There's also a huge range of outdoor game sets, like volleyball and badminton nets.

Al Hamur Marine & Sports Equipment

Opposite Jumeirah Centre mall, Beach Road, Jumeirah (344 4468). **Open** 8.30am-1pm, 4.30-9pm Thur-Sat; 8.30-11am, 4.30-9pm Fri.
Credit MC, V. **Map** p284 D9.

An excellent shop for underwater equipment. Wetsuits, diving kit, masks and fins are all here, alongside a good showing of fishing rods, some body boards and various beach balls.

Picnico

Al Bahr Marine, Beach Road, Jumeirah (394 1653).
Open 9am-9pm Sat-Thur; 4.30-9pm Fri. **Credit**
AmEx, MC, V. **Map** p284 D9.

Picnico specialises in camping equipment, with a decent range of tents, sleeping bags and barbecue sets. Rounding out the stock are handheld GPS systems, penknives and gadgets galore.

Souvenirs

See also p122 **Golden opportunities.**

Gifts Tent

Shops Nos.52 & 53, Block D, Karama market area (335 4416). **Open** 9am-10.30pm Sat-Thur; 4-10.30pm Fri. **Credit** AmEx, MC, V. **Map** p285 J7.

Perfect for picking up touristy knick-knacks: shisha, backgammon boards, pashminas (from Dhs10) and even cuddly, singing camels.

Gift World

Shop No.209, Block T, Karama market area (335 8097). **Open** 9am-10.30pm Sat-Thur; 4-10.30pm Fri. **Credit** AmEx, MC, V. **Map** p285 J7.

Gift World is a good place to buy embroidered bedspreads from India or thick Syrian table covers, plus silver trinkets and striking ornaments.

Arts & Entertainment

Festivals & Events

The lure of big money and grateful audiences keeps the stars coming.

In its efforts to become a world player in the tourist industry, Dubai has poured countless dirhams into a number of high-profile events designed to entice visitors. The majority of these spectacles take place on the sporting field, with both government and private sponsors – particularly Emirates Airlines – spending big to attract top-drawer stars. The most renowned event in the city's sporting calendar is the **Dubai World Cup**, which sees all horse-loving eyes turn to the Emirates for the world's richest race. The day itself epitomises the country's melting-pot mentality: be-hatted Western and Levantine expats teeter about in their finery, sipping champagne in the many bars

Concerted efforts: from opera to rock.

and eateries; serious Emirati racehorse owners in gold-trimmed dishdashes (ankle-length shirts) celebrate the return of their winning jockeys to the enclosure; and Sudanese, Indian and Yemeni race-goers cheer from the stands, ripping up their programmes into confetti to honour celebrity jockeys and victorious members of the Maktoum family.

Other star-drawing events include the **Dubai Duty Free Tennis Open**, which normally takes place in March and boasts Andre Agassi, Roger Federer and the Williams sisters among its illustrious alumni; the **Dubai Desert Golf Classic**, which has attracted the likes of Tiger Woods and Colin Montgomery; and the **Dubai Rugby Sevens**, part of the IRB World Sevens series.

When it comes to cultural events, Dubai lags a few steps behind. The (hopefully annual) **Desert Rock** festival brings bands of the calibre of The Darkness and Sepultura to town, attracting legions of metal fans, while the **Dubai International Jazz Festival** is a rather more sedate. Current highlight of the cultural calendar is the **Dubai International Film Festival** (*see p157* **Keeping it reel**), an orgy of quality celluloid and top celebrities.

If you're after a little tradition, the holy month of Ramadan, followed by the celebration of Eid Al Fitr, allows a glimpse of the real Arabia. For non-Muslim residents and tourists, Ramadan is only a dry-ish month nowadays, alcoholic drinks are served after sundown in most hotels and atmospheric Iftar (fast-breaking) tents offer a rare opportunity to share the evening with Emirati and other Arab hosts and guests. Dubai's Heritage Village and other traditional spots come into their own over the festive days at Eid, which is celebrated with fireworks, dancing, singing, huge platters of dates and other delicacies, and hour upon hour of shisha smoking.

Meanwhile, Dubai's 'ethnic majority', the Indian population, makes the most of **Diwali**, dressing up apartment blocks in bright lights and candles, and partying family-style in the streets and restaurants of subcontinental neighbourhoods such as Karama and Satwa.

And then there's Dubai's other religion: shopping. What other city in the world would dare, with a straight face, to put on a festival

Arts & Entertainment

Anyone for tennis? The **Dubai Duty Free Tennis Open**.

that's dedicated to conspicuous consumption? Nevertheless, it's a true success: the month-long extravaganza that is the **Dubai Shopping Festival** packs planes, hotels and malls with shoppers intent on hoovering up bargains.

The big events are crammed into the high season (October to May), although steps have been taken to attract visitors in the hot summer months, especially families from other Gulf states, with the **Dubai Summer Surprises** kids' festival. Here we've focused on the best annual events; many are dependent on the international sporting calendar or Ramadan, so precise dates tend to vary each year. Other one-off events featuring visiting bands, musicians and theatre companies take place in the winter months outside Ramadan – pick up a copy of *Time Out Dubai* each week for up-to-the-minute information.

Tickets are available from the venues listed below, or from the **Time Out ticketline** (800 4669, www.itptickets.com).

Spring

Dubai Duty Free Tennis Open
Dubai Tennis Stadium, Aviation Club, Garhoud Road (282 9166/316 6969/www.dubai tennischampionships.com). **Map** p281 K3. **Date** mid Feb-early Mar.

A fantastic opportunity to see the world's best players slamming it out in a laid-back atmosphere devoid of the queues, rain and soaring ticket prices typical of Wimbledon – tickets for the Dubai Open start from Dhs30. Regular members of the Aviation Club suddenly find themselves changing alongside the likes of Tim Henman and Andy Roddick, and players can often be spotted strolling through the Irish Village 'pub garden', which lays on champagne and strawberries for the occasion. In a switch from convention, the fortnight-long event begins with the $1 million ATP Men's Open before the ladies take over for the WTA Women's Open.

Dubai Desert Golf Classic
Emirates Golf Club, off Interchange 5, Sheikh Zayed Road (295 6440/www.dubaidesertclassic. com). **Map** p278 A5. **Date** early Mar.

Dubai's greening of the desert – the city has eight golf courses, and more are planned – attracts swingers from around the world. Come March each year, fans welcome the likes of Tiger Woods, Colin Montgomerie (who has his own eponymous course in Dubai) and three-times-winner Ernie Els for the four-day event, part of the European Professional Golf Association Tour; they compete for an impressive total of US$2.2 million. Tickets cost Dhs145 for a day pass, Dhs500 for a season ticket (concessions half-price). The event is held on the beautiful Majlis Course, belonging to the Emirates Golf Club, but there's talk of moving the event to one of the city's other courses.

Fun for little ones: **Dubai Summer Surprises**.

wedding reception in history. (For information on how to watch the horses being put through their paces at Nad Al Sheba, *see p77*.)

Summer

Dubai Summer Surprises
Various venues (www.mydsf.com).
Date early June-late Aug.
An effort to draw in the crowds over Dubai's stifling three months of summer, DSS (as it's known locally) features occasional bargains and an endless stream of children's entertainment, mainly taking place in the city's shopping malls. DSS is presided over by the slightly irksome Modhesh, a bright yellow cartoon character who appears in 'person' at various malls and in caricature on every street corner and roundabout. *See p149* **Dubai Summer Surprises**.

Autumn

Desert Challenge
Various venues (www.uaedesertchallenge.com).
Date Oct.
The second largest motorsport event in the Middle East, the UAE Marlboro Desert Challenge pits the world's finest endurance riders and cross-country drivers against each other. The last round of both the FIA Cup and FIM World Championship for Cross Country Rallies, the UAE Challenge is the final shakedown before January's Paris–Dakar Rally. While it's the cars that grab the headlines, there are separate categories for an assortment of trucks and bikes. The five-day drive begins with a prologue event and continues with four other stages, starting on the Corniche in Abu Dhabi and continuing across the remote deserts of Abu Dhabi and Dubai emirates, with bivouacs sited at Mizaira'a in the Liwa Oasis, on the edge of the Rub Al-Khali (Empty Quarter). Grab a spot at the finish (at the Dubai International Marine Club) and take in the awards ceremony, or head out to Liwa yourself to see determined motorheads tackle some of the world's biggest sand dunes.

Ramadan
Various venues. **Date** varies (early Oct 2005; mid Sept 2006).
During Ramadan, Muslims are required to fast from dawn until dusk – an imperative extended to non-Muslims in public areas of Dubai, apart from some screened-off cafés in hotels. Non-Muslim expats and visitors can, nowadays, quietly drink alcohol in many hotels in the evenings, although live or loud music remains a definite no-no. Be sure to make the most of the large, canvas Iftar tents that spring up around the city, where you can share the breaking of the fast every evening with Emirati and other Muslim hosts and their guests. (For further tips on how to behave, *see p250* **Attitude & etiquette**.) Many of the five-

Dubai Desert Rock
Dubai Country Club (333 1155/www.csmentertains. com). **Map** p278 C4. **Date** mid Mar.
This one-day mosh fest shakes Dubai to its hastily laid foundations every March, having brought about the unlikely pairing of the City of Gold with the shaggy world of heavy metal. The inaugural event in 2005 saw the Darkness, Sepultura and Machine Head thrill the city's surprisingly large contingent of rock fans, before the big day itself. This organisers CSM promise there are bigger things to come.

Dubai World Cup
Nad Al Sheba Racecourse, off the Dubai–Al Ain Road (332 2277/336 3666/www.dubaiworldcup. com/www.emiratesracing.com). **Map** p278 C4.
Date Mar.
The Dubai World Cup is famous as the richest horse race in the world: prize money in 2005 totalled US$15,250,000, with the seventh and most prestigious race netting the competitors a cool US$6 million. Over the years the meet has expanded to include a month-long 'Racing Carnival', taking in four racing evenings and plenty of social and fashion events, before the big day itself. This is when you'll see Dubai at its grandest: all facets of UAE society attend, in all manners of dress and levels of sobriety, and the atmosphere in the free stands can be pretty electric – never more so than when a member of Godolphin (which is the Royal Family's stable) romps home first, ridden by the much-loved celebrity jockey Frankie Dettori. The attached and licensed international village (tickets to enter start at Dhs150) resembles the largest

Arts & Entertainment

Dubai Shopping Festival

Only Dubai, with its recent, zealous conversion to consumerism in all its forms, could pull off dedicating an entire festival to the art of shopping. But pull it off it has: the month-long extravaganza (mid January to mid February) sees flights and hotels – not to mention shopping malls – packed with bargain-hunters.

Depending on your level of shopaholism, it's either a dream come true or the worst holiday imaginable. Some airlines even offer excess baggage allowance, two-seats-for-one and similar deals. Towards the end of the festival, the airport begins to resemble a warehouse, with shoppers struggling to check in box-loads of fridges, electronic goods and clothes – not to mention bags of frozen chickens and other bizarre must-haves. The most enthusiastic shoppers tend to hail from the former USSR, the Gulf states and India but, cynicism aside, there's something in it for everyone.

In recent years, some of the more upmarket boutiques have declined to join in, but most of the bigger shops have sales, some with discounts of up to 75 per cent. The malls lay on entertainment, kids' activities and more raffles than you can wave a credit card at. There's also a huge fun fair by the Creek, and firework displays every evening.

More bohemian shoppers will marvel at the scrum of bargain-seekers at **Global Village** – a vast, glorified, global souk featuring kitsch pavilions from 32 Middle Eastern, African and Asian countries. In 2004 the Village was on the Creek by Garhoud Bridge, at the site of the forthcoming Dubai Festival City, but in 2005 it moved to a permanent site off the Emirates Road and stayed open an extra month. Beware: take a taxi, limber up beforehand, sharpen your elbows and – especially in the evenings – prepare yourself to experience shopping hell. Over three million people now visit annually, many with sugar-pumped kids in tow.

But the crush is worth it. You can load up on gifts (for yourself or others) for years: from India there are chic chiffon coats and cheap summer pashminas; from Thailand, beautiful silk handbags; from Yemen, silver *khanjar* (traditional knives) and antique jewellery; from Palestine, top-quality olive oil and traditional crockery; from Iraq, Afghanistan and Iran, a massive selection of contrasting styles of low-priced carpets, plus an array of unusual antiques.

Throughout the month, the Heritage Village and museums lay on special activities, including an Arabian Bedouin Lifestyle Festival, and there are exhibitions, concerts and other shows (the listings in *Time Out Dubai* have the details), but these are merely a pretence that the event is about something more than snapping up suitcase-loads of bargains. If you can take the pace, it's all yours. See www.mydsf.com for further details.

star hotels really go to town, erecting tents with spectacular decorations, straight out of Arabian Nights, as well as lavish spreads of dates, sweets, meze and rows of gleaming shisha – try the Ritz-Carlton's Bedouin village, which comprises four types of tent (Moroccan, Iranian, Egyptian and Syrian). The sweet smell of fruit-flavoured shisha smoke pervades the air, and the click-clack of backgammon and chess games can be heard above the chatter. For many locals and visitors, Ramadan is a welcome taste of the old days.

Diwali

Various venues. **Date** mid Oct-mid Nov.
The 'Festival of Lights' – which is the Hindu equivalent of the Western New Year or Muslim Eid Al Fitr – is celebrated during the month of Ashwin, normally falling between mid October and mid November. The Indian population lays on colourful, noisy festivities that go on for around five days. The entrances to villas, restaurants and shops are decorated with Rangoli designs (symmetrical images that depict gods, goddesses, dancers and other figures) and candles to welcome Lakshmi, the goddess of wealth and prosperity, and drive away evil spirits. Come evening, children race down from blocks of flats to let off firecrackers, and communal firework parties take place all over town. If you don't manage to wangle an invitation to a party yourself, you're best off soaking up some of the cheerful atmosphere in one of Dubai's Indian neighbourhoods, preferably over a cheap-as-chips meal in one of the many curry houses in Karama or Satwa (*see pp90-91*).

Winter

Eid Al Fitr

Various venues. **Date** varies (early Nov 2005; mid Oct 2006).
The timing of Eid Al Fitr – 'Feast of the Breaking of the Fast' – is dependent on the date set for the conclusion of Ramadan (*see p144*): in 2005 the three-day Eid festival should fall at the beginning of November, in 2006 it will be around the middle of October. Taking advantage of what is the longest Muslim holiday, many Dubai residents head off on camping trips or go abroad, but staying in town is no bad thing. The end of the month of abstinence is celebrated in time-honoured Arabian style. Unless you are lucky enough to be invited to a family party by Emiratis or expat Arabs, it's best to celebrate at one of the restaurants along the Creek (such as Fatafeet; *see p84*) or at the Heritage & Diving Village (*see p66*), which has a shisha and meze café and Emirati restaurant. Each evening there will be a firework display that never seems to end, and Emiratis and other Muslims will get together to sing and dance to traditional bands. You'll also find stalls are set up to sell traditional food, including fresh oysters, and handicrafts. For Eid Al Adha, *see p147*.

Camel racing

Nad Al Sheba Camel Racetrack, off the Dubai–Al Ain Road (338 2324). **Map** p278 C4. **Date** early Nov-Apr.
The camel-racing and horse-racing seasons begin in early November and continue through to April. Whether it's the sport of kings or the ungainly efforts of the ships of the desert that grab you, the races attract all strata of UAE society and a fair number of visitors. Camel races tend to take place on Thursdays and Fridays, around 7am; you can watch training sessions most mornings around 10am (*see p74*). The season reaches its peak in March, with prize-races attended by the ruling Emirati families. Responding to increasing international criticism, the UAE government are now cracking down on the use of under-age jockeys. According to Emirati law, riders must be at least 15 years old and weigh over 45 kilograms. The law also specifies that all camel jockeys must have proof of age and have been issued with a medical certificate by the Camel Racing Federation. That said, there are concerns that the law is still being breached, with children as young as six employed by unscrupulous camel owners.

Horse racing

Nad Al Sheba Racecourse, off the Dubai–Al Ain Road (336 3666/www.nadalshebaclub.com/www. drc.co.ae). **Map** p278 C4. **Date** every Thur from 7pm Apr-early Nov (9pm during Ramadan).
Horse racing at the grand Nad Al Sheba track, featuring local and international steeds and their jockeys, takes place each week during winter, with races every half an hour. In accordance with Muslim beliefs, no betting is allowed, although various competitions offer cash prizes. Entrance to the Maktoum and Millennium stands is free; day membership, giving access to the clubhouse and Del Mar bar, costs Dhs60; those lucky enough to possess an owner's badge, hobnob with binocular-bearers in the more exclusive boxes and bars. For more details, *see p75*.

Dubai Rugby Sevens

Dubai Exiles Club, 6km (4 miles) east of Dubai on the Al Awir Road (321 0008/www.dubairugby7s. com). **Map** p281 K5. **Date** early Dec.
Recently granted International Rugby Board status, this annual World Sevens Series tournament features 16 international and huge numbers of local and regional teams, competing for a variety of trophies over three days. Rugby fans can enjoy watching their sporting idols in action, and then take in a local game featuring teams from around the Gulf. The event is much loved by residents and overseas visitors alike – some 20,000 people attended in 2005 – and Dubai (or its expat population at least) properly lets its hair down in the Rugby Village. The festivities culminate in Rugby Rock, which is a huge party with live bands, held on the final day. Tickets to the matches cost Dhs80 for a day pass, up to Dhs150 for a season ticket.

World Offshore Powerboat Championship & Lifestyles Festival

Dubai International Marine Club, Le Meridien Mina Seyahi Hotel, Al Sufouh Road, Jumeirah (399 4111). **Map** p278 A5. **Date** mid Dec.

The UIM Class I World Offshore Powerboat Championship races, to give them their full name, take place over two days in mid December. Top teams from around the world compete for a place on the podium. Sadly, as a spectator sport the racing leaves much to be desired – you can see some boats in the middle distance, with little or no clue as to who is winning. No matter: the Victory Team are local heroes and the racing is accompanied by a classy fashion and jazz festival.

Dubai International Film Festival

Various venues (www.dubaifilmfest.com). **Date** mid-late Dec.

A non-competitive festival, DIFF is a week-long celebration of quality film from around the world. Expect to see moderately left-field slices of Hollywood and the best Arabic and Indian cinema (*see p157* **Keeping it reel**).

Dubai Shopping Festival

Various venues (www.mydsf.com). **Date** mid Jan-mid Feb.

A month-long festival of bargain shopping, with various bits of entertainment thrown in *(see p145)*.

Dubai International Jazz Festival

Dubai Media City, off Sheikh Zayed Road (391 1196/www.chilloutproductions.com). **Map** p278 A5. **Date** Jan.

Who would've thought that a love affair between a Gulf state and that all-American music form, jazz, could be struck up so quickly? The first Dubai International Jazz Festival in January 2003 was a resounding success, which helped attract such world-class musicians as Stanley Gordon, Mike Stern and Bobby Durham to grace its stages in the following years. After the completion of the outdoor concerts (day pass Dhs150, 3-day pass Dhs295), jam sessions continue at hotel bars into the small hours. The festival lasts three days.

Eid Al Adha

Various venues. **Dates** vary (early Jan 2005 & 2006).

The Festival of the Sacrifice takes place on the tenth day of the Islamic month Dhul-Hijjah (the last month of the Islamic calendar). Although only the pilgrims in Mecca can participate fully, other Muslims all across the world join with them by also celebrating on the correct days. In Dubai there is a four-day holiday. Celebrations tend to be based in individual homes and are far less ostentatious than those that mark the Eid Al Fitr (*see p146*). No alcohol is served on the day that precedes Eid Al Adha.

Dubai World Cup. *See p144.*

Arts & Entertainment

Children

Aquatic games, beachside sports and theme parks galore.

As a winter holiday destination for those with young children, Dubai has a lot to offer. This family-oriented society, with safe beaches and an array of kids' clubs at the hotels, is an ideal option for parents in search of a worry-free getaway between October and May. Active youngsters will be in their element with scuba diving, sports parks and water sports all available. The summer months are a little more trying, as sky-rocketing temperatures and humidity force families into the often-maddening confines of the air-conditioned indoors. The government's **Summer Surprises** (*see p149*) programme attempts to wage war on heat-induced boredom with mall-based 'edutainment' but a seven-foot talking dinosaur doesn't really compensate for being stuck indoors for three months; those who can, tend to take their children and flee the country for more hospitable climes.

Children's City.
See p153.

The city's restaurants and cafés are generally child-friendly and most places, particularly those in hotels and malls, have children's menus. However, they are not always equipped with high chairs, so it's worth checking in advance. Streetside independent restaurants often come with 'family rooms' and are always welcoming regardless. Many Friday brunches (*see p97* **The brunch bunch**) are aimed at visiting families and come with clowns, face-painters and other child-pleasers. Particular family favourites are those at the **Dusit** (*see p52*) and **Le Meridien Dubai** (*see p48*). Pubs don't tend to be so child-friendly, so your best bet for an outing is to head for alfresco venues that also serve food such as **The Irish Village** (*see p111*) and **Barasti Bar** (*see p113*).

Dubai Museum and other heritage centres are not particularly child-oriented, but Dubai does boast a fantastic, dedicated **Children's City**, a vast construction in Creekside Park, billed as the world's fifth-largest 'infotainment' facility.

The town's older kids and teenagers are less well catered for, with Dubai's offerings limited to sports activities, arcade games centres and shopping – the clothes stores in Karama and Satwa are full of imitation designer gems for the teenage shopper (*see p136* **Market values**). For mid to late teens, there are occasional 'rain parties' and other non-alcoholic raves, as well as a few local bands that play in unlicensed venues. Sadly, these events are few and far between; see *Time Out Dubai* magazine for listings.

Dubai is an astonishingly safe city, where the sun and the traffic are the only potential pitfalls for parents. The importance of keeping kids covered up, sunscreened and away from the busy roads cannot be overstated at any time of year.

If you are planning a trip to Dubai, be sure to ask your hotel in advance about babysitting services and kids' clubs. If you're stuck for ideas during a holiday visit, need advice or are planning a longer stay, the local community group **ExpatWoman** (www.expatwoman.com) will be able to help. Another useful resource to check out is **Rent-A-Crib** (050 588 7917, www.angelfire.com/in4/rentacrib), which will hire out everything from children's car seats and cots to toys.

Exploring the city

Bastakia & the Creek

With kids in tow, Dubai's heat, hard edges and multi-lane roads can make urban exploring an unrelenting nightmare. There are, however, spots where you can leave the highways behind and take off on foot, interspersing your journey with brief taxi rides. An exploration of the **Creek**, with its abra stations and dhow wharfage, plus Children's City, makes an ideal half-day family wander.

While energy levels are high, you could begin at **Dubai Museum** (*see p64*) in Bastakia, Bur Dubai side. Some displays of artefacts can be a little boring for younger kids – although older ones might enjoy the traditional weaponry – but the mock souk, halfway through the museum, is spooky enough to grab the attention of wandering minds, and the pearl-diving display is also interesting. Entrance is a mere Dhs1 for children (under-fives free, adults Dhs3).

Further round on the Bur Dubai side is the **Heritage & Diving Village** (*see p66*) – particularly worth visiting in the winter evenings, when children can take donkey and camel rides, and watch traditional singing and dancing. The Heritage & Diving Village can be sleepy during the summer and some weekday evenings: phone in advance to check whether special activities are taking place.

Just a five-minute walk down to the Creek from the museum will take you to the **abra stations** – the kids will love packing on to the water taxis with Dubai's workers and chugging across to the Deira side (it only costs Dhs1 too), although little ones will need hanging on to, as there's not much protection. Abras can be hired for longer trips (around 30 minutes) up and down the Creek; this is a fun way to check out the Deira cityscape, Bastakia wind towers and all those dhows, each packed with goods bound for Iran. You have to haggle over the cost of the trip, but don't agree to pay more than Dhs50.

Teenagers will really enjoy the souks in Deira, but you may be better off catching the abra back again with any younger ones and heading upstream by (road) taxi to the lush, green Creekside Park and **Children's City** (*see p153*), an interactive centre that's aimed at five- to 15-year-olds. A couple of highlights here are the the giant open-backed computer and the larger-than-life internal phones.

If you push on further upstream, there's more entertainment. Just before Garhoud Bridge, you'll find **Wonderland Theme & Water Park** (*see p153*), a kids-oriented leisure centre that includes a 'Desert Extreme' skate park, funfair rides, karting, paintballing and Splashland, complete with nine water rides and several pools. It's good clean fun but – compared to Children's City – is definitely beginning to show its age.

Dubai Summer Surprises

Unashamedly uncool, Dubai Summer Surprises is nonetheless a godsend for parents desperate for a break from the rugrats while they shop or enjoy a coffee in peace.

Offering weeks of mall-oriented 'surprises' and a rather annoying mascot Modhesh ('surprise' in Arabic), a cuddly, bright yellow, punk-haired cartoon character, it's an idea singletons may scoff at, but step out of August's 40°C-plus temperatures into a chilled shopping mall, and you'll come across bevies of grateful adults who would otherwise be at a loss as to how to entertain the cooped-up kids.

DSS runs from the middle of June through to the end of August. Each week is themed, with activities, shows, competitions and giveaways taking place in malls and around the city,

organised by different government departments. Children can look forward to baking cakes, making sweets, creating various 'works of art', getting showered in petals and being crowned flower queen for the day, not to mention performing in an ice show and hunting for treasure. As a further incentive, many shops and malls feature sales or special discounts throughout the summer.

The programme changes each year, but you can expect Colour Surprises, featuring laser and light shows; the very popular Ice Surprises, with sporting events and a daily ice show; and Heritage Surprises, including falconry, mock Bedouin wedding ceremonies and other elaborate folkloric entertainment. For more information, go to www.mydsf.com.

Gloriously green **Al Safa Park**. *See p152.*

Jumeirah & Umm Suqeim

Jumeirah and its long strip of public and private beaches (*see p205* **City hotspots: parks and beaches**) is not just Dubai's best-heeled neighbourhood; its seaside lifestyle and residential, family-oriented atmosphere make it an ideal base for holidaying with children. Jumeirah's public beach can fill up quickly at weekends – good alternatives are heading up the coast to Wollongong or Umm Suqeim beaches, or paying the Dhs5 entrance fee to Jumeirah Beach Park, a green, shady area with showers and picnic tables (Saturdays are for women and children only).

Dubai Zoo (*see p69*), on Beach Road, is long overdue a transfer to more spacious grounds in the desert. For now, the animals tend to be crammed into small cages, which can make for unpleasant viewing. Still, it remains a popular distraction for some families. The various malls along the Beach Road – **Mercato** (*see p120*), **Palm Strip** (*see p120*), Town Centre and Beach Centre – all offer fast food, coffee bars and other refreshments, plus shopping and some games centres.

The more arty visitor might prefer to indulge in some painting at **Café Céramique** (*see p154*), where kids and adults can pick a ceramic bowl, plate, mug, piggy bank or other item, and paint and glaze it while enjoying a coffee, juice or bagel. Children can be left for a couple of hours if booked into a workshop, or there's a great terrace with sea views where you can while away the hours. Jumeirah is also home to the **Dubai International Arts Centre** (*see p154*), which has classes in everything from pottery to marble mosaics for children, teenagers and adults (classes need to be booked in advance).

Heading up the coast to **Umm Suqeim**, next to Dubai's most recognisable landmark, the Burj Al Arab, is **Wild Wadi** water park (*see p153*). With 23 rides, a wave pool, eateries and a shipwreck, this is a day's activity in itself – and the kids will no doubt pester you to return.

Outdoor fun

While those few notorious months of soaring temperatures see Dubai's residents dive desperately for air-conditioned environments, the sun-drenched city does offer excellent opportunities to get outdoors. Many an expat parent will tell you that their child's ability to play outside almost all year round is reason enough to relocate to Dubai. Adults can enjoy immaculate beach parks (*see p205* **City hotspots: parks and beaches**) and various water sports (*see pp190-201*), but there are plenty of activities for kids too.

Family fun at **Wild Wadi** water park. *See p153.*

Parks & play areas

Al Mamzar Park

Al Mamzar Creek, by the Sharjah border (296 6201).
Open 8am-11pm Sat-Wed; 8am-11.30pm Thur, Fri.
Admission Dhs5. **No credit cards. Map** p279 D1.
Looking out over a blue lagoon to the emirate of
Sharjah, this grassy park has three beaches and
plentiful barbecue areas, providing one of the most
entertaining places for children in the city. There
is also an impressive large wooden fort and an
amphitheatre that regularly lays on family shows.
On a Friday the park has a fantastically laid-back
atmosphere; the place fills up with Indian, Arab
and Emirati families enjoying their barbecues and
celebrating a day off by singing and playing drums.
Note that every Wednesday the park is open only
to women and children.

Al Safa Park

*Near Choithram supermarket, on Al Wasl Road,
Jumeirah (349 2111).* **Open** 8am-11.30pm daily.
Admission Dhs5. **No credit cards. Map** p280 G5.
Al Safa Park, a firm favourite with the prosperous,
Jumeirah crowd, has large stretches of grass that are
perfect for football or cricket, plus plenty of shady
trees to relax under. Weekends are often extremely
busy with barbecuers and sauntering couples, and
the amusingly bouncy tarmac path running around
the perimeter attracts pre- and post-work joggers
and powerwalkers in droves. The tiny boating lake,
miniature funfair (with a small Ferris wheel) and
play areas dotted about are perfect for children. The
slightly run-down but ludicrously cheap tennis
courts are handy for older kids, but you may have
to wait your turn before getting on to one. The park
is open to women and children only on Tuesdays.

Umm Suqeim Park

Near Jumeirah Beach Hotel, off Beach Road, Jumeirah (348 4554). **Open** 8am-10.30pm Sat-Wed; 8am-11pm Thur, Fri. **Admission** free. **No credit cards. Map** p278 B4.
Situated opposite the public beach, this modest and slightly tired-looking park has a reasonable array of educational apparatus for children and pleasant shaded gazebo areas for parents. It's ideal as an alternative to the beach.

Theme & water parks

Luna Park

Al Nasr Leisureland, Oud Metha (337 1234). **Open** 9am-10.30pm daily. **Admission** *Leisureland, incl Luna Park* Dhs10; Dhs5 concessions. **Credit** AmEx, DC, MC, V. **Map** p281 J3.
A permanent funfair, offering a range of rides that are suitable for four-year-olds and up, including bumper cars, go-karts and a rollercoaster. Further attractions in Leisureland include an ice rink and a giant outdoor pool with three-foot waves and a tiled 'beach', plus six slides and a water playground with water cannons (pool admission is an extra Dhs40 for adults and Dhs20 for children).

Wild Wadi

Next to Jumeirah Beach Hotel, Beach Road, Jumeirah (348 4444/www.wildwadi.com). **Open** *Winter* 11am-6pm daily. *Summer* phone for times. **Admission** Dhs120; Dhs100 concessions; free under-3s. **Credit** AmEx, DC, MC, V. **Map** p278 B4.
Dubai's Arabian-themed premier water park has 23 fun-filled rides for kids and adults. Wind your way in leisurely fashion round Whitewater Wadi, propel yourself up Summit Surge, then whoosh down the 33m-high (108ft) Jumeirah Sceirah (read 'scarer'). Plenty of lifeguards are on hand to make sure you and your rubber ring don't part company, but it's down to you to hold on to your shorts. Kids love the shipwreck with squirting cannons, and there are plenty of fast-food restaurants to feed them in afterwards. Parents, meanwhile, can take turns to chill out for the day in Breaker's Bay.

Wonderland Theme & Water Park

Creekside Park, near Garhoud Bridge, Garhoud (324 1222). **Open** *Theme Park* 2-10pm Sat-Wed; noon-11pm Thur, Fri. *Splashland* 10am-7pm daily. **Admission** Dhs75; Dhs55 concessions. *Splashland only* Dhs45; Dhs35 concessions. **Credit** AmEx, DC, MC, V. **Map** p281 K3.
Wonderland includes a theme park, Splashland and the Desert Extreme skate park, which has half-pipes, trick boxes, rail slides and ramps for BMXers, skateboarders and inline skaters (over-fives only); helmets are compulsory and all equipment can be hired. Besides Splashland, with its nine water rides and activity pools, there's a huge variety of indoor and outdoor rides, food outlets, paintballing, go-karting and, for the less adventurous, camel rides. Timings are liable to change, so phone to check.

Scuba diving & snorkelling

Al Boom Diving

Near the Iranian Hospital, Al Wasl Road, Satwa (342 2993). **Cost** *Bubblemaker course* Dhs250. *Seal course* Dhs1,000. *Junior Open Water course* Dhs1,700. **Credit** MC, V. **Map** p284 E9.
Al Boom runs the PADI Bubblemaker courses (a 60- to 90-minute basic introduction to diving for over-eights), PADI Seal courses (basic principles for over-eights, taught over 12 hours) and PADI Junior Open Water courses (for kids ten years and over, 30 hours) in two fully equipped classrooms and a swimming pool.

Scuba Arabia

Le Meridien Mina Seyahi Hotel, Al Sufouh Road, Jumeirah (399 3333/2278). **Cost** *Seal course* Dhs800. *Junior Open Water course* Dhs1,700. **Credit** AmEx, DC, MC, V. **Map** p278 A5.
Eight- to ten-year-olds can become PADI Seal team members and discover the thrill of under-water diving in the safety of the Club Mina hotel pool. Over-tens are able to move on to the Open Water course; they must be accompanied by an adult to do so, but it earns them a certificate that will allow them to dive anywhere in the world.

Indoor fun

Activity centres

Children's City

Creekside Park, entrance on Riyadh Road (334 0808). **Open** 9am-9.30pm Sat-Thur; 4-9.30pm Fri. **Admission** Dhs15; Dhs40 family; Dhs10 concessions. **Credit** AmEx, MC, V. **Map** p281 K3.
Children's City is a huge Duplo-style centre in Creekside Park, a brightly coloured blocky building that boasts myriad educational zones, designed to stimulate the curiosity of toddlers and teenagers alike. These 'edutainment' zones include the Toddler area, Discovery Space section, Physical Science zone, Computer & Communication Gallery, The Way We Live area and Nature Centre. There are also culture blocks dedicated to the history of the UAE, with profiles of Arab intellectuals, and a planetarium and amphitheatre. The displays are imaginative, interactive and highly entertaining (our favourite is a giant computer with rideable mouse). The centre also has a Malik Burger joint for refreshments, a library and an early-learning shop.

Encounter Zone

Level 3, Wafi City mall, Oud Metha Road (324 7747/ ezone@emirates.net.ae). **Open** 10am-10pm Sat-Tue; 10am-11pm Wed, Thur; 1-10pm Fri. **Admission** *Galactica* Dhs25/hr. *LunarLand* Dhs20/hr. *All zones* Dhs45/day. **Credit** DC, MC, V. **Map** p281 J3.
Encounter Zone has two parts: LunarLand, for the under-eights, has a Snow Capsule, Komet roller-coaster, and the slides and tunnels of Skylab; for

Arts & Entertainment

over-eights there is Galactica, with network games, an indoor skate park, a chamber of horrors house, an anti-gravity racing simulator, a 3-D cinema and the mentally challenging Crystal Maze, with its medieval, future and ocean zones. Kids can be left here under the drop 'n' shop deal; enquire about other packages.

Fun City

Oasis Centre mall, Sheikh Zayed Road (339 1302). **Open** 10am-10pm Sat-Thur; 2-11pm Fri. **Admission** free. *Rides & games* Dhs2 each. **Credit** AmEx, DC, MC, V. **Map** p278 B4.
Fun City has a lot to offer children of all ages. The area for under-fives ('Fun and Learn') has several make-believe areas, including a kitchen, a library, a fair, an art studio and a shop. Slightly older children can enjoy a good-sized two-tier soft-play maze (at the Oasis and Mercato branches), a substantial bouncy castle, and a smallish area for bumper cars.
Other locations: Mercato mall, Jumeirah (349 9976); BurJuman Centre mall, Bur Dubai (359 3336).

Magic Planet

City Centre mall, Beach Road, Jumeirah (295 4333). **Open** 10am-midnight daily. **Admission** free. *Rides & games* from Dhs2 each; unlimited-ride wristband Dhs50. **Credit** AmEx, DC, MC, V. **Map** p281 K2.
Whizzing and whirring, Magic Planet is possibly the noisiest of Dubai's indoor play areas. It boasts dozens of arcade games and fairground rides (including a Ferris wheel, a traditional carousel, bumper cars and a little City Train, which snakes its way through the 'planet'), as well as sand art and pinball stations, so you'll have a tough time tearing kids away. The easily accessible food court allows you to watch over your children in the

big soft-play cage, but the place is, in general, unsupervised, so don't expect any babysitting service. There's also a ten-pin bowling centre.

Toby's

Level 3 Food Court, BurJuman Centre, Trade Centre Road, Bur Dubai (355 2868). **Open** 10.30am-10pm Sat-Tue; 10.30am-11pm Wed, Thur; 2-10.30pm Fri. **Admission** Dhs15-Dhs25/2hrs. **No credit cards.** **Map** p283 J5.
Here under-fours get to romp in their own ball pit and soft-play area, while bigger kids can frolic in a larger zone of slides, punch bags, space hoppers and swinging inflatables. There's a cafeteria, where parents and minders can sit and keep an eye on the tinies, and a mall and food court just outside if they prefer to leave over-fours in the capable hands of Toby's staff – the play pit is gate-controlled, so there's no chance of any escapees.

Arts & crafts centres

Café Céramique

Town Centre mall, Beach Road, Jumeirah (344 7331). **Open** 8am-midnight daily. **Admission** *Studio fee* Dhs25; Dhs15 concessions. **Credit** AmEx, DC, MC, V. **Map** p286 C12.
This is indeed a café, but the name is a hint as to its raison d'être. Customers here, whether adults or children, are encouraged to select an unpainted item of ceramic crockery and let their creativity run wild on the decorations.

Crafters Home

Shop No.M-59, mezzanine floor, Mazaya Centre mall, Sheikh Zayed Road (343 3045). **Open** 9am-9pm Sat-Thur; 4.30-9pm Fri. **Admission** *Studio fee* Dhs25; Dhs15 concessions. **Credit** MC, V. **Map** p287 E14.
This in-shop studio enables you can satisfy your artistic desires using various materials and not-as-hard-as-they-look techniques.

Dubai International Arts Centre

Beach Road (turn right towards the sea opposite Commercial Bank of Dubai), Jumeirah (344 4398). **Open** 8.30am-6.30pm Sat-Wed; 8.30am-3.30pm Thur. **Admission** *School holidays* Dhs75-Dhs150 per workshop. *Term-time* phone for membership details. **Credit** AmEx, DC, MC, V. **Map** p284 D9.
Dubai's only arts centre has a well-deserved reputation for recruiting friendly, professional teachers. Hands-on classes here include mixed media, ceramics, photography, silk painting, dress-making and calligraphy.

Jam Jar

Umm Hurair Road, near Lamcy Plaza, Bur Dubai (334 8706). **Open** 10am-10pm Sat-Thur; 2-10pm Fri. **Credit** MC, V. **Map** p281 J3.
A hands-on arts studio, the Jam Jar helps visitors to create their own art masterpieces. All the materials and some helpful advice are on hand at this splattery funhouse.

Easel does it at the **Jam Jar**.

Learn by art

In recent years Dubai has seen a new wave of child-friendly craft workshops open their doors to the city's young – and young at heart. The concept is simple: gather together art utensils and materials (usually attached to a coffee shop) and, for a flat rate plus the price of materials, patrons are free to indulge their inner Picasso.

The first of these arty-crafty places was **Café Céramique** (*see p154*). It is also the most successful, and remains a perfect way to while away a few hours getting messy with your paintbox. Select an unpainted item of ceramic crockery from the hundreds on display and decorate it with your own designs. Staff then glaze and fire your handiwork, which is ready for collection a couple of days later. There is a great winter terrace with sea views, plus a programme of kids' workshops and activities. Studio fees are Dhs25 for adults and Dhs15 for children; items start at Dhs10. The studio fee is halved on weekday mornings.

Brush & Bisque-It (285 5444), in Jumeirah Plaza, follows Café Céramique's blueprint to the letter. Pay Dhs20 plus the cost of the item (from Dhs15 to Dhs500) and receive plain pieces of crockery and all the artist's materials you can shake an acrylic-laden brush at to create your own mugs, plates and dishes. There's no time limit to your visit and the store, a blindingly brightly coloured affair, is open until 10pm seven days a week, giving you plenty of time to finish your design.

The newest DIY art space on the block is the excellent **Jam Jar** (*see p154*), a small, open, warehouse-like location, littered with easels and dressed with paintings suspended from the high ceiling. A three-hour session, inclusive of all supplies, is priced at Dhs170. First you choose a canvas, ranging from the sweetly small to the wall-hoggingly mammoth. You then help yourself to the giant tomato ketchup-style dispensers, filled to the brim with globules of richly coloured acrylic paints. Finally, you pick out your tool of choice from an array of sponges and bristling brushes. Once you're happy with your masterwork, it's time to take it home and display it in the living room. The Jam Jar also regularly holds exhibitions.

Finally, **Crafters Home** (*see p154*) is an exhaustively stocked in-shop studio where you can create your own designs on ceramic, wood, plastic and other materials. Get artistic with all sorts of folk art, including sand art, jewellery-making, foam flower art, vegetable carving, parchment craft and bead-weaving. The cost of individual items is not included in the Dhs25 (Dhs15 children) studio fee.

Arts & Entertainment

Film & Theatre

New venues and a dedicated festival of film are signs of what's to come, but for now Dubai is still all about the mainstream.

Film

The cinema scene in Dubai sits very firmly in the mainstream. The city is awash with multiplexes – there's one in pretty much every decent-sized mall – and all are dominated by the latest Hollywood or Bollywood blockbusters and action flicks, films that go straight to video anywhere else in the world (Jean-Claude Van Damme could make a claim to be the Emirates' favourite actor). Despite efforts to generate home-grown talent and the success of the first Dubai International Film Festival (*see p157* **Keeping it reel**) there's no art house scene to speak of. Private clubs host the occasional screening (see *Time Out Dubai* magazine for details) but indie fare rarely makes it into the multiplexes. Alfresco screenings are becoming increasingly popular, though, and many hotels erect screens in their grounds for evening showings. Due to its large Indian population, Dubai has a booming Bollywood scene, and many smaller, older cinemas are dedicated to the very latest Hindi, Malayalam and Tamil films; these too rarely make into the multiplexes. Films are screened mere days after their home debut and often sell out, particularly on a Thursday night.

LOCATION, LOCATION, LOCATION

Dubai is striving to establish itself as a major location destination for international film shoots and offers attractive tax breaks and incentives to lure in the crews. Bollywood has been particularly well courted, and Indian film stars can often be spotted holidaying at the top-notch hotels, eating in the new Indian-fusion restaurants and partying at some of the trendier clubs. Some even find time to shoot a film or two. Hollywood, it seems, is following suit. The George Clooney/Matt Damon vehicle *Syriana* shot scenes in the Emirates and the Nickelson Entertainment/Mirage Group have announced plans to build a state-of-the-art 170-acre (30ha) studio. It will have the world's largest soundstage, at 100,000 square feet (9,300 square metres), and 500,000 square feet (46,500-square metres) of off-lot water tank. The local government intends to exploit this trend fully and is planning a dedicated site for film studios, dubbed (in typical Dubai style) 'Film City'.

CENSORSHIP

The government censors – currently two employees of the Ministry of Information and Culture – have gradually eased regulations over the years, but sex scenes are usually cut, as is any overtly religious content. On occasion the reasons for cuts are somewhat opaque – for example, Morgan Freeman's part as God in the 2003 Jim Carrey film *Bruce Almighty* was entirely cut, making a nonsense of storyline, yet *The Passion of the Christ* was shown in its entirety.

When it comes to politics, as in many other Arab countries, any recognition of Israel is a definite no-no – in fact the word itself can be beeped out, as in the 2001 Robert Redford/Brad Pitt vehicle *Spy Game* – and censors have also been known to chop anything sensitive regarding the Arab world and

George Clooney, on location here in 2005.

Keeping it reel

The huge success of the inaugural **Dubai International Film Festival** (www.dubaifilmfest.com) in December 2004 shocked pretty much everyone. Although it is undoubtedly bolstered by the presence of Hollywood stars such as Morgan Freeman and Orlando Bloom, celebrity-spotting came well behind film-watching as cinema-starved Dubaians filled up on quality celluloid. A non-competitive event, the festival showcased 76 films in venues across the city, including a giant outdoor screen at Dubai Media City and the Madinat Jumeirah, which acted as the festival's base. Split into nine categories, screenings included regional films, breakout

European and Asian art house, and some thought-provoking offerings from both Bollywood and Hollywood. A smattering of directors and stars were in attendance to host lively Q&A sessions, the most interesting of which came courtesy of the makers of Al-Jazeera doc *Control Room*. Mark Achbar, director of *The Corporation*, was also excellent, and showed unlimited patience when dealing with such inane enquiries as 'Why aren't you funny, like Michael Moore?' With the festival scheduled to run at the Madinat Jumeirah for a week each December, the promise of more films and directorial interaction sessions is bringing hope to the city's frustrated cinephiles.

its leaders. Violence and bad language, however, are rarely censored and many films pass without any cuts nowadays.

Censors claim that they are gradually adapting their rules to suit the times. Quizzed as to its motives, the Ministry insists it is merely following the wishes of the Emirati population at large and that, after all, Dubai's ruling sheikhs and their governments have a paternal duty to 'protect' the people and their traditions.

PIRACY
Piracy is a huge problem in Dubai as many frustrated cinephiles, whether they are anti-censorship or simply after a wider selection of movies, turn to Dubai's cut-price DVD market. The souks are buried in illegal copies of DVDs and VCDs, and many offices and flats

are served surreptitiously by hawkers carrying holdalls stuffed with knock-off films. The government and the Arabian Antipiracy Alliance (AAA) are attempting to crack down on the problem with police raids, but so far to limited effect.

LOCAL TALENT
Home-grown cinema in the UAE has been making steps forward in recent times. Emirati students began making short videos about their lives and experiences in the late 1990s; they now compete for prizes in Abu Dhabi's Emirates Film Competition every March, and some have managed to make it to international film festivals.

These young filmmakers, particularly women, have produced some bold shorts about the massive changes that have taken

Arts & Entertainment

place in Emirati society over the past 40 years. Some documentaries and fictional tales tackle taboo subjects, such as contact between young, unmarried men and women; *wasta*, the local system of using influence to gain favours; and incidents of poverty among Emiratis. Given their determination, and the influence of a few passionate local film buffs, the UAE could produce the first generation of filmmakers from the Gulf.

CINEMAS

Dubai's multiplexes are mostly located in malls; they are served by just a handful of distributors, so they tend to show a similar selection of Hollywood and some other English-language films. Due the Thursday/Friday weekend, new films are released on a Wednesday evening rather than the traditional Friday in Europe. This means the UAE is often the first country to screen summer blockbusters: films such as *Star Wars Episode III: Revenge of the Sith* and the final part of the *Lord of the Rings* trilogy both made their debut in Dubai before the rest of the world. The films are subtitled (none are dubbed) in Arabic and – if the

reel is imported from Lebanon – French as well. Occasionally unsubtitled films appear from Egypt's commercial studios, or a Hindi blockbuster crops up with Arabic, not English, subtitles and nonetheless gets its big-screen airing in the multiplexes. Smaller cinemas around town tend to show a mix of Hindi, Malayalam and Tamil films.

Films open on a Wednesday, often with a midnight showing for bankable titles. More unusual films and non-US English-language films can make it on to the distributor's schedule at any time, with some even appearing months after the DVD release. Late-night showings on Thursdays and Fridays are popular, especially with Emirati males, but you'll rarely need to book a seat for daytime and weeknight screenings. As we went to press, the region's first IMAX cinema was set to open in late 2005 as part of the 20-screen **Grand Megaplex** in the Ibn Battuta mall. All cinemas run air-con, sometimes to quite frosty temperatures, so take a long-sleeved shirt or cardigan. Be warned: Emiratis tend to see cinemas as a social activity and not as a place of quiet absorption. Screenings often suffer from whole rows of chatterers and, despite attempts to create mobile-free theatres, it's also not uncommon to be disturbed by a young man or woman with a penchant for text messages or even full-blown phone conversation mid-film.

Time Out Dubai magazine lists and reviews the month's screenings, but distributors and cinemas can change the programme with little warning, so it's always best to phone to check in advance. If taking children with you, do also check with the cinema for the rating that has been assigned to the film – G (General), PG (Parental Guidance), 15 (aged 15 and above) and 18 (18 and over); while the UAE uses a similar certificate system to the USA and UK, it sometimes gives the film a different category or age bracket.

Multiplexes

These all show a similar programme of English-language (mainly Hollywood) films, with a smattering of Egyptian and Hindi blockbusters.

Century Cinema
Mercato mall, Beach Road, Jumeirah (349 8765). **Tickets** Dhs30. **Screens** 7. **Credit** AmEx, DC, MC, V. **Map** p286 C12.

CineStar
Deira City Centre mall, Garhoud (294 9000). **Tickets** Dhs30. **Screens** 11. **Credit** AmEx, DC, MC, V. **Map** p281 K2.

Anorak of Fire at **Madinat Theatre**. See p161.

Grand CineCity
Above Spinneys supermarket, in Al Ghurair City mall, Al Rigga Road, Deira (228 9898). **Tickets** Dhs25-Dhs35. **Screens** 8. **Credit** AmEx, DC, MC, V. **Map** p283 K3.

Grand Cineplex
Next to Wafi City mall, Garhoud (324 2000). **Tickets** Dhs25-Dhs30. **Screens** 10. **Credit** AmEx, DC, MC, V. **Map** p281 J4.

Grand Megaplex
Ibn Battuta mall (366 9898). **Tickets** Dhs30. *IMAX* Dhs50. **Screens** 20 plus IMAX screen. **Credit** AmEx, DC, MC, V. **Map** p278 A5.

Metroplex Metropolitan Hotel
At Interchange 2, Sheikh Zayed Road (343 8383). **Tickets** Dhs25. **Screens** 8. **Credit** AmEx, DC, MC, V. **Map** p280 G5.

Local cinemas

The following independent cinemas show a mixed programme of Malayalam, Tamil and Hindi films, which are usually screened with Arabic subtitles rather than English.

Dubai Cinema
Near JW Marriott, Muraqqabat Street, Deira (266 0632). **Tickets** Dhs15-Dhs20. **Screens** 1 (Hindi films). **No** credit cards. **Map** p281 K1.

Galleria Cinema Hyatt Regency
Al Khaleej Road, Deira (273 7676). **Tickets** Dhs20. **Screens** 2 (Malayalam & Tamil films). **No** credit cards. **Map** p279 J1.

Lamcy Cinema
Next to Lamcy Plaza mall, Oud Metha (336 8808). **Tickets** Dhs20. **Screens** 2 (Hindi films). **No** credit cards. **Map** p281 J3.

Al Nasr Cinema
Near Al Nasr Leisureland, Oud Metha (337 4353). **Tickets** Dhs15-20. **Screens** 1 (Malayalam & Tamil films). **No** credit cards. **Map** p281 J3.

Plaza Cinema
Opposite Bur Dubai taxi stand, Al Ghubabai Road (393 9966). **Tickets** Dhs15-Dhs20. **Screens** 1 (Hindi, Malayalam & Tamil films). **No** credit cards. **Map** p282 G4.

Theatre

After so many years without a playhouse, Dubai gave an especially warm welcome to the **Madinat Theatre** when it opened in the Souk Madinat Jumeirah complex in 2004. Since then, the venue has been a shot in the arm for the city's commercial arts, having staged touring versions of *Art, The Woman in Black* and *Anorak of Fire*, as well as performances by the English National Ballet and the Band of HM Royal Marines. The venue seems set to be joined by a new **Dubai Community Theatre**, expected to open in September 2005, after years of fundraising, as part of the Mall of the Emirates. Once completed, it will cover more than 129,100 square feet (12,000 square metres) and be split into a 500-seat main theatre, a 150-seat studio theatre and rehearsal spaces.

The major importer of shows to the region is currently **Streetwise Fringe**, a company that specialises in English-language shows from the UK. The main Hindi theatre company, **Rangmanch**, recently set up an academy presided over by actor Kader Khan, but continues to organise its occasional mini theatre festivals, typically starring actors well known on the Indian theatre circuit. Details of performances by local amateur groups, such as the Chamber Orchestra, Big Band and Chorus, are listed each week in *Time Out Dubai* magazine.

OTHER PERFORMING ARTS
Public performances in Dubai of Emirati poetry, song and dance are mainly limited to ceremonial occasions and traditional displays at the **Heritage & Diving Village** (*see p66*). While the strong tradition of poetry and storytelling, sometimes set to music, is handed down from nights around the camp fire, many of the songs actually originated on the pearling dhows. In the face of brutally hard work, team spirits would be buoyed by the singing of sea shanties, led by a *naha'an* (professional song leader), with each song appropriate to the task at hand.

At Eid and other celebrations, you're also likely to see *ayyalah* performances, re-enactments of battles and hunting expeditions of (recently) bygone days, with groups of men beating sticks, and hurling swords or rifles high into the air. Dressed in the bright *abayas* (cloaks) of the desert, groups of women engage in separate *na'ashat* dances, swinging their long hair and swaying to music. Local bands are made of players of the *tubool* and *rahmani* (different drums), the *daf* (tambourine), and the *nai* and *mizmar* (wind instruments). As for expat dance, there are some ballet schools and a lively salsa scene, but performances of Western classical dance are very rare.

As for the city's classical music scene, it is still in its infancy: local musicians recently formed an orchestra and there are some enthusiastic amateur choirs, but the really dedicated travel to Abu Dhabi for international concerts, often held at the

Madinat Theatre.

Cultural Foundation (*see p217*). Check *Time Out Abu Dhabi* magazine each month for details of current performances.

Theatres

Madinat Theatre
Souk Madinat Jumeirah, Beach Road (366 6546/ www.madinatjumeirah.com). **Tickets** prices vary. **Credit** AmEx, DC, MC, V. **Map** p278 A4.
As we went to press, the Madinat Theatre was still Dubai's only playhouse, a luxurious 424-seat arena located in the Madinat Jumeirah. Reflecting its solitary position in the city's art world, the venue hosts a broad array of performances. These range from opera and ballet to improvised comedy and English-language theatre.

Theatre companies

Dubai Drama Group
333 1155/050 551 5407/www.dubaidramagroup.org.
Despite the city's lacklustre performing arts scene, this amateur, non-profit English-language theatre group lays claim to more than 100 members. From

highbrow plays to thigh-slapping pantomimes, the group puts on a decent number of performances of varying quality each year, usually staging them at the Dubai Country Club (Map p281 L5).

Rangmanch Theatre Company & Academy
Office 21, Block 13, Knowledge Village, near Interchange 4, Sheikh Zayed Road (391 3441/3442/ 366 4523/mail@rangmanch.net). **Map** p278 A5.
Rangmanch runs mini theatre festivals throughout the year, featuring theatre companies from India at various venues. All the plays are in Hindi. Actor Kader Khan's academy – the first theatre school in the Gulf – offers courses in all aspects of theatre, in both English and Hindi.

Streetwise Fringe Theatre
331 1111/050 652 6920/www.streetwisefringe.com.
Streetwise imports plays, musicals and one-man shows from the UK, including pre-London runs and hits from the Edinburgh Fringe. Streetwise productions often feature young, upcoming actors, and the monthly performances (October to May), which are usually held at the Madinat Theatre or the Crowne Plaza Hotel (*see p51*) on Sheikh Zayed Road, are generally of a high standard.

Galleries

A handful of impressive arthouses champion a scene that's still in its infancy.

Dubai is far from gaining renown as an artistic hotspot. Instead, the city is rightly famed as a consumer paradise that appeals more to sun-seekers than culture vultures. That said, there have been recent attempts to restore and preserve the traditional Arabian way of life that has been largely swept away in the rush to modernity, and to create opportunities for contemporary art, music and theatre to develop. The most visible example of this culturally minded approach is in the Bastakia area of Bur Dubai (*see p64* **Customs and exercise**). Not only did this wind-towered suburb survive the bulldozers of the 1980s, it is also now a protected heritage area and home to a clutch of galleries, the most rewarding of which is the **Majlis Gallery**; just round the corner from Majlis lie **Ostra** and **XVA**. As with all galleries in town, this arty triumvirate are commercial enterprises and serve half as art showcase and half as art showroom.

Away from Bastakia, Dubai has two serious commercial galleries: **Total Arts at The Courtyard**, on a fascinating 'street' within a warehouse in the industrial area of Al Quoz, and the **Green Art Gallery** in Jumeirah. The latter shows quality work by artists, mainly painters, from the Arab world in a charming villa setting, and is a must for collectors. Total Arts is a large gallery, set over two floors, which runs a programme that mixes conservative calligraphers, innovative tribal and contemporary artists from Iran and the Arab world, and rare Persian rugs, kilim and tribal weavings. Dariush Zandi, a photographer, architect and off-road specialist, built the quirky Courtyard housing Total Arts himself. It is intended as a paean to Soho in New York, and the gallery and adjoining 'street' are an aesthetically pleasing mishmash of European, local and North African architecture. Here you'll find a coffee shop, interiors gallery, photography studio and other arty outlets.

Other 'galleries' range from quality antiques, art and design outlets – such as **Hunar Gallery**, the **Creative Art Centre** and **Showcase Antiques** – to interiors shops (*see pp137-139*). Here we've listed the best contemporary galleries, plus some art and antique showrooms; for full weekly listings, pick up a copy of *Time Out Dubai* magazine. Local artists tend to congregate at the **Dubai International Arts Centre** in

Jumeirah (344 4398), while other practical centres for budding artists can be found in *Time Out Dubai*.

Perhaps spurred on by Sharjah's success in the contemporary arts field – its Biennial is well respected in the world of contemporary arts (*see p226*) – Dubai showing renewed interest, with public galleries, theatres, museums and opera houses now included in its grand development plans. But, for the moment, many local and international artists end up displaying work in hotel lobbies and shopping malls – no bad thing for busy visitors.

Still, members of the first generation of expats actually born in Dubai, now in their twenties and thirties, show a commitment to fostering local art and importing cutting-edge talent from across the Arab world, Iran and their diasporas. The **9714 Productions** crew (www.9714.com), for example, a mix of young Arab, Iranian and Emirati culturalists, stage excellent regular cultural nights in their **Five Green** clothes shop-cum-art space (*see p129*). Events can include exhibitions by local and international artists, photographers, architects, video screenings, live musicians or poetry readings, and are usually attended by enthusiastic audiences.

Contemporary art galleries

Green Art Gallery
Street 51, Villa 23, behind Dubai Zoo, Jumeirah (344 9888/www.gagallery.com). **Open** 9.30am-1.30pm, 4.30-8.30pm Sat-Thur. **Admission** free. **Map** p284 D10.
Housed in a typical Jumeirah villa, Green Art Gallery stocks a diverse selection of original paintings, limited edition prints, crafts and sculpture by established and upcoming contemporary artists from Lebanon, Syria, Iraq, Jordan and the rest of the Arab world. Regular solo and group exhibitions take place during the winter months.

Majlis Gallery
Al Fahidi roundabout, Bastakia, Bur Dubai (353 6233). **Open** 9.30am-1.30pm, 4.30-8pm Sat-Thur. **Admission** free. **Map** p282 H4.
Having opened in the late 1970s, the Majlis became a mainstay of the small commercial arts scene that emerged in Dubai in the 1990s. This old wind tower house has a delightful courtyard and its series of exhibition rooms stocks antique and new country-style furniture from India and

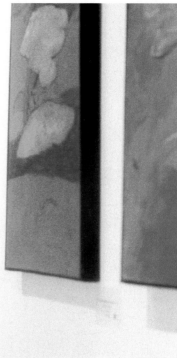

XVA.

the Gulf, plus Bedouin and contemporary jewellery and a range of ceramics and other interior accessories. In the winter months, there are regular shows by local and international artists, mainly watercolourists and designers.

Ostra

Behind Majlis Gallery, Al Fahidi roundabout, Bastakia, Bur Dubai (050 624 2070). **Open** 9.30am-8pm Sat-Thur. **Admission** free. **Credit** AmEx, DC, MC, V. **Map** p282 H4.

Specialising in high-end contemporary art and sculpture, Ostra occupies a small white space in a beautiful old Bastakian building. Run by an enthusiastic businessman with a good eye for unusual pieces, it's a small place (you could easily saunter round in 15 minutes), but full of thought-provoking work. Alongside the items for sale there are more novel installation works; some beautifully bound local books complete the collection.

Total Arts at The Courtyard

Off Sheikh Zayed Road, between Interchanges 3 & 4, just before Mercedes-Benz showroom, Al Quoz (228 2888/347 5050/www.courtyard-uae.com). **Open** 10am-1pm, 4-8pm Sat-Thur. **Admission** free. **Credit** AmEx, DC, MC, V. **Map** p278 B4.

At the end of a street of arty shops and businesses is the biggest gallery in Dubai. Through its atrium entrance are two floors of contemporary art, design and weavings. Like its owner and designer, Dariush Zandi, many of the artists hail from Iran – you're as likely to come across a huge show of rare, reasonably priced kilim and tribal weavings as you are traditional calligraphy or contemporary photography. Exhibitions frequently feature installations and contemporary work by local and international artists, plus occasional shows from renowned Iranian masters.

XVA

Behind Majlis Gallery, Al Fahidi roundabout, Bastakia, Bur Dubai (353 5383). **Open** 9.30am-8pm Sat-Thur. **Map** p282 H4.

Part hotel (*see p58*), part local residence and part art gallery, XVA pays tranquil homage to the sleepy old fishing village that was swallowed up by the modern city. The gallery exhibits modern art, contemporary jewellery and pretty outlandish fashion, while the central courtyard often houses ostentatious installations. The climb up on to the roof is rewarded with great views of the area's wind towers, minarets and winding streets.

The only traditional Russian cuisine and entertainment in Dubai

TROYKA SPECIALS

Majlis Gallery, the city's first and finest commercial art space. *See p162.*

Art & antiques showrooms

Creative Art Centre
Behind Choithram supermarket, Beach Road, Jumeirah (344 4394/www.arabian-arts.com). **Open** 8am-6pm Sat-Thur. **Admission** free. **Credit** MC, V. **Map** p286 C12.
These two villas display art, antiques, gifts and souvenirs. Collectors' items include chests, old Omani doors (made into coffee tables) and Bedouin silver, while gifts (from Dhs15) include freshwater pearls. Staff can assist with furniture restoration and interior design; there's also a framing service.

Four Seasons Ramesh Gallery
Ground floor, Al Zomorrodah Building, Zabeel Road, Karama (334 9090/www.fourseasonsgallery.com). **Open** 9am-9pm Sat-Thur; 5-9pm Fri. **Admission** free.
The gallery holds a large collection of historical images of the UAE by renowned photographer Ramesh Shukla, plus prints, paintings and interior design objects, from classical to contemporary.

Hunar Gallery
Street 49, Villa 6, Rashidiya (286 2224). **Open** 9am-1pm, 4-8pm Sat-Thur. **Admission** free. **Credit** MC, V. **Map** p279 E2.
Fine art from all corners of the world, including artistically decorated Japanese tiles and Belgian pewter and glass pieces, plus old Persian paintings and contemporary art.

Majlis Al Ghorfat Umm Al Sheif
Beach Road, past Dubai Zoo, Jumeirah 3 (394 6343). **Open** 8.30am-1.30pm, 3.30-8.30pm Sat-Thur; 3.30-8pm Fri. **Admission** Dhs1; free under-6s. **No credit cards. Map** p278 B4.
Built in 1955 as a summer residence for Sheikh Rashid Bin Saeed Al Maktoum, this atmospheric dwelling is now open to visitors. It's always very quiet here, giving you a chance to appreciate the peaceful, traditional *majlis* (meeting room), with its display of old coffee pots, carpets and other antique interior accessories. While you're here, do take the time to enjoy the palm tree garden, with its traditional *falaj* irrigation system.

Showcase Antiques, Art & Frames
Beach Road, off Interchange 3, Sheikh Zayed Road, Umm Suqeim (348 8797/www.showcaseantiques.net). **Open** 10am-1pm, 4-8pm Sat-Thur; 4-8pm Fri. **Admission** free. **Credit** AmEx, DC, MC, V. **Map** p278 B4.
Here you can count on a good display of antiques and art, including dowry chests, silver Bedouin jewellery, silver *khanjar* (knives), antique coffee pots and tables, plus furniture from Europe and the Near East. Upstairs is a selection of British antiques. The staff are knowledgeable and well worth quizzing for ideas.

Arts & Entertainment

Nightlife

Expecting tranquil Arabian nights? Think again. After dark, Dubai's clubs and pubs are booming.

MIX. *See p169.*

First-time visitors to Dubai are often shocked by the vibrancy and variety of Dubai's nightlife. Tourists expecting to find a chaste Muslim city find themselves in a hedonistic playground packed with all kinds of drinking establishments, each filled with an enthusiastic clientele. Things were not always so vibrant. In the 1980s visitors and expats were stuck with a smattering of British-style boozers and little else, but the 1990s saw the arrival of the Lebanese and with them the ostentatious revelry of Beirut. Cue swanky venues with stunning light and sound systems; over-dressed, over-coiffed clientele; and wall-to-wall house music. Other clubbing communities followed suit and these days, whether you're in the market for buckets of lager and cheesy disco or wallet-busting cocktails and roomfuls of wafer-thin Russians, there's a scene for every taste.

Most clubs open until 3am, but patrons push 'fashionably late' to the extreme – meaning places don't get going until 1am, leaving two hours of hardcore mayhem before bedtime. Dubai's clubbers are a notoriously fickle crowd

and one month's 'in' place is passé almost before the paint has dried. The result is a cynical, and cyclical, club scene where nightspots desperately try to out-hip each other with big-name DJs, outrageously expensive drinks and escalating levels of exclusivity – occasionally culminating in bars so elitist they have no customers. However, this one-upmanship has led to some truly stunning locations opening, from lavish clubs such as **Trilogy** (*see p175*) and **Kasbar** (*see p175*) to the popular-as-breathing **Peppermint Lounge** (*see p169*) at the Fairmont. Most of these upmarket joints enforce a strict dress code, so you won't be able to get away with trainers or scruffy garb, although jeans are usually permitted. In a bid for equality, this applies to both men and women.

Perhaps as a backlash against this cooler-than-thou ethos, there's a new generation of down-to-earth pubs opening their doors to hordes of pint-hungry punters. Places like **Waxy O'Conner's** (*see p174*), **Fibber Magee's** (*see p172*) and **The Lodge** (*see p173*) pull in the patrons with such delights as karaoke competitions, yards of ale and lightweight pop music, creating an almost Benidormian ambience. These venues will welcome you no matter what your get-up: trainers are pretty much the norm and shorts are fine during the daytime.

A Dubai weekend varies depending on which sector you work in: most local companies take Thursday and Friday off, while Westerners generally opt for Fridays and Saturdays. This means that Thursday is always the big night of the week, and for many party people Fridays are spent nursing hangovers in Dubai's variety of brunch spots (*see p97* **The brunch bunch**). However, unlike weekend-obsessed Europeans, Dubai drinkers will celebrate on pretty much any day ending in 'y' and there is something going on every night of the week. Tuesday night, for example, is a citywide ladies' night, when women can crawl their way to inebriation courtesy of free drinks promotions at most bars. The schedule of touring DJs also sees big-league beat merchants playing midweek.

Despite the stiff competition, drinking in Dubai is still an expensive business. By law, every alcoholic outlet has to be housed in a hotel or hold a special licence, usually only awarded to social clubs or large sporting grounds. This means paying top whack for pick-me-ups: you'll struggle to find a tipple below Dhs15, and in classier joints you'll pay up to Dhs30 for a bottle of beer; on average, expect to pay Dhs20 for beers, wine and spirits. When you chuck in taxi rides, admission prices and post-club munchies you're unlikely to get much change from Dhs200 for your night out. Despite being based in hotels, most venues have a separate entrance to keep well-oiled patrons away from guests. Entry is mostly free, except for in the very top hotels (such as the Burj), but drinkers are not entitled to use the leisure facilities (pools, health clubs and so on).

SCENE AND HEARD

Due to the extreme heat in summer and the lack of pedestrian-friendly areas, it was, until recently, almost impossible to orchestrate a decent pub-crawl in the city. The opening of the Madinat Jumeirah has changed this. Housing over 40 food and drink outlets under one roof, it has become the nightspot de rigueur for bar hoppers, most of whom end up at Trilogy, current king of the super-clubs. If you are commuting between pints, cabs are cheap and plentiful, although the rather erratic driving can prove troublesome if you're feeling a little the worse for wear. Should the

The best Venues

For a chilled one
The vast terrace at **The Irish Village** (*see p175*) is best for a tranquil pint. At the other end of the swank scale is **Sho Cho's** (*see p179*), a must-see shoreside setting.

For lowbrow delights
Groove to the pop classics of days gone by at **The Lodge** (*see p173*), **Jimmy Dix** (*see p169*) and **Zinc** (*see p169*).

For dedicated dancing
Gigantic **Trilogy** (*see p175*) is the current mainstay for those seeking house in all its guises, **Peppermint** (*see p169*) owns Friday night, and **MIX** (*see p169*) hosts international DJs at least once a month.

For outdoor schmoozing
The gorgeous **Rooftop** and classy **Koubba** (for both, *see 179*) will have you sipping on the ceiling; **Barasti** (*see p178*) boasts cracking views, a casual dress code and a lively atmosphere; **QD's** (*see p174*) has the Creek's best alfresco panorama.

inevitable happen, there is no clean-up charge, but Dubai's cabbies work long hours for little pay, and a decent tip goes a long way.

The Achilles heel of Dubai nightlife is live music. Although big-name acts do occasionally grace these shores (Destiny's Child, 50 Cent and The Darkness have all commanded sell-out audiences in recent times), they are too easily outweighed by legions of fading pop stars cashing in on Dubai's hunger for gigs – take a bow The Scorpions, Bryan Adams and Julio Iglesias.

There are currently two annual festivals in the city, drawing big acts from very different musical worlds. Each January the **Dubai International Jazz Festival** (*see p147*) attracts quality jazz and blues musicians from around the globe, with heavier emphasis on respected veterans than on household names. It draws a mighty crowd and is a precious highlight of the musical year. The **Dubai Desert Rock** festival (*see p144*) in March is a more populist affair, boasting The Darkness and Sepultura among its alumni.

The local scene is rather more depressing. Hotel bars are by and large clogged with bland, synth-heavy cover bands churning out soft-rock hits, while the city's handful of original groups are either too young or too inept to

Arts & Entertainment

secure a venue. The more down-at-heel bars in Bur Dubai and Deira have developed their own scene (*see p172* **Off the beaten track**), with a host of cracking Indian, African and Filipino bands banging out the hits. Although covers still rule, the delivery and reception is far more passionate than at most five-star bars, but you may find yourself in a room full of prostitutes (*see p181* **Sex and the city**).

Dubai's 'birds of a feather' mentality means that clubbing is almost entirely segregated in the city, with few hedonists venturing outside their own cultural clique. At its worst this 'stick to your own' policy translates into pure racism, disguised as a members-only policy. Certain bars, predominantly old-school pubs patronised by Western expats, will block the admittance of anyone they feel is 'unsuitable',

claiming you have to be a member to enter. While many bar licences do depend on operating such a system, if you are white you are likely to breeze through unhampered. Maddeningly, there is little that can be done short of boycotting such establishments, and arguing with the bouncer is liable to yield nothing more than laryngitis.

Regardless of your particular brand of hedonism, you're bound to find a scene that suits you. However, the fast pace of Dubaian clublife means venues close or rebrand at a moment's notice, beach parties spring up for the winter season before dying off in summer, and today's hot venue can be stone cold by tomorrow. To keep absolutely up to date, it's always worth picking up the latest copy of *Time Out Dubai* magazine.

Peppermint people getting Friday right. *See p169.*

Bur Dubai

DJ bars/clubs

Ginseng
Wafi Pyramids, at Wafi City mall, Oud Metha Road (324 8200). **Open** 7pm-1am Sat, Sun, Mon; 7pm-2am Tue-Fri. **Admission** free. **Credit** AmEx, DC, MC, V. **Map** p281 J3.
Ginseng is a cosy Asian-themed venue that can't quite work out whether it's a bar, a restaurant or a nightclub. There's a large array of fierce cocktails, and while the place is stylish it isn't as pretentious as many similar bars in the city. That said, entry is still very much dependent on your look and the company you keep, meaning that all-male posses will be politely moved along. Once inside, you're privy to one of the most eclectic record boxes in town, with chill-out mixes woven through the week. *See also p87.*

Jimmy Dix
Mövenpick Hotel, 19th Street, Bur Dubai (336 8800). **Open** 6pm-3am daily. **Admission** free. **Credit** AmEx, MC, V. **Map** p281 J3.
A meat market cast from the same no-frills mould as the Rock Bottom Café (*see below*), Jimmy Dix attracts an up-for-it throng out to drink themselves steadily into oblivion. The poorly-ventilated scarlet interior might give you the impression you've been trapped in the lung of a chain smoker, but the decent cover band and resident DJ can whip up an something approaching a storm with their airings of old-school pop, rock and lightweight dance music. Jimmy Dix is also worth a visit for one of their intermittently excellent Laughter Factory comedy nights, which happen once a month.

MIX
Grand Hyatt Hotel, Oud Metha Road (317 1234). **Open** 6pm-3am Sun-Fri. **Admission** free. **Credit** AmEx, MC, V. **Map** p281 K3.
A musical monolith, MIX is a three-tier clubbing complex that, until the equally monstrously proportioned Peppermint Lounge (*see below*) and Trilogy (*see p175*) arrived, possessed the Middle East's largest dancefloor. Music here varies from night to night, but the main room tends to err on the side of house, while the smart upstairs area specialises in R&B and commercial hip hop. The sheer size of MIX makes it hard to generate much of an atmosphere, but the high-calibre guest DJs (David Morales and John Digweed played here in 2004) can usually get the place jumping.

Peppermint Lounge
Barajeel Ballroom, Fairmont Hotel, Sheikh Zayed Road (050 552 2807). **Open** 10pm-3am Fri. **Admission** Dhs50. **Credit** AmEx, MC, V. **Map** p285 G9.
Arguably the most popular night out in Dubai, Peppermint Lounge should be easy to hate: a higher than average number of posers turn up sporting sunglasses, there are queues longer than a Dubai traffic jam, and the bouncers have all the charm of Secret Service interrogators. But once inside the plush Barajeel Ballroom, all pretensions seem to be left at the door. The glamorous, up-for-it crowd is goaded into a frenzy by the host of top house DJs, flown in specially for the evening, and the dancefloor fills up with people more interested in moving than seeing what their reflection looks like. A must-visit – if you can stick around long enough to get past the velvet rope.

Rock Bottom Café
Regent Palace Hotel, World Trade Centre Road (396 3888). **Open** 7am-3am daily. **Admission** free. **Credit** AmEx, DC, MC, V. **Map** p283 J5.
Although it's officially a bar and restaurant rather than a club, Rock Bottom only comes alive as other bars reach kicking-out time. Something of a cattle market, RB's pulls an impressive crowd with its proven blend of Bullfrogs (a highly potent cocktail utilising all the white spirits plus the magic of Red Bull), a resident DJ and a live band, pumping out the pleasers until closing time. There's even an in-house shoarma joint should your dancing bring on an attack of the munchies.

Tangerine
Fairmont Hotel, Sheikh Zayed Road (332 5555). **Open** 8pm-3am daily. **Admission** free. **Credit** AmEx, DC, MC, V. **Map** p285 G9.
Tangerine has forged itself quite a reputation among Dubai's capricious clubbing fraternity by hosting some red-hot house nights. The interior is lavishly decorated in low-lit, Arabian boho style and a hallowed VIP area lies behind the red rope stage left. As you would expect from somewhere styled to within an inch of its life, drinks can be a little on the pricey side.

Zinc
Crowne Plaza Dubai Hotel, Sheikh Zayed Road (331 1111). **Open** 7pm-3am daily. **Admission** free. **Credit** AmEx, DC, MC, V. **Map** p285 G10.
A popular venue with flight crew, Zinc has a large central bar, a separate dining area and a pretty decent in-house covers band. The decor is metallic chic, but the general atmosphere is more down-to-earth than in other venues along the Sheikh Zayed Road. An unabashed crowd-pleaser, Zinc's DJ supplies a soundtrack of mainstream chart hits, with occasional inoffensive dance tracks thrown in; the live band plays a set led by rhythm and blues numbers. The venue also hosts the great Laughter Factory night once a month.

Live music venues

Garden Rooftop
Wafi City mall, Oud Metha Road (324 7300). **Open** *Winter* 8pm-midnight Fri, Sun. **Admission** free. **Credit** AmEx, DC, MC, V. **Map** p281 J3.
Situated between two other bars – Carters (*see p110*) and Seville, both of them perfectly fine

Rack 'em up at **Aussie Legends**.

drinkeries in their own right – lies the Garden. It's a combination of fake rocks and real grass, with a sunken volleyball court, constructed in a sort of amphitheatre style, that doubles as a music venue. On Fridays throughout winter, this alfresco venue hosts Peanut Butter Jam, with a number of bands peddling their wares to a crowd that lounges on the luminous beanbags. The atmosphere is terrific, even if the bands vary in quality. If you're more of a cinephile than a music buff, the Rooftop also hosts Movies Under the Stars every Sunday – definitely worth looking into.

Pubs/bars

The Agency
Emirates Towers Hotel, Sheikh Zayed Road (330 0000). **Open** 12.30pm-1am daily. **Admission** free. **Credit** AmEx, DC, MC, V. **Map** p280 H4.
An upmarket city-style wine bar, the Agency attracts affluent, well-dressed and well-behaved thirtysomethings. The bar's chilled-out interior, a blend of dark wood and crimson velvet furniture, is perfect for intimate conversation. It's a crying shame, then, that the exterior is so uninspiring: sat on ideas-above-their-station patio furniture and flanked by potted plants, you gaze out on to... a fine pair of escalators. On the other hand, it does have one of the best wine lists going. *See also p110.*

Aussie Legends
Rydges Plaza Hotel, Satwa roundabout, Satwa (398 2222). **Open** 3pm-3am Sat-Wed, Fri; noon-3am Thur. **Admission** free. **Credit** AmEx, DC, MC, V. **Map** p284 F8.
Set on the ground floor of Rydges Plaza, the ever-popular Aussie Legends is, as the name implies, a 'down under' theme bar and grill with a small dancefloor and a well-used pool table. Antipodean tipples abound, including bottles of Crown lager and, when supplies allow, the joy that is Victoria Bitter. Any big-screen sporting action will draw impressively large crowds.

Blue Bar
Novotel, behind World Trade Centre, Sheikh Zayed Road (332 0000). **Open** noon-2am daily. **Admission** free. **Credit** AmEx, DC, MC, V. **Map** p285 G10.
The Blue Bar has carved itself a bit of a live music niche, thanks to its regular jazz night on Thursday. Located on the ground floor of the business-like Novotel, the Blue Bar combines fashionable decor, a chilled-out vibe and an unusually good selection of draught Belgian beers to potent effect. Regular nights see a bevy of TV screens churning out the usual MOR pop pap, meaning the place resembles the hotel bar that it is. But it's still a nice enough venue to enjoy some quality lager.

Arts & Entertainment

Chameleon & Vice

Wafi City (324 0000). **Open** 7pm-2am daily. **Admission** free. **Credit** AmEx, MC, V. **Map** p281 J3.
Taking its cue from some of the hippest hangouts across the globe, Chameleon attempts to blend beats with eats in a shimmering temple to design. For the most part it pulls it off. The food is decent, the range of cocktails exhaustive and the staff well-versed in the importance of offering stimulating conversation. But that isn't where the fun ends: upstairs you will find Vice, a thimble-tiny outlet offering sushi, champagne and vodka. While it has struggled to command the crowds on a Friday, Thursdays are hotting up very nicely indeed.

Fibber Magee's

Sheikh Zayed Road (332 2400). **Open** noon-1am daily. **Admission** free. **Credit** AmEx, MC, V. **Map** p285 F10.
Fibber McGee's is one of Dubai's rare independent boozers. Found behind the swanky, glass-fronted skyscrapers on Sheikh Zayed Road, Fibber is a half-hearted copy of a Dublin spit 'n' sawdust drinking den, complete with farm machinery and Guinness posters. As Irish as Tony Cascarino, it's still a good bet for hearty pub grub and a jar of the black stuff. A firm policy of showing big Premiership football games helps draw a loyal expat crowd.

Off the beaten track

Dubai's cultural diversity has given birth to a vibrant musical sub-scene, far removed from the swanky bars of the city's five-star hotels. Mostly based around the Rigga area of Deira and Bank Street in Bur Dubai, a clutch of Russian, African, Indian and Filipino clubs offer an alternative to Westernised hangouts. These bars are usually in three-star hotels and often provide a joyously unpretentious atmosphere, although their location can occasionally attract prostitutes (*see p181* **Sex and the city**). The bars recommended here operate a strict no-hookers door policy, but things do change so be wary. And (except where specified) expect to pay in cash.

Club Africana

Rush Inn Hotel, Kahlid Bin Al Waleed Road (Bank Street) (352 2235). **Open** 9pm-3am daily. **Map** p283 J5.
Housed deep within the confines of the Rush Inn Hotel, Club Africana is one of Dubai's best-kept secrets. The house band is a 12-strong Congolese collective who lay on free-form African rapping, harmonising and soliloquising to heart-stopping effect. Visit at 1am and the bar is invariably packed, a throbbing sinew of electrified energy. Alternatively, pop along at around 11pm for a couple of hours of laid-back ethnic tunes. It's like the Buena Vista Social Club, only African and in Dubai.

Maharlika's President Hotel

Trade Centre Road, Karama (334 6565). **Open** 6pm-3am daily. **Admission** free. **Credit** AmEx, DC, MC, V. **Map** p285 J6.
Maharlika's is one of Dubai's finest live music venues – presuming, that is, that your favourite tunes come from Filipino cover bands. While lots of venues offer this kind of thing, Maharlika's does it with unashamed style, drawing a huge crowd pretty much every night of the week. The bands change occasionally, but the theme remains the same: a six- or seven-piece Filipino band, heavy on the guitars, and lithe young women with lots of flailing hair. Expect to hear Led Zep's 'Stairway to Heaven', the Cranberries' 'Zombie' and some choice Guns N' Roses. Requests are most welcome.

Moulin Rouge

The Broadway Hotel, Deira (221 7111). **Open** 7pm-3am daily. **Map** p283 K3.
An unpolished diamond in Deira, the Rouge is a paean to multiculturism: where else in the world can you can sip Belgian lager in a Parisian-named, *EastEnders*-style nightclub, while scantily clad Slavs blast you with Arabic, French and English? The sheer insanity of the entertainment is staggering and, having seen a variety show of dancers, singers and mime artists, you'll be uttering more exaltations than an evangelist on Ecstasy.

Rasputin's

Al Khaleej Holiday Hotel (227 6565). **Open** 9pm-3am daily. **Map** p283 K3.
An expansive Russian club that really gets jumping in the smallest of hours. The house band clearly dine from a varied musical menu, with everything from traditional Turkish to old-school Arabic and soft-rock standards tickling their, and indeed our, fancy. In truth they're so staggeringly attractive they could be reciting the telephone directory with a voice like a bullfrog with tonsillitis and we would still be captivated.

Chameleon & Vice. *See p172.*

Harry Ghatto's

Tokyo @ the Towers, Emirates Towers Hotel, Sheikh Zayed Road (330 0000). **Open** 10pm-3am daily. **Admission** free. **Credit** AmEx, DC, MC, V. **Map** p280 H4.

Dubaians can be split into two camps: those who love karaoke and those who hate it, but secretly wish they were up on stage crooning 'Suspicious Minds'. If you have confronted your inner diva, then Harry Ghatto's is the best place in Dubai to belt out a few classics. Nestled in the back room of a sushi restaurant, it combines can't-swing-a-cat cosiness with a twin microphone set-up to inspire a brothers-in-song feel. Dutch courage comes courtesy of imported Japanese brews and sake but don't worry if you're still nervous: the staff are always on hand to show you how it's done.

The Lodge

Al Nasr Leisureland, near the American Hospital (336 9774). **Open** noon-3am daily. **Admission** free. **Credit** AmEx, DC, MC, V. **Map** p281 J3.

A cross between a British working men's club and a Costa del Sol slosh-pit, the Lodge is a legend among long-term expats. It's home to nine bars, two dancefloors and a massive outdoor arena, which sees up to 1,000 clubbers going mad for it during the winter months. The sheer size of the place can be daunting on an empty Monday night, but it's invariably stuffed to the gills on Thursdays. Drinkers range from tottering trolley dollies to hard-nosed alcoholics. But the atmosphere is more bleary-eyed happiness than football hooligans on

the piss, an ambience maintained by the Lodge's cunning fun formula: the provision of cheap drinks and crowd-friendly music.

Long's Bar

Towers Rotana Hotel, Sheikh Zayed Road (312 2202). **Open** noon-2.30am daily. **Admission** free. **Credit** AmEx, DC, MC, V. **Map** p280 H4.

The main claim to fame of this hotel basement bar is that it has the Middle East's longest bar counter. Unfortunately this also means that there's hardly any space for the punter to relax in, despite the separate restaurant area and small dancefloor. During daylight hours, the bar tends to be littered with elderly sun-shunners drawn to the big-screen televisions. In the evening, the average age drops to the early thirties as Sheikh Zayed Road's business types stop by to chew the fat while knocking back monkey nuts. The later hours see the arrival of far too many older Brits with their young Filipina girlfriends.

Scarlett's

Emirates Towers Hotel, Sheikh Zayed Road (330 0000). **Open** noon-3am daily. **Admission** free. **Credit** AmEx, DC, MC, V. **Map** p280 H4.

Scarlett's is a popular bar/restaurant/nightclub, with a Dixieland theme looser than Miss O'Hara herself. It has become a bit of a Dubai institution, with its young, mostly affluent and invariably well-dressed crowd investing serious time drinking and attempting to strike up conversation with members of the opposite sex. The ladies' night on a Tuesday is particularly popular.

Arts & Entertainment

Vintage

Vintage, Wafi Pyramids, Oud Metha Road (324 4100). **Open** 6pm-midnight Sat-Wed, Fri; 4pm-1am Thur. **Admission** free. **Credit** AmEx, DC, MC, V. **Map** p281 J3.

There's something about Vintage's chic interior and stupendous cellar that soothes the soul. The wine bar is constantly buzzing with sophisticated chatter and there's a good cheeseboard on hand to soak up the excess alcohol.

Vu's Bar

51st floor, Emirates Towers Hotel, Sheikh Zayed Road (330 0000). **Open** 7.30pm-1am daily. **Admission** free. **Credit** AmEx, DC, MC, V. **Map** p280 H4.

Laid-back elegance at premium prices has well-heeled conversationalists heading up to this swanky 51st-floor bar, where high-vaulted ceilings and impeccable good looks open on to one of the finest views in Dubai. Head up early on to watch the sun go down and the lights go up across the city. Make sure you wear a collar or the fashion police will throw you out. *See also p86.*

Waxy O'Conner's

Ascot Hotel, Kahlid Bin Al Waleed Road (Bank Street) (352 0900). **Open** noon-2am daily. **Admission** free. **Credit** AmEx, MC, V. **Map** p282 H5.

In no way affiliated to the popular UK chain, Waxy's is an Irish theme bar that has become popular with air stewardesses and determined old soaks. The reason for the sun-starved pint pit's success is simple: the proprietors have lined up a deluge of deals to entice in the budget-conscious boozer. The biggest bargain is the Friday funky brunch, at which Dhs50 will get you a full Irish breakfast, five drink tokens and a buffet carvery. However, connoisseurs of quality nourishment be warned: the food element plays second fiddle to the drinking, which means the place attracts the city's less salubrious old-school siphons. This lends itself to a rather charged atmosphere as the day wears on, but the craic is good early on.

Deira

DJ bars/clubs

Oxygen

Al Bustan Rotana Hotel, Casablanca Road, Garhoud (282 0000). **Open** 6pm-3am daily. **Admission** free. **Credit** AmEx, MC, V. **Map** p281 K2.

The only regular dance club on the city's east side, Oxygen hands over its sound system to touring DJs as well as a range of local talent. The club's original novelty factor – an air bar dishing out blasts of O_2 to out-of-breath clubbers – has long since fallen by the wayside, with the management now banking on drinks promotions and top DJs to pull in the punters. Despite being a relatively small venue, Oxygen has managed to attract some of the biggest names in dance – Danny Rampling and

Goldie have both manned the decks in recent years – but it struggles to find a crowd on regular nights. For the restaurant, *see p95.*

QD's

Dubai Creek Golf & Yacht Club, Garhoud Road (295 6000). **Open** 6pm-2am daily. **Admission** free. **Credit** AmEx, DC, MC, V. **Map** p281 K3.

QD's is definitely on the must-visit list during the winter months. A classy open-air affair in the grounds of a newly glossy Dubai Creek Golf & Yacht Club, this wood-decked bar offers superb views across the creek, a wood-burning pizza oven and all the shisha you can smoke. The regular DJ can be a bit hit and miss, but if you can block out his musical missteps, watching the sun crash down beyond the Creek with a cocktail in your hand is about as good as it gets. *See also p111.*

Live music venues

Up on the Tenth

InterContinental Dubai Hotel, Baniyas Road (205 7333). **Open** 6pm-3am daily. **Admission** free. **Credit** AmEx, DC, MC, V. **Map** p283 J3.

Up on the Tenth is a heart-warming (if wallet-straining) jazz bar, though the Manhattan-style decor looks increasingly dated. The in-house band is excellent and the views across the Creek are great, but somehow it's impossible to forget that you're in a somewhat sterile hotel bar rather than steamy downtown New Orleans.

Velvet Lounge

Al Khaleej Palace Hotel, Al Maktoum Road (223 1000). **Open** 6pm-3am daily. **Admission** free. **Credit** AmEx, DC, MC, V. **Map** p283 J3.

This swanky bar on the tenth floor of the Al Khaleej Hotel may be in an unfashionable part of town but the atmosphere is chilled and the music intriguing. Depending on which night you choose visit, you can expect to find a conventional guitar band, a new funk DJ or, if you're really lucky, a bearded hippy hunched over a turntable, squeezing out electronic yelps while a girl scrapes a melody out of a violin. A mile away from the current trend for generic 1980s-style, neon-lit bars, Velvet Lounge's low, seductive lighting and mix-'n'-match Arabic-style furniture gives the place an intimate air. Sadly, drinkers are reluctant to venture over the river, which can leave the place almost dead midweek.

Pubs/bars

Dubliners

Le Meridien Dubai Hotel, Airport Road, Garhoud (282 4040). **Open** noon-3am daily. **Admission** free. **Credit** AmEx, DC, MC, V. **Map** p281 L2.

An intimate Irish bar serving some of the best pub grub (and biggest pies) in town, the Dubliners is decorated with plenty of dark wood, Guinness posters and the back end of a truck, at the expense of windows. The drinkers are a friendly bunch

The Irish Village.

though and the place is packed during televised sporting events. There is an outdoor courtyard to cope with overspill, but it is not exactly attractive, comprising only a solitary tree that appears to have died from loneliness.

The Irish Village

Dubai Tennis Stadium, Garhoud Road (282 4750). **Open** 11am-1.30am daily. **Admission** free. **Credit** AmEx, DC, MC, V. **Map** p281 L3.

A Dubai institution, the Irish Village – or 'IV' as it's colloquially known – is situated along the exterior of Dubai Tennis Stadium and is frequently packed with residents and tourists alike. The major draw during winter months is a fantastic outside terrace that hugs a never-used micro golf course and a quaint duck pond, yet the vast assortment of draught beers available – including Old Country favourites Guinness and Kilkenny – keep people flooding in all year round. An absolute must. *See also p111.*

See also p111.

Jumeirah

DJ bars/clubs

Boudoir

Dubai Marine Beach Resort & Spa, Beach Road (345 5995). **Open** 7.30pm-3am daily. **Admission** free. **Credit** AmEx, DC, MC, V. **Map** p284 D8.

This swanky, wannabe Parisian club ranks as one of the most exclusive venues in the city. Boudoir attracts a predominantly Lebanese crowd, and if you want to get past the door staff you should be dressed to impress and preferably in a couple. There are different theme nights, ranging from R&B on Wednesdays to Eastern dance fusion on Fridays, but it's the lure of sparkling wine (aka free champagne) for women on Tuesdays that really gets the place jumping. *See also p101.*

Kasbar

One&Only Royal Mirage Hotel, Al Sufouh Road (399 9999). **Open** 7pm-3am Sat, Mon-Fri. **Admission** Dhs50. **Credit** AmEx, DC, MC, V. **Map** p278 A5.

Arranged on three huge levels, each decked out with authentic Moroccan decorations, the Kasbar is a super-chic nightclub for the super-rich. It has a full complement of private booths, a large dance-floor and a pool table in the basement. Opulence rules throughout, with Kasbar's prosperous patrons unlikely to be troubled by the staggering booze bills.

Trilogy

Souk Madinat Jumeirah, Jumeirah Beach Road (366 8888). **Open** 9pm-3am daily. **Credit** AmEx, MC, V. **Map** p278 A4.

Dubai's undisputed king of the nightclub scene, this three-floor monster is always full at the weekends. Trilogy manages to attract big-name DJs on

Arts & Entertainment

Business as usual,
But a stay that's truly special.

- Located in close proximity to the airport as well as commericial and shopping centres.
- A choice of speciality restaurants serving scrumptious food and beverage.
- 115 well-appointed deluxe rooms and suites with garden and airport views.
- Warm and friendly service to cater to your every need.

Tex Mex **International** **Pub Grub** *Da Vinci's* *The friendliest Italian in town*

MILLENNIUM AIRPORT HOTEL
DUBAI

el : +971 (0)4 282 3464 Fax: +971 (0)4 282 3781 E-mail: sales.airdxb@mill-cop.com Website: www.millenniumhotels

a regular basis, but the highlight here has to be the Rooftop bar, which offers a stunning view of the Persian Gulf and hosts intimate midweek nights and weekend VIP bashes. Be careful when you try to find it though: it's easy to get lost in the labyrinth of back rooms and dancefloors.

Live music venues

DMC Amphitheatre
Dubai Media City, off Interchange 5, Sheikh Zayed Road (391 4555). **Open** varies. **Admission** varies. **No credit cards. Map** p278 A5.
An expansive outdoor area set in the middle of the city's separate media enclosure, the Amphitheatre comes complete with real grass and its own lake. It hosts a number of one-off events – Destiny's Child, Mark Knopfler and Alicia Keys have all played here in recent times – and provides a home for the Dubai International Jazz Festival (*see p147*) each year.

JamBase
Souk Madinat Jumeirah (366 8888). **Open** 7pm-2am Sat, Mon-Fri. **Admission** free. **Credit** AmEx, DC, MC, V. **Map** p278 A4.
The best live music venue in this scene-starved city, JamBase prizes style as highly as substance. There's a strict door policy, the furniture is artfully angular and the decor is calculated art deco chic. Thankfully the place just about has the mouth to back up its immaculately cut trousers – the most vocal part being a mighty fine house band that's tighter than a shrink-wrapped Scotsman.

Malecon
Dubai Marine Beach Resort & Spa, Beach Road (346 1111). **Open** 7pm-3am daily. **Admission** free. **Credit** AmEx, DC, MC, V. **Map** p284 D8.
Malecon isn't related to its more famous overseas namesakes, but it's a funky salsa spot with a solid in-house Latino troupe. The blue messageboard

Trilogy. *See p175.*

walls have already been graffitied to the max. Malecon is a restaurant in the early evening, but the smaller hours see some serious action on the dancefloor as a regular collective of merengue maniacs cut some rug.

Pubs/bars

The Alamo
Dubai Marine Beach Resort & Spa, Beach Road (346 1111). **Open** noon-3am daily. **Admission** free. **Credit** AmEx, DC, MC, V. **Map** p284 D8.
The Alamo is everything Dubai used to be – and evidently, for some, still is. Popular for many years with middle-aged British male expats who still think they are in their local at home, the Alamo has some – Dubai-style – olde-worlde charm. The doorman is a vertically challenged Thai, dressed in American Civil War fatigues (the Alamo and all that). Things are only marginally less surreal once you get through the swing doors. Yet, in spite of the time-warp Tex-Mex feel, it's still possible to have a good night here. Drop by on a Friday for the ever-popular brunch deal.

Barasti
Le Meridien Mina Seyahi Hotel, Al Sufouh Road (399 3333). **Open** 8pm-2am daily. **Admission** free. **Credit** AmEx, DC, MC, V. **Map** p278 A5.

This is a cracking outdoor venue, perched on its own elevated platform above the Mina's private beach and extends around the hotel pool. As you'd expect, dress is reasonably casual, and the place remains the busiest spot uptown for sundowners. Besides the usual alcoholic treats, the bar does a nice line in shisha and offers the perfect setting to have a puff overlooking the sea. Despite being set in one of Dubai's most touristy locations, Barasti generates a cheery local ambience. *See also p101.*

Bar Zar
Souk Madinat Jumeirah (366 6348). **Open** 5pm-2am Sat-Wed; 5pm-3am Thur; noon-3am Fri. **Admission** free. **Credit** AmEx, DC, MC, V. **Map** p278 A4.
As chilled as an Arctic Rastafarian, Bar Zar's water-side terrace is one of the most popular drinking spots in the city. Set in the bustling Souk Madinat, the bar pulls in punters with a variety of drink deals and promotions. The place is huge, covering two floors indoors in addition to the patio. Big-screen TVs play a mix of muted MTV and sports events.

Boston Bar
Jumeirah Rotana Hotel, Al Diyafah Street (345 5888). **Open** noon-2am Sat, Tue, Fri; noon-3am Wed, Thur. **Admission** free. **Credit** AmEx, DC, MC, V. **Map** p284 F8.

Authorised alcohol

Having a detailed chapter on drinking options in the city may suggest otherwise, but Dubai is still strictly a Muslim state and as such alcohol is tolerated rather than celebrated. So here's the lowdown on legal drinking.

Bringing it in
It is perfectly permissible to bring alcohol into the UAE – in fact, once you're through passport control, the first thing you'll see is a Duty Free shop. At present you're limited to four items per person, so whether it's mother's ruin or a drop of firewater, choose wisely. *See also p252* **Customs**.

Buying it there
Residents can buy alcohol from one of the city's two alcohol suppliers MMI (209 5000) and a+e (222 2666) providing they have a valid licence. Only one licence is awarded per household, with a limit set dependent on salary. *See also p87* **Buying booze**.

The law demands that all bars be housed within hotels or private clubs, but often these links are tenuous to say the least, and most establishments will have their own entrances away from the hotel lobby. Although it is illegal

for drinking establishments to encourage Muslims to break their faith by serving them alcohol, don't be surprised to chance upon a local in national dress happily supping a pint; this is one law quite openly flouted.

Drunk and disorderly
Public displays of drunkenness are frowned on and there is zero tolerance when it comes to the city's strict under-age drinking and drink-driving countermeasures. You must be 21 to purchase or consume alcohol, and many bars will require photo ID before they serve baby-faced boozers. Drive with the faintest whiff of alcohol on your breath and you can expect to do some time in one of Dubai's far-from-friendly prisons, as well as having to pay a small fortune in punitive fines. (It is worth bearing this in mind the morning after a heavy night – stay off the road until the last traces are out of your system.)

Dubai isn't really geared up for punters walking from pub to pub, so opt instead for one of the city's inexpensive and omnipresent taxis, which will ferry you between as many cocktail lounges and gin joints as you wish.

Bar Zar. *See p178.*

Based on the bar in Cheers, the Boston is an unpretentious expat boozer that's typically full of Brits. It can get very lively if there's a football match on, and dancing on the bar, although heavily discouraged, does occasionally break out.

Koubba

Al Qasr, Madinat Jumeirah (366 8888) **Open** noon-2am daily. **Credit** AmEx, MC, V. **Map** p278 A4.
Perched on the swankiest corner of the Madinat Jumeirah, Koubba's jaw-flooring views across the Gulf alone are worth the trip. The ambience is less pints and pork scratchings than champagne cocktails and crudités, and the loungey soundtrack and smartly attired clientele reflect this. A great choice for a few leisurely drinks.

Left Bank

Souk Madinat Jumeirah (366 8888). **Open** noon-2am daily. **Credit** AmEx, MC, V. **Map** p278 A4.
Neon lighting, low seating and minimalist decor are the order of the day here. Left Bank's interior is doubtless a bit All Bar One for the scenesters, but the waterside terrace is surely worthy of a visit.

The Rooftop

Arabian Court, One&Only Royal Mirage Hotel, Al Sufouh Road (399 9999). **Open** 5.30pm-1am Sat, Mon-Fri. **Admission** free. **Credit** AmEx, DC, MC, V. **Map** p278 A5.
A sedate sipping station, the Rooftop remains one of the most magnificent drinking venues in the city. The views, which take in the serene Gulf and the maddening Palm Island, can't be beaten and the soundtrack of cryogenically chilled beats, with the odd classic tossed in to add spice to the mix, is perfectly judged. While you might experience an occasional onset of dancing, it's far more likely the crowd will be ogling the star-filled sky from the comfort of the Arabian-themed seating. Highly recommended.

Sho Cho's

Dubai Marine Beach Resort & Spa, Beach Road (346 1111). **Open** 7pm-3am daily. **Admission** free. **Credit** AmEx, DC, MC, V. **Map** p284 D8.
With a gorgeous terrace overlooking the Gulf and manga movies projected on to walls studded with fish tanks, Sho Cho is a super-hip Japanese bar

Dubai Creek
More than just golf...

The Boardwalk

O'ds

aQuarium restaurant

Lake View

The Academy

Legends STEAKHOUSE

by dg

with an animé twist. Sophisticated, classy and dead trendy, this is where the beautiful people go when they want to play, pose and look pretty: you won't see an ounce of spare body fat anywhere inside. The staff and clientele can be a little snobby, it's true, but with a setting this good you can just about forgive their coldness.

Sky View Bar

Burj Al Arab Hotel, Beach Road (301 7438). **Open** 11am-2am daily. **Admission** Dhs200 (redeemable against drinks & food). **Credit** AmEx, DC, MC, V. **Map** p278 A4.

Despite being housed in what is the world's most exclusive hotel, the Sky View Bar is a haven of tack. In fact, the interior looks more like a gaudy 1980s disco or a wobbly *Dr Who* set. But the panoramic vista is extraordinary, with the large windows affording you ample opportunity to gaze out across the Arabian Gulf, the neon-lit city or the expansive Palm Island. One word of warning about the drinks: they're every bit as expensive as you'd expect.

Trader Vic's

Crowne Plaza Hotel, Sheikh Zayed Road (331 1111). **Open** 7-11.30pm daily. **Admission** free. **Credit** AmEx, DC, MC, V. **Map** p285 G10.

An intriguingly odd-looking Mai Tai lounge, where a Polynesian band meets the most potent cocktails in the UAE and end up creating a magnificently carefree atmosphere. Seating is fairly limited and the bar is often crowded, so be sure to arrive early if you want to take the weight off your feet. You'll also then be able to make the most of the happy hours, during which prices drop from astronomical to merely expensive. *See also p92 and p113.* **Other locations**: Souk Madinat Jumeirah (366 5646).

Sex and the city

Somewhat surprisingly for a country that prides itself on its principled social structure, prostitution has become an increasingly open phenomenon in the UAE in recent years. No accurate statistics are available, but the most recent attempt at an official survey – a 'Country Report on Human Rights Practices' released by the US Department of State on 31 March 2003 – cites 'credible reports of trafficking in women to the country'. While the document states clearly that prostitution is strictly illegal in the UAE, it goes on to assert that 'substantial numbers of women [have] arrived from the states of the former Soviet Union, Africa, East Asia, Eastern Europe, and other states of the Middle East for temporary stays during which they engaged in prostitution and possibly other activities connected with organized crime.'

Visitors straying from the city's more glamorous nightspots will testify to this continuing influx: the problem is hard to ignore in certain districts, where a single man will soon find a scantily clad woman attaching herself to his arm, and where a single woman can expect to attract unwanted attention from expectant curb-crawlers no matter how she dresses. The lower end of the business culminates in a number of oriental and Eastern European girls looking for company in certain dingy Bur Dubai and Deira bars. A handful of establishments appear actively to encourage harlotry, charging admission on the door and occasionally assigning different floors to different 'types'. These are without exception very depressing places, where down-on-their luck hookers crowd the doorways desperate to catch a meal ticket come closing time.

While prostitution is acknowledged widely to exist, it is not a topic that receives critical attention in the local media. In April 2005, *Gulf News*, a Dubai-based daily newspaper, brought the case of Amali Wijiyatunga into the public domain. 'The Sri Lankan housemaid escaped from being forced into prostitution by jumping from an apartment,' ran the article. Wheelchair bound, she was left stranded in the hospital for weeks while her repatriation claim was processed. Despite occasional articles like this, the US Department of State report maintains that the UAE government does not officially address the issue because of 'societal sensitivities'. Nonetheless, in an effort to combat the epidemic, Dubai police are conducting special patrols in areas frequented by prostitutes, while immigration teams are conducting various raids and sting operations to address the problem. Authorities have also restricted the number of visas issued to single women between the ages of 30 and 40.

According to UAE law, prostitutes must be caught in the act if a conviction is to be secured. The official punishment is lashing, followed by a term of imprisonment. However, it is not uncommon for those arrested for prostitution to be detained for a brief period, before being deported from the country and placed on a blacklist that prevents them from returning.

Arts & Entertainment

Active Dubai

Spectator Sports

Presiding over a new era of sports tourism, Dubai is luring top athletes to perform – and hosting the crowds of fans that follow.

Nowhere has Dubai's renowned marketing machine enjoyed greater success than in the world of sport. Despite the city's youth and limited cultural stature, its sporting calendar is crammed with professional tournaments, from the well-attended **Rugby Sevens** and **Dubai World Cup** to more reserved contests in golf, tennis and water sports.

Drawn no doubt by the warm weather, sumptuous hospitality and generous purses, the top names in their respective games have walked down Dubai's red carpet. While Ernie Els, perennially ranked as one of the top

Federer and Agassi atop the Burj Al Arab.

golfers in the world, scooped the **Desert Classic** in 2005, world number one Roger Federer breezed his way to success in the **Dubai Duty Free Tennis Open** and top-seed Lindsay Davenport held her nerve to claim the US$1 million women's section of the event.

Some stars simply want a break from the harsh northern European winter, including a growing number of British soccer teams who choose to hold training camps or practice matches here. Newcastle United enjoyed midwinter training in Dubai so much that the players came back to attend the **Dubai World Cup** in March 2005. Several England players have even bought houses on Palm Island *(see p26 The silly isles)*, to great media interest.

Ultimately, if Dubai has been good for sport, then sport has also been extremely kind to the emirate, primarily as a highly effective marketing tool for the tourism sector. Shots of Federer and Agassi trading volleys on the Burj Al Arab helipad *(pictured left)* or Kournikova trying on jewellery in the Dubai gold souk have bounced around the world, securing TV airtime and publicity that cash simply could not buy. If appearance cheques have changed hands (rumour has it Tiger Woods was last paid US$1 million for just turning up at the Desert Classic), there have been no complaints about value for money.

The sole disappointing aspect is that the local sporting public has not always taken full advantage of these chances to observe the big names at close range. Hundreds of football fans from Glasgow faithfully flew over to watch Paul Gascoigne headline a Rangers v Celtic Veterans match, but local residents have been far more apathetic and attendances at the men's and women's tennis tournaments have been consistently disappointing.

Golf

The shining jewel in Dubai's golfing calendar is undoubtedly the **Dubai Desert Golf Classic** *(see p143)*. This professional tournament is a respected fixture on the European PGA Tour, luring world-class players like Colin Montgomerie, Darren Clarke, Mark O'Meara and Ernie Els to the wealthy emirate in pursuit of prize money worth over US$1.2 million.

Colt from the blue

Few success stories in the world of sport can rival that of Godolphin (www.godolphin.com), the racing stable established by the Maktoum Royal Family. But while it has ruled the flat-racing roost for the past decade, Godolphin retains an air of mystery thanks to the closed-door policy of its Dubai and British stables, as well as the royal profile of its owning syndicate.

From humble beginnings in 1994, Godolphin – named after one of the three founding stallions, each of them a modern thoroughbred – has grown to become a revolutionary force in racing around the world, with Dubai at its epicentre. Legend tells of the Godolphin Arabian, an 18th-century horse who ended up in England and won everything in sight before going to stud. There he enjoyed still greater success, with leading sire titles in 1738, 1745 and 1747. His influence was ultimately immense; each

of the first 76 British Classic winners had at least one strain of him in their pedigree.

The Dubai-based operation chalked up their first local winner at Nad Al Sheba in 1992. Since then their record is without peer: Godolphin has won Group One races in no less than 11 countries, while Frankie Dettori, Godolphin's retained jockey, can claim 470 wins from 1,463 rides. The stable also bred the great Dubai Millennium, unleashed to win the race seemingly made for him – the Dubai World Cup 2000 – when he beat an international field by more than six lengths. Tragically, the horse, still commonly regarded in Dubai as the best ever, died a year later after a week-long battle with grass sickness. Much like the dynamic city in which Godolphin has built a home, this racing network continues to exceed all expectations, defying logical limitations in everything they do.

Frankie Dettori at the **Dubai World Cup**. *See p187*.

Active Dubai

Sporting calendar

The oppressive summer heat forces anyone with any sense to retreat into air-conditioned comfort from May to August, so Dubai's sporting line-up is effectively squeezed into an eight-month period: most events fall between October and March, with plenty of high-quality action for spectators to watch. Tiger Woods, Frankie Dettori, Venus Williams and Anna Kournikova are among the many stars who have visited Dubai in recent years. In typical Dubai fashion, specific dates for the following events (despite their being annual fixtures) will not be finalised until much later in the year. We recommend you contact the organisers, listed below, closer to the time. See also pp142-147 **Festivals & Events**.

October

Camel racing: The season kicks off at Nad Al Sheba, with races every Thursday and Friday. Season ends April 30.
Contact Nad Al Sheba Club (338 1168).
Marlboro Desert Challenge: Expect to see 4x4s, motorbikes and trucks tearing up the desert. The rally begins with a prologue from Jebel Ali Racecourse.
Contact UAE Desert Challenge (266 9922, rallyuae@emirates.net.ae).

November

Horse racing: Another season of floodlit racing gets underway at Nad Al Sheba, ending mid April 2006.
Contact Dubai Racing Club (332 2277, info@dubairacingclub.com).
Dubai Rugby Sevens: Sixteen international teams and several social outfits compete over three days for various plates and shields. Rowdy fun for all – particularly people who like to get drunk.
Contact Promoseven Sports (321 0008, www.dubairugby7s.com).

December

Offshore Powerboating: The UIM Class 1 World Offshore Championship combines with a festival of local and international musicians in a celebration of the great outdoors.
Contact Dubai International Marine Club (399 5777, www.dimc-uae.com).

January

Dubai Marathon: It's not about winning – register to run the full city circuit and help to raise money for research into blindness and

sight restoration. Also on offer are a 3km fun run and 10km road race.
Contact www.dubaimarathon.org.

February

Dubai Tennis Championships: The world's top male and female players battle it out in the intimate Dubai tennis stadium. Guarantees day-long sunshine and non-British finalists. The championships begin late Feb and end in the first week of March.
Contact Dubai Duty Free (216 6444, www.dubaitennischampionships.com).

March

Dubai Desert Golf Classic: Expect some immaculate greens and the greatest swingers of the day at this PGA European event. Such stars as Colin Montgomerie, Ernie Els and Mark O'Meara usually attend; autograph-hunters and hospitality-freeloaders alike will find plenty to satisfy them.
Contact UAE Golf Association (399 5060, www.dubaidesertclassic.com).
Dubai World Cup: Dubai hosts the highest-stakes horse race in the world at Nad Al Sheba. Visiting celebs, free-flowing bubbly and ridiculous hats are the order of the day.
Contact Dubai Racing Club (332 2277, www.dubaiworldcup.com).

Ernie Els at the **Dubai Desert Golf Classic**.

Active Dubai

Golf is big business in Dubai, and the city now boasts no fewer than five premium courses. The Desert Classic has been staged at both the **Emirates Golf Club** and the **Dubai Creek Golf & Yacht Club** (for both, *see p196*), the latter reopening to great acclaim in 2005 after significant redevelopment. But various courses in the city enjoy the attention of stars in need of a practice session before the main event and security is consistently low-key; it's perfectly possible to come away with treasured autographs and photos. The **Jebel Ali Golf Resort & Spa** (883 6000, www.jebel ali-international.com) hosts a curtain-raiser in the guise of a nine-hole challenge match. The Classic itself is well attended, drawing many amateur residents who play the same world-beating courses all year round. Besides the hangers-on most interested in all-you-can-drink corporate hospitality, the tournament enjoys its fair share of legitimate golf fans, happy to chase around after the pros.

Horse & camel racing

Holding its own in several sports, Dubai really only pulls ahead of the chasing pack in the equine arts. Known these days as the new international centre for horse-racing, the emirate can boast the unrivalled excellence of the Maktoum's Godolphin operation *(see p185* **Colt from the blue***)*. Yet while the Royal Family's private stable has proved itself on tracks around the world, it's still a special experience to watch some of the best horses on the planet strut their stuff on home turf.

The **Nad Al Sheba** horse-racing track *(see p77)*, a short drive from the downtown area of the city, is the focal point and flagship facility for racing in the UAE, boasting a 2,000-metre (6,500-foot) turf course sitting inside a 2,200-metre (7,200-foot) dirt track, which can be configured to three different lengths. Each year this prestigious stretch of turf hosts the world's richest horse race, the US$6 million **Dubai World Cup** *(see p144)*, as well as the season-long Dubai Racing Carnival, established in 2004. The World Cup meeting is regularly attended by some 50,000 people. In 2005 Roses in May took World Cup victory to became the 43rd winner of the Racing Carnival, which began on 20 January. Some 200 horses from 20 countries, representing 79 trainers, came to Dubai to compete for a total of US$25 million in prize money.

The World Cup is the place to rub shoulders with the great and the good of the city, and there's as much action off the track as on it, not least at the Fillies & Fashion event, which has generous prizes for the best-dressed ladies. However, racing in Dubai is about far more than one big day out in the sun. The **Dubai Racing Carnival** features 55 races (20 on turf, the rest on dirt) over a ten-meeting, nine-week period, leading up to the World Cup at the end of March. Admission to racing at Nad Al Sheba is free, apart from the World Cup meeting, but the bad news for visitors who like to indulge in a flutter is that betting in the UAE is strictly illegal. Instead, prizes are on offer for correct predictions of race results.

As well as the Nad Al Sheba track, there are also a sand-and-oil-surface racing track at **Jebel Ali** (call 347 4914 for details) and a fibreturf track at **Ghantoot** in Abu Dhabi (02 562 9050); both are a 30- to 40-minute drive south from downtown Dubai, or 45 minutes from the city centre. No visit to Dubai, though, is complete without a trip to another type of racing – the nearby **camel track** *(see p74)*, also in Nad Al Sheba. The days of local residents climbing aboard one of these 'ships of the desert' for a gruelling trip across the sands to Abu Dhabi or Al Ain may be long gone, but camels remain revered in many Middle Eastern societies for their unique abilities. Racing camels are a breed apart, and the strongest and fastest specimens change hands for millions of dirhams. The camel-racing season in Dubai starts in November and runs through to April. Admission is free to the races at Nad Al Sheba, which usually begin on Thursdays and Fridays at 7am and are over by 8.30am (timings are later in Ramadan). For more information, *see p146*.

There had been international criticism that young children were being illegally press-ganged into becoming jockeys, their light frames allowing the speeding camels were able run faster. UAE authorities have been sensitive to these concerns, and have taken steps to regulate the sport. Camel owners were first threatened in 2003 with fines and jail sentences for breaking existing laws, which state that jockeys must be aged at least 15, weigh a minimum of 35kg (just over 77lb), be certified medically fit and have a valid UAE residence. Jockeys were issued with identity cards and are now subject to spot checks. In 2005, somewhat bizarre experiments have been authorised by various Gulf governments to create lightweight robot jockeys in an attempt to progress beyond the days of child riders. Designed to look like a small man with an electronic whip, the robots are controlled by human hand via a joystick and computer screen. Future models will feature cameras to give operators a jockey's-eye view of the track.

Active Dubai

Dubai's Olympians

Whether or not the Olympic Games are held in Dubai in 2016 – the government was tabling a bid as we went to press – the 2004 Athens Olympics will be etched in the memory of all Emiratis because **Sheikh Ahmed bin Hasher Al Maktoum** (*pictured*) made history for the UAE when he won the country's first ever gold medal. Competing in the men's double trap shooting event, Sheikh Ahmed put on an unrivalled display of marksmanship at the Markopoulo Range, hitting an Olympic record 144 of 150 clay pigeons in qualifying and 45 of 50 in the six-man final to take the gold.

Also in the squad were **Sheikh Saeed bin Maktoum bin Rashid Al Maktoum**, who represented the UAE in skeet shooting, athlete **Ali Mohammed Murad** and swimmer **Obaid Ahmed Obaid**. Middle-distance runner Ali Mohammed competed in the 800 metres,

while Obaid contested the 100-metre freestyle. Another UAE national, artist **Juwairia Abdul Rahman Al Khaja**, also travelled to Athens. Her work entitled *Minding Sports* won eighth prize in the Sports and Arts Olympiad 2004, organised by the International Olympics Culture and Educational Committee.

Motor sports

Bahrain may have beaten Dubai in the race to host Formula One Grand Prix racing in the Middle East, but the emirate has trumped its competition with the opening of the region's first fully integrated motor sports facility. Located a short drive out of town along the Emirates Road, the **Dubai Autodrome** (294 9490, autodrome@unionproperties.com) boasts a world-class 5.3km (three-mile) motor-racing track, an international-standard pit-lane complex and a grandstand able to accommodate more than 5,000 spectators.

Aston Martin confirmed in early 2005 that it will run an Autodrome-based racing team of two DBR9s and several high-profile drivers, including Sheikh Maktoum bin Hasher Maktoum Al Maktoum, in the world's GT Series. The Dubai GT Team should debut in November's LG Super Racing Weekend, held at the Autodrome, before racing in earnest in 2006 across Europe, Asia, the USA and the Middle East.

Away from the relative comfort of the tarmac, the Emirates Motor Sport Federation organises several high-octane events, among them the Emirates Rally Championship, the 1,000 Dunes Rally and the Autocross Championship. Dubai traditionally stages the final leg of the Middle East Rally Championship, usually in December, and also hosts the **Desert Challenge** (*see p144*), a renowned local rally-driving event held over

five days in October. This dune-bashing affair consistently attracts many of the world's leading drivers and is the final round of the FIA Marathon World Cup.

Tennis

While most Dubaians relish the city's homegrown sporting calendar – watching local petrolheads attempt the Desert Challenge, or applauding the clash of expat veterans in the boisterous Rugby Sevens – there's a school of thought that hankers after the true international stars of sport. The British Lions don't entertain the Wallabies in Dubai, for example. But Dubai's Tennis Championships really do bring the sport's premium racketeers to town. From Venus Williams and Anna Kournikova to Boris Becker and Tim Henman, the top players have all taken part in the annual back-to-back WTA and ATP tournaments known as the **Dubai Duty Free Tennis Open** (*see p143*). The world number ones of both sexes – Roger Federer and Lindsay Davenport – took the honours in 2005, and should be back to defend their titles in 2006.

The action unfolds at the purpose-built stadium in Garhoud. Many spectators take pub grub and liquid refreshment at the Irish Village (*see p175*) between games, but the restaurants of the Century Village on the other side of the stadium also lay on lunch deals. While the players flock to Dubai to take full advantage of the city's magnificent hospitality and attractions (not to mention a healthy purse), it's also true that the general public has been a bit slower to show its enthusiasm, with early rounds routinely played out in front of thin crowds. However, the finals tend to attract a packed house and home-grown players are treated to an encouraging reception, even if expats tend to save the most rousing cheers for stars hailing from their respective home countries.

Water sports

Dubai traditionally plays host to the finale of the **World Offshore Powerboat** racing season (*see p147*). The emirate is the base of the appropriately named **Victory Team** (www.victoryteam.org.ae), one of the most successful Class One outfits in the sport. A string of world titles, records and trophies have been secured since it was formed in 1989, with throttleman Saeed Al-Tayer earning a place in the record books as the first Arab to win a hat-trick of Class One championships back in 2001. So it is, that each December, Dubai hosts the last leg of the annual UIM Championship Class One World Offshore season.

February sees Dubai host an **International Sailing Week Regatta**, the only event of its kind in the world. This growing spectacle pits ten- to 17-year-olds, racing in optimist and laser categories, against each other. The Regatta pulls in over 100 competitors from 14 nations each year. Dubai also hosts the region's biggest annual boat show in March, at which manufacturers from across the globe display all manner of seacraft, from lightweight jet skis to luxury cruisers and yachts.

The **Dubai International Marine Club**, which is based at the Meridien Mina Seyahi hotel (*see p48*), is the body responsible for the growth of water sports in the UAE. It organises various meets each year to promote jet skiing, traditional rowing sports and dhow sailing, as well as setting up race opportunities for modcatamarans and lasers. The venues used by the Club include the Mina Seyahi, Dubai Creek, Abu Dhabi, Ras Al Khaimah and Fujairah. Because many of these races take place some distance from the coast, spectator numbers tend to be rather low. Nonetheless, the competitive sailing season in the UAE (from October to May) is keenly contested. The crowning highlight of the dhow sailing season is the **Sir Bu Nu'air Dhow Race** from the island of the same name to Dubai. This event takes place during May – it is the third and final race of the 60-foot category and the final race of the watersports season. The 58-nautical-mile race attempts to recapture the glory of the pearling fleet as it struck for home at the height of the pearling trade. In recent years, fields of over 90 dhows have crossed the finishing line.

Sir Bu Nu'air Dhow Race.

Participation Sports

With world-class golf courses, warm Gulf waters and year-round sunshine,
Dubai will get the most ardent couch potato up and running

In a city where real-estate development is rife, sports fans will be pleased to discover that plenty of investment is being ploughed into new sporting facilities. The single biggest change to Dubai's skyline will surely be **Sports City**, part of the ongoing (and mind-boggling) Dhs18 billion Dubailand development. In the interim, top sports acts like Premiership football clubs are still proving receptive to Dubai's open invitation, but currently the city lacks the venues to do their performances justice. The answer? A multi-purpose stadium equipped with 25,000 seats, designed to host football matches and track and field events, should be open for business from 2007. A separate indoor stadium will host conventional hard-court sports like tennis, ice hockey and boxing, to be joined by purpose-built cricket (holding another 25,000 spectators) and field hockey stadiums (10,000). The remarkable cash investment seems to be working: in 2005 the International Cricket Council (ICC) agreed to move its headquarters from the UK to Dubai's Sports City on completion of a new cricket academy for promising kids.

Of course, Sports City wouldn't truly be a Dubaian development without a shopping mall thrown in for good measure. Plans have also been tabled for a Grand Plaza, offering a car park for 10,000 cars and access to an all-new retail mall. Covering an area of more than 19 million square metres (206 million square feet), Sports City is also about championing the local sports scene. It will house facilities to encourage all manner of athletic pursuits, from extreme sports (think rock-climbing, in-line skating and kiteboarding) to high-octane thrills like motocross and dune-buggying.

There isn't anything the Dubai authorities won't aspire to creating – doubters need look no further than Dubai's latest believe-it-or-not project, the region's only indoor ski slope, which opened its doors to the public in September 2005 as part of the monolithic Mall of the Emirates (*see p120*). Dubbed **Ski Dubai**, it holds over 6,000 tonnes of snow at any given time and has taken its place in the history books as the third largest indoor snow dome in the world.

The Arabian Gulf team – **rugby** remains popular at grass-roots level. *See p199.*

Dubai has long been a golfer's paradise, with several outstanding courses that impress even those pros that flow into the city for the Desert Classic tournament (*see p143*). New courses springing up in Dubai have taken the emirate's total to no fewer than eight different venues, including the **Dubai Creek Yacht & Golf Club**, which reopened in 2005 after extensive redevelopment and landscaping. It's now entirely possible to camp down in a five-star hotel a few miles from the airport and a three-iron from one of Dubai's prestigious fairways; small wonder that a new breed of golfing visitor played an average of five rounds per trip in 2004.

Not that an active life in Dubai necessarily requires spending a small fortune in clubs, kit and green fees. Thanks to a cosmopolitan population and pleasant climate, the city offers a wealth of sports and games to be played in the great outdoors. The presence of thousands of workers from the subcontinent means that cricket is played widely and with great enthusiasm, both at an organised level and with impromptu games staged on patches of waste ground around the city every Friday. Football, which boasts a multicultural amateur expat league as well as a domestic professional league, is popular, while the city's beach culture ensures all water sports have a healthy following, including the relatively new activity of kitesurfing: initiates to the sport will find sun-kissed Dubaians performing aerial tricks at dawn along the emirate's pristine shoreline.

Archery

Dubai Archers Club
Dubai Country Club, Al Awir, off the Ras Al Khor road south of Dubai (344 2591/linton@emirates. net.ae). Meets 3pm Thur, Fri. **Price** Dhs30. **No credit cards. Map** p281 L5.
Archery enthusiasts meet here weekly for target practice. All standards are welcome, and the entry fee includes equipment hire.

Badminton

Dubai Country Club
Al Awir, off the Ras Al Khor road south of Dubai (333 1155/www.dubaicountryclub.com). **Open** 8.30pm Sun; 9pm Mon; 8.30pm Wed. **Price** Dhs25 members, Dhs35 non-members. **Credit** AmEx, DC, MC, V. **Map** p281 L5.
Dubai's badminton facilities are a little thin on the ground, but courts are available at the popular Country Club. You should come equipped wih your own racquets and shuttlecocks. For more details, email milesaarons@hotmail.com.

Where to...

...get aggressive
George Micouris teaches Thai boxing at **Club Mina** (318 1420; *see p203*) four times a week, alongside regular courses in kickboxing.

...go hot-air ballooning
Take in the scenery with **Zodiac Balloons** (390 3505) or try **Amigos Balloons** (289 9295), who offer breakfast and a certificate, as well as a bird's-eye view of Al Ain.

...jump out of a plane
Take tandem jumps at Umm Al Quwain Aeroclub with the **Emirates Parachutes Sports Association** (06 768 1447).

...learn to fly-fish
Expert Suzy gives JR Hartley a run for his money at **Nautica 1992** (050 426 2415), managed from the Metropolitan Resort and Beach Club, Jumeirah.

...hike into the sunset
Dubai's Desert Rangers (340 2408; *see p79* **Tour operators at a glance**) organise a number of trips and safaris; call for details of their latest footslog.

...pitch and putt
Try playing against the glorious backdrop of **Dubai Creek Golf & Yacht Club** (205 4646; *see p196*), but beware the dress code. Warm up with a Dhs25 bucket of balls on the driving range, then plump for a quick round of nine holes for just Dhs60.

...ride horses
Dhs60 buys you a 30-minute private lesson in the paddock at **Jebel Ali Golf Resort** (804 8058); seasoned riders can pay Dhs115 for a one-hour desert ride.

...shoot guns
Whether you indulge in skeet or trap, you can squeeze off a few rounds at the **Jebel Ali Shooting Club** (883 6555).

Basketball

Intersportz
Next to Modern Bakery, behind Spinneys warehouse, off Sheikh Zayed Road, Interchange 3 (347 5833). **Open** 9am-10pm daily. **Price** Dhs25 per person (incl basketball). **Credit** (min Dhs200) MC, V. **Map** p278 B4.
This indoor sports centre is starting to show its age, but the low prices keep it popular, and the

Active Dubai

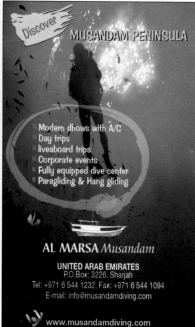

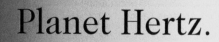

five-a-side football pitches can be easily converted to accommodate fans of the hoop. But be warned: the air-conditioning system only just about allows you to play through the summer.

Bowling

Al Nasr Leisureland
Behind the American Hospital, Oud Metha (337 1234). **Open** 9am-midnight daily. **Price** *Entrance fee* Dhs10; Dhs5 under-10s; Dhs7 per game (incl shoes). **Credit** MC, V. **Map** p281 J3.
Al Nasr is markedly less plush than other lanes in town, but it has one important advantage over the competition: it's licensed. Bowlers thirsty for a beer can make group bookings for a big night out, but resevation details have to be faxed through in advance to 337 6832.

Thunderbowl
Near Defence roundabout, off Sheikh Zayed Road, Interchange 1 (343 1000). **Open** 9am-midnight daily. **Price** Dhs10 per game (Sat-Wed); Dhs15 per game (Thur, Fri). *Shoe hire* Dhs2. **Credit** DC, MC, V. **Map** p287 E13.
The first bowling alley of its kind in the region, Thunderbowl has an impressive 20 computerised lanes. It is always busy, particularly at weekends.

Climbing

Pharaohs' Club
Wafi Pyramids, Oud Metha Road (324 0000). **Price** Dhs40 (1hr class). **Open** 7am-10pm Sat-Thur; 9am-9pm Fri. **Map** p281 J3.
Assuming you don't suffer from vertigo and do like scaling inanimate objects, there's no better place to spend some time than Pharaohs' textured climbing wall. It includes a boulder cave about 3.5m (11.5ft) high and a 1.5m (5ft) overhang.

Cricket

Dubai Cricket Council Pitches
Behind Dubai Police Officers' Club, Sharjah Road, Jaddaf (information: Emirates Cricket Board, Sharjah, 06 542 2991).
The Dubai Cricket Council has 17 pitches, including two grass wickets (one floodlit) on a huge expanse of land behind the Dubai Police Officers' Club. The pitches are the venue for any number of leagues, with social, corporate and inter-hotel competitions all played here, and matches taking place virtually all year round, even in summer.

Intersportz
Next to Modern Bakery, behind Spinneys warehouse, off Sheikh Zayed Road, Interchange 3 (347 5833). **Open** 9am-10pm daily. **Price** Dhs25 per person. **Credit** (min Dhs200) MC, V. **Map** p281 B4.
Indoor five-a-side football courts here are easily turned into cricket nets. The ancient air-conditioning system just about makes it possible to play in the

Little monkeys enjoying **Pharaohs' Club**.

summer, but you should be prepared to sweat it out a bit. The price includes 'indoor' cricket bats and balls. Intersportz also hosts its own cricket league.

Fencing

Metropolitan Hotel
Sheikh Zayed Road, Interchange 2 (343 0000). **Open** 6.30-8pm Sat, Mon, Wed. **Price** Dhs35 per class; Dhs300 for 12 classes. **Credit** AmEx, MC, V. **Map** p280 G5.
Learn fencing (épée, foil and sabre) or brush up your expertise at the International Fencing Club of Dubai with Master Zahi El Khoury, a former world championship finalist and Arabic champion.

Quay Health Club
Mina A' Salam Hotel, Al Sufouh Road, Jumeirah (366 8888/www.dubaifencingclub.com). **Open** *Advanced* 7.30pm Sat, Wed; 6.30pm Mon. *Beginners* 7.30pm Tue; 6.30pm Fri. **Price** *Members* Dhs35 per session. *Non-members* Dhs45 per session. **Credit** AmEx, DC, MC, V. **Map** p278 A4.
At the time of writing, Mihail Kouzev was the head coach of this popular club; he represented Bulgaria in the pentathalon world championships. Fencers of all ages and standards are welcome. In addition to the sessions listed above, junior training takes place at 9.30am every Friday at Jumeirah Beach Club (*see p43*). Kids can also arrange one-to-one sessions with Maria (050 684 2935).

Active Dubai

Fishing

Dubai is a prime source of offshore bonding experiences if you can get like-minded friends on board one of several commercial craft operating along the Jumeirah coast. Reliable sunshine, calm seas and good fish can be found throughout the year, including the noble sailfish – its numbers are now protected by a conservation effort based in Abu Dhabi, despite the best efforts of illegal Iranian trawlers plundering all and sundry. Prime fishing months are January through to March, and during this period advance booking is strongly recommended.

Bounty Charters

Dubai International Marine Club, Le Meridien Mina Seyahi Hotel, Al Sufouh Road, Jumeirah (050 552 6067). **Open** advance bookings only. **Price** Dhs1,700 4hrs; Dhs1,900 6hrs; Dhs2,400 8hrs; Dhs2,600 10hrs. **No credit cards. Map** p278 A5.
South African sailor Richard Forrester, a veteran sailor in the region's waters, takes the helm at Bounty Charters. His 11m (36ft) Yamaha Sea Spirit game fishing boat can be booked for tailor-made fishing trips all year round, taking out groups of up to a maximum of six people.

Club Joumana

Jebel Ali Hotel, Sheikh Zayed Road, Exit 13 (past Interchange 7) (883 6000/www.jebelali-international.com). **Open** 8am-noon, 2-6pm daily. **Price** Dhs1,500 4hrs; Dhs2,700 8hrs. **Credit** AmEx, DC, MC, V. **Map** p278 A5.

Club Joumana has just one boat, the streamlined Kingfish, which holds a maximum of seven people per trip. Full- and half-day excursions are available. For the price (either length of voyage) you get a friendly crew, who are experienced enough in these waters to steer you to the better spots; the use of tackle; plus refreshments in the form of soft drinks, tea and coffee, plus Danish pastries and croissants.

Dubai Creek Golf & Yacht Club

Opposite Deira City Centre mall, Garhoud (205 4646). **Open** *Fishing trips* 7am-6pm daily. **Price** Dhs1,875 4hrs (7-11am, 8am-noon, 1-5pm); Dhs2,125 5hrs (7am-noon, 1-6pm); Dhs2,375 6hrs (6am-noon; noon-6pm); Dhs2,850 8hrs (7am-3pm, 8am-4pm). **Credit** AmEx, DC, MC, V. **Map** p281 K2.
The Dubai Creek club's own 10m (32ft) single-cabin boat 'Sneakaway' is available for trips for up to six people. The various prices includes the cost of tackle, bait and fuel, as well as a good supply of soft drinks (but for food and additional drinks you will pay extra). Although landlubbers may find a full day on the high seas to approach overkill, the Sneakaway crew unsurprisingly recommend the eight-hour trip (and an early start) to maximise your chances of making a memorable catch.

The Image

Moored in Jumeirah (282 2783/050 653 3496/ sailing@theimageworks.ae). **Open** times & departure points vary. **Price** Dhs1,100 1hr.
Following a leisurely afternoon sojourn on this nifty catamaran, you'll probably decide the life of a salty seadog is the life for you. The boat is just about perfect for a spot of lazy fishing, and there's

Sport fishing in the Gulf.

a Jacuzzi net and doughnut ride should the fish refuse to bite. The boat takes a maximum of 20 people, which works out as a meagre Dhs55 per person if you happen to be popular.

Le Meridien Mina Seyahi Beach Resort & Marina

Le Meridien Mina Seyahi Hotel, Al Sufouh Road, Jumeirah (399 3333/www.lemeridien-minaseyahi. com). **Open** *Fishing trips* depart 7am, 1pm daily. **Price** Dhs1,725 4hrs. **Credit** AmEx, DC, MC, V. **Map** p278 A5.

Tackle, bait, soft drinks and water are included in the price of these regular trips to some of the best fishing grounds in the Gulf; the maximum allowed per trip is six people, and you'll be asked to leave a 50 per cent deposit on your credit card. Look out for The World site (*see p31* **Coming attractions**) on your way out to sea. After it's over, fishermen in the know usually nip into the hotel's Barasti Bar (*see p113*) for a quick sundowner.

Yacht Solutions

Jumeirah Beach Hotel Pavilion Marina, Beach Road, Jumeirah (348 6838/www.yacht-solutions.com). **Open** for trips 7am-6pm daily. **Price** from Dhs1,600 for 4hrs to Dhs2,500 for 8hrs. **Credit** AmEx, DC, MC, V. **Map** p278 B4.

Yacht Solutions run one of the biggest operations in Dubai and offer a friendly, flexible service. There are three boats available for hire (each will take up to six passengers per fishing trip), and multiple fishing lines ensure you're trawling for sharks while drifting for kingfish while catching some rays and enjoying a cold one.

Football

Dubai Expat League

Information: Gary Foote (050 458 1087).

The Expat League is an expanding 11-a-side league of like-minded male footie fans, buoyed up with sponsorship from Umbro. A dozen teams currently participate, meeting weekly to do battle in parks and on pitches. Points games, invariably held at the Dubai Exiles Rugby Club (*see p199* **Rugby**), are friendly but competitive. There's also a seven-a-side tournament that runs in the summer. Gary Foote, Neil Jenson (050 553 6042) or chairman Ray Nickson (raynickson@dpa.co.ae) introduce ringers and new Dubaian residents to local team captains needing to make up the numbers. There are also indoor five-a-side pitches at Intersportz (*see p191* **Basketball**).

Women's Football League

Dubai Exiles Rugby Football Club (050 784 5758).

The women's league is always on the lookout for fresh talent. All levels of experience are welcome, but you must be over 16 to participate. For more details, call Suzannah on the above number or email her at dubaiwf@hotmail.com. Training sessions take place at 7pm on a Sunday.

Golf

An explosion in the number of visiting tourist golfers means facilities here are first class, although costs can be steep. Courses justify this by citing the extra expense built into green fees here – millions of gallons of desalinated water are required each day to prevent the desert reclaiming these modern oases. Bookings for tee times for several clubs listed below can be made through the central reservations office (390 3931, www.dubaigolf.com). The **UAE Golf Association** (www.ugagolf.com) is the governing body for the sport in this country; yearly membership is Dhs200, which entitles players to reductions on green fees, lessons and merchandise at all UAE clubs.

Al Badia Golf Resort

Dubai Festival City, Al Rebat Street, Ras Al Khor, Deira (285 5772/www.albadiagolfresort.com). **Open** 7am-2.30pm (last tee-off) daily. **Price** *Non-members* Dhs490 Thur-Sat, Dhs395 Sun-Wed. *UGA members & course residents* Dhs440 Thur-Sat, Dhs355 Sun-Wed. All green fees incl 18 holes & shared cart. **Map** p281 L3.

Dubai's most recent addition to the golfing fraternity sits Creekside a short drive from Garhoud Bridge, in the direction of Ras Al Khor. Open to pay & play visitors from early 2005, the 18-hole Al Badia resort was designed by renowned golf course architect Robert Trent Jones II, with a clubhouse, sports academy and boutique hotel.

Club Joumana

Jebel Ali Hotel & Golf Resort, Sheikh Zayed Road, Exit 13 (past Interchange 7) (883 6000 / www.jebelalihotel.com). **Open** 7am-3.30pm (last tee-off) daily. **Price** non-resident 18 hole, mid-week Dhs215, weekend Dhs230. Cart fee Dhs50. Club hire Dhs85 per set. Set of 50 range balls Dhs20. **Credit** AmEx, DC, MC, V. **Map** p278 A5.

A nine-hole, par-36 course, with superb views of the Arabian Gulf, a salt-water lake and the colourful presence of preening peacocks. The facilities include a driving range, 27-hole putting green and indoor swing room. There are also a variety of coaching packages to choose from depending on whether you are a virgin swinger or hardened pro; five half-hour lessons start at Dhs595.

The Desert Course

Arabian Ranches, Emirates Road, off Junction 4 (884 6777). **Open** 6.30am-7pm daily. **Price** Dhs345 (Sat-Wed); Dhs425 (Thur-Fri, national hols). **Map** p278 C5.

Laid out in association with Nicklaus Design, this par 72 course is the brainchild of golfing hero Ian Baker-Finch. Part of a bigger residential complex located some distance out of town, the course boasts a floodlit driving range, as well as par three pitch-and-putt facilities to hone your short game.

Active Dubai

Dubai Creek Golf & Yacht Club.

Dubai Country Club

Al Awir, off the Ras Al Khor road, south of Dubai (333 1155/www.dubaicountryclub.com). **Open** 8am-6pm daily. *Driving range* 8am-8.30pm daily. **Price** Dhs65 per game, plus Dhs30 for piece of artificial turf. **Credit** AmEx, DC, MC, V. **Map** p281 L5.

Dubai's first golf club opened in 1971 and it is still a popular option, although the competition gets noticeably stiffer year by year. The club boasts 18- and nine-hole courses on sand; players buy and then carry a piece of artificial turf to play off, except for on the 'browns' (sand equivalents of greens), which are brushed regularly to ensure a smooth roll. Players must wear flat-soled shoes.

Dubai Creek Golf & Yacht Club

Opposite Deira City Centre mall, Garhoud (295 6000). **Open** 7.30am-2.50pm (last 18-hole tee-off) daily. **Price** *UGA members* Dhs295-Dhs525 (Sat, Thur, Fri); Dhs325-Dhs385 (Sun-Wed). *Non-members* Dhs325-Dhs475 (Sat, Thur, Fri); Dhs295-Dhs425 (Sun-Wed). **Map** p281 K2.

This luxury 18-hole, par 71 course closed for a full year in December 2003 to allow for a redesign of its front nine by local legend Thomas Björn. Now open again, it also has a renovated back nine, widened driving range and new par three course, which opened in April 2005. The par five 18th crowns what is a stunning course. Luxury villas line the avenue leading to the landmark clubhouse, a towering building designed to look like a sail. The meandering road also passes a 225-room Hyatt hotel, still under construction as we went to press. Prices are lower in summer than winter.

Emirates Golf Club

Sheikh Zayed Road, off Interchange 5 (380 2222/www.dubaigolf.com). **Open** 6am-3pm (last tee-off) daily. **Price** Dhs525 daily. Non-members should book 18-hole rounds at least 1wk in advance. **Credit** AmEx, DC, MC, V. **Map** p278 A5.

Home to two fine courses and a Bedouin tent-inspired clubhouse, this is the most eye-catching golfing facility in the region. The 7,101-yard Majlis course, as well having been the first grass facility to open in the Middle East, is home to the Dubai Desert Classic (*see p143*). Since 1996 it has been complemented by the 7,127-yard Wadi course, which features 14 lakes and numerous bunkers. Both are par 72 courses and make good use of the naturally rolling desert terrain to create a serious test for players of all abilities. Many experts regard this as the premier golf club in Dubai.

The Montgomerie

Emirates Hills, Sheikh Zayed Road, off Interchange 5 (390 5600/www.themontgomerie.com). **Open** 7am-1.50pm (last tee-off) Sat, Thur, Fri; 7am-4pm (last tee-off) Sun-Wed. **Price** *UGA members* Dhs440 (Sat, Thur, Fri); Dhs340 (Sun-Wed). *Non-members* Dhs550 (Sat, Thur, Fri); Dhs425 (Sun-Wed). **Credit** AmEx, MC, V. **Map** p278 A5.

The Montgomerie, designed by Scottish Ryder Cup star Colin Montgomerie, covers more than 200 acres (81ha) of undulating links-style fairways. With 14 lakes and the small matter of 72 bunkers to avoid, drive placement is key. Look out for the 13th hole, with what is claimed to be the largest single green in the world, covering a staggering

5,394sq m (58,000sq ft). Golfers who feel they need a bit more practice before tackling the course proper can head to the Academy, by Troon Golf. There you'll find a state-of-the-art swing studio, a nine-hole, par-three course, a short-game area, some putting greens and even a 'dummy' fairway, all of them under floodlights.

Nad Al Sheba

Off the Dubai–Al Ain Road (336 3666/www.nad alshebaclub.com). **Open** 7.30am-8pm (last 18-hole tee-off) daily. **Price** *Non-members* Dhs220 (7.30am-3pm Sat-Wed), Dhs325 (3-8pm Sat-Wed); Dhs220 (4-8pm Thur, Fri). *Members only* Dhs260 (7.30am-4pm Thur-Fri). **Credit** AmEx, DC, MC, V. **Map** p278 C4.

The oldest floodlit 18-hole course in the Emirates has recently had a facelift, focusing on the back nine holes, all of which are inside the track of the world-famous Nad Al Sheba racecourse (*see p77*). A Scottish-style links course, it boasts a huge number of pot bunkers and its greens now feature a new variety of dwarf grass, ensuring a more consistent putting surface. Facilities also include a rebuilt short-game area and new grass practice tees. The 'learn golf in a week' course is always popular.

Ice hockey

Al Nasr Leisureland

Oud Metha (337 1234/www.dubaimightycamels.com/ www.dubaisandstorms.com). **Price** *Membership* Dhs1,000 Mighty Camels; Dhs700 Sandstorms (youth team). **No credit cards. Map** p281 J3.
Ice hockey in the desert? You better believe it. There are two thriving clubs based at Al Nasr's ice rink.

The Mighty Camels comprise a dozen nationalities, in addition to the mainstay Canadians, amounting to more than 90 members; they practise twice a week (8.30-11pm Sun, Tue). The Camels play in regular tournaments overseas, and even host their very own competition in Dubai at the end of the season, which runs from September to April. The Sandstorms, meanwhile, have four separate teams: novice (ages 5-8), junior (9-10), intermediate (11-13) and senior (14-18). They practise on three different days each week (4.30-9pm Sat; 7-9pm Mon; 5.30-7.30pm Wed).

Ice-skating

Galleria Ice Rink

Hyatt Regency Hotel, Deira Corniche (209 6550). **Open** 10am-1.30pm, 2-5.30pm, 6-9pm Sat-Thur; 10am-1.30pm, 2-5.30pm, 6-8pm Fri. **Price** Dhs25 incl skate hire. **Credit** AmEx, MC, V. **Map** p283 J1.
This rink is in a somewhat surreal location, slap-bang in the middle of the small shopping mall that's attached to the Hyatt Regency Hotel. Lessons are available (from Dhs80 for half an hour) – expect a gaggle of bemused onlookers, with shopping bags.

Al Nasr Leisureland

Oud Metha (337 1234). **Open** 10am-noon, 1-3pm, 4-6.30pm daily. **Price** Dhs5 plus Dhs5 skate hire. **Credit** MC, V. **Map** p277 J3.
Leisureland is a popular venue for ice-skaters of all ages, particularly during the summer when the out-door temperature soars. It is advisable to call before you go to check the rink is open to the public: with ice hockey played here almost every day (*see above*), it can interfere with door times.

Pitch perfect

The only time you'll need jumpers in Dubai – voilà, instant goalposts!

Organised sports clubs abound in Dubai, but you don't need oodles of kit and cash to have a kickabout with friends and family. Whatever the shape of your bat, ball or Frisbee, the desert emirate has cultivated great swathes of soft green stuff to cushion your very own cup final.

There are immaculate grass pitches available for both rugby and football at the **Dubai Country Club** (333 1155) and nearby **Dubai Exiles Rugby Football Club** (333 9664), the latter boasting a no-frills but sociable bar. **Emirates Golf Club** (347 3222) offers both grass (Dhs300 per hour) and astroturf (Dhs200 per hour) surfaces. If there's a small matter of pride at stake, you might make use of **Al Wasl Football Club** (324 3333), next to Al Wasl Hospital on the opposite side of Al Qutaeyat Road to Wafi

City. At a wallet-decimating Dhs1,000 an hour, the Al Wasl pitch is the most expensive in town, but it's also the best. At the other end of the spectrum is picturesque **Al Safa Park** (349 2111), with a pitch marked out by the first gate and many large areas available. Entry is a mere Dhs5 at weekends, and the park fills up quickly with men who should know better squeezed into various bits of AC Milan and Man Utd kit – stake your claim early.

Basketball fans can play outdoors in a **public court** by Rydges Plaza on Al Dhiyafa Street or, if the sun is just too fierce, you might try **Intersportz** (347 5833) off Sheikh Zayed Road. Its small courts are perfect for basketball and five-a-side footie, but it's tough going in summer with air-conditioning that's modest at best. The indoor surface is also pretty unkind to knees and elbows.

Active Dubai

Karting

Dubai Autodrome

Off Interchange 4, Sheikh Zayed Road (367 8700).
Open 10am-6pm daily. **Price** Dhs80 per 10min
session. **Map** p278 C5.

This FIA-approved track might one day host F1
racing but, in the meantime, you can have a go on
one of the incredibly nippy pro-karts. 'Arrive and
drive' sessions began at the Kartdrome in May 2005;
the organisers plan to introduce retail shops dedicated to racing, as well as corporate packages for ten
to 100 guests – usual opening hours do not apply
when a corporate event is scheduled. Not for the
faint-hearted, the 13-horsepower karts skim the
ground mere centimetres from the track, but hit
speeds of 130kph (80mph).

Emirates Kart Centre

Near Jebel Ali Golf Resort (050 559 2131). **Open**
noon-9pm. **Price** Dhs100 per 30min session.
Map p278 A5.

The floodlit outdoor track is fairly tricky, with its
hairpin bends and chicanes. Notoriously busy on
the weekends, advance booking is a must; the
centre can also cater to groups numbering from
ten to 200 drivers at a single booking. Junior karts
are available for kids and safety kit is provided.

Kitesurfing

Arabian Gulf Kite Club

*Jumeirah Beach, near University of Wollongong,
Beach Road, Jumeirah (050 455 5216/www.fatima
sport.com).* **Open** varies. **Price** varies. **No credit
cards. Map** p278 B4.

This spectacular hybrid sport has become the
coolest activity in Dubai, and if you head down to
Jumeirah you'll be able to watch some more serious
aquatic aerobatics being displayed. The Kite Club
is manned by friendly hobbyists who are more than
happy to help get you started.

Mini golf

Golf Park

Hyatt Regency, Deira Corniche (209 6802). **Open**
4-10.30pm daily. **Price** Dhs10. **Map** p283 J1.

The Hyatt Regency has a small but perfectly
formed crazy golf course that is cheap as chips to
play. You could also try your hand on the hotel's
nine-hole, which costs a mere Dhs15 per round,
with sand wedge and putter thrown in (a ball costs
Dhs8). Fun, but not for serious swingers.

Mountain biking

Desert Rangers

*Dubai Garden Centre Building, Sheikh Zayed Road
(340 2408/www.desertrangers.com).* **Open** 9am-6pm
Sat-Thur. **Price** from Dhs300 per person (min 4
people per trip). **Credit** MC, V. **Map** p278 B4.

Desert Rangers organises tailor-made treks for
riders of all ages, abilities and strengths. Guides,
bikes, pick-ups and drop-offs are all included.

Paintballing

Wonderland Theme & Water Park

*Creekside Park, near Garhoud Bridge, Garhoud
(050 651 4583).* **Open** varies. **Price** Dhs50 per
100 paintballs; Dhs120 rental of mask, clothing
& paintgun. **No credit cards. Map** p281 K3.

The only paintballing centre in Dubai is a fenced-
off 'zone' of desert scrubland, with strategically
placed barricades to create choke-points and
vantage-points. Groups are divided into opposing
teams before being given protective overalls, face
masks, 'guns' and paintballs, followed by a safety
demonstration. The organisers claim they'll open
at any time, day or night, to accommodate visitors.

Pool

While the following dedicated pool halls don't
serve alcohol, there is still healthy competition
for a spot at their tables. Die-hard cue-pushers
will enjoy playing in Dubai's dimly lit snooker
clubs, but more casual punters might prefer
to grab a game at one of the several bars
equipped with pool tables (*see pp166-181*
Nightlife). *See also p200* **Snooker.**

Billiard Golden Hall

*Al Habtor Building, near Ramada Continental
Hotel, off Al Ittihad Road, Deira (262 9290).* **Open**
9am-3am Sat-Thur; 2pm-3am Fri. **Price** Dhs15
per hr before 5pm; Dhs2 per hr after 5pm. **No
credit cards. Map** p279 D1.

This bright Deira hall lacks the dank mustiness
that characterises most other venues, boasting lava
lamps in the place of trademark pink, tasselled
lampshades. Eight- and nine-ball is fast but friendly.

Emirates Billiards Centre

*Behind Ramada Continental Hotel, off Al Ittihad
Road, Deira (262 4499).* **Open** 10am-2am Sat-Thur;
2pm-2am Fri. **Price** Dhs25 per hr. *Amateurs* Dhs5
per game. **No credit cards. Map** p279 D1.

This dark but spacious pool hall offers 11 tables
and is a firm favourite with local players. There's
a 'winner stays, loser pays' policy, but you can
book in advance to avoid playing with strangers.

Millenium Avenue

*Off Abu Hail Road, near Galadari roundabout,
Deira (266 6595).* **Open** 10am-2am Sat-Thur; 2pm-
2am Fri. **Price** *Members* Dhs5 per hr mornings;
Dhs10 afternoons & evenings. *Non-members*
Dhs15 mornings; Dhs20 afternoons & evenings.
No credit cards. Map p279 D2.

The only pool joint in town with round tables: the
balls are snooker size (smaller than pool balls) and
you win 25 points every time you sink a ball, but
miss it and you give up 25 points to your opponent.

Shoot to thrill: **Wonderland Theme & Water Park**. *See p198.*

There is no triangle. This version of the game may make the oblong tables seem boring, but they're just as popular – you'll have to queue for either.

Rugby

If you're in town for a while and fancy watching a game, or even kicking a point or two, the following clubs welcome spectators and might just take on a gifted ringer.

Dubai Dragons

Dubai Exiles Rugby Football Club, next to Dubai Country Club, Al Awir, off the Ras Al Khor road south of Dubai (050 455 9237/www.eteamz.com/ dubai_dragons_rugby). **Map** p281 K5.
The Dragons are tenants of the Dubai Exiles (*see below*), their biggest rivals, with both typically in the hunt for local league honours. The Dragons have a second XV that plays in the Emirates League, and are always on the lookout for new members. Contact Matt Seale on the number above for more details, or call John Mamea (050 358 9690) to find out about the Young Dragons.

Dubai Exiles

Dubai Exiles Rugby & Football Club, next to Dubai Country Club, Al Awir, off the Ras Al Khor road south of Dubai (333 1198/www.dubaiexiles.com). **Map** p281 K5.
The oldest rugby club in Dubai, the Dubai Exiles are the self-professed 'Pride of Dubai', and still the biggest outfit in town. The club boasts four grass

pitches and a welcoming bar, as well as running second XV and veterans', women's, mini and junior sides. Contact James Hane (050 764 4765) for more information.

Dubai Hurricanes

Dubai Country Club, Al Awir, off the Ras Al Khor road south of Dubai (333 1155). **Map** p281 K5.
They have traditionally been regarded as a purely social team, but the Hurricanes are increasingly a force to be reckoned with.

Sailing

Club Joumana

Jebel Ali Hotel, Sheikh Zayed Road, Exit 13 (past Interchange 7) (883 6000/www.jebelali-international.com). **Open** 10am-4pm daily.
Price Dhs80 (non-hotel guests) entrance fee; Dhs80 per hr catamaran; Dhs60 per hr laser.
Credit AmEx, DC, MC, V. **Map** p278 A5.
Club Joumana has a choice of two 16-foot Prindle catamarans and a single laser boat available to hire from its sailing hut. If they're already in use, relaxed watersports like banana-boat rides and dingy rides are also on offer.

Dubai Offshore Sailing Club

Beach Road, by Wollongong University, Jumeirah (394 1669/www.dosc.org). **Open** 8am-12.30am daily. **Price** Dhs25 (non-members) entrance fee; Dhs180 2hr private lesson; Dhs100 group lesson.
Credit DC, MC, V. **Map** p278 B3.

Active Dubai

This non-profit-making club is typically abuzz with eager sailors. Recognised by the Royal Yachting Association, the DOSC offers courses all year round in optimists, lasers and toppers (the Cadet Club, held on Thursdays and Fridays, is popular with younger enthusiasts). There are races every Friday, mooring facilities are provided and the club puts on a full social calendar.

Jebel Ali Sailing Club
Near Dubai International Marine Club (Le Meridien Mina Seyahi Hotel), Al Sufouh Road, Jumeirah (399 5444/www.jebelalisailingclub.com). **Open** 9am-8pm Sat-Wed; 9am-10pm Thur, Fri. **Price** *Lessons* from Dhs450 (members); from Dhs650 (non-members). **Credit** AmEx, MC, V. **Map** p278 A5.
Weekly races for adults and children are held here in a variety of vessels, ranging from toppers and catamarans to lasers and cruisers. For children, three-hour Cadet Club sessions take place every Thursday (10am-noon, Dhs40); experienced adult sailors get free Laser 4.7 training.

Scuba diving & snorkelling

It's possible to dive and snorkel all year round off Dubai, but it should be noted that the dive sites off the UAE's east coast (*see pp238-240* Fujairah) are widely regarded as superior in terms of visibility and marine life. Most Dubai-based diving outfits organise trips to the east coast (about two hours' drive away). You can pick up snorkels, masks and fins at the dive centres listed below, or find less-expensive flippers and face masks in the tourist shops of any beachside hotel.

Al Boom Diving
Opposite the Iranian Hospital, Al Wasl Road (342 2993/www.alboommarine.com). **Open** 10am-8pm Sat-Thur. **Price** Dhs1,700 PADI open water course; Dhs1,000 Advanced open water course. **Credit** MC, V. **Map** p284 E9.
This one-stop dive shop is arguably the most comprehensive in the city, good both for casual visitors who just want to test the waters with a sample dive and for more experienced divers who are looking for a specific course. Dive trips can be arranged, and the shop also rents equipment and handles maintenance and servicing. A complete range of Suunto diving computers and Sea Quest accessories is available, along with fashion items.

Pavilion Dive Centre
Jumeirah Beach Hotel, Beach Road, Jumeirah (406 8827/www.jumeirahinternational.com). **Open** 9am-6pm daily. **Price** Dhs320 Discover scuba course; Dhs1,750 open water course. **Credit** AmEx, DC, MC, V. **Map** p278 B4.
This centre, based in a luxury hotel, claims to be the first and only Golden Palm five-star training institute in Dubai. It offers a comprehensive range of courses, from beginner through to instructor

development (twice a year, usually in May and October). Daily trips leave the marina at 10am, weather permitting, and return before 3pm.

Scubatec
Sana Building, Trade Centre Road, Karama (334 8988/scubatec@emirates.net.ae). **Open** 9am-1.30pm, 4-8.30pm Sat-Thur. **Price** varies. **Credit** MC, V. **Map** p285 H7.
Scubatec's qualified instructors are licensed by both the PADI and TDI organisations, and provide a full range of courses. They are usually flexible enough to accommodate both residents and visitors. Services and repair facilities are available.

Snooker

See also p198 **Pool.**

Dubai Snooker Club
Just off Maktoum Bridge, behind the Dubai Printing Building, Bur Dubai (337 5338). **Open** 9pm-2am Sat-Thur; 3pm-1am Fri. **Price** Dhs15 per hr. No credit cards. **Map** p281 J2.
A total of 15 full-size tables are available at this popular venue, which also offers pool tables and PC games. It gets very busy in the evenings.

The Snooker Club
Metropolitan Hotel, Sheikh Zayed Road, Interchange 2 (343 0000). **Open** 6pm-1am daily. **Price** free. **Credit** (drinks only) MC, V. **Map** p280 G5.
The only place in Dubai where you can enjoy a free game of snooker – on the proviso you buy drinks at the licensed bar. Hardly visited, comfortable and well air-conditioned, it's a great place for chilling out. Darts are also available.

Snooker World
Opposite Dubai police headquarters, next to new labour office, Hor Al Anz East, Deira (268 5566). **Open** 10am-3am Sat-Thur; 2pm-3am Fri. **Price** Dhs22 per hr. No credit cards. **Map** p279 E1.
This is a peculiar club, with a strong winner-stays-on policy. Snooker World also offers internet use (Dhs10 per hr), shisha and a screen in the coffee shop that plays two of the latest films every night for free. Tournaments are locals only, but apart from that everyone is welcome to play.

Squash

Al Nasr Leisureland
Oud Metha (337 1234). **Open** 10am-11pm daily; booking essential. **Price** *Per court* Dhs20 (non-members); Dhs10 (members). *Individual lessons* Dhs45 (non-members); Dhs40 (members). *Group lessons* Dhs25 (non-members); Dhs20 (members). **Credit** MC, V. **Map** p281 J3.
Leisureland may be showing its age, but the still-popular centre is one of very few places in town that offers access to squash courts to visitors who haven't been blessed with a stay in one of Dubai's better-equipped hotels.

Club Joumana.

Tennis

CF Tennis
The Aviation Club, off Sharjah Road, Garhoud (282 4540/www.cftennis.com). **Open** 6.30am-11pm daily. **Map** p281 L3.
One of Dubai's most popular fitness clubs provides several outdoor courts. Lessons cater to every level of player, with 14-week group courses starting from Dhs600. The Aviation Club is also home to Dubai's annual tennis championships. *See also p206.*

Wakeboarding

Dubai Water Sports Association
Jadaf (324 1031/www.thewakeboardschool.com). **Open** 8am-6pm daily. **Price** *Facilities* Dhs30, plus Dhs15 entrance for non-members. *Lessons* Dhs75 (non-members); Dhs50 (members). **Credit** AmEx, MC, V. **Map** p281 K3.
Set on Dubai Creek, the WSA has two tournament ski boats, a slalom course and a full-sized jump. It's a far cry from the emirate's pristine beaches, but some will find the clubhouse's faded charm makes a refreshing change from the overrun beach clubs. Facilities include a lawn, swimming pool, Jacuzzi, children's playground and barbecue area. To get there, take the exit to Jadaf from Sheikh Zayed Road near Garhoud Bridge. Proceed to the docks and

follow the fence round to the right. The paved road becomes a dirt track, but venture on and you'll find signs to the nearby ski club.

Water-skiing & windsurfing

Club Joumana
Jebel Ali Hotel, Sheikh Zayed Road, Exit 13 (past Interchange 7) (883 6000/www.jebelali-international.com). **Open** 8am-noon daily. **Price** Dhs80 per 30mins. **Credit** AmEx, DC, MC, V. **Map** p278 A5.
Non-hotel guests must pay an entrance fee of Dhs80 to use the facilities here, and booking in advance is advisable. Your friendly and encouraging instructor is likely to take a mixed bag of tourists out on to the water as a group, if sufficient hotel guests are interested. For more information on other club facilities, *see p199* **Sailing**.

Dubai Water Sports Association
Jadaf (324 1031/www.thewakeboardschool.com). **Open** 8am-6pm daily. **Price** *Facilities* Dhs30, plus Dhs15 entrance for non-members. *Lessons* Dhs75 (non-members); Dhs50 (members). **Credit** AmEx, MC, V. **Map** p281 K3.
The versatile wakeboard team will as happily instruct you on two skis as on a single board. For details of other facilities and how to get to WSA, *see above* **Wakeboarding**.

Active Dubai

Health & Fitness

If you've got it, here's where to flaunt it. If you haven't, skip ahead to Dubai's toughest fitness clubs.

Beach clubs

Most holiday shows on TV open their coverage of Dubai with a camera panning along the emirate's coastline, taking in the clean white beaches, gently lapping waters of the Arabian Gulf and the odd lofty palm tree offering a little splash of shade – before throwing in a gratuitous shot of the Burj Al Arab for good measure. The cliché is maintained for good reason: most hotels located on Dubai's coast operate beach clubs to impeccably high standards, and almost all are open to the public – the exceptions being the One&Only Royal Mirage, Dubai Marine Beach Resort & Spa and the Jumeirah Beach Club, which can be used only by hotel guests, club members and members' guests.

Unfortunately, there is currently a fly in the ointment in the guise of construction. Unsightly cranes and heavy congestion are the result of massive developments in Jumeirah, from ongoing work at Dubai Media City and Palm Island (*see p26* **The silly isles**) to the high-profile Jumeirah Beach Residence and lesser known real-estate projects like Lake Shore Towers and Liwa Heights. Work

isn't loud or ugly enough to ruin a holiday at one of Dubai's five-star beachside properties, but the experience of getting to and from your hotel will be a miserable one until Jumeirah's extraordinary landscaping efforts are finished.

Despite the rigours of city life – perhaps because of them – beach clubs remain hugely popular with the more affluent Dubai residents and tourists, and at weekends (Friday and Saturday) a large segment of the Jumeirah crowd head down to hang out at venues like the Meridien Mina Seyahi's **Club Mina** and the **Ritz-Carlton Beach Club**, which charge them anything from Dhs5,000 to Dhs10,000 a year for the privilege.

For a daily fee, visitors get access to the hotel grounds, private beach and swimming pool, and the attentive service you'd expect from such oases of calm. However, if you want to use the hotel's other facilities, such as a spa, health club, tennis courts or water sports – virtually all beach clubs offer a complete range of marine activities – you are almost certain to incur extra costs. So the experience doesn't come cheap, but as a special treat it's hard to beat.

Poolside at **Dubai Marine Beach Resort & Spa**. *See p209.*

Caracalla Spa & Health Club

*Le Royal Meridien Hotel, Al Sufouh Road, Jumeirah
(399 5555/www.leroyalmeridien-dubai.com).* **Open**
8am-8pm daily. **Price** (non-members) *Sat-Thur*
Dhs100; Dhs40 concessions. *Fri* Dhs150; Dhs60
concessions. **Credit** AmEx, MC, V. **Map** p278 A5.

A long, long period of time on the waiting list has
to be endured by any resident Dubaian determined
enough to make Caracalla's annual membership
scheme. The admission fee gives free access to the
beach and swimming pool, but additional charges
are levied for the gym, sauna, steam room, Jacuzzi
and hammam pools (which are a set of five pools,
each at a different water temperature), tennis and
squash courts. A full range of water sports is, of
course, also available, and guests can further
indulge themselves with a wide variety of massage
and aromatherapy 'treatments'.

Club Joumana

*Jebel Ali Hotel, Sheikh Zayed Road, Exit 13
(past Interchange 7) (883 6000/www.jebelali-
international.com).* **Open** 7am-7pm daily.
Price (non-members) *Sat-Thur* Dhs80; Dhs40
concessions. *Fri* Dhs180; Dhs90 concessions.
Credit AmEx, DC, MC, V. **Map** p278 A5.

Located about 40km (25 miles) south of town, the
Club Joumana is known both for the extreme
friendliness of its staff and for the unbroken peace
and quiet you'll enjoy while you're there. Miles
from the bustle of the city centre, you might
equally choose to stretch out and doze on the
club's lush lawns or to indulge in the variety of
water sports that are available from the private
beach; activities include water-skiing, windsurfing,
banana boating and sailing (catamaran and laser),
while boat and fishing trips can also be organised.
Back on dry land, Club Joumana boasts four floodlit tennis courts, two glass-backed squash courts
and a badminton court, plus a gym, Jacuzzi and
sauna. There are also two freshwater pools with
swim-up bars, a seawater pool and a children's
pool. Nearby is a par-36 nine-hole golf course (*see
p195*) and practice facilities.

Club Mina

*Le Meridien Mina Seyahi Hotel, Al Sufouh Road,
Jumeirah (399 3333/www.lemeridien-minaseyahi.
com).* **Open** 6am-9pm daily. **Price** (non-members)
Sun-Wed Dhs100; Dhs200 incl lunch. *Sat, Thur-
Fri* members only. **Credit** AmEx, DC, MC, V.
Map p278 A5.

One of the trendier clubs in town, Club Mina has
a private beach that stretches for about half a
kilometre and hosts many of the city's beautiful
people whenever a powerboating race comes to
town. You can't beat 'em, so you might as well join
'em: the relaxed beachside Barasti bar (*see p178*)
is a terrific place to chill out. Club Mina's pure
reputation for swank is borne out by excellent
facilities, from three large swimming pools and
two smaller shaded pools for children to a grass
footie pitch and expanded gym with aerobic studio.

Jumeirah, Dubai's 'golden mile'.

Hiltonia Health & Beach Club

*Hilton Dubai Jumeirah Hotel, Al Sufouh Road,
Jumeirah (318 2227/www.hilton.com).* **Open**
Beach & pool 7am-7pm daily. *Health club* 7am-
10pm daily. **Price** (non-members) Dhs75;
Dhs30 concessions. **Credit** AmEx, DC,
MC, V. **Map** p278 A5.

There's no shortage of things to do here: water
sports include parasailing, kayaking, jet-skiing,
knee-boarding and fishing trips. The health club
has a well-equipped gym, sauna and steam room.
For those on an extended stay, monthly memberships are available (Dhs550; Dhs650 couple).

Jumeirah Health & Beach Club

*Sheraton Jumeirah Beach Resort, Al Sufouh Road,
Jumeirah (399 5533/www.starwood.com).* **Open**
7am-10pm daily (no lifeguards after 7pm). **Price**
(non-members) Dhs100; Dhs50 concessions; free
under-6s. **Credit** AmEx, DC, MC, V. **Map** p278 A5.

As well as two swimming pools, a couple of floodlit tennis courts and a pair of squash courts, this
club has a gym packed with the usual array of bikes,
steppers, rowing machines and treadmills. Add in
volleyball, a range of water sports, a sauna and a
steam room, and you won't run out of things to do
in a hurry. Or you could just treat yourself to the
Aqua Centre Spa, which offers facials and a range
of different massages and aromatherapy.

Metropolitan Resort & Beach Club

*Metropolitan Hotel, Al Sufouh Road, Jumeirah
(399 5000/www.methotels.com).* **Open** 8.30am-
7.30pm daily. **Price** (non-members) *Sat-Thur*
Dhs95. *Fri, public hols* Dhs120. *Concessions* Dhs25.
Credit AmEx, DC, MC, V. **Map** p278 A5.

Active Dubai

Al Mamzar Park (*see p205*), a forgotten haven of peace, miles from Jumeirah's beaches.

In 2005, the Metropolitan's fitness club benefited from a massive facelift. It now offers a convenient (and brand new) gymnasium, as well as a spa and squash and tennis facilities. The beach is pleasant, if fairly busy, and those easily bored of sunbathing will find a slew of entertaining water sports, from water-skiing to scuba (24hrs notice required).

Oasis Beach Club

Oasis Beach Hotel, Al Sufouh Road, Jumeirah (315 4034/www.jebelali-international.com). **Open** 9am-9pm daily. **Price** (non-members) *Sat-Wed* Dhs85; Dhs50 concessions. *Thur, Fri* Dhs160; Dhs50 concessions. **Credit** AmEx, DC, MC, V. **Map** p278 A5.

Archery and pétanque are just two of the sports on offer at this lively four-star club, which tends to attract a younger, active crowd and families. There is a floodlit tennis court, beach volleyball and soccer, and water sports include windsurfing, wakeboarding, water-skiing, banana boats and snorkelling. A large pool with swim-up bar and the Coco Cabana beach-side restaurant make for a lively atmosphere. It's still all good value for money, but popularity of the club has meant its prices have jumped in the last year. Non-guests at the hotel can apply for a 'Neighbourhood Privilege Club' membership. This is free and entitles holders to half-price admission during the week (Dhs15 discount at weekends), as well as a 25% discount on food and drink.

Ritz-Carlton Beach Club

Ritz-Carlton Dubai Hotel, Al Sufouh Road, Jumeirah (399 4000/www.ritzcarlton.com). **Open** 6am-10pm daily. **Price** (non-members) *Sat-Wed* Dhs150; Dhs60 concessions; free under-4s. *Thur-Fri* members only. **Credit** AmEx, DC, MC, V. **Map** p278 A5.

Despite the mess of construction edging closer and closer to this haven of tranquillity, the Ritz-Carlton Beach Club is still a spectacular place. For starters there is a 350m (120ft) stretch of private beach and vast landscaped gardens. Then there are typically impressive facilities: four floodlit tennis courts, a grass soccer pitch, two squash courts, a pitch-and-putt golf course and a comprehensively equipped gym. Personal trainers are always on hand to answer fitness questions, and the classes available include power yoga and women-only 'aerotennis', which is a cross between the racket sport and normal aerobics. The Ritz-Carlton spa features two women-only treatment rooms, taking the overall total to ten, and offers a range of seductive treatments that stretches from Balinese-style massage to Scentao hot stone therapy. Water sports can be organised on request at an additional cost.

Health clubs

Given the dominance of beach culture and alfresco lifestyles in the UAE, it should hardly be a surprise that there is high demand for fitness training and health advice. Many visitors also choose Dubai and its lack of obvious sightseeing tours in order to achieve some quality personal time on the beach, in the gym or stretched out in the spa. Health clubs are certainly big business, and the variety (and range of quality) of instruction is broad: annual memberships can stretch from Dhs3,000 to the unfeasibly extortionate. Given that it's not as easy to pop from one side of the city to the other as it used to be, and

City hotspots: parks and beaches

Dubai's residents are finally making use of the city's low-key suntraps, as rising prices, sluggish traffic and ever-growing crowds of tourists make a weekend at the city's premium hotel beach clubs (*see pp202-204*) less desirable than it used to be. It's not a bad idea to join them, but bear in mind that in rough weather the Dubai coast is plagued by strong offshore undertows, and swimming without trained lifeguards on hand can be dangerous. It's not unheard of to see red flags warning against taking a dip in the water and young men ignoring the sensible advice. You're also not allowed to take dogs on public beaches, a rule enforced by the police.

For sun lovers who prefer flora and fauna to sand and surf, the city is well endowed with lush green parks, maintained at phenomenal expense and tended with care. The three main family-centric parks are **Al Mamzar**, **Al Safa** and **Umm Suqeim** (for full descriptions, *see pp152-153*), all of which have excellent facilities for children. Otherwise, you should try basking in the hotspots listed here. Do bear in mind, however, the only public place where flesh can be shown is the beach; in the parks your shorts and T-shirts must remain firmly on.

Creekside Park

Umm Hurair, near Wonderland (336 7633). **Open** 8am-11pm Sat-Wed; 8am-midnight Thur, Fri. **Admission** *Park* free. *Cable car* Dhs25; Dhs10 concessions. *Children's City* Dhs15, Dhs10 concessions. **Map** p281 K3.
An enormous stretch of greenery that runs along 2.5km (1.5 miles) of prime Creek frontage, Creekside Park has acres of pristine lawns and gardens where you can roll out a rug and get tanning. Those who wish to fish can do so from dedicated piers that jut out into the Creek. Joggers are well catered for with purpose-built tracks, in-line skating is permitted, and bikes can be hired from Gate 2. A cable car (the emirate's first when it opened in 2000) gives an aerial view over the water.

Jumeirah Beach Park

Jumeirah 2, next to Jumeirah Beach Club (349 2555). **Open** 8am-10.30pm Sat-Wed; 8am-11pm Thur, Fri; women & children only Sat, Sun. **Admission** Dhs5; Dhs20 per car incl occupants. **Map** p286 A15.
A popular hangout thanks to its ample, well-manicured gardens, which tumble down to a narrow but well-maintained strip of beach,

Jumeirah Beach Park is a pleasant place to start working on your tan. The park is particularly busy on Friday afternoons, when people gather around barbecue pits for all-day burger-eating and socialising.

Kite Beach

Umm Suqeim 4, behind Wollongong University. **Map** p278 B4.
Kitesurfing and parasailing have taken off in a big way in Dubai and the long stretches of undeveloped sand at the southerly end of Jumeirah are collectively named after this popular activity. For surfers these beaches offer unbroken expanses of ocean, free from breakwaters. For those who have less strenuous pursuits in mind, fear not – there's plenty of space to stretch out and sunbathe.

Mushrif Park

Near Mirdif (288 3624). **Open** 8am-11.30pm daily. **Admission** Dhs3; Dhs10 per car. *Swimming pool* Dhs10; Dhs5 concessions. *Train* Dhs2. **Map** p279 F3.
Is this park still the best-kept secret in Dubai? To get here, drive past the airport and continue out of town. Ten minutes later, just past the residential area of Mirdif, you'll find yourself at Mushrif Park, a surprisingly huge swathe of green, filled with wildlife and crossed by a dinky train service. You can assert your tourist credentials by leaping aboard a camel for a ride, before soaking up the rays in your very own landscaped plot.

Russian Beach

Jumeirah 1, next to Dubai Marine Beach Resort & Spa. **Map** p284 D9.
One of the city's best-known public beaches and the closest one to the centre of town, Russian Beach (also known as Open Beach) is popular with an eclectic mix of residents because it offers easy access and (during calm weather) safe bathing. It's also free, and draws an increasingly varied crowd – not all of whom are there to gaze at the horizon. The once-pristine shore now suffers views of construction and passing ships, and there's an increasingly depressing amount of litter where the sand meets Jumeirah's Beach Road. Still, the numerous beaches that nestle within man-made breakwaters are reliable suntraps, and when you've had enough fun you're just a stone's throw from the many cafés and stores lining the northern end of Beach Road.

Active Dubai

despite the excellent facilities that are still provided by Jumeirah's beach clubs, these listings reflect the new breed of inner-city fitness club that is winning over time-sensitive Dubaians.

The Aviation Club

Off Sharjah Road, Garhoud (282 4122/www. *aviationclubonline.com).* **Open** 6am-11pm daily. **Price** (annual membership only) Dhs5,000 men; Dhs3,750 women (plus Dhs2,500 one-off joining fee). Discounts are available for couples & corporate membership. **Credit** AmEx, MC, V. **Map** p281 L3.

Home to Dubai's prestigious tennis tournament and one of the few clubs to establish itself on the Deira side of the Creek, the Aviation Club is incredibly popular. An extensive upgrade had been completed by the middle of 2005, ensuring the place remained at the forefront of the fitness scene with the construction of separate spas for ladies and gents, and the addition of new group exercise studios. There's an impressive list of facilities, including six floodlit tennis courts, a swimming pool with 25m lap lanes, two squash courts, a dedicated spinning studio, a sauna, a steam room, plunge pools and a nine-hole par-three golf course, in addition to the fully equipped gym. The aerobics studio is still the biggest and busiest in Dubai, hosting several fat-busting classes a day.

The Big Apple

Emirates Towers Boulevard mall, Sheikh Zayed Road (319 8661/www.jumeirahinternational.com). **Open** 6am-10pm daily. **Price** *Gym* Dhs30 per day. *Classes* Dhs25. **Credit** AmEx, DC, MC, V. **Map** p280 H4.

Tucked away in the lower levels of the Emirates Towers, the Big Apple is a highly polished chrome and steel affair, the epitome of the modern urban fitness centre. It lacks swimming, sauna or steam room facilities, but is armed to the teeth with Nautilus, Startrak, Stairmaster and Concept II equipment. Aerobic classes cover everything from BodyPump to spinning. Membership packages are available for less than Dhs3,000 per year, which, considering the swanky location, represent excellent value for Dubai.

Club Olympus

Hyatt Regency Hotel, Deira Corniche (209 6802/ www.dubai.regency.hyatt.com). **Open** 7am-11pm daily (incl swimming pool). **Price** *Hotel guests* free. *Non-guests (ID required)* Dhs50 per day Sat-Wed; Dhs60 per day Thur, Fri. **Credit** AmEx, DC, MC, V. **Map** p283 J1.

The friendly, professional staff attract a varied clientele to this city-centre club. Classes range from salsa to karate, and you'll also find a Nautilus gym and a running track that circles the two floodlit tennis courts. A pair of squash courts, outdoor swimming pool, spa, sauna, steam room, Jacuzzi and splash pool complete the line-up of facilities; the outside deck is particularly popular when the cooler winter months come round.

Dimension Health & Fitness Club

Metropolitan Hotel, Sheikh Zayed Road, Interchange 2 (407 6704). **Open** 6am-midnight daily. **Price** *Facilities* Dhs40 per day. *Classes* Dhs20-Dhs35. **Credit** AmEx, DC, MC, V. **Map** p280 G5.

The Metropolitan is one of the older complexes in Dubai, but Dimension packs a well-equipped gym with an assortment of Nautilus equipment and free weights. Its 25m outdoor swimming pool is one of the main attractions, although there is also a Jacuzzi, steam room and sauna. The studio runs various classes, including fencing (*see p193*) and kickboxing. In fact, the Dimension Club is a bit of a one-stop shop, with Indian and Chinese massage available if you're too tired to pump another iron.

Fitness Planet

Al Hana Centre, Dhiyafah Street, Satwa (398 9030/www.bgroupme.com). **Open** *Mixed gym* 6am-11pm Sat-Thur; 4-10pm Fri. *Women's gym* 7am-9pm Sat-Thur. **Price** (non-members) *Facilities* Dhs30 per day. **Credit** AmEx, MC, V. **Map** p285 F8.

The emphasis at this busy gym is on free weights and resistance machines, so expect to see serious bodybuilders and weightlifters. For women who might find the main mixed gym a bit intimidating, there's a separate women's area, Fitness Planet Hers, on the mezzanine level. Other facilities include a Jacuzzi, a steam room and a sauna. Membership packages start at three months.

Lifestyle Health Club

Sofitel City Centre Hotel, Port Saeed (603 8825/ www.accorhotels.com). **Open** 6.30am-11pm Sat-Thur; 8am-8pm Fri. **Price** *Facilities* Dhs50 per day. *Aerobics classes* Dhs30. **Credit** MC, V. **Map** p281 K2.

This hotel-based club stretches over three floors: the reception, two squash courts and the sauna and steam room are on one level; the gym and aerobics studio are on the next; and an outdoor swimming pool and the floodlit tennis court are on the roof. The gym is decked out with the full complement of cardiovascular and resistance machines, and different aerobic classes are held each day in the studio. Residents have a choice of membership schemes: you can either pick up a green card (Dhs3,000) for full access for a year, or get yourself a yellow card (Dhs2,300) which allows you to use the gym and pool.

Nautilus Academy

Al Mussalla Towers, Kahlid Bin Al Waleed Road (Bank Street), Bur Dubai (397 4117). **Open** 6am-11pm daily. **Price** *Membership* Dhs900 per mth. *Classes* Dhs30. **Credit** AmEx, DC, MC, V. **Map** p282 H4.

One of Dubai's best-equipped gyms, fielding all manner of Nautilus machines (as you might expect) and cardiovascular equipment, this fitness club is located right in the heart of the city. Increasingly popular, Nautilus no longer sells day passes as a rule, but it will sometimes makes an exception for short-term visitors on quiet days. Separate studios

No pain, no gain at **Club Mina**. *See p203.*

exist for spinning classes and aerobics, and there are two squash courts, a small outdoor swimming pool, a steam room, a sauna, a Jacuzzi and a café.

Nautilus Fitness Centre

Crowne Plaza Hotel, Sheikh Zayed Road (331 4055).
Open 6am-10pm Sat-Wed; 8.30am-8.30pm Thur, Fri. **Price** *Membership* Dhs400 per mth. *Facilities* Dhs50 per day. *Classes* Dhs25 (non-members); Dhs15 (members). **Credit** MC, V. **Map** p285 G10.
The focus at this centre is, of course, on Nautilus training techniques, but there are also free weights and an array of cardiovascular machines. The long list of aerobic classes stretches from powerpump to Tae-Bo and yoga, and even belly dancing for those who want something a bit more exotic. Other facilities include a squash court, table tennis, a sauna, a steam room and an outdoor swimming pool.

Pharaohs' Club

Wafi Pyramids, at Wafi City mall, off Oud Metha Road (324 0000/www.waficity.com).
Open 7am-10pm Sat-Thur; 9am-9pm Fri.
Price *Monthly membership* Dhs1,000. *Annual membership* Dhs5,500 (discounts for couples). *Swimming pool* (members & guests only) Dhs60. **Credit** AmEx, DC, MC, V. **Map** p281 J3.
Still one of the most prestigious clubs in Dubai, Pharaohs' offers members luxurious surroundings and an impressive array of facilities. There are well-equipped gyms for men and women, with the latter benefiting from exclusive use of the main gym on Wednesday and Sunday mornings, until 1pm. Steam rooms, plunge pools and Jacuzzis are provided, as well as a large swimming pool and a separate pool in which, with a flick of a switch, you can attempt to swim against the tide. The club also boasts a climbing wall, three floodlit tennis courts, two squash courts and a comprehensive range of fitness classes. Best of all, members qualify for an enticing 25% discount on treatments at the adjoining Cleopatra's Spa (*see p209*).

Spas

Perhaps because expats demand to be spoilt, arguing that life is all about enjoying the finer things, there has been a veritable explosion in spa culture in Dubai over the last few years. Much of the emirate's success has been built on supplying five-star services at three- and four-star prices, and the story of the city's spas follows that pattern exactly: here body and soul pamperings of every conceivable philosophy and substance are firmly within the financial reach of tourists and residents alike. Better yet, the quality and scope of the competition keeps most of these spas at the very top end of the market in terms of surroundings and quality.

Assawan Spa & Health Club

Burj Al Arab Hotel, Beach Road, Jumeirah (301 7338/www.jumeirahinternational.com). **Open** 6.30am-10pm daily. **Price** Dhs300 1hr basic massage. **Credit** AmEx, DC, MC, V. **Map** p278 A4.
This lavishly decorated club is located on the 18th floor of Dubai's iconic landmark hotel, providing spectacular views of the Arabian Gulf. There are separate male and female areas boasting a total of eight spa treatment rooms, a sauna, a steam bath, a plunge pool, a Jacuzzi and a solarium. Espa and La Prairie facials are offered, as well as wraps, massages and hot stone treatments. Don't expect any of this to come cheap, but if you're seeking a truly once-in-a-lifetime experience then this is the place to explore. Non-guests can book treatments here, but subject to availability.

Ayoma Spa

Taj Palace Hotel, Al Maktoum Street, Deira (211 3101/www.tajhotels.com). **Open** 10am-10pm daily (last booking 8pm). **Price** Dhs250 1hr basic massage. **Credit** AmEx, MC, V. **Map** p283 A3.

Weird science

Do you find Balinese massage mainstream in the extreme? Are hot energy-filled batu stones from Indonesia so last century? Fear not. There's a fast-growing fringe of spiritual healers in Dubai itching to unblock your aura and manipulate your meridians – let the healing begin.

Bach Flower Remedies

In the 1930s, respected Harley Street physician Dr Edward Bach began to recognise stress as the catalyst for many illnesses and he ultimately became dissatisfied with orthodox approaches to medicine. Instead, he hit upon the notion of the healing power of flowers, and spent years in search of flora that would counteract what he identified as the 38 negative states of the human mind. The result was a series of flower remedies, prepared droplets of essence that hold the healing vibrations of their parent petals. Patients can take the droplets in a drink or directly on the tongue; dilution doesn't affect efficacy. Those in search of flower power should contact the **General Naturpathic Centre** (344 1778) on Beach Road, Jumeirah. An hour's consultation costs up to Dhs250.

Bowen Therapy

The brainchild of intuitive healer Tom Bowen, and developed in Australia in the 1960s, Bowen Therapy assists the body's healing processes through non-invasive manipulation of the body's connective tissues. The theory goes that the body's water levels can become imbalanced and, if flowing improperly, have a knock-on effect on every interconnected organ. Gentle pressure applied to the body compresses and stretches key ligaments, creating heat in certain areas so that the body responds by transporting rehydrating water as the healer directs. The process

works the body, but no oils are involved and clothing can be worn. Certainly the experts at the **Healing Zone** (394 0604), Umm Suqeim, argue that Bowen Therapy is a very different thing to a simple massage.

Pranic Healing

Lost in history for years before its rediscovery in 1987, this ancient medical system maintains that the body can heal itself. Chakras – energy centres in your aura – channel prana from the sun to keep your organs functioning by throwing out body toxins. When emotional problems like stress interfere with your prana, internal organs are deprived of much-needed energy. That's when a healer from the **Pranic Therapy Centre** (336 0885), Karama, should be called to 'scoop' out your bad prana so that the body can thrive again. A consultation costs Dhs100 and, much like other hands-on holistic treatments, the client remains fully clothed throughout.

Spiritual Healing

Around since the dawn of time, in one way or another, this school of healing has acquired the status of New Age fad following various modern interpretations. The basic premise maintains that your physical being is a shell for your real, spiritual self. Illness is seen as an outward sign of inner imbalance, sparked off by negative thoughts and actions. Through the laying on of hands (figuratively speaking), the healer channels higher vibrations of energy into the patient's form, increasing the frequency of the denser, unhelpful vibrations. According to the gurus at **MindBody Dynamixs** (348 5798), also based in Umm Suqeim, the restorative effects can be compared to experiencing comfortable sights and sounds, like hearing the voice of a friend or breathing in fresh sea air. Consultations cost Dhs250.

Far away from plush beachside Jumeirah, hidden away in Deira's Taj Palace, there's an atmospheric and relaxing spa. Three different styles of massage are available here, progressing from Ayurvedic to Balinese and Swedish, and the friendly staff will happily recommend an appropriate in-depth treatment to you, depending on the desired effect. For something a little less committed, facials and a range of other acts of delightful pampering are also available. As well as the separate saunas and steam rooms, this spa features a swimming pool and the obligatory Jacuzzi.

Caracalla Spa

Le Royal Meridien Hotel, Al Sufouh Road, Jumeirah (399 5555/www.leroyalmeridien-dubai.com). **Open** 9.30am-8pm daily. **Price** Dhs240 1hr basic massage. **Credit** AmEx, DC, MC, V. **Map** p278 A5.

This spa is normally open only to hotel guests and members of the Caracalla club (*see p203*) – but treatments can be booked by other visitors and residents if there are any free slots, a rare occurrence indeed, such is the popularity of this venue. Dedicated steam and sauna rooms, plus a Jacuzzi and hammam with five plunge pools, serve both men and women. Treatments include excellent 50-minute aromatherapy massages, one-hour 'well-being' (face and body) massages and exotic facials.

Cleopatra's Spa
Wafi Pyramids, at Wafi City mall, off Oud Metha Road, Bur Dubai (324 7700/www.waficity.com).
Open *Women only* 9am-8pm Sat-Thur; 10am-8pm Fri. *Men only* 10am-10pm Sat, Mon-Fri; 10am-7pm Sun. **Price** Dhs230 1hr basic massage. **Credit** AmEx, DC, MC, V. **Map** p281 J3.
For the ultimate in spa treatments you can't go far wrong amid the luxury at Cleopatra's. As the name implies, the whole facility has an Egyptian theme, with larger-than-life statues outside Wafi Pyramids give way to a far more sophisticated and visually stunning interior. The usual facials and wraps complement some very different treatments, including the gorgeous aroma stone massage, in which the body is massaged with hot energy-filled batu stones from Indonesia and exotic oils. Ayurvedic treatments are also offered, as is Ionithermie, a detox and slimming treatment. A sports therapist is on hand for specialised and remedial massage.

Dubai Marine Beach Resort & Spa
Beach Road, Jumeirah (304 8081/www.dxb marine.com). **Open** 10am-7pm daily. **Price** Dhs250 1hr basic massage. **Credit** AmEx, DC, MC, V. **Map** p284 D8.
Guests staying at the secluded chalets of the charming but well-worn Beach Resort & Spa are usually people who appreciate private downtime. This low-key spa boasts six qualified therapists, using upmarket Guinot and Espa beauty products. There are three treatment rooms for relaxing massages, facials and body treatments.

Indian Ayurveda
Shop B201, Al Attar Centre, Kuwait Street, Karama (396 0469). **Open** 9am-1pm, 4.30-9.30pm Sat-Thur; 9am-6pm Fri. **Price** Dhs100 1hr massage. No credit cards. **Map** p283 J5.
A far cry from Jumeirah's brand hotels, Karama's no-frills finest offers a full body, face and head massage at the hands of trained masseurs from Kerala in southern India. Treatments here have a proven feel-good formula, but lack the luxurious frippery you may or may not wish to pay for. Shower facilities are available.

One&Only Royal Mirage Spa
One&Only Royal Mirage Hotel, Al Sufouh Road, Jumeirah (399 9999/www.royalmiragedubai.com). **Open** *Women only* 9.30am-1pm daily. *Mixed* 2.30-7pm daily. **Price** Dhs275 1hr basic massage. **Credit** AmEx, DC, MC, V. **Map** p278 A5.
The magnificent Health & Beauty Institute at the Royal Mirage Spa covers an area of 2,000sq m (21,500sq ft), divided over two levels. On the upper floor, the Givenchy Spa has separate areas and opening times for women; the rest of the time, it's mixed. It features 12 treatment rooms, including an exclusive suite for private consultations, a resting

area, an organic juice bar and a Givenchy boutique. The lower floor is proud home to an authentic oriental hammam with a traditional heated marble massage table, plus two steam rooms and two private massage rooms. The institute marries modern cleanliness with the hotel's Moroccan-fort theme; the result is arguably the most heavenly escape in Dubai. Two Jacuzzis, a whirlpool and a plunge shower are also on offer.

Ritz-Carlton Spa
Ritz-Carlton Dubai Hotel, Al Sufouh Road, Jumeirah (399 4000). **Open** 6am-10pm daily (massages 9am-6pm daily). **Price** Dhs265 1hr basic massage. **Credit** AmEx, DC, MC, V. **Map** p278 A5.
The heady Balinese theme at the Ritz-Carlton Spa is a well-executed concept, running thoughout the decor and artwork, and extending to all-Balinese staff. The treatments available include a Balinese Boreh massage and a Nirvana herbal body wrap. There are no less than eight treatment rooms and a salon dedicated to doing your hair and enhancing your beauty, as well as a Jacuzzi, sauna and steam room. European and marine spa treatments are available, using minerals, salts from the Dead Sea and natural sponges. Additional treatments include waxing, electrolysis, vibromassage and reflexology. Individual treatment times vary, ranging from a half-hour or one-hour session up to the two top treatments that last six hours: guests with time to spare can choose the marine-based Calming Sea package or the Eastern Delight Oriental treatment.

Royal Waters Health Spa
Al Mamzar Centre, Sharjah Road, Deira (297 2053). **Open** *Women only* 9am-5pm daily. *Mixed* 5pm-midnight daily. **Price** Dhs225 1hr basic massage. **Credit** AmEx, MC, V. **Map** p279 E1.

One&Only Royal Mirage Spa.

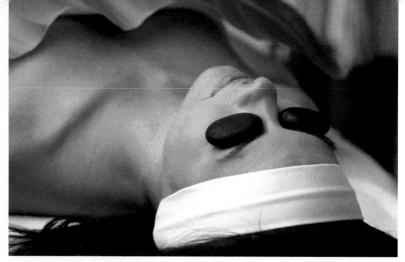
Bed of heaven: the Madinat Jumeirah's new **Six Senses Spa**.

The Royal Waters Health Spa is certainly high-tech, but it's also less intensely posh than rival hotel-based establishments. Perhaps lacking a little glamour, it nonetheless avoids the formulaic feel of some hotel spas, and should offer uneasy spa-virgins an experience that's more intimate and less intimidating than they'd get elsewhere. Available treatments include a full hydrotherapy circuit, Eastern and Western massage, and slimming treatments. The spa also contains a swimming pool, sauna and steam rooms.

Satori Spa
Jumeirah Beach Club Hotel, Beach Road, Jumeirah (310 2754/www.jumeirahinternational.com). **Open** 9am-9pm daily. **Price** Dhs250 1hr basic massage. **Credit** AmEx, DC, MC, V. **Map** p286 A15.
The list of treatments at this exclusive club is seemingly endless, from eye lifts and facials to sessions in Thai massage and reflexology. Although this is technically a members' and hotel-guests' club, it was possible as we went to press for non-members to book a fully self-indulgent day of pampering for Dhs499 (be sure to book at least 24hrs in advance). This covers two spa treatments, lunch, and access to the gym and beach.

Six Senses Spa
Madinat Jumeirah, Al Sufouh Road (366 8888/www.jumeirahinternational.com). **Open** 9am-10pm daily. **Price** Dhs350 1hr basic massage. **Credit** AmEx, DC, MC, V. **Map** p251 A4.
True to the Madinat philosophy, Dubai's newest spa is built around a labyrinth of paths and waterways, courtyards and studios. Guests of the resort will enter the spa on board a silent abra (or water taxi), which is relaxing in itself. Otherwise, you should head for Al Qasr hotel until you see signs to the spa. Regardless of your method of arrival, the beautiful landscaped gardens and sculpted scenery soon set the tone for a serious bliss-out

session. Many different types of ethnic treatment are on offer to rejuvenate tired travellers, from massages with exotic oils to more scientific healing and wellness therapies. Indeed, the business of relaxation is taken seriously at Six Senses: every visitor is given a free health assessment to ensure that the most appropriate treatment is offered.

Spa Thira
Opposite Jumeirah Beach Park, Beach Road, Jumeirah (344 2055). **Open** 9am-8pm Sat-Wed; 9am-2pm Thur. **Price** Dhs300 90min facial. **Credit** DC, MC, V. **Map** p286 A15.
A women-only one-stop beauty shop in the heart of Jumeirah, Spa Thira offers a range of treatments, from facials and manicures to soft-laser hair removal and light Moroccan-style massages. Once you've had the full treatment, it's a good idea to go and flaunt your new, ultra-relaxed look by topping up your tan in neighbouring Jumeirah Beach Park (*see p205* **City hotspots: parks and beaches**).

Willow Stream Spa
Fairmont Hotel, Sheikh Zayed Road (332 5555/www.fairmont.com). **Open** 6am-midnight daily. **Price** Dhs250 1hr basic massage. **Credit** AmEx, DC, MC, V. **Map** p285 G9.
Expect high-quality pampering and treatments at the sublime, high-design Willow Stream Spa, which covers a little under 4,000sq m (40,000 sq ft). As well as separate whirlpools, saunas and steam rooms for men and women, it also boasts two large outdoor swimming pools, positioned so that one catches the sun in the morning and the other gets the sun in afternoon. There is a wading pool for children and a lounge that's open to all. Guests get to enjoy a vast range of seductive treatments, including everything from a sea-scrub body polish to a detox hydrobath treament, as well as facials, skin treatments and waxing. Which are exactly what the Fairmont's high-flying clientele ordered.

Active Dubai

The UAE

Getting Started

Aside from the fast-living fun of Dubai, the UAE has an abundance of attractions to explore.

Although it was the British who brought the seven emirates of Abu Dhabi, Ajman, Dubai, Fujairah, Ras Al Khaimah, Sharjah and Umm Al Quwain together as the Trucial States, it was the late Sheikh Zayed Al Nahyan – the much-mourned former leader of Abu Dhabi, whose death in 1994 brought dignitaries here from all over the world (*see p12* **Sheikh Zayed, architect of the UAE**) – who cemented them in the name of the UAE. The year was 1971, and buoyed by the collective strength of the union and the foresight and fortunes of Abu Dhabi in particular, each emirate has grown in status since then.

The UAE is situated on the south-eastern tip of the Arabian peninsula. To the north-west is Qatar; Saudi Arabia is to the west and south and Oman to the south-east and north-east (for map, *see pp274-275*). It goes without saying that Dubai leads the way in terms of accommodating and entertaining tourists, but away from the glitz lies the wider UAE's tapestry of sun-drenched beaches, cool mountain escapes and bustling cities rich with cultural experiences. Just short of two hours south of Dubai is the capital, **Abu Dhabi** (*see p213*), and closer still, to the north, there are unexpected pockets of quiet reflection amid the chaos of **Sharjah** (*see p226*). Adventure abounds further north in the wild reaches of **Ras Al Khaimah** (*see p233*), while superb snorkelling abounds at **Fujairah** (*see p238*) and along the east coast.

Be warned, however, that public transport remains fairly primitive here. Buses are as cramped as they are economical, and rarely would you see a tourist aboard one; there are no trains whatsoever. Nonetheless, the government's determination to build smooth efficient highways is paying off. Our advice if you're heading out of Dubai is take to the wheel of a 4x4 on short-term hire and explore the UAE's delights at your own speed.

The UAE

The ever-changing skyline of **Abu Dhabi**.

Abu Dhabi

So long in the shadow of Dubai, the UAE's capital is beginning to boom as new developments shape a truly modern city.

Abu Dhabi's transformation from tiny fishing village to bustling capital city in such a short space of time is testament to the incredible foresight of Sheikh Zayed bin Sultan Al Nahyan. It was less than 50 years ago that the entire emirate of Abu Dhabi was near-empty desert, populated by Bedouin tribes and dotted by a minute amount of villages. Its initial elevation to economic prominence was the result of pearl cultivation, until global recession coupled with a thriving cultivated pearl industry in Japan put to paid to that and relegated Abu Dhabi to the position of poorest emirate. But the discovery of huge offshore oil reserves in 1958 and the subsequent rule of Sheikh Zayed totally transformed its fortunes. As recently as 30 years ago the capital city was still short of a reliable electricity supply and roads. Now its expanse of roads are always chock-full of cars and the whole city has been transformed into a powerhouse capital that's the envy of nations across the globe.

STRIKE IT LUCKY

Having noted the island stood as a natural stronghold – and also offered fine fishing – the Ban Yas Bedouin tribe settled in Abu Dhabi in the 1760s. They dubbed the region Abu Dhabi ('Father of the Gazelle') and would thereafter lead a largely unchanged existence for nearly 200 years. Legend tells that the city owes its unorthodox name to gazelle tracks found by a wandering party of Bedouin hunters. The nomads followed the tracks into a shallow inlet of the sea only to discover they emerged again on the shore of the facing island and ended at a spring of fresh water. They quickly returned to their base in the Liwa oasis and reported the discovery to their leader, Sheikh Dhiyab bin Isa, who decreed that the island should thereafter be known as Abu Dhabi in honour of the auspicious find.

The discovery of a freshwater well encouraged the ruling Al Nahyan family to relocate from their home in Liwa to Abu Dhabi, securing the city's first steps on its rise to prominence. And the good times continued through the 1800s, as residents grew prosperous from the seemingly endless supply of pearls that were found off Abu Dhabi's lengthy coastline. Then came the aforementioned worldwide pearl recession and

Abu Dhabi's inevitable decline, which forced potentate Sheik Shakhbut bin Sultan to investigate other potential sources of revenue. Somewhat fortuitously, he granted drilling rights to the British – who had been present in the region since 1892 in the role of overseers of a protectorate – and the search for oil began. In 1958 huge offshore oil reserves were found; Abu Dhabi became the first of the Gulf States to export oil in 1962, earning an estimated US$70 million per year that decade from black gold. Today, roughly two million barrels of oil are exported around the globe every 24 hours. Current estimates suggest this will continue for the foreseeable future.

The British left the Gulf region in 1971 and the seven factional emirates united to form the UAE, declaring Abu Dhabi the provisional capital. Sheikh Zayed Al Nahyan was welcomed as the new state's first president and duly returned to power every five years before his death saw his son assume control. In 1996 the word 'provisional' was dropped from Abu Dhabi's title, making it the official, permanent capital city.

CAPITAL GAINS

It may be busier and more bustling than at any point in its short history, but the modern city of Abu Dhabi is essentially unhurried, a proud, reserved place set by the clear waters of the Arabian Gulf. Wide boulevards are lined with trees that belie the city's desert origins, running through a 20th-century grid-based traffic system amid clusters of high-rise blocks. A beautiful and recently developed – to the tune of millions – corniche runs the length of the city, curled between the coast and the less-than-picturesque highway that stretches on to Dubai. There is an oddly engaging range of finely manicured – and often statue-bedecked – roundabouts, a liberal scattering of fountains, and more green than you'll find anywhere else in the UAE, bar the Garden City of **Al Ain** (*see p224*). The greenery is a lasting testament to the environmental commitments of Sheikh Zayed Al Nahyan, which won him worldwide acclaim.

There is, though, a concerted effort by the current authorities to build on the near Dhs100 billion facelift that Sheikh Zayed Al

Abu Dhabi

A   **B**   **C**

1

Ras Laffan

Khor Laffan

Port Zayed

A R A B I A N

G U L F

2

Jazirat Bu
Ash Shu'um

The Club

Iranian souk

AL MEENA

Al Diar Capitol Hotel

Le Meridien
Hotel

Abu Dhabi Mall

Sheraton
Hotel

Cemetery

Mosque
Gardens

Beach Rotana
Hotel

Cemetery

Sadiyat
Bridge

Abu Dhabi Grand
(Le Royal Meridien)

Nina

AS SALAM ST

QASR EL BAHR

Millennium Hotel

Al Lulu

Volcano
Fountain

Capital
Gardens

BANI YAS

3

Clock
Tower

Crowne
Plaza
Hotel

MADINAT
ZAYED

SEA PALACE
ROAD

AL ITTIHAD
SQUARE

Cemetery

AL
DHAFRAH

EASTERN RING

AL HOSN

Old Fort
& Al Husn
Palace

Cultural Foundation

Grand
Mosque

AL MANHAL

Central
Hospital

SHEIKH RASHID BIN SAEED AL MAKTOUM ST

AL WAHDAH

NEW AIRPORT ROAD

Al Mahnal
Palace

AL
KARAMAH

National
Theatre

4

Breakwater

AL TABBIYAH

MUSSALA
EL EID

Municipality

AL KHALIDIYAH

Khalidiya
Garden

AL ROWDAH

Khalifa
Gardens

Marina Mall

Khalidiya
Childrens
Garden

Municipal
Market

Mushrif Palace

Hilton Hotel

Ministry
of State

Ras Al Bateen

AL KHALEEG AL ARABI STREET

Emirates
Palace
Hotel

Police Station

Cemetery

Cemetery

Golf &
Equestrian
Club

AL KHOBEIRAH

AL BATEEN

Bateen
Palace

Race
Track

Bainunah Street

InterContinental
Hotel

SULTAN BIN ZAYED STREET

AR RAS
AL AKHDAR

SAEED BIN TAHNOON S

5

Khor Al Bateen

Hideriyyat

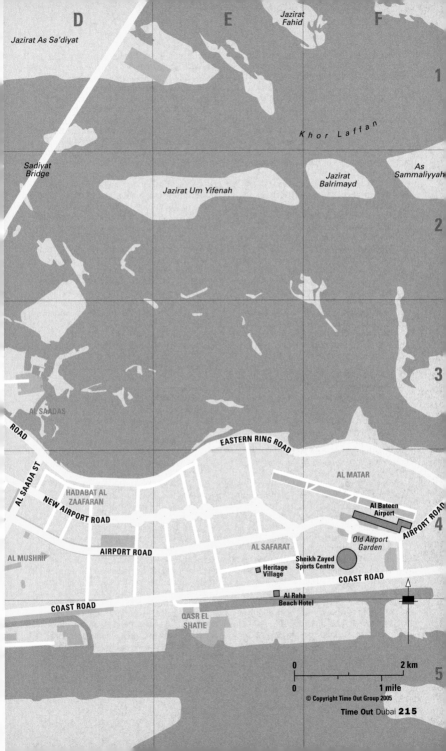

D

E

F

Jazirat As Sa'diyat

Jazirat Fahid

1

Khor Laffan

Sadiyat Bridge

Jazirat Um Yifenah

Jazirat Balrimayd

As Sammaliyyah

2

3

AL SAADAS

ROAD

EASTERN RING ROAD

AL SAADA ST

HADABAT AL ZAAFARAN

NEW AIRPORT ROAD

AL MATAR

Al Bateen Airport

AIRPORT ROAD

4

AL MUSHRIF

AIRPORT ROAD

AL SAFARAT

Heritage Village

Sheikh Zayed Sports Centre

Old Airport Garden

COAST ROAD

COAST ROAD

Al Raha Beach Hotel

QASR EL SHATIE

0   2 km

0   1 mile

© Copyright Time Out Group 2005

5

Nahyan oversaw in the city during his tenure. Certainly, in terms of tourism, business is booming. Abu Dhabi International Airport services more than 40 competing airlines, Etihad Airways, the Emirates' own airline, among them. And a radical overhaul of the entire site will see the airport double its passenger and cargo capacity to more than seven million and 300,000 tonnes respectively. Nearly all the hotels in the city are able to point to year-on-year growth, and the further influx of tourists will have an increasing number of luxury hotels compete for their custom. The official opening of the imposing **Emirates Palace** (*see p223*) isn't scheduled until the end of 2005, but its mere presence has already drawn the eyes of the world to Abu Dhabi: *The Sunday Times* listed the city among its 50 hottest holiday destinations of 2005. At its heart though, Abu Dhabi remains a traditional Middle Eastern city, which means it is advisable to watch your behaviour even when passing through. Overt drunkenness and lasciviousness should be confined to private places, and revealing outfits are best avoided. Gone are the days when such things would result in jail time, but too much skin on show will still attract slack-mouthed stares from pretty much everyone you meet.

Sightseeing

It has yet to reach Dubai's level of glamour – and has no pretensions to do so – but Abu Dhabi can be a near perfect place to relax. Whether lazing on a private beach, stretching your legs in an oasis of lush greenery or exploring the unique arrangement of islands off the emirate's northern coast, the capital boasts inspirational sights aplenty – if you only know where to look.

Just east of Abu Dhabi you'll find Al Maqtaa Fort, next to Al Maqtaa Bridge on the Airport Road. Now some 200 years old, the fort was originally built to keep bandits away from the city's riches. Another fortification to have witnessed great change is Qasr Al Husn, or the White Fort, which stands on the corner of Khalid Bin Waleed and Al Nasr Streets (Map p214 B3). Built at the end of the 1700s, it once served as the official residence of the rulers of Abu Dhabi but is now open to the public. Residents will tell you that Abu Dhabi is the cultural heart of the UAE, and the **Cultural Foundation** takes pride of place. The only facility of its kind in the region, it hosts temporary art exhibitions and local performances, between visits from international artistes; expect dinner theatre, amateur dramatics and the occasional touring ballet group. For other live entertainment, try the **Al Raha Theatre** (02 556 0176). Opened in 2003, it's one of the most sophisticated auditoriums in the Middle East – and, at Dhs81 million, one of the most expensive.

To realise just how far the city has come in such a short space of time, get a glimpse of the past at the **Dhow Harbour**, still worked by doughty craftsmen, and the **Heritage Village**, a faithful representation of a small nomadic camp. A less interactive but fairly comprehensive account of Abu Dhabi's oil-based boom can be had at the **Petroleum Exhibition**. Follow this with a tour of the grandiose **Emirates Palace** (*see p223*). Largely in an attempt to prevent large numbers of sightseers from wandering around its cavernous interior, the Palace offers guided tours throughout the day free of charge. Just ask at reception for details of timings, which tend to vary.

Arabia is famous worldwide for its racing thoroughbreds, its ancient bloodlines and the passion with which the Emirati people hold the equestrian arts. The breeding of winning horses is a serious business and the **Golf & Equestrian Club** (02 445 5500; Map p214 C4) holds races every Sunday from November to April. In a surprisingly efficient use of space, there is a par-72 golf course located within the racetrack, which closes two hours before the racing begins. Non-member green fees for 18 holes are Dhs230 (Saturday to Wednesday) or Dhs240 (Thursday and Friday). More fun but less prestigious is a round at **Al Ghazal Golf Club** (02 575 8040), an 18-hole sand course chiselled into land alongside the airport. It's open to anyone – even transit passengers with a few hours to kill. Non-member green fees for 18 holes are a mere Dhs100.

While it's not Paris, the city also boasts a surprisingly decent network of **parks**. Slap bang in the centre of the city is Capital Gardens (Map p214 B3), a delightful assortment of manicured lawns gathered around a central pond – known to erupt into aquatic action whenever the mood takes it. Refreshments come courtesy of vending machines and a small cafeteria. Be prepared to pay a dirham to get in, should you be able to get the little man's attention. The New Corniche park (Map p215 D4), found on the east side of the island, is a haven for birdwatchers and anglers. Picnic tables are popular on warm winter evenings, and it's always well lit and clean. Khalidiya Garden (Map p214 B4) doesn't have a cafeteria, but does offer vending machines and lawns like billiard tables. For a quiet stretch, the Old Airport Garden (Map p215 F4), next to the

Al Ghazal Golf Course.
See p216.

ice-skating rink, has swings for the kids, is beautifully ornamental and manages to remain tranquil. Trainspotter types might even fancy a gander at the largest flagpole in the world (Map p214 A4), which resides at the end of Abu Dhabi's breakwater.

Cultural Foundation

Opposite Etisalat building, Airport Road (02 619 5223). **Open** 8am-2pm, 5-9.30pm Sat-Thur; 5-8pm Fri. **Admission** varies. **Map** p214 B3.

This vast centre for the arts is proof of a very real desire to stimulate artistry in a land where so much energy is put into making cold hard cash. As you might expect from a building with such a noble purpose, there's a hushed atmosphere throughout the network of corridors and arched courtyards. The summer months excluded, the Foundation fills its lecture halls with residents drawn to international acts, primarily musicians, but speakers and actors too. The Foundation publishes a wealth of Islamic texts and is home to the National Archives.

Dhow Harbour

Al Bateen. **Admission** free. **Map** p214 B2.

A step back into the ancient Arabic world of ship-building, the famous Dhow Harbour provides an intriguing look at maritime skills that have been all but lost to the modern Gulf region. It's a hive of activity, and when they're not too busy the local craftsmen are (in the most part) happy to talk about their work and allow photographs to be taken of the task they're working on.

Heritage Village

Behind the Abu Dhabi Exhibition Centre, Mussafah Road (off Airport Road) (no phone). **Open** 8.30am-5pm daily. **Admission** free. **Map** p215 E4.

A faithful representation of the small nomadic camps typical of the Bedouins who roamed the land before the oil boom, the village is a hands-on attempt to show what life was like a century ago. Make rope from date-palm husks, ride on a camel, or drink the terribly pungent Arabic coffee. On odd occasions there are demonstrations of ancient crafts and farming, while Fridays give you the chance to watch falcons swoop to their waiting handlers. A traditional (in all but price) souk sells a range of tourist mementos.

Petroleum Exhibition

Corniche Road East, near Volcano Fountain (02 626 9715). **Open** 7am-2pm Sat-Wed. **Admission** free. **Map** p214 B3.

Although it's a rather dry account of the city's rise from the riches of pearling to the riches of the oil industry, the Petroleum Exhibition is the most comprehensive account available of how the small desert hamlet of Abu Dhabi transformed itself into one of the world's largest oil producers.

Beaches & islands

The majority of the city's five-star abodes have their own stretch of sand, which non-guests can use for a charge of generally between Dhs80 and Dhs100 for a day pass.

The UAE

Public art on Abu Dhabi's Airport Road.

Alternatively, Abu Dhabi boasts several
public beaches and, unlike in the other
emirates, they're off limits to vehicles
so you won't have to dodge Pajeros every
few minutes or suffer loud car stereos.
There are countless scenic if rugged
stretches around the peninsula (near
the Khalidiya Palace Hotel and up past the
InterContinental Hotel), but without facilities
like changing rooms and shops. Otherwise,
the best beach in town is **Al Raha**, easily the
most convenient in terms of amenities and
refreshments. For a little more exclusivity,
women can avoid the male of the species
altogether at **Al Dana Ladies' Beach**.

There is no need for the more adventurous
tourist to stop at the shore, however. Abu
Dhabi is unique among the emirates in
its wealth of islands. Over 200 of them lie
just off the coast, various in size and level of
habitation. Small wonder that hopping from
island to island is one of the emirate's more
popular pastimes. If you don't own a boat
you'll need to hire one – with driver – from
a hotel beach club. This is the safer option in
any case, as the water is dangerously shallow
in places and would-be captains must be able
to navigate the treacherous dredged channels.

The rather large island opposite the
corniche is **Lulu Island** (Map p214 A3), a
man-made lump that's famous for having
been built with no real purpose in mind.
Depending on what you read, it is destined

to become a Fun Island theme park or an
entertainment complex. It is also due to be
linked to Abu Dhabi by means of bridges and
tunnels, which were still being built as we
went to press. Slightly further out is **Sa'diyat
Island** (Map p215 D1), a popular destination
for overnight and weekend trips. The island
is home to basic facilities in the form of boat
moorings, chalets and an entertainment hall.
It's commonly used as a base for water sports,
including jet-biking and water-skiing.

Motor about five kilometres (three
miles) or some ten minutes south of Abu
Dhabi and you'll come to **Futaisi Island**,
an inhabited island, some 15 miles (40
kilometres) square, which is privately owned
by Sheikh Hamad bin Hamdan Al Nahyan.
Home to old quarries from which stone for
Abu Dhabi's forts was once dug, the island
is now a tourist retreat and nature reserve.
Here you can rent a chalet and ride horses.
West of Abu Dhabi is **Sir Bani Yas Island**
(*see p234* **Gimme shelter**), home to a nature
reserve and conservation programmes.

There are many other small, uninhabited
bits of green dotted around out to sea, but
still within easy reach of the city. Popular
outcrops include Bahraini, Cut and
Horseshoe, but all are good for a day's
exploring and secluded sun-soaking. You'll
often find a cluster of windsurfers taking brief
respite on Surf Reef, gathering themselves
amid the swirling offshore breezes.

Al Dana Ladies' Beach
Just past the Hilton Hotel, Corniche Road (02 665 0129). **Open** noon-6pm Sat-Wed; 10am-6pm Thur, Fri. **Admission** Dhs10. *Parking* Dhs5. **Map** p214 A4.
Besides boasting a totally man-free environment, Al Dana beach offers a cafeteria and swimming pool. It is typically open until dusk (around 6pm).

Al Raha Beach
Past Umm Al Nar roundabout. **Admission** free.
A clean and relatively recent beach development, Al Raha is one of the city's favourite sun traps. A small section is cordoned off for women only, but the rest is accessible to all. A small cafeteria sells snacks and soft drinks.

Where to eat & drink

As Abu Dhabi boasts an array of five-star hotels, it's no surprise that the restaurants they house are of high quality. But should you be in search of the humble hamburger or something altogether more adventurous, you won't fail to find it here either. Standards of service are, for the most part, impeccable.

Art Cauldron
Al Falah Street, opposite Navy Gate (02 644 4309). **Open** noon-4pm, 6pm-midnight daily. **Main courses** Dhs30-Dhs45. **No credit cards**. **Map** p214 C3.
Not located in a hotel – and therefore not permitted to serve alcohol – this bohemian basement hideaway has a lot of atmosphere and great decor. It serves an inventive international menu, in huge portions and with top-notch ingredients and service. We can particularly recommend the penne contadina, served in a delicious sun-dried tomato sauce.

Bice
Hilton Hotel, Corniche Road (02 681 1900). **Open** noon-3pm, 7-11pm daily. **Main courses** Dhs40-Dhs60. **Credit** AmEx, DC, MC, V. **Map** p214 A4.
Bice is a truly wonderful place in which to dine. Polished oak floors, beautifully crafted chairs and a splendid in-house pianist define a setting that is rich in atmosphere. Be sure to try the sweet, crumbly and crispy crab cake, which is served with avocado tartare – which is like guacamole, only a smoother and creamier – and drizzled waves of bell pepper sauce, accompanied by one of the sommelier's recommendations from the lengthy list of impressive wines.

Al Fanar
Le Royal Meridien, Khalifa Bin Zayed Street (02 674 2020). **Open** 6-11am, 12.30-3pm, 7.30-11pm daily. **Main courses** Dhs40-Dhs60. **Credit** AmEx, DC, MC, V. **Map** p214 B3.
Revolving restaurants may be the epitome of 1970s uncool, but here it's done with a certain style. Al Fanar prides itself on its popular Friday brunch, which affords diners the opportunity to drink an unlimited amount of bubbly. And unless you suffer from vertigo, or indeed carouselophobia, you're sure to enjoy the experience. The food and music are pleasant, the atmosphere is leisurely and relaxed, and the views are excellent.

Finz
Beach Rotana Hotel, next to Abu Dhabi Mall, north end of Ninth Street (02 644 3000). **Open** 12.30-3.30pm, 7-11pm daily. **Main courses** Dhs60-Dhs80. **Credit** AmEx, MC, V. **Map** p214 C2.
From a comfy vantage point in this spacious and beautifully designed restaurant you can peer into the large open kitchen and see the staff preparing the seafood; in the other direction, you are able to enjoy end-of-the-jetty views of the fish-laden sea. Finz is built out of wood imported from New Zealand, and boasts a head chef imported from California, so don't be surprised to discover an menu with global scope, the pick of which is a tangy hammour massala.

The Fishmarket
InterContinental Hotel, Bainunah Street (02 666 6888). **Open** 12.30-3pm, 7.30-11pm daily. **Main courses** Dhs50-Dhs100. **Credit** AmEx, MC, V. **Map** p214 A4.
A novel design concept is the main draw of the Fishmarket: one side of the restaurant is taken up with stalls displaying fresh fish of all kinds, as well as huge heaps of vegetables, each labelled with a price per kilo. Your waitress accompanies you to the stalls, armed with an old-fashioned wicker basket, into which she drops whichever fishy friend takes your fancy. You then choose how you want it cooked, before delving into a dazzling array of sauces – from oyster to lemony garlic to red curry. Throw in the veggies and your choice of noodles or rice, and you've got as tailored a dining experience as you could hope to find.

La Mamma
Sheraton Hotel, Corniche Road (02 677 3333) **Open** noon-4pm, 7-11.30pm daily. **Main courses** Dhs40-Dhs50. **Credit** AmEx, MC, V. **Map** p214 B2.
From the bright red sun motif painted on the domed ceiling to the rustic linen blinds and happy yellow and green colour scheme, La Mamma is the kind of place you can visit for lunch and then spend most of an afternoon still sat there, quietly day-dreaming. Find yourself a window table, where an abundance of greenery filters out the fierceness of the sun, indulge in a jug of house wine and take a wander around the towering buffet display. By night, the restaurant becomes the perfect romance-kindling eaterie.

Nina
Khalifa Bin Zayed Street (02 672 2267). **Open** 8am-12.15pm daily. **Main courses** Dhs20-Dhs30. **Credit** AmEx, MC, V **Map** p214 B3.
Abu Dhabi's coolest café is home to the city's most celebrated fruit cocktail: a quad-layered wonder, with sweet avocado base; thick, none-too-grainy

The UAE

Bice, serving contemporary Italian in the capital. *See p219.*

pear fluid; insatiably sweet liquidised mango; and, to top things off, the unmistakably summery taste of fresh strawberry juice. It's a simply winning combination. Drink a couple of these alongside a dish of fresh tabouleh, prepared with mild sprigs of parsley and tangy tinsels of mint, and boasting a sharp citrusy finish. To idle the time away, you can watch Arabic music videos, browse Nina's huge selection of magazines, then grab another fruit cocktail to go – they really are that good.

Rodeo Grill
Beach Rotana Hotel, next to Abu Dhabi Mall, north end of Ninth Street (02 644 3000). **Open** 12.30-3.30pm, 7-11pm daily. **Main courses** Dhs60-Dhs80. **Credit** AmEx, MC, V. **Map** p214 C2.
This upmarket steakhouse serves the best slabs of meat in Abu Dhabi. Among their finest works is a wondrous wagyu beef. Traditionally, Japanese cattle are pampered with beer and saké to enhance the quality of their meat; it seems to work – the wagyu meat here is intensely marbled, giving it an amazingly soft texture and creating a sweet, almost nutty flavour.

Sayad
Emirates Palace Hotel, Corniche Road (02 690 8888). **Open** 12.30-3pm, 6.30-11.30pm daily. **Main courses** Dhs150-Dhs200. **Credit** AmEx, DC, MC, V. **Map** 214 A4.
Despite being one of the priciest restaurants in the city, Sayad is far from the stuffy, extravagant venue its palatial setting may suggest. Indeed, posh and casual are willing bedfellows here. The

excellent food makes it a successful fine-dining destination, but the incredibly friendly, chatty service makes it feel relaxed. Be sure to sample the the flavourful saffron-infused seafood broth, or the thoroughly rich foie gras, before feasting on the finest duck the city has to offer.

Soba
Le Royal Meridien, Khalifa Bin Zayed Street (02 695 0450). **Open** 1-3.30pm, 7-10.30pm Sat-Wed; 1-3.30pm, 7pm-midnight Thur; 7pm-midnight Fri. **Main courses** Dhs40-Dhs60. **Credit** AmEx, DC, MC, V. **Map** p214 B3.
Everything about Soba, from the decor to the dessert menu, is a stylish fusion of modern and traditional. Coloured glass, light wood and geometric patterns are offset by floaty white curtains and pretty screens, which give a hideaway feeling to what is essentially a fairly narrow and thus unprepossessing ground-floor room. There is a resident DJ, but the sound is so unobtrusive as to be almost forgotten at times. Soba has set out to please everyone – and succeeds. Whether you want to share sushi, grab a quick bowl of noodles or tackle the towers of tempura with a group of friends, you'll find your corner here.

Talay
Le Meridien Abu Dhabi, north end of Sheikh Zayad Second Street (02 644 7800). **Open** 12.30-3.30pm, 7-11.30pm daily. **Main courses** Dhs50-Dhs60. **Credit** AmEx, DC, MC, V. **Map** p214 C2.
Talay is the pick of the restaurants located in Le Meridien's picturesque culinary village, its delights best enjoyed at one of the beachside tables – even

The UAE

though you'll have to arrive early to be sure of securing one. Try the signature tom yam seafood soup, with its squid, shrimp and serious chunks of oyster mushroom deftly seasoned with coconut milk and lemongrass. Most of the dishes strike a delicately lip-tingling balance between flavour and heat, but those marked spicy are spicy indeed.

Vasco's

Hilton Hotel, Corniche Road (02 681 1900). **Open** noon-3pm, 7-11pm daily. **Main courses** Dhs40-Dhs60. **Credit** AmEx, DC, MC, V. **Map** p214 A4.
Vasco's has long been a bastion of excellence in the capital. Perched on the waters of the Gulf, it is still the city's must-have dining experience. Although its meat and seafood are second to none, Vasco's adventurous salads simply have to be sampled. Plump for the thoroughly impressive asparagus and avocado affair, complete with perfectly ripened tomatoes – they're a real rarity in the UAE – or the 'Breakwater', which is nearly as impressive, comprising succulent and fulsomely flavoured hunks of sesame-soaked chicken. Whether you choose to sit by the sea or indoors to take in the sounds of the bustling open kitchen, you'll have a fine meal.

Nightlife

Abu Dhabi is home to an ever-expanding expat community that makes the most of a social scene that's really rather quiet. Apart from a few clubs and off-licences (as in Dubai, you need a licence to shop at these), the sale of alcohol is restricted to the city's hotels. While this seems a burdensome set-up, in practice there are still a handful of very good venues in town – and they really come alive when the sun dies down.

a.m.p.m.

InterContinental Hotel, Bainumah Street (02 692 5214). **Open** 6pm-2.30am Sat-Wed; 6pm-4am Thur; 6pm-2.30am Fri. **Admission** free. **Credit** AmEx, DC, MC, V. **Map** p214 A4.
Chrome-wrapped and ultra-modern in design, this smart, spacious club lacks a bit of atmosphere. Although the music is as upbeat as it is loud, there are often more people in the DJ booth than on the dancefloor. It does, however, host some decent one-off nights, with many popular Lebanese artists visiting throughout the year.

Captain's Arms

Le Meridien Abu Dhabi, north end of Sheikh Zayed Second Street (02 644 7800). **Open** noon-1am Sat-Wed; noon-1.30am Thur; noon-1am Fri. **Admission** free. **Credit** AmEx, DC, MC, V. **Map** p214 C2.
The Captain's Arms is an attempt by Le Meridien to relocate a traditional English pub in the heart of the desert. It certainly meets with the approval of expat punters, though this may have less to do with the nautical theming than the cheap pints available during regular happy hours, hours that

stretch well beyond the regulation 60 minutes. During the cooler months, a pretty, if diminutive, terrace is the busiest place in town.

Heroes

Crowne Plaza Hotel, Hamdan Street (02 621 0000). **Open** noon-1.30am Sat-Tue; noon-3am Wed-Thur; noon-1.30am Fri. **Admission** free. **Credit** AmEx, DC, MC, V. **Map** p214 B3.
This American-themed diner is primarily for sports enthusiasts or those with appetites to rival Desperate Dan, given multiple screens and portions that would outweight the behemoth. Regular drink deals and decent in-house entertainment – a monthly comedy club, the Laughter Factory, is held here – ensure Heroes is busy most nights of the week, remaining a popular choice for expats seeking a slice of home comfort.

Jazz Bar

Hilton Hotel, Corniche Road (02 681 1900). **Open** 7pm-1am Sat-Tue; 7pm-2am Wed, Thur. **Admission** free. **Credit** AmEx, DC, MC, V. **Map** p214 A4.
The Jazz Bar has long enjoyed a special place in the hearts of all Abu Dhabians, combining excellent food with amiable staff and a near-perfect ambience. The Bar's candlelit tables cannot be pre-booked, so they often fill up early doors, but they do afford patrons a fine view of the stunning house singer, fronting the best band in town. If you're not one for house and hip hop – the prevailing genres in the city's few clubs – this is surely the place for you.

LAB

Beach Rotana Hotel, next to Abu Dhabi Mall, north end of Ninth Street (02 644 3000). **Open** 7pm-2.30am Sat-Wed; 7pm-3am Thur; 7pm-2.30am Fri. **Admission** free. **Credit** AmEx, MC, V. **Map** p214 C2.
Arguably Abu Dhabi's slickest bar, LAB is also one of the city's busiest hangouts, thanks in no small part to a candlelit terrace on which large groups of pretty people relax, making use of the ultra-comfortable beanbags and soaking up the sound of the sea. To heighten the mood, ladies can sup on sparkling wine free of charge on a Monday, while bountiful beats ensure the large expanse of dancefloor rarely much less than full.

Rock Bottom

Al Diar Capitol Hotel, Meena Street (02 678 7700). **Open** 8pm-2.15am daily. **Admission** free. **Credit** AmEx, MC, V. **Map** p214 B2.
A quick perusal of this bar's clientele and you'll be in little doubt as to why it is so named: the live entertainment oscillates between ear-splittingly loud band and DJ playing run-of-the-mill tracks to a dancefloor full of unsuspecting tourists, touchy-feely ladies and denim-clad bikers. It's the kind of place that only ever springs to mind at around 1am when you're trying to think of somewhere that serves alcohol and is still open. In short, it's where you'll end up because your alcohol-addled brain has learned its lesson yet.

The UAE

Sax

*Le Royal Meridien, Khalifa Bin Zayed Street
(02 674 2020).* **Open** 7pm-2am daily. **Admission**
free. **Credit** AmEx, MC, V. **Map** p214 B3.

Although a new kid on the block, Sax hasn't taken
much time to endear itself to the capital's crowds,
possibly because it followed the blueprint of
the Jazz Bar (*see p221*) to a tee, definitely because
what it offers is a cut above most competition.
Low-lit and relatively snug, Sax is the perfect
place to head if you're seeking a good meal with
impressive entertainment, coming courtesy of a
talented South African sextet.

Trader Vic's

*Beach Rotana Hotel, next to Abu Dhabi Mall,
north end of Ninth Street (02 644 3000).* **Open**
7pm-midnight Sat-Wed, Fri; 7pm-1am Thur.
Admission free. **Credit** AmEx, MC, V.
Map p214 C2.

A gem of a bar that couples quality cuisine with an
exhaustive list of cocktails. If you're in for the
night, we recommend you try the potent Queen's
Park Swizzle or an equally mind-numbing Rum
Keg. Trader Vic's isn't a haunt for the bargain
hunter, though: more like reassuringly expensive.

Zenith

Sheraton Hotel, Corniche Road (02 677 3333).
Open 9pm-2.30am Sat-Wed, Fri; 9pm-3.30am
Admission free. **Credit** AmEx, MC, V.
Map p214 B2.

In its attempt to live up to its own billing as the
capital's most cutting-edge club, Zenith made
something of a stuttering start: it was being
rebranded as we went to press, mere months after
the grand opening. It has, though, already hosted
some true DJ greats – Norman Jay among them –
and its lighting, sound and stylish decor mean it's
one of Abu Dhabi's better options should be in
need of somewhere to party. On the downside,
drinks here are some of the dearest in the city, so
come prepared to part with your pennies.

Shopping

Shoppers used to modern malls will be
heartened by the presence of the twin
colossi of the **Abu Dhabi** and **Marina Malls**:
these similarly sized American-style shopping
centres offer quick and easy food courts,
cinemas and wares ranging from domestic
goods to designer labels.

But by far the most interesting (and hectic)
shopping experience in the capital is at the old
and new **central souks** (Map p214 B3). They
are your prime source of traditional Arabic
knick-knacks and the usual (suspect) range of
Celvin Kline and Adidas clothing. Expect to
find all the market favourites: cheap shoes,
bags, clothes and toys... you name it, it's here –
and it's never too expensive if you haggle like a

demon. (Never pay more than Dhs70 for a fake
Rolex, for example.) A bridge links the two
markets, running between Hamdan (Fifth) and
Khalifa Streets. Over 500 shops and stalls open
at seemingly random times between 8am and
11pm, depending on the enthusiasm of the
owners. Far more predictable is the afternoon
siesta, which ensures all trade stops between
1.30pm and 4pm. Most shops will appear rather
dingy and dirty on the outside – and also inside,
to be honest – but there are plenty of bargains.

It's also well worth paying a visit to the
Iranian souk (Map p214 B2), found near
Port Zayed. Goods fresh off the boats from
Iran arrive every three or four days: on sale
are all manner of Iranian carpets, ornaments,
terracotta trinkets and the like. Haggling is
regarded as a kind of sport in these parts, so
you should indulge in a round or two as much
to pass the time as to procure bargains.

Abu Dhabi Mall

North end of Ninth Street (02 645 4858). **Open**
10am-10pm Sat-Wed; 10am-11pm Thur. **Map**
p214 C2.

Connected to the Beach Rotana Hotel, this large
shopping centre keeps attracting bigger and better
brand names to complement an already great range
of outlets. Featuring familiar designer brands like
Levi's and Guess, it also has gems like Nails and
Massimo Dutti, a cinema and a host of eateries.

Marina Mall

The Breakwater (02 681 2310). **Open** 10am-10pm
Sat-Tue; 10am-11pm Wed, Thur; 2-10pm Fri.
Map p214 A4.

The standard of shops at Marina Mall falls short of
its rival, but it has great views of the sea and the
city, thanks to a commanding position on the
break-water. A favourite with young families, it
offers a huge kid's playland and a cinema, besides
one-stop shops like IKEA and Carrefour.

Where to stay

Beach resorts

Beach Rotana Hotel & Towers

*Next to Abu Dhabi Mall, north end of Ninth Street (02
644 3000/fax 02 644 2111/www.rotana.com).* **Rates**
Dhs550-Dhs1,150 single/double; Dhs900-Dhs9,000
suite. **Credit** AmEx, DC, MC, V. **Map** p214 C2.

Perfectly placed adjacent to the expansive Abu
Dhabi Mall, the Beach Rotana is without doubt one
of the city's premier hotels. It's supremely elegant
inside, with a wonderfully welcoming lobby and
rooms that are as spacious as they are stylish. The
top-class rooms have luxury bathrooms with
Jacuzzi baths and rain showers. The beach, too, is
well sized and a children's pool sits next to the
adult one. If you wish to keep fit while away from
home, there is also a state-of-the-art gymnasium.

Al Raha Beach Hotel.

and guests enjoy unlimited access to an excellent beach club, which sports an outstanding private beach and spa. The hotel is arguably home to the finest food and beverage outlets in Abu Dhabi.

InterContinental

Bainunah Street, Al Khalidya (02 666 6888/fax 02 665 6158/www.ichotelsgroup.com). **Rates** Dhs650-Dhs950 single/double; Dhs1,590-Dhs8,250 suite. **Credit** AmEx, DC, MC, V. **Map** p214 A4.

The InterContinental is not only home to the best beach in town, but also has a picturesque marina, in fairly green surroundings, and provides first-class facilities. The rooms may be a touch dated in terms of furnishings, but they are exceptionally comfortable. Located slightly away from the main hustle and bustle of central Abu Dhabi, the hotel is close enough to be convenient, but far enough away to ensure you can lounge on the beach relatively undisturbed. Great views.

Le Meridien

Tourist Club area, north end of Sheikh Zayed Second Street (02 644 6666/fax 02 645 5715/ www.lemeridien.com). **Rates** Dhs700-Dhs1,300 single/double; Dhs2,500-Dhs6,000 suite. **Credit** AmEx, DC, MC, V. **Map** p214 C2.

Le Meridien is another international standard hotel, situated by the beach and centred on the tranquil Meridien Village, a stretch of greenery around which congregate a variety of excellent alfresco food and beverage outlets. There's an on-site spa centre that offers soothingly traditional Turkish hammam treatments.

Al Raha Beach Hotel

Al Raha Beach, Shahama city (02 508 0555). **Rates** Dhs900-Dhs1,200 single/double; Dhs3,200-Dhs6,500 suite. **Credit** AmEx, DC, MC, V. **Map** 215 E4.

Set apart from the cluster of hotels in the city centre by a 15min drive, the Al Raha Beach Hotel is a new five-star property that is unique in Abu Dhabi for the fact that it has a number of two-, three- and four-bedroom beach villas. These can be rented for either a short holiday or a more extended stay, and they are wonderfully decorated, each one representing a private paradise. The lovely infinity pool boasts unspoilt views of the Gulf, while those seeking a bit of action will be pleased to hear the UAE's largest nightclub opens here before the end of 2005.

Sheraton

Corniche Road (02 677 3333/fax 02 672 5149/www. starwood.com/sheraton). **Rates** Dhs600-Dhs650 single/double; Dhs1,400-Dhs5,150 suite. **Credit** AmEx, DC, MC, V. **Map** p214 B2.

The Sheraton boasts the best outdoors area in the capital: a luxurious little oasis with wonderful pools for children and adults alike, set among palm trees. The rooms have very modern decor and are fully equipped, but they are slightly on the small side. Nevertheless, if it's a touch of finery that you seek, there are few better options.

Emirates Palace

Corniche Road (02 690 9000/fax 02 690 9999/ www.emiratespalce.com). **Rates** Dhs2,200 single; Dhs2,400 double; Dhs5,500, Dhs9,000 & Dhs49,000 suites. (Prices exclude 20% tax). **Credit** AmEx, DC, MC, V. **Map** p214 A4.

The jewel in the capital's crown, this stunning building is an incredible landmark, sat proudly at the end of the corniche. Luxurious in every sense, rooms come with plasma screens as standard; top-of-the-range accommodation provides private butlers to take care of your needs. The beach and pool areas are outstanding, and the lush green gardens that surround them are equally stunning. By the end of 2005, the Palace will also house a spa and marina. *See also p225* **Crystal palace**.

Hilton Abu Dhabi

Corniche Road (02 681 1900/fax 02 681 1696/ www.hilton.com). **Rates** Dhs600 single/double; Dhs1,100-Dhs3,200 suite. **Credit** AmEx, DC, MC, V. **Map** p214 A4.

Set in a fine location overlooking the Arabian Gulf, the majority of the Hilton's rooms have recently received a makeover and are much the better for it. The beds are the most comfortable in the city,

The UAE

City hotels

Crowne Plaza

Hamdan Street (Fifth Street) (02 621 0000/fax 02 621 7444/www.crowneplaza.com). **Rates** Dhs890 single/double; Dhs1,500 suite. **Credit** AmEx, DC, MC, V. **Map** p214 B3.

Centrally located, the Crowne Plaza is in prime position to take full advantage of Abu Dhabi's shopping and beach-based activities. The Roman-style rooftop pool is a major plus for all visitors here; the hugely popular basement bar Heroes (*see p221*) offers entertainment for the evenings.

Millennium Hotel

Khalifa Bin Zayed Street (02 626 2700/fax 02 626 0333/www.millenniumhotels.com). **Rates** Dhs500-700 single/double; Dhs850-Dhs12,000 suite. **Credit** AmEx, DC, MC, V. **Map** p214 B3.

From its chandelier-dominated reception to the chunky brass doorknobs, the Millennium Hotel oozes quality. This luxury abode overlooks both the capital gardens and the corniche, with great views whichever side of the building you are in. On the downside, the hotel lacks a little atmosphere. The decor is a nice mix of dark woods and marble, though, and competent staff conduct their business with unobtrusive efficiency.

Le Royal Meridien

Khalifa Bin Zayed Street (02 674 2020/fax 02 674 2552/www.lemeridien.com). **Rates** Dhs550-Dhs950 single/double; Dhs1,700-Dhs3,000 suite. **Credit** AmEx, DC, MC, V. **Map** p214 B3.

This plush 31-storey hotel resembles an ordinary city skyscraper in all respects bar the revolving Al Fanar restaurant (*see p219*) that slowly slides around the roof of the building. Rooms in the royal tower have recently been refurbished to great effect, and the rest of the hotel's rooms are due to undergo the same treatment by the end of 2005. The Meridien also has some great restaurants and bars.

Resources

Hospitals

Al Noor Khalifa Bin Zayed Street (02 626 5265). **Map** p214 B3.

Corner of Al Karamah & Bateen Streets (02 621 4666). **Map** p214 B3.

Internet

Street Net Café *Abu Dhabi Mall, north end of Ninth Street (02 645 4141).* **Price** Dhs15 per hr. **No credit cards. Map** p214 C2.

Police station

Police HQ *Sheikh Zayed First Street (02 446 1461).* **Map** p214 B4.

Post office

Central post office *East Road (02 621 5415).* **Open** 8am-8pm Sat-Wed; 8am-6pm Thur. **Map** p210 B2.

Tourist information

Ministry of Information & Culture *Near police station, Airport Road (02 444 0444/info@abu dhabitourism.ae).* **Open** 7.30am-2pm Sat-Wed. **Map** p214 C4.

There are plans to move the tourist office to the city centre; contact them for up-to-date details.

Getting there

By car

From Dubai, simply get on to Sheikh Zayed Road and keep on in a straight line for 150km (95 miles); the closer you get to the city, the more road signs you'll see. The road turns into Airport Road as you enter Abu Dhabi.

By bus

Minibuses from Bur Dubai bus station cost Dhs20; there are no specific departure times, as drivers wait for the bus to fill up before they will set off (meaning they are usually rather cramped as a consequence). The minibus will drop you off at the bus station in the centre of Abu Dhabi.

By taxi

The journey from Dubai to Abu Dhabi will cost you Dhs220-Dhs250 if you flag a taxi down in the street. However, Al Ghazal Express – an Abu Dhabi-based taxi operator – will come to collect you in Dubai and take you to the capital for a flat fee of Dhs120. Bookings can be made by calling 02 444 5885. If you're travelling alone, you could take a shared taxi from Bur Dubai bus station at a cost of Dhs50. The taxi waits until there are four passengers before departing, so you could be sat waiting for anything from ten minutes to an hour.

Al Ain

Owing to its wealth of greenery, the emirates' second largest city is known as 'the Garden City'. There is plenty to savour in this quiet retreat of tree-lined boulevards and low-rise buildings, including the UAE's **Natural History Museum** (Al Khubaisi, 03 761 2277); **Al Ain Museum** (Zayed Bin Sultan Street, 03 764 1595), the country's largest collection of historical artefacts; and the UAE's biggest zoo, the **Al Ain Zoo & Aquarium** (Zoo roundabout, near the traffic police HQ, 03 782 8188). About 160 kilometres (100 miles) east of Abu Dhabi and the same distance south-east of Dubai, Al Ain is a 90-minute drive from both, but there are also domestic and international flights to Al Ain International Airport (03 785 5555). The best time to visit is winter, when time can be spent exploring ancient archaeological sites, the hot springs in the Jebel Hafeet mountains and the smelly but entertaining camel market.

Al Ain InterContinental

Near Al Ain Mall, Ernyadat Road (03 768 6686/ fax 03 768 6766/www.ichotelsgroup.com). **Rates** Dhs600 single/double; Dhs1,000-Dhs3,000 suite. **Credit** AmEx, DC, MC, V.

A sprawling complex that's the focal point of the Garden City's social life in the evenings, the Al Ain InterContinental has a series of top-notch outlets and clean, functional rooms. Popular with families for its network of pools and the laid-back attitude of the staff, this is a fine hotel indeed.

Al Ain Rotana Hotel

Zayed Bin Sultan Street (03 754 5111/fax 03 754 5444/www.rotana.com). **Rates** Dhs350-Dhs700 single/double; Dhs1,600-Dhs6,000 suite. **Credit** AmEx, DC, MC, V.

The low-rise Rotana boasts a stunning pool and modish, nicely turned-out rooms. Tennis courts, a well-stocked gym and ace massage facilities round off what is the poshest hotel in the city.

Hilton Al Ain

Follow signs from city centre to Sarroj (03 768 6666/ fax 03 266 0000/www.hilton.com). **Rates** Dhs500-Dhs650 single/double; Dhs700-Dhs900 suite. **Credit** AmEx, DC, MC, V.

This good-value branch of the Hilton empire has large, comfy rooms, equipped with balconies on which you can take your time to grapple with the generous breakfasts. Sink-in armchairs, bouncy beds, myriad satellite channels and speedy room service make this a good option if you'd rather enjoy a lazy weekend than head out on the town.

Crystal palace

Its branding as a seven-star hotel may be no more than a media myth (notwithstanding the **Burj Al Arab**, *see p47*, no commendation above five stars exists), but **Emirates Palace** (*see p223*) is certainly seated in the lap of utter luxury. It cost an estimated Dhs14 billion to build, making it the most expensive hotel ever, and simply walking around you would cover a distance of more than two kilometres. It boasts a dome larger than that on St Paul's Cathedral, lush gardens covering over a million square metres, 110,000 cubic metres of marble, and an abundance of silver and gold. If staying here would write off rather than merely dent your credit card, it will at least suffer no more than superficial damage should you stop by for a Dhs45 coffee. Alternatively, a day's lounging on the Palace's 1.3km stretch of beach will set you back a jaw-dropping Dhs350 per man, Dhs200 per woman and Dhs200 per child. Tours of the Palace can be undertaken at no cost; they depart at varying times, so it's best check with the front desk when you arrive.

The UAE

Northern Emirates

Synonymous with rich tradition and unspoilt beauty, the northern Gulf dishes up equal portions of cultivated sightseeing and unadulterated adventure.

As fabulous as plastic fantastic Dubai is, sometimes one needs to escape the glitz in search of some old-world Arabic charm. A trip up north is the perfect antidote for those sick of the shopping, swimming and clubbing scene. And the great thing about leaving the city is that you don't have to go terribly far to notice the vast changes in your surroundings. The further north one ventures, however, the more obvious the differences are, and dazzling Dubai soon fades into the distant background as the urban sprawl of **Sharjah** and **Ajman** is taken over by the desert, mountains, plains and empty stretches of endless beaches at the outer reaches of **Umm Al Quwain** and **Ras Al Khaimah**. Not too daunting in size, this northern strip is ideal road-trip territory.

Sharjah

With its abundance of museums, galleries and theatres, it's hardly surprising that Sharjah holds the title of cultural capital of the Arab world. With the UAE's severest laws on decency and conduct, and a ban on alcohol, this is rather an odd choice for an art-centric emirate, yet concealed in the crowded city are some of the country's best museums and markets. Home to the **Al Hosn Fort**, the **Art Museum** and the **Arabian Wildlife Centre at Desert Park**, all are impressive and, suitable for all ages and nationalities, offer invaluable insight into Arab and Islamic history, as well as local wildlife.

Don't be put off by the Dubai–Sharjah road, notorious for deeply unimaginative high-rise apartment blocks that invite gusty sand storms in summer and off-putting flood water in winter. Once you've battled through the insane traffic, confusing road system and bad signposting, you'll be glad you made the effort.

History

Sharjah's roots lie to the north of its modern location, in and around what is now the emirate of Ras Al Khaimah (see p233), which replaced the ancient capital of Julfar as a local trading hub some time in the 17th century. Sharjah grew as a competing power to Ras Al Khaimah,

with things coming to a head in 1814, when Sultan Ibn Saqr, a former Ras Al Khaimah ruler, seized Sharjah and declared it a separate sheikhdom. He then annexed Ras Al Khaimah to his new base, following the sacking of the city by a British expedition in 1819.

Thus began a game of chess, in which Ras Al Khaimah would move in and out of Sharjah's fold several times. Sharjah became signatory to the 1820 General Treaty of Peace between the British and nine local Arab sheikhdoms. Despite the British installing a garrison in the region and a political agent in Sharjah, different factions continued to feud. The British became more active, signing a treaty to create a six-month truce during the pearling season with the principal sheikhs in 1835. This was renewed for ten years in 1843. In 1853, a 'perpetual maritime truce' was signed, giving the area the name 'The Trucial Coast'. By 1893, the British had effectively turned the Trucial Coast into a protectorate, even though the British flag did not fly anywhere other than from its military bases and agents' buildings.

However, the swings back and forth of family politics did not end under British dominance: coups in Sharjah took place in 1951 and 1965, and there was an assassination only months after the British withdrawal in 1971. An attempted coup in 1987 was ended by consultation between the ruling families of all the emirates. Despite the intrigue, Sharjah grew rapidly from the 1960s onwards. It has become today a major trading hub and manufacturing base despite, or perhaps because of, the oil that has helped Abu Dhabi and Dubai to prosper. Sharjah's trading history still stands it in good stead today, though it has also been aided by investment from Saudi Arabia.

Sightseeing

Uninformed arty cynics may well dispute the difficulty of achieving the status of cultural capital of the Arab world. Bestowed this title by UNESCO in 1998, with no less than 15 museums (out of a total of 21 in the UAE) and with plans underway for further contemporary galleries and work spaces, one cannot dispute

Khaled Lagoon, a popular setting for powerboat races.

Sharjah's worthiness for this accolade. Several galleries face on to Arabic Calligraphy Square, a haven of artistry that seems miles away from industrial Sharjah. It's also worth an educational stroll around the Heritage Area, a complex of old buildings and renovated structures clustered just a minute's walk from Rolla Street taxi stand.

Archaeological Museum

Halwan District, off Cultural Square (06 566 5466). **Open** 9am-1pm, 5-8pm Sat, Mon-Thur; 5-8pm Fri. **Admission** free.

This large museum presents local archaeology beautifully. Stretched across several halls full of audio-visual wonder, man's first and subsequent steps across the Arabian Peninsula are documented in chronological order. Clear displays of finds from Sharjah's many Stone Age, Iron Age and Bronze Age sites sit alongside lovingly wrought models of the emirate's first houses. Touch-screen computers provide images from the museum archives and also educational games for children.

Art Museum

Al Shuwaiheyn, behind the bazaar, close to the waterfront (06 568 8222). **Open** 9am-1pm, 5-8pm Sat, Sun, Tue-Thur (Wed afternoon women & children only); 5-8pm Fri. **Admission** free.

Paintings, documents and maps, dating to the 18th century and taken from the personal collection of the ruler of Sharjah, sit alongside occasionally awful abstract art. The permanent collection is brightened by an active programme of exhibition exchanges with international museums, and the

museum is home to the Sharjah International Art Biennial, held in spring (usually April) every odd-numbered year. There is a handy coffee bar in the museum, and basement parking is available.

Desert Park & Arabian Wildlife Centre

Sharjah Airport Road (direction Al Dhaid), Interchange 9 (06 531 1999). **Open** 9am-6.15pm Sat-Wed, public hols; 11am-6.15pm Thur; 2-6.15pm Fri. Last tickets 5.30pm. **Admission** Dhs15; under-15s free. **No credit cards**.

This world-class educational and research facility houses the most important captive breeding centre for endangered species in the whole of Arabia. There's an incredibly advanced public zoo in the Arabian Wildlife Centre, plus an innovative natural history museum (06 531 1411) and an excellent children's education park. More than 100 species of animal roam the various re-created habitats, while in the vast indoor aviary thousands of birds swoop mere inches above your head.

Heritage Museum

Al Shuwaiheyn, between the waterfront & Al Hosn Avenue (Bank Street) (06 569 3999). **Open** 9am-1pm, 5-8pm Sat, Sun, Tue-Thur; 5-8pm Fri. **Admission** free.

Around the courtyard of the former home of the Al Naboodah family, the buildings of the Heritage Museum are a fascinating example of traditional UAE architecture. Inside, you'll find displays of old clothing and heritage items. For the modern-day equivalent, take in the nearby Al Arsah Souq, an alley packed with antiques and jewellery.

The UAE

Al Hosn Fort

*Al Hosn Avenue (Bank Street), Heritage Area
(06 512 9999).* **Open** 9am-1pm, 5-8pm Sat, Sun,
Tue-Thur (Wed afternoon women & children
only); 5-8.30pm Fri. **Admission** free.
Al Hosn Fort was built in 1820 by Sultan Ibn Saqr,
the first of the Qawasim sheikhs (*see p230*) to
make Sharjah his capital. The fort was the political centre of the emirate until it was demolished
in 1969 to make way for the modern buildings that
now typify the city; only two walls and a 12m (40ft)
tower were left standing. Original 19th-century
structures were renovated in 1996, and the rest
of the complex was rebuilt to its original design;
the fort now houses a museum, with a series of
exhibition rooms surrounding the central courtyard. Inside are weapons, coins, jewellery and
information about the pearl trade of old.

Islamic Museum

*Al Gharb, off Al Hosn Avenue (Bank Street), Heritage
Area (06 568 3334).* **Open** 9am-1pm, 5-8pm Sat,
Sun, Tue-Thur; 5-8pm Fri. **Admission** free.
Along a narrow lane behind Arabic Calligraphy
Square you'll find the old wooden door of Sharjah's
single-storey Islamic Museum. This houses an
important collection of rare Arabic manuscripts,
a major Islamic mint exhibition featuring silver
dinars and dirhams from the Abbasid and Umayyad
periods (from the sixth century AD), plus archaeological artefacts from the Islamic era. Particularly

fascinating are navigational instruments used
by ancient Arabic seafarers and an extraordinary
'upside down' map of the world that was drawn
1,000 years ago by Sharif Al Idrisi.

Museum for Arabic Calligraphy & Ornamentation

*Al Gharb, off Al Hosn Avenue (Bank Street),
Heritage Area (06 568 3334).* **Open** 9am-1pm,
5-8pm Sat, Sun, Tue-Thur; 5.30-8.30pm Fri.
Admission free.
Walk west to the large defensive tower that's
visible from Al Hosn Fort, turn north into Arabic
Calligraphy Square, and you'll find this intriguing
museum. The galleries are filled with beautiful
works by Arab, Persian and Turkish artists, while
the calligraphy and ceramics studios, in the cool
of winter, host students developing their ideas.

Shopping & souks

For a break from the increasingly popular
and pristine malls, immerse yourself in local
culture with a trip to the traditional souks at
the Ar-Ruba flyover end of the Corniche
Road. In the single-storey **vegetable souk**
opposite the Oil Supply Post, the date stall –
with produce from Iran, Iraq, Saudi Arabia and
the UAE – provides the best value for money:
a kilogramme of sweet sticky Saudi dates costs

Sea and sun, **Sharjah**-style.

a mere Dhs10. Popular with Sharjah's diverse community of residents, one might be surprised at the rather high prices of other fruits (six tangerines, for example, cost Dhs5), but with the local climate as hot as it is, most of the produce has to be imported.

On the opposite side of the road is the **fish souk** (open 5-11am). Here, dhows berth and offload their catch direct to around 50 fresh fish shops facing the quay on Khaled Lagoon.

Further up the corniche is the fantastically comprehensive **plant souk**, and behind this flea market of flora lies the **livestock souk** (follow signs for 'Bird and Animal Market' on the Corniche Road), offering cows, sheep and goats from Somalia and Pakistan, as well as young bulls that will be fattened in Fujairah for fighting (or, more accurately, butting; *see p239*). With chickens running around and Bedouin boys driving pick-ups with goats in the back, this is a more accurate example of modern UAE country ways than any number of heritage museums.

From here, walk through to the poultry pushers of the **bird souk**. Another long, slim building, this souk is lined with shops selling every kind of bird imaginable, including pheasants, peacocks, baby ostriches, song birds and parrots. Be warned, though: many birds are in the sort of cramped conditions that you may find unpleasant to witness.

Blue Souk
Al Majaz, Corniche Road, close to Khaled Lagoon. **Open** 9am-1pm, 4-11pm Sat-Thur; 9am-noon, 4-11pm Fri. **No credit cards.**
Also known as Souk Al Markazi, the Blue Souk is set in a huge green space dotted with fountains, looking much like a cross between a European central train station and a mosque – a perfectly atrocious example of Sharjah's modern, wedding cake-style architecture. The crème brûlée colours of the interior and fiddly wrought iron don't help to dispel that image, but you're here to shop, not critique the architecture, especially as the souk is fully air-conditioned, allowing for proper browsing even in the height of summer.

There are around 600 shops in the Blue Souk, making it the largest single wholesale and retail market for handicrafts and textiles in Arabia. It is not an Arab market in the true sense: the vast majority of goods sold are Indian in origin. And don't expect to find genuine antiques. If you are told that what you are looking at is over five years old, be very careful. But if you find a shopkeeper you are comfortable with, sit down, drink tea and bargain away to your heart's content.

There are, in effect, two identical souk buildings, connected by bridges. The ground floor of the building nearest the lagoon is mostly taken up with gold, textiles, perfume and camera shops; the one

further away sells finished clothes and electronics. Look out for wooden furniture from Jaipur in Rajasthan, Iranian and Pakistani carpets, and hand-made textiles. Highest quality pure silk Nepalese pashminas should cost less than Dhs250, and you can get Indian pure wool pashminas for around Dhs90. Among the best bargains are the 1.5m-long (5ft) chain-stitched rugs from Kashmir – you should be able to pick one up for less than Dhs150.

Sahara Centre
Al Nahda Street (06 531 6611). **Open** 10am-10pm Sat-Wed; 10am-11pm Thur; 2-11pm Fri. **Credit** MC, V.
Sharjah's mall mania manifests itself in the snake-like sprawl of the Sahara Centre, with hundreds of shops coiling along the underbelly of the first floor. While Dubai's usual suspects are all featured, there are several more interesting stores, such as the venerated Shuh Shoes. The biggest attraction is probably the indoor Adventureland (06 531 6363) on the second floor, which boasts two thrilling rollercoasters (one for teens and one for kids), Wacky Racer mini dodgems and a Log Jam water ride. Prices range from Dhs7.50 to Dhs8. And if in all the excitement you've worked up an appetite, you can stuff yourself silly at the food court.

Sharjah City Centre
Al Wahda Street (06 533 2626). **Open** 10am-10pm Sat-Thur (Carrefour 9am-midnight); 2-10pm Fri (Carrefour 9-11am, 1.30pm-midnight). **Credit** MC, V.
This mall has the same Lego-like colour and feel as Dubai City Centre (in fact, it's owned by the same company), but with less variety of shops. Its Carrefour is similar to its counterparts in Dubai, and huge enough to sell absolutely everything.

Souq Al Majarrah
Corniche Road, next to Masjid Jamila Mosque. **Open** 9am-1.30pm, 4-10.30pm daily. **No credit cards.**
Souk Al Majarrah is a gorgeous structure, with vaulted ceiling and Corinthian columns styled, in part, on the most beautiful souks of Damascus and Aleppo in Syria. The shops cater exclusively to Arab women's and men's fashions, notably selling abayas (cloaks), handbags, shoes and perfume. The only shop not selling some form of fashion is Mujezat Al Shifa Honey (06 565 8707), where you can pick up 500g jars of Afghani-Pakistani lotus honey for Dhs50. For those who don't subscribe to Viagra, royal jelly is Dhs30 for a 15g pot or there's ginseng at Dhs25 for 20g.

Where to eat, drink & stay

Coral Beach Hotel
Coral Beach roundabout, Beach Road (06 522 9999). **Rates** Dhs500 single; Dhs550 double. **Credit** MC, V.
With its coastline dominated by massive ports, Sharjah hardly feels like a coastal resort – until you visit Coral Beach Hotel. A small and slightly cranky four-star, it has an excellent private beach (actually

a man-made cove), there's a large raised swimming pool overlooking the beach, a 'rockery' for kids, slides and a circular 'bar' area (this is Sharjah, though, so no alcohol is served). A second pool is right outside the hotel, in reasonably extensive gardens.

Radisson SAS
Ahmed Bin Dareish Square, Corniche Road (06 565 7777). **Rates** *Sept-Mar* Dhs500 single; Dhs600 double. **Credit** MC, V.
The Radisson SAS may be getting on a bit, but its pyramidal blue-glass-and-cream cladding hides what is still one of the loveliest (and largest) atriums in the world. The lobby has a gift shop that is, for some inexplicable reason, filled with Dubai tat, and the exorbitantly priced Cappuccino coffee shop (tea and coffee, Dhs11.50; average meal, Dhs38). But the whole atrium is filled with calming noise from what lies inside: an indoor arbour, or as the hotel likes to call it, a 'tropical rainforest'. With that famous forest animal, the duck, waddling happily in its streams, a meal on the decking downstairs in the Calypso Café is charming, even if the food is the usual hotel fare (fish and chips, Dhs45; meze, Dhs35). There's a very 1970s-looking beach, with wooden parasols dotted along a little curved bay.

Sharjah Rotana Hotel
Al Khaleej Square, Ar-Ruba flyover (06 563 7777). **Rates** Dhs500 single; Dhs600 double; Dhs700-Dhs2,000 suite. **Credit** AmEx, MC, V.
A clean and functional four-star, the Sharjah Rotana is a proven respite from the maelstrom of the city outside. The Al Dar Restaurant on the first floor serves decent Western food, including sandwiches, salads and steaks, with the piped jazz music fitting in nicely with the place's general plastic feel.

Resources

Hospitals
Kuwaiti Hospital *Kuwait Road (06 5242 111).*
Al Dhaid Hospital *Al Dhaid, 50km (30 miles) inland from Sharjah (06 882 2221).*
Al Zahra Private Hospital *Opposite the clock tower, Al Zahra Square (06 561 9999).*

Internet
Radisson SAS Hotel *Corniche Road (06 565 7777).* **Price** Dhs30 per hr.

Police station
Traffic Police HQ *Abu Tina (06 554 1111).*

Post office
Central post office *By Municipality roundabout, Al Soor (06 572 2219).* **Open** 8am-8pm Sat-Wed; 8am-6pm Thur.

Tourist information
Sharjah Commerce & Tourism Development Authority *Off Ar-Ruba Road, towards the Corniche (06 556 6777/www.sharjah-welcome.com).* **Open** 7.30am-2pm Sat-Wed.

Essentials

It is illegal for women to wear clothes that show their upper arms or too much leg, or to be in a car with someone who is not related to them (this is mainly aimed at stopping prostitution). Alcohol is strictly illegal anywhere in Sharjah, including its enclaves on the east coast. Unlike Dubai, you cannot expect English to be spoken everywhere – it may be a cliché, but it's true: a few words in Arabic go a long way (*see p264* **Language**).

Getting around

Taxis in Sharjah are generally cheaper than in Dubai. However, they are unmetered, and we've heard complaints of travellers being ripped off. No ride within Sharjah city should cost more than Dhs10. Note also that many drivers won't take you if they don't understand you. If you're stuck, **Delta Taxis** (06 559 8598) will pick you up.

Getting there

By car
Sharjah is clearly signposted on Dubai's major roads. The easiest option is to cross Garhoud Bridge and continue north straight along the freeway to Sharjah.

By bus
Buses leave from the Deira taxi stand near Al Nasr Square whenever the bus is full (normally every 20-30 minutes). They cost Dhs5 and stop anywhere en route to Sharjah's Rolla Square.

By taxi
From Dubai you can take any of the usual metered cabs at roughly Dhs20 from Deira, Dhs40 from Bur Dubai and Dhs60 from Jumeirah. However, if you get an unlicensed cab you can haggle for a cheaper price. Unfortunately, when returning you must use a Sharjah taxi; these tend to be older than their Dubai equivalents, unmetered, and driven by men who haven't learnt what indicators or brakes are for. Expect to pay around Dhs40 to travel back as far as Bur Dubai.

Ajman

After working up a thirst museum hopping in teetotal Sharjah, Ajman is the place to head to for a little boozing in a plastic-table-and-bottled-beer-only style. Aside from perfecting the art of the eastern Arabian waterhole, Ajman boasts a rich history. When, in the mid 18th century, the seafaring Qawasim tribe took control of the lower Gulf coast, the tiny coastal strip of Ajman fell under their sway. But soon after they destroyed the

Qawasim fleet at Ras Al Khaimah in 1819, the British declared Ajman independent, leaving power firmly in the hands of the Al Abu Khurayban clan of the An-Naim tribe. Ajman was signatory to British Trucial treaties of 1820, 1835, 1843 and 1853, and became subject to the Residency of the Persian Gulf in 1892.

Vestiges of this era remain in several locally built *burj* (defensive towers) which dot the coast, and the large and well-renovated 18th-century fort, now inland at the centre of the city – ask for Dowar Al Hosn or Al Hosn roundabout. Alternatively, at the roundabout before the Ajman Kempinski hotel, look for the Ajman Chamber of Commerce building on your righthand side. Turn right here and continue straight over the next roundabout. The fort is on the left and houses the **Ajman Museum**.

Fishing has always been the main industry in the emirate, which covers just 259 square kilometres (100 square miles); traditional fishing vessels can still be seen all along the coast. Ajman port, located on the northern side of the creek a few kilometres from the town centre, has been transformed into a major dhow-building centre and important dockyard. But, without oil resources, Ajman has been largely dependent on federal money for its development since joining the United Arab Emirates in 1971.

Still, hundreds of companies are being incorporated at Ajman Free Zone and Ajman Industrial Area which means the population has grown from around 80,000 in 1992 to around 256,000 in 2005. Indeed the expansion of Dubai, Sharjah and Ajman now means that the emirate is part of a coastal conurbation that starts at Jebel Ali in Dubai and ends at Ajman's northernmost border with Umm Al Quwain, a distance of around 100 kilometres (60 miles). With rent here so cheap, many people now live in Ajman but work in Sharjah or Dubai.

Ajman Museum

Al Hosn roundabout, Aziz Street, by Central Square (06 742 3824). **Open** times vary, phone to check. **Admission** Dhs4; Dhs2 under-7s. **No credit cards.** Displays depicting weird and wonderful medical and religious practices give a fantastic if eerie insight into life as it must have been led for centuries among the coastal Bedouin. It isn't a large collection, but it certainly delves deeper than most displays of so-called heritage. There is also a working wind tower in one corner of the fort, under which one can sit to feel the breeze created by the traditional design.

Where to eat, drink & stay

The emirate's costliest and newest resort is the five-star **Ajman Kempinski** (06 745 1555). Prices start at Dhs1,560, rates that aren't so steep as to deter the German and Russian tour operators who regularly make block bookings. Guests here tend to stay within the hotel confines and sun themselves happily on the private beach, which is in truth far more inviting than the stretch of sand called Ajman Corniche.

With little else to do in Ajman besides tan and eat, the hotel offers excellent restaurants: for Italian there's **Sabella's Trattoria & Pizzeria**, while **Bukhara** does some great North Indian food. There is also a lovely veranda café, the 24-hour **Café Kranzler**, where you can sit out just metres from the sea. **Hai Tao** is the Kempinski's Chinese outlet, but for a meal that's equally good but costs less (albeit in considerably more basic surroundings) try the **Blue Beach Restaurant** halfway down Ajman Corniche, on the opposite side of the road to the sea. The charming family running the place are from Shanghai, and specialise in food from that area (superb braised duck, Shanghai style, is Dhs45, but you can eat a lot cheaper if you wish).

Close by is the four-star **Safir Dana Resort** (06 742 9999). The name is a slight misnomer, since it doesn't actually have a private beach. Staff will, however, bring parasols and serve you on the public beach opposite the hotel's **Al Seef Café**. Rooms in the Safir Dana Resort used to go for Dhs100 a night in low season, but since the last edition of this guide they've escalated dramatically and the cheapest room now costs Dhs400.

The **Ajman Beach Hotel** (06 742 3333) – not to be confused with the Ajman Beach Resort, the first resort hotel in Ajman – hasn't raised its prices at all, but this restaurant and bar complex is full of Russian and Chinese 'entertainers', which usually sees guests only staying for a few hours. If you do want a full night's sleep, it will cost Dhs250 for a single room and Dhs350 for double (including tax). The beach is uninspiring, but the hotel's an acceptable choice if other places are booked.

Resources

Tourist information

Ministry of Information & Culture *Near Kempinski Hotel, the Creek end of Arabian Gulf Street (06 744 4000/www.uaeinteract.com).* **Open** 7.30am-2pm Sat-Wed.

Getting there

By car

From Dubai, get on to Sharjah's Ar-Ruba Street by turning left underneath Sharjah Gate Square. Cross Khaled Lagoon, and then at the Khaleej Square roundabout turn left to the coast. The Ajman/ Sharjah border is at the Coral Beach Hotel roundabout, just by the sea.

By bus

Dubai Transport buses leave for Ajman from the Deira taxi stand (near Al Nasr Square). They cost Dhs7, and leave when they are full.

By taxi

Metered taxis from Dubai to Ajman Corniche cost around Dhs40-Dhs50 from Deira, Dhs60-Dhs70 from Bur Dubai and Dhs80-Dhs90 from Jumeirah.

Umm Al Quwain

If burning rubber, hurling yourself out of the sky or letting rip on a shooting range floats your boat, then Umm Al Quwain is the adrenalin-pumping adventure playground for you. The UAE's answer to extreme sports capital of the world New Zealand, Umm Al Quwain's seemingly rustic serenity – in the form of mangroves and sandbars – provides the perfect setting to let loose the action man or woman inside.

Take the **Emirates Car & Motorcycle Racing Club** (06 768 1166), a rather clever effort by the ruler of Umm Al Quwain to keep local lads from killing each other in high-octane motorway death duels that has spawned a fast-growing racing scene. The Racing Club now has full drag, motocross, autocross and even supercross tracks. Every Thursday and Friday night, upwards of 15,000 people come to watch local teams compete in some of the world's fastest cars. If you want to watch Nissan Skyline GTs charging round a circuit like a scene from *The Fast and the Furious*, head 15 kilometres (9.5 miles) north of the Umm Al Quwain roundabout – the club is opposite the beached Ilyushin-76 cargo plane that marks the Aeroclub's territory. Lines get crossed at 6pm and entrance is Dhs10-Dhs20.

On the other side of the road, the Umm Al **Quwain Aeroclub** (06 768 1447) is another thrill-junkies' dream. Here you can skydive from 9am to sunset. Tandem jumps go for Dhs800, while qualified jumpers can have a go from as little as Dhs85 (plus an extra Dhs40 for parachute hire and Dhs25 for packing); a parachute student's 'accelerated free fall package' is Dhs6,000. Opposite the Aeroclub is the **Umm Al Quwain Shooting Club** (06 768 1900). You used to be able to shoot everything from Uzis to AK-47s here, but in 2003 the federal ministry in charge withdrew these licences across the UAE; you are now limited to single- and double-barrelled shotguns. You can shoot these daily, except

Wednesdays, from 1pm to 9pm; 25 cartridges will cost you Dhs65.

If all this fills you with abject horror, head a bit further up the road to **Dreamland Aqua Park** or the **Umm Al Quwain Fort** (06 765 0888), a positively calming experience.

Dreamland Aqua Park

Umm Al Quwain–Ras Al Khaimah road (06 768 1888). **Open** 10am-6pm Sat-Wed; 10am-8pm Thur, Fri. **Admission** Dhs70; Dhs40 5-11s; free under-4s. **Credit** AmEx, MC, V.
This haven of family-friendly near sanity might be bang in the middle of nowhere, but the water rides and food stalls easily match the fun of Jumeirah's Wild Wadi (*see p153*), albeit in a less swanky setting.

Umm Al Quwain Fort

Al Lubna Road, Old Town (06 765 0888). **Open** 8am-1pm, 5-8pm Sat, Sun, Tue-Fri; 8am-1pm Mon. **Admission** Dhs4; free under-16s. **No credit cards.**
Very similar to other forts in the region, but with better access to rooms and walkways, Umm Al Quwain Fort has an well-laid-out jewellery collection, an in-depth weapons display, and a couple of rooms showing material from the Ad-Dur archaeological site. Most interesting of all, however, is the amazing story pinned to a wall of one of the towers. It relates (if you can decipher the slightly obscure English) the story of the murder of ruler Ahmed bin Ibrahim Al Mualla by his cousin-servant in 1929, and how the people of Umm Al Quwain punished the murderer by burning him alive inside the tower.

Where to eat, drink & stay

The **Flamingo Beach Resort** (06 765 0000) is one of those odd, desolate coastal resorts on the lower Gulf that puts you in mind of the Eagles' 'Hotel California'. Still, it has good service and is reasonable value for money – prices seem to have stuck at around Dhs300, for which you get a double room and the opportunity to lounge around a large, open, grassy space with pool, bar and incredibly cheap booze – no food is served after 10pm but, as the concierge says, 'liquor is 24 hours'. The hotel offers an unusual pastime: crab hunting. For Dhs125, you can be taken out to the creek by motor launch for a couple of hours of night-diving along the shores of Al Siniyyah Island. The trip includes snacks and dinner; staff barbecue your catch on the beach.

We regret that we can't recommended a stay at the **Barracuda Hotel** (06 768 1555): first, it is expensive at from Dhs250 to Dhs550 (depending on whether you choose old or new accommodation); second, the smell of sewage on the tide is well-nigh unbearable.

You shouldn't feel obliged to stay in Umm Al Quwain at all. If you've got this far, you probably came by car, and there are only a few more kilometres to drive north until you reach to the more attractive **Bin Majid Beach Resort** or **Al Hamra Fort Hotel** (for both, *see p235*).

Tourist information

Ministry of Information & Culture *Off Abu Bakr Al Siddiq Road (06 765 6663/www.uaeinter act.com)*. **Open** 7.30am-2pm Sat-Wed.

Getting there

By car

Take the Dubai–Sharjah Road and keep going north until you hit UFO roundabout (so-named because of the concrete, UFO-shaped building on one side), then take the second exit towards Cultural roundabout. From Cultural roundabout, take the second exit. Filter right at the next major junction, take the third exit left, and head straight for about 20km (12.5 miles) until you hit Umm Al Quwain roundabout. Turn left to go into town, or head 15km (9.5 miles) straight on to reach the Aeroclub.

By bus

Dubai Transport buses leave for Umm Al Quwain from the Deira taxi stand near Al Nasr Square. Buses cost Dhs10, and depart once they are full. To return, take a taxi (around Dhs60).

By taxi

A metered taxi from Dubai to Umm Al Quwain town centre costs around Dhs180 from Deira, Dhs200 from Bur Dubai and Dhs240 from Jumeirah. Ras Al Khaimah taxis (they wait behind Deira bus station) will be cheaper. Haggle.

Ras Al Khaimah

Driving into the northernmost emirate of the UAE is like stepping into a scene from the 1972 Clint Eastwood film *Joe Kid*: you're confronted by harsh, yet hauntingly beautiful scenery, dominated by desert, arid plains, massive mountains and sea. The inhabitants reflect their uncompromising surroundings, being resilient and blunt in manner. Ras Al Khaimah's diverse history extends back into antiquity and a pioneering project, announced in May 2005, aims to propel the emirate into the future. The Dhs221 million venture marks the beginning of a long series of projects in the region, set to completely transform an area of previously untouched coastal property.

But first, the history. Pottery found in archaeological excavations has been dated back as far as the Ubaid Period (5000-3800 BC) and reveals the settlement of an advanced civilisation. While most of Europe was still in the grip of the Stone Age, the Ras Al Khaimah locals buried their dead accompanied by painted beakers, spouted jars, incised stone bowls and personal ornaments, suggesting a highly sophisticated society.

Named Julfar by the 12th-century Arab explorer Al Idrisi, the region then fell under the sway of the Kingdom of Hormuz, the growing island-empire based in the sea straits separating the Musandam (in modern-day Oman, *see p237*) from Persia. Its flourishing wealth did not go unnoticed: the Portuguese

The life aquatic: diving at **Dibba Rock**. *See p236.*

Gimme shelter

Only 30 years ago there was nothing but sand and volcanic mountains on what is now known as **Sir Bani Yas**, the largest island in the UAE. Then along came Sheikh Zayed bin Sultan Al Nahyan, who had decided to set about creating his very own Noah's Ark.

First taking it upon himself simply to protect the endangered Arabian oryx and sand gazelle, and live among these animals on the island, the project evolved into something far more ambitious. Not quite two of every sort did Sheikh Zayed bring unto the land, but he did manage a fairly impressive mix of over 60,000 animals. Three artificial plastic-bottomed lakes were built and over 6,000 acres (15,000 hectares) of trees planted, including 3,000 olive groves cultivated for local markets. Using the underground natural springs on the island (Sir Bani Yas translates into 'the place where the water stands'), the Sheikh ensured arid land became a hydro-powered isle that generated its own water and electricity. And the Sheik saw everything that he had made and, behold, it was very good.

A boat whisks you from Sir Bani Yas jetty at 8.15am to a haven of landscapes that smack of the savannahs of Africa. A kaleidoscope of browns and greens confronts you, strikingly offset by fuchsia-pink bougainvillea. But, this being the UAE, the conservation park and important agricultural research centre is by no means a peace, yoghurt and wholegrain socks kind of hippy affair. Home to no less than three Bedouin-style palaces (one of which is sans helipad), it also boasts an ornate lift for those unable, or unwilling, to make the ascent to the viewing point.

The tour itself needs reworking: after clambering in and out of the mini bus for the umpteenth time, trudging from one lot of gazelle pooh to the next to take another photo of (yet more) buck, you may feel as worn out as the languid llama, too hot to even spit at you. Each animal does, however, have its own idiosyncratic charm: the Dhabis (spangled-legged deer that gave the emirate its name) are so adorable its difficult to refrain from popping one into your handbag; the Oryx are challengingly elusive; the emus, with ears resembling cigarette burns, appear constantly perplexed; and the majestic giraffes parade their patchwork patterns with great pride. If you are lucky, you may even pass a school of dolphins en route.

Apart from reclaiming acres of dry land, some of the plantations are part of food-growing experiments which test new ideas and find species that show the maximum tolerance for Abu Dhabi's arid climate. And those who chose to make the island their home have found a refuge and staging post with a safe anchorage, excellent fishing and treasured pearling beds in the Gulf nearby.

Keen conservationists and curious tourists alike will enjoy a trip to this crown jewel of the Arabian waters. Refreshments come in the form of cold drinks and sandwiches with the crusts cut off, and what the guide lacks in command of the facts, she makes up for with her sunny personality.

The Danat Resort

02 801 2222.
Tours 8am-12.15pm Thur, Fri. **Cost** Dhs100.

---

invaded the Empire of Hormuz in 1507, sacking tributary cities along the east coast of Oman and taking Hormuz itself in 1514. But constantly harried by local tribes, the Ottomans and their Omani vassals, not to mention the Dutch, British and Persians, the Portuguese were finally ousted in 1622, leaving a tumult of competing powers and navies. Julfar increasingly lost importance as first Safavid Persia, then the Al Yaruba Omani Empire took loose control of the area. Eventually it was abandoned, with the centre of trade moving four kilometres (2.5 miles) south. The new town was named Ras Al Khaimah, which literally translates as 'the Head of the Tent'. This became the home base for a local tribal confederation known

as the Qawasim. The decline in Omani power in the area allowed Qawasim sailors to take control of the trade along the Gulf, Musandam and northern Omani coasts – as well as of commerce in the Indian Ocean. The Qawasim declared the independence of Ras Al Khaimah and the growing town of Sharjah from the Omani empire in 1749.

With the collapse of the world pearl market in the early 20th century, Ras Al Khaimah, as with all of the towns of the lower Gulf, fell into abject poverty. Limited oil production from 1969 onwards helped matters, but while Ras Al Khaimah sought to remain independent from the Federation of United Arab Emirates (lasting for 44 days after the other emirates signed on 2 December 1971), but joining a federation backed by Abu Dhabi's oil reserves was really the only option. The emirate received a boost with the discovery of the offshore Saleh oil field in the 1980s and has since worked hard to develop export industries in cement and ceramics, but it remains far poorer than Abu Dhabi or Dubai, and thus maintains its reputation as Arabia's 'Wild West'.

Sightseeing

The creek, Khor Ras Al Khaimah, cuts the city of Ras Al Khaimah into two sections, connected by a single bridge. In the west, the original old town houses the **National Museum** and a number of souks, while the newer Al Nakheel district serves as the commercial and business zone, with a few hotels and the new Manar Mall.

National Museum of Ras Al Khaimah

Old Town (07 233 3411). **Open** *June-Aug* 8am-noon, 4-7pm Sat, Sun, Tue-Fri. *Sept-May* 10am-5pm Sat, Sun, Tue-Fri. **Admission** Dhs2; Dhs1 children; permission to take photos Dhs5. **No credit cards.**
From the Umm Al Quwain highway, head straight towards old Ras Al Khaimah at the first (Clock Tower) roundabout. Go left at the second roundabout and the fort is a few hundred metres away, on your right. Past the rather sullen guards, you'll find a lovely tree-lined courtyard with pearling, fishing and pottery-making exhibits – and the most detailed labelling in Arabic and English of any of the northern Emirati forts. Most interesting are the reproduction paintings of the first British naval expedition of 1809. Depicting the attack on Ras Al Khaimah, they are accompanied by text promoting the thesis of Sharjah's current ruler, Sheikh Dr Sultan bin Mohammed Al Qasimi, that the Qawasim weren't responsible for piracy in the area (read the cited references and make up your own mind). Silver tribal jewellery and a Baker Rifle, the British army's first standard-issue rifle, are also displayed.

Ras Al Khaimah Shooting Club

Khuzam Road, first right after walled Ruler's Palace (07 236 3622). **Open** 3-8pm daily. **No credit cards.**
Marksmen used to come to this club from far and wide, as the RAK Shooting Club is the best such public facility in the UAE. They once shot the likes of M16s, AK-47s and 9mm Brownings, but these big boys' toys were spirited away shortly before the palace coup of June 2003. This leaves shotguns available for skeet and trap shooting at a cost of Dhs50 for 25 cartridges – a whole Dhs15 cheaper than at the Umm Al Quwain Shooting Club.

Tower Links Golf Course

Khuzam Road, opposite walled Ruler's Palace (07 227 9939). **Open** 7.30am-10.30pm daily (last tee-off 8pm). **Rates** Dhs225 (incl golf cart & bucket of balls).

Tower Links, the latest addition to the UAE's remarkable golfing boom, only opened in January 2005. It comprises an 18-hole floodlit course was unveiled, along with clubhouse, academy, restaurant, bar, gym and spa. Designed by the American Gerald S Williams and built by Hydroturf, Tower Links is unusual in that it abuts the huge mangrove reserve sited at the base of Ras Al Khaimah's creek. Consequently, the grass used on the course is not the usual Bermuda, but an entirely new, specially saline-tolerant species, called *paspallum.*

Where to eat, drink & stay

Bin Majid Beach Resort

Umm Al Quwain–Ras Al Khaimah coast road, just before RAK Ceramics (07 244 6644). **Rates** Dhs490 single/double; Dhs525 suite, incl breakfast, lunch & dinner. **Credit** AmEx, MC, V.
This four-star beach chalet hotel is peaceful, but it does have a ramshackle air about it that suggests the Costa del Sol, circa 1975. You'll find several bars, coffee shops, an 'Indian' nightclub and what must be one of the smallest hotel gift shops in the world (it's only about 2.5m or nine feet wide).

Al Hamra Fort Hotel

Umm Al Quwain–Ras Al Khaimah coast road, 25km (15 miles) from Dreamland, 20km (12.5 miles) from Ras Al Khaimah centre (07 244 6666/www.alhamra fort.com). **Rates** Dhs800 single; Dhs850 double. **Credit** AmEx, MC, V.
With distinctive wind towers on top of its villas and two kilometres (1.25 miles) of private beach, unique for the area, this hotel is a hidden gem. Enjoy some water sports, before having a drink at the delightful covered bar outside, or visit the Italian and Arabic restaurants indoors. It's well worth dropping in to take afternoon tea in the lobby café (Dhs14 for two), even if you're heading further north. Ask about villa rates.

Hilton Ras Al Khaimah

New Ras Al Khaimah, by the bridge (07 228 8888). **Rates** (incl breakfast & tax) Dhs500 single; Dhs550 double; Dhs800-Dhs1,000 suite. **Credit** AmEx, MC, V.
The Hilton's five stars hang by a thread, but even if decor is cheap and cheerful, the service is by and large efficient and friendly. The food is pretty good too, and there is a great wood-panelled bar called Havana for unwinding after a hard day's wander.

Al Nakheel Hotel

Al Muntasir Street, opposite Dubai Islamic Bank, Al Nakheel (07 228 2822). **Rates** (incl taxes) Dhs100 single; Dhs150 double. **Credit** MC, V.
Not the most salubrious establishment in town, but definitely the quirkiest. Al Nakheel has the northernmost bar in the Emirates. It rejoices in the name Churchills, and is a hangout for expat Brits, Omani oilmen and Filipino workers. Rooms are grubby and bare, but the hotel's cheap and friendly.

To dive for

There's a staggering array of marine life right here in the UAE, so get tanked up, strap on those fins and prepare to get wet in these local aquatic hotspots. If you need a bit of training before you head out, *see p200.*

EAST COAST (GULF OF OMAN)

Visibility on this coast can reach 20 metres (65 feet), making it an ideal place for learner divers and snorklers.

Dibba Rock

This small sloping island is swamped with hard and soft coral. It's a 20-minute boat ride from Al Aqah Beach and offers dives ranging from three metres (ten feet) to 14 metres (46 feet). There's very little current here, so it's perfect for open water divers. As well as turtles, there are bags of moray eels, putterfish, boxfish, moses sole, clownfish, lionfish and pipefish – which are closely related to seahorses.
Scuba 2000 *Al Aqah Beach (09 238 8477).*

Martini Rock

A favourite among east coast dive instructors, this underwater outcrop is ten minutes by boat from Khorfakkan Harbour and renowned for its range of corals. You can expect to see teddybear corals and whipcorals, as well as nudibranches – marine snails decked out in rather garish colours. Suitable for learner divers, this is also somewhere you can participate in night dives.
Divers Down Khorfakkan Dive Centre *Oceanic Hotel (09 237 0299).*
Scuba International Diving College *Fujairah International Marine Club (09 222 0060).*
7 Seas Divers *Near Khorfakkan souq (09 238 7400).*

Shark Island (aka Khorfakkan Island)

Turtles are a common sight here and, in winter, you might see blacktip reef sharks.

Snoopy Island

The only shore dive along the coast, this is perfect for divers with their own equipment. Expect to see big mouth mackerel, moral eels, colourful anemones, comic-looking parrotfish and, if you are lucky, blacktip and guitar sharks (which are, in fact, rays).
Sandy Beach Diving Centre *Al Aqah Beach (09 244 5555).*

MUSANDAM (GULF OF OMAN)

With the rocky Hajar Mountains rising directly from the sea, the Omani enclave to the north of Dibba is not only stunning with its fjord-like scenery, but presents marvellous diving opportunities. With sightings of all sorts of sharks, eaglerays, coral, scorpion fish and sunfish, this is as good as diving gets.

The Caves

The main chamber of this limestone cavern recedes about 20 metres (65 feet) and its 10-metre (33-foot) depth makes it ideal for less experienced divers. Take a torch and you'll spot spiny lobsters and crayfish.
Al Boom Diving Club *Le Meridien Al Aqah (04 342 2993).*

Ruqq Suwayk/Ras O'Shea

If you are going to catch a notoriously rare sight of a whale shark in the UAE, then the advanced divers' paradise of Ruqq Suwayk is the place it's going to happen.
Khasab Travel and Tours *(0968 830 464).*
Al Marsa *(06 544 1232, 050 462 1304).*

Resources

Tourist information

Ministry of Information & Culture *Off King Faisal Road (06 765 6663/www.uaeinteract.com).* Open 7.30am-2pm Sat-Wed.

Getting there

By car

Take the Dubai–Sharjah Road and keep right on going north until you hit UFO roundabout (so-named because of the concrete, UFO-shaped building). Take the second exit to Cultural roundabout and, once there, take the second exit again. Filter right at the next major junction, and take the third exit left. Head straight past Umm Al Quwain (at about 20km or 12.5 miles) to the first roundabout (perhaps a further 46km or just under 30 miles). Continue straight ahead for Ras Al Khaimah old town or, for the newer side of the city, keep going and turn right two roundabouts later to cross the bridge.

By bus

Dubai Transport buses to Ras Al Khaimah leave from the Deira taxi stand near Al Nasr Square, but they won't set off until they're full; you'll pay Dhs20. To return, take a Ras Al Khaimah taxi, which should cost around Dhs90.

By taxi

A metered taxi from Dubai to Ras Al Khaimah town centre will cost about Dhs200 from Deira or maybe Dhs230 from Jumeirah. Ras Al Khaimah taxis can be found waiting behind Deira station, and should cost around Dhs80. Haggle.

Musandam

Formed during the Cretaceous and Miocene ages 1,850 million years ago, the craggy and unspoilt peninsula of Musandam pushes itself out of the extreme north of the Sultanate. Originally just part of the Zagros Mountain range, the peninsula was split from them by earthquakes and volcanic activity to form the Hajar mountain range. The Strait of Hormuz, the 60-kilometre-wide (37-mile) passage between the Zagros and Hajar ranges, is of critical importance to Oman, with 90 per cent of all the Gulf's oil trade passing through this area. Up until ten years ago no tourists were allowed into this imposing high security area because of its strategic military position.

Belonging to Oman, these 'Fjords of Arabia' are best reached by hiring a boat from the port in Khasab. Be prepared to haggle to get the right price for your half-hour ride to **Telegraph Island**. Even in the height of summer, a trip here is idyllic and you can always slip over the side for a quick swim. Secluded azure bays, frolicking dolphins, excellent snorkelling and quaint local villages at the foot of rugged mountains that plunge directly into the sea are just some of the sights that await. You can also plan a longer trip and camp out on a beach.

It is not possible to rent diving gear in Khasab, so come fully equipped or book a diving trip ahead of time through **Khasab Travel & Tours** (266 9950). A half-day dhow trip (9am to noon) costs Dhs150 per person; a full-day trip (9am to 4pm) is Dhs250, or Dhs300 with diving – a speedboat and cylinder will be provided. An overnight camping trip (for a minimum of ten people) costs Dhs650 each. You can also rent a 4x4 from the same company at Dhs800 for a full day and Dhs450 for half a day. Tours need to be organised before going to Khasab, as availability is far from guaranteed.

Once back in port, drive to the top of **Jebel Harim** mountain for breathtaking views and temperatures that become some eight degrees cooler as you approach 2,000 metres (7,000 feet) in altitude. You can continue past the military dome on the summit for a little way, but must return on the same path as no access is allowed through the checkpoint at the bottom of Wadi Bih.

Golden Tulip Hotel

Khasab coast road (00 968 2673 0777). **Rates** Dhs380 single; Dhs460 double. **Credit** AmEx, MC, V.

The Golden Tulip Hotel is nestled conveniently on the coast as you make your way into Khasab. The 60 rooms here are compact, but clean; there are also a swimming pool, a restaurant and a bar. They all have terrific sea views.

Khasab Hotel

Khasab coast road (00 968 2673 0271).
Rates Dhs200 single; Dhs300 double; Dhs600 apartments (6 people). **Credit** AmEx, MC, V.

For many years the only hotel to greet you in the Musandam was the Khasab. It has 15 rooms and the service is genuine and friendly. There are also four apartments, each of which sleeps six people. The hotel restaurant is refreshingly old-fashioned, serving food that is basic but tasty, and the hotel can also sometimes arrange a rental car for you – check when making your reservation.

Tourist Information

Omani Consulate *Off Khalid bin Al Waleed Road, Bur Dubai, Dubai (397 1000).* **Open** 7.30am-2.30pm Sat-Wed.

Essentials

Visa regulations

Gaining a visit visa to enter Oman seldom causes any problems, usually taking no more than about ten minutes (depending on your nationality) at the Omani border post or at Khasab Airport; but don't forget your Omani car insurance, as you will need to show proof of coverage. The major issue is being allowed to re-enter the UAE: any single-entry visit visa is cancelled when you cross the border. This trip is therefore only possible if you come from one of the 33 countries eligible for a visit visa on arrival back in the UAE; it's best to check with **Dubai Tourism & Commerce Marketing** (223 0000) to find out whether this applies to you.

Getting there

By car

It takes just over 2hrs to reach Khasab from Dubai, depending, of course, on how quickly you manage to get through the border. The trip from Ras Al Khaimah is just 70km (45 miles), but for much of that distance it is rewardingly picturesque.

By plane

Oman Air flies Dubai to Khasab daily. Flights are at 8.20am, 13.50pm, 5.15pm, 9.35pm and 10.15pm, take 45mins, and cost from Dhs920 to Dhs5,540. Contact the airline's Dubai office on 351 8080 for details.

The UAE

East Coast

Defined by its rugged mountains and long stretches of sand, the east coast provides a welcome escape from the city.

Fujairah.

Even if you are only in the UAE for a short time, making a trip to the strikingly beautiful east coast of the Emirates should be a high priority, no matter how full your itinerary. Whether it's a weekend camping break, a day spent snorkelling around the infamous Snoopy Rock (see p236 **To dive for**), a more challenging diving course off the amazing coastline or simply the opportunity to enjoy the simpler pace of life, a trip through the rugged **Hajar Mountains** and down to the Gulf of Oman offers the perfect getaway – and it should only take you a couple of hours to get there.

Tumbling down to the Indian Ocean from the interior, cleft by wadis and dotted with villages, the dramatic Hajar mountain barrier make the drive through this area a treat in itself. The youngest of the seven emirates, until 1952 **Fujairah** was part of Sharjah, and its relatively newfound independence makes it the only emirate to be located entirely on the east coast. It has become increasingly popular with tourists, who still tend to overlook the

unique treasures found in areas to the south and west of it. Use Fujairah as a base to visit the inviting hot springs of **Ain Al Gamour**; or to explore **Khor Kalba**, a village on a tidal estuary that's home to the oldest mangrove forest in Arabia. The ruined houses at **Wadi Hayl** and the T-Shaped Tomb of **Al Bithnah** are also well worth a visit, while if you venture north to **Dibba** and the border of the Musandam peninsula (see p237), you will be rewarded with some of the finest and most remote beaches in the whole of the UAE, as well as getting to enjoy such world-class diving sites as Khor Fakkan and Al Aqah.

Fujairah

The golden sands and coral reefs off the coast of Fujairah make it ideal beach holiday territory. Throw in the surrounding hillsides scattered with mysterious ancient forts and watchtowers and a thriving city centre crammed with character, and you have an utterly charming package on offer.

The UAE

Fujairah was part of the Qawasim sheikhdom based in Sharjah, until the local Al Sharqi branch of the Qawasim gained some autonomy in 1903. The British recognised Fujairah as independent from Sharjah in 1952, but it is not local politics that gives Fujairah its distinct atmosphere. With the Hajar mountains running parallel to the east coast from Al Ain to Ras Al Khaimah, Fujairah has always been cut off from the rest of the UAE: the first all-weather road through the mountains only opened in 1975. Despite new high-rises along the main drag, the city is mainly a one-storey sprawl that seems to be in a different time zone to the rest of the UAE.

Fujairah is the second-busiest refuelling port in the world, and it is common to see hundreds of ships queuing up offshore, which unfortunately means that some illegally empty their holds out at sea before heading to the Gulf to upload more oil. This has clearly had a detrimental effect on the wildlife in the area, but the fishing remains excellent. Aside from sea trawling and the variety of water sports on offer, Fujairah is also a prime place to watch birds en route to Africa and Asia.

In the winter season, the stretch of beach between the Hilton and the Khor Kalba area takes on a Mediterranean feel, as crowds gather to watch the ancient (and bloodless) Portuguese sport of bull butting. More humane than bull fighting, a winner is determined after two big bulls have butted each other about in a head-to-head duel.

For an equally outlandish sport, you can watch 'slippery soccer', a game of football on a multicoloured oiled pitch, where keeping your balance is the biggest challenge. No one is quite certain as to the origins of this sport, but if you head down to Al Gurfa Street off the Plaza Cinema, you'll be able to come up with some of your own deductions.

On your drive to Fujairah, if you keep going straight after Manama, after 20 kilometres (12.5 miles) you'll dip down into a bowl of gravel lined with stalls. Known as **Friday Market**, it sells carpets, plants, pottery and fresh fruit, and presents a perfect opportunity to put your haggling skills to the test. You can buy pretty pottery candle covers for Dhs15 or less; kitsch Pakistani carpets are another favourite (those featuring Sheikh Zayed's face are top of our shopping list). Don't get fleeced: none of the items are old and few are worth much. The most expensive goods are the attractive Iranian patterned silk carpets, which you should be able to pick up for less than Dhs450. You can also stop for snacks such as fresh corn-on-the-cob for less than Dhs4, and grab a chai (thick, sweet Indian tea) for 50fils at the New Restaurant.

Fujairah Museum

Head inland & follow signs from Coffee Pot roundabout, Al Gurfa Street (09 222 9085). **Open** 8.30am-1.30pm, 4-6pm Sun-Thur; 2-6pm Fri. **Admission** Dhs3; Dhs1 children. **No credit cards.** This bizarre building is close to collapse, with a ceiling that would be at home in an Edwardian parlour. Yet it houses a fabulous collection of archaeological remains, taken from local sites, which easily rival those in Sharjah's more prestigious Archaeological Museum (*see p227*). The building is supposed to be a temporary measure until restoration of the 360-year-old fort behind it is complete; as we went to press, the move looked to still be some time off.

Where to eat, drink & stay

At the Coffee Pot roundabout, just before the Hilton Hotel, is Al Owaid Street, which takes you towards the shoreline where you'll find the teapot-shaped **Fujairah International Marine Club** (09 222 1166). It houses the Armada Bar, serving excellent pub grub to an interesting mix of locals, expats, dive-centre workers and the occasional crew from visiting boats. You can also replenish yourself at the **Fujairah Youth Hostel** (09 222 2347), on the lefthand side of Al Faseel Street, parallel to the Corniche.

Hilton Fujairah

Just off Coffee Pot roundabout, Al Gurfa Street (09 222 2411). **Rates** Dhs700 single; Dhs750 double. (Summer rates from Dhs350.) **Credit** AmEx, MC, V.
The Hilton is a charming retreat, where delicate fountains surround a shady courtyard and spill into mosaic-lined swimming pools. The hotel has a private stretch of beach, and the bar and beach huts lend a Mediterranean feel. Having been refurbished a few years ago, the rooms are still clean and attractive. Staff are friendly and competent, and the hotel can arrange jet-skiing, windsurfing, water-skiing and fishing or diving trips.

Resources

Tourist information
Ministry of Information & Culture
Off Jerusalem Road (09 222 4190/www.uae interact.com). **Open** 7.30am-2pm Sat-Wed.

Getting there

By car
The 130km (80 mile) drive from Dubai to Fujairah via Al Dhaid is a treat in itself, taking you through deep desert and mountain villages. Spectacular new mountain roads are being built (already passable in two-wheel-drive vehicles) from Ras Al Khaimah on the Arabian Gulf coast (*see p233*) to Dibba and Fujairah, and from Sharjah to Kalba,

but at the time of writing the Al Dhaid route was simplest. From Dubai, jump on to the E44 Emirates link road west (direction Al Awir/Hatta/Oman). From the Bu Kidra Interchange at the end of Dubai Creek, travel 18km (11 miles) to the third interchange and go left (north) on to the E611, heading for Sharjah/Al Dhaid. After 19 kilometres (12 miles) go west towards Al Dhaid on the E88. This takes you through rolling dunes, and finally you come over the crest of a hill to find the oasis of Al Dhaid stretched before you.

Go left at the first roundabout in the town, then right at the next roundabout towards Manama. Keep going straight on. After 20km (12.5 miles) or so you'll dip down towards the Friday Market.

Further on through the mountains lies the nondescript town of Masafi (Ras Al Khaimah's mountain enclave), best known for its mineral water production. The first junction you come to takes you left (north) to Dibba at the northern tip of the UAE's east coast before the Musandam peninsula, or right (south) to Fujairah town and Kalba at the Oman border, passing via the small townships of Diftah, Blaydah and Al Bithnah.

By bus

Buses to Fujairah go every half hour from Deira taxi stand, near Al Nasr Square, and cost Dhs35. You can't return by bus, but will have to take a taxi instead.

By taxi

Dubai's metered cabs will cost Dhs190 to Dhs240, depending on pick-up point and destination. In Fujairah, you can pick up taxis from the Karachi Durbar side of Plaza Cinema roundabout. A local taxi (taking up to six people) will cost around Dhs80 for a journey back to Dubai.

Khor Kalba

Bird life is particularly plentiful in Khor Kalba, the oldest mangrove forest in Arabia and the most northerly in the world. The Khor Kalba conservation area supports a distinctive eco-system and it is the only place you'll have the chance of spotting two of the rarest birds on the planet: the Khor Kalba white-collared kingfisher (*kalbaensis*) and the Sykes's warbler. Even those not enthralled by birdwatching will be in awe of the stunning natural beauty and tranquillity of the area.

From Fujairah, turn southwards down the coast towards **Kalba**, which is only about 10 kilometres (six miles) away. Drive through the town and, on reaching the beginning of the swamps on your lefthand side, take a left on to a well-used track that hugs the outer edge. Follow this track round quite naturally and take the bridge on to the sandy area between the sea and the swamps.

Tracks along the shore are suitable for four-wheel drivers, but under no circumstance drive over vegetation or close to the waterfront.

Contact Dubai-based **Desert Rangers** (*see p79* **Tour operators at a glance**) to organise canoes to watch the wildlife.

Just a few kilometres south of Kalba, and inland from the coast, the tiny Fujairan village of **Awalah** sits on the north side of a wadi that runs from east to west. Sitting atop a terrace overlooking the wadi is a mud-brick fortified house, dating to the 19th century. The building covers the western corner of an Iron Age fortified enclosure, which still boasts visible defensive walls more than 2.3 metres (seven feet) thick and up to 60 metres (200 feet) long, preserved in places to almost 1.5 metres (five feet) above today's ground level.

Ain Al Gamour

For a rejuvenating dip, head to the hot springs at Ain Al Gamour, surrounded by a lush oasis of trees and vegetation. Strong, steaming bubbles in which you can immerse yourself feed a small pool near the parking area. This little haven can be reached by driving south past Kalba, keeping an eye out for the Adnoc service station. Pass the roundabout for the main road up into the mountains and take the next turn right on to a graded track 1.3 kilometres (0.75 mile) later. After some 2.5 kilometres (1.5 miles), take the next fork left and follow the signs for Ain Al Gamour.

Al Bithnah

In the Hajar Mountains, 13 kilometres (eight miles) outside Fujairah, sits the historic village of Al Bithnah. Notable mainly for its ancient fort and important archaeological sites, discoveries have also revealed that it was once a stopover for trading caravans from the Far East. The village can easily be reached from the Fujairah–Sharjah road, while if you drive through the village and the wadi you will access the fort, which used to control the main east–west pass through the mountain. What was used as a burial chamber from approximately 1350 BC to 350 BC is now known as the T-Shaped Tomb or the Chambered Tomb. It has had to be sealed off and covered to protect it from the elements, but the **Fujairah Museum** (*see p239*) provides fascinating information about this famous archaeological site.

Wadi Hayl

Wadi Hayl is situated in startlingly beautiful scenery, and is home to an abandoned village and the best-preserved mountain fort in the

Snoopy Island.
See p243.

UAE. This is a short off-road trip, and as such is perfect to link with a visit to the east coast.

From the outskirts of Fujairah, jump on to the Masafi–Fujairah road from the roundabout and go less than a kilometre west, looking left for signposts opposite the police station to Hayl Castle or Palace (22 kilometres/13.5 miles from Masafi). Two-wheel drive cars can easily reach the fort by turning left towards the quarry (the signpost reads 'Al Hayl Palace 4km') after turning off the main road. Four-wheel drives can continue straight on through the abandoned village of Hayl.

The village's ruined houses and terraces follow the watercourse and its tributaries. You should keep an eye out for the hundreds of 4,000-year-old petroglyphs – depicting animals, horses and riders – that cover boulders on either side of the wadi.

Bear right at the fork at the end of the track after the village and you will find the fort (some call it a fortified house) perched on an isolated outcrop. The fort has been dated to between AD 1470 and 1700, though much of today's structure is not thought to be more than about 100 years old, when it doubled as the palace of Sheikh Abdullah bin Hamdan Al Sharqi. It is built with natural materials – stone and mud-bricks mixed with straw, and wooden floors. There is a watchtower on the hill behind, and numerous ruins of smaller houses surrounding it. The main track continues past the fort and, although it doesn't lead to any other specific areas of interest, it's an attractive drive. You can leave the track at any point and explore further up one of the side wadis.

Getting there

By car

The simplest way to get to explore the south and west is to start at Fujairah itself (see pp238-240). To pass through breathtaking mountains and incredible tunnels, head east from Dubai to Hatta (see pp73-74). Pass Hatta's main roundabout (with Hatta Fort Hotel on your left) and 2.8km (two miles) further on take the next tarmac left towards Huwaylat and Munay. The twisting road from here on in is a lovely drive. After 11km (seven miles), take the second exit left at the Huwaylat roundabout towards Munay. In 9km (5.5 miles), at Munay, turn right, down on to the motorway heading east. This takes you past mountain strongholds and through an amazing feat of engineering in the shape of the 1.2km-long (just over half a mile) Gillay tunnel.

The road then snakes down through Wadi Moudiq on the other side of the Hajar to Kalba's first roundabout – just follow the coast north (left) past the swamps to Kalba and on to Fujairah. If you get lost anywhere along the coast don't be afraid to ask the (older) locals. A smattering of Arabic is useful (see p264 **Language**), and a map even more so.

Khor Fakkan

Bordered by two headlands, this popular coastal town at the base of the Hajar Mountains is also known as 'Creek of the Two Jaws'. Attracting a steady stream of divers, the second largest town on the east coast is popular for the inland trip getting there, as well as the fact that it is by far the cleanest town in this region.

Wide streets and well-tended gardens make it a pleasant place to wander, even if there are few specific attractions worth visiting. If you're low on vitals and need to hit the shops, the covered souk at the container terminal at the far south of the port is perfect for fresh produce. Known as Chorf to Venetian jeweller Gasparo Balbi in 1580, Khor Fakkan has the remains of a Portuguese fort, most likely destroyed during hostilities when the Persian navy invaded the east coast in 1623 under Omani Sheikh Muhammad Suhari's command. According to the German traveller Carsten Niebuhr, Khor Fakkan belonged to a sheikh of the Qawasim by 1765, and today the town is another east coast enclave belonging to the Qawasim emirate of Sharjah. Khor Fakkan's most notable inland sight is **Wadi Wurrayah**. Guaranteed to provide cool, shady, watery relief from baking temperatures and blazing sun, its waterfall is an area of natural beauty spoilt only by graffiti and litter left by misguided visitors.

The entrance to Wadi Wurrayah is off the main road that runs north between Khor Fakkan and Dibba. There are therefore two sides from which you can approach the entrance to the wadi. Travelling north up from Fujairah, then from the roundabout at the Oceanic Hotel in Khor Fakkan, continue for almost five kilometres (three miles) and make a U-turn just beyond the third roundabout. Double back on yourself for 700 metres (slightly more than a quarter of a mile) before taking the tarred road off to your right. If you're coming at it from the opposite direction, from Dibba, then the turning will be on your right, around 2.4 kilometres (1.5 miles) from the Badiyah roundabout. This tarred road continues straight, forking after roughly five kilometres (three miles). At the fork you can take either road, as they join up just over a kilometre further on. The turning not to miss is in the second major dip in the wadi, one kilometre (half a mile) after the forked roads join up again. 4x4s can turn right into the wide wadi bed at this point, but normal cars should keep to the left and follow the tarred road for just under three kilometres (two miles), at which point you'll have a great view from above the waterfall. You can park and climb down from here, but be careful: the gravel can be very loose.

If you are following the 4x4 track, the wadi gets quite narrow and twists and turns between high stony walls. The surface is quite rough and stony, and the going will be pretty slow for the next few kilometres. There is a fair amount of vegetation along the edges that adds to the atmosphere and when the wadi opens out, you'll find the deep, all-year-round pool, fed by the waterfall. Inevitably, the size of the waterfall depends on the season, with it becoming little more than a trickle in the hot summer months.

Where to eat, drink & stay

Note that, as it is part of the Emirate of Sharjah, no alcohol is served in Khor Fakkan.

Khor Fakkan Youth Hostel

Opposite Oceanic Hotel, follow signs from northern roundabout, Coast Road (09 237 0886). **Rates** *(4-bed room) YHA members* Dhs30 per person. *Non-members* Dhs45 per person. **Credit** AmEx, MC, V.

A charming and cheap alternative to the Oceanic Hotel, with many visitors using the 24-bed hostel as their base while making the most of the Oceanic's dive centre. The hostel is squeaky clean, has kitchen facilities, and is run by a charmingly efficient Filipino called Rudy. If you are a single woman and it's appropriate, Rudy will give you a separate room.

Oceanic Hotel

Near Khor Fakkan dam, follow signs from northern roundabout, Coast Road (09 238 5111). **Rates** *Oct-mid May* Dhs400 single; Dhs500 double. *Mid May-Sept* Dhs300 single/double. **Credit** AmEx, MC, V.

At the top end of the quality scale, the Oceanic tucks into a knoll of rock on the Indian Ocean. It has a funky, if musty, 1970s kitsch feel, mature gardens, a great swathe of white-sand beach and a good diving centre. Rates are reasonably high, though you can negotiate outside high season.

Badiyah

The tiny village of Badiyah's biggest claim to fame is that it is home to the oldest mosque in the UAE. The **Badiyah Mosque** dates back to 1446, predating the Portuguese invasion of the area by more than 50 years and representing a unique feat of engineering for its time, with four small domes supported by a central pillar, stone carvings and special shelves for the holy Koran. Also known as Al Masjid Al Othmani, it sits at the side of the main Khor Fakkan–Dibba road (about 38 kilometres or 24 miles from Fujairah) and, unusually for mosques in the UAE, can be visited outside prayer times if accompanied by a guide (who lives next door). The imam (leader of prayers) is friendly and will engage you in conversation given half a chance. It's also worth a short hike up the mountain to look at the two watchtowers perched behind the mosque and take in the view.

Ideal for divers: Al Aqah's laid-back **Sandy Beach Motel**.

Al Aqah

Situated 16 kilometres (ten miles) from Khor Fakkan and 18 kilometres (11 miles) from Dibba, there's something for tourists at both ends of the spectrum at Al Aqah. Moneyed holidaymakers can be pampered in the five-star **Meridien Beach Resort**; outdoorsy, salt-of-the-earth types will appreciate the faded charms of the **Sandy Beach Motel** – not least its proximity to Snoopy Island.

Where to eat, drink & stay

Le Meridien Al Aqah Beach Resort

From Dubai, head east towards Sharjah, through Al Dhaid to Masafi, then take the Dibba Road & follow the signs for 35km/22 miles (09 244 9000). **Rates** Dhs500-Dhs800 single; Dhs800-Dhs1,000 double; Dhs2,400-Dhs12,000 suites. **Credit** AmEx, MC, V. Love it or hate it, you can't miss the colossal glass and concrete construction jutting out of its remote setting between the mountains and the Indian Ocean. Le Meridien would blend in perfectly on the Dubai coastline, although critics say that this uncompromising structure looming up unexpectedly is incongruous here. As a guest, though, you can't dismiss the impressively spacious rooms, with their spectacular views of the ocean and the Hajar mountains. The services and facilities (which include a beautiful beach, good restaurants, a health club and a nightclub) also make the place worthy of each and every neutron of its five stars.

Sandy Beach Motel

Head east from Dubai towards Sharjah, through Al Dhaid to Masafi, then take the Dibba Road & follow the signs for 35km/22 miles (09 244 5555). **Rates** (incl tax) Dhs303 single; Dhs385 double; Dhs660 chalet. **Credit** AmEx, MC, V.
Squatting in the shadow of Le Meridien, the far simpler Sandy Beach Motel is a favourite among divers and expatriates who want to get away from everything Al Aqah stands for. With mature gardens, a lovely beach and one of the best dive centres in the area, the motel is a serene sanctuary with its faded decor setting it worlds apart from Dubai's big hotel chains. Arguably, Sandy Beach's greatest attraction is the fact that it is located directly opposite Snoopy Island (*see p236* **To dive for**), an outcrop in the ocean so-called because it vaguely resembles the shape of the cartoon dog reclining on top of his kennel. The area around the rock is great for snorkelling and diving, though the dive centre at the motel also offers more technical dives in the Omani waters of the Musandam. The restaurant is basic, with the best dishes tending to be those that include meat and grilled fish from the local markets.

Dibba

Described by some as the most beautiful part of the emirates, Dibba is steeped in a rather volatile history. A walk through the old part of town, paying special attention to the ornate doors of the compounds, is one of the highlights of a trip here. You won't come across many

The UAE

Westerners in town, which lends an even more special feel to your adventure.

There are actually three Dibbas: Dibba Muhallab (also called Dibba Al Fujairah – belonging to Fujairah), Hosn Dibba (belonging to Sharjah) and Dibba Bayah (Oman). There are no border posts here and it is possible to cross into any part of the conurbation without hindrance – just don't have a car crash in Dibba Bayah without Omani insurance. The three Dibbas share an attractive bay, fishing communities, Portuguese fortresses, wadi waterfalls and exceptional diving locations.

To access an appealing beach, well known for camping, snorkelling and picnics, follow the coastline until you reach the tiny Dibba port ('Mina Bayah' in Arabic) on the far northern edge of the town, just a few hundred metres from the Globe roundabout. An active fishing harbour, you can see the day's catch spread out on the ground and the air is loud with locals bartering. If so inclined, you can charter a fishing boat or dhow from here for a short trip. Once past the port, continue along the main road away from town and then take the sandy track that forks right, bringing you towards a stretch of beach by the mountains in the very corner of the bay. Which makes for an altogether calmer setting when compared to Dibba's prior, battle-filled years.

Before the coming of Islam, no state had ever been able to control the tribes of Arabia. The Persian Sassanids, Byzantium and even the Southern Arabian states all tried but failed. The final battle in the AD 633 Ridda Wars (Wars of Apostasy) ended this tradition of complete independence from external powers. Many Arabian Bedouin tribes had sworn their personal allegiance to the Prophet Mohammed, so when he died in AD 632, so did the Bedouin allegiance. By refusing to accept the leadership of Mohammed's successor, his father-in-law Abu Bakr, they were challenging outside control – as they had done for hundreds of years. But now they were also challenging Islam and Abu Bakr was having none of it. The huge battles at Dibba (there are 10,000 gravestones in a cemetery here) marked the end of the Muslim reconquest of Arabia, the beginning of state control from Mecca (in modern-day Saudi Arabia), and the beginning of Islamic expansion beyond it.

Where to eat, drink & stay

Holiday Beach Motel

Head east from Dibba towards Khor Fakkan, for 5km/3 miles along the coast road (09 244 5540). **Rates** *Oct-June* Dhs385 studio chalets; Dhs485 single chalets; Dhs685 double chalets. *July-Sept* Dhs325 studio chalets; Dhs400 single chalets; Dhs585 double chalets. **Credit** AmEx, MC, V.

A superb place to dive from, though the hotel is at the ramshackle end of the quality measure, its chalets overlooking a distinctly underwhelming expanse of grass and a basic pool. However, Maku Dive Centre (09 244 5747), run by great instructors, comes highly recommended. Prices here start at Dhs1,600 for four-day course. The motel has Indian and Pakistani nightclubs open nightly until 3.30am, but as with all nightlife spots on the east coast, both border on the tacky.

Getting there

By car

If you don't want to get to the north via the Masafi–Dibba–Fujairah loop (*see pp239-240*), there is a road being built to connect Ras Al Khaimah (*see p233*) with Dibba through the startlingly harsh and beautiful Ruus Al Jibal, part of the Hajar mountains. With graded tracks leading on and off perfect tarmac, it is passable even in a two-wheel-drive vehicle – just beware rock transporters along the way.

By taxi

To travel directly to Dibba and the north by taxi, Dubai's metered cabs will cost Dhs250 to Dhs260, depending on pick-up point and destination. On the way back, in the unlikely event that a local cab driver won't take you all the way to Dubai, have him drop you in Fujairah, and get a cab from there.

Dibba.

The UAE

Directory

Directory

Getting Around

Arriving & leaving

By air

Dubai International Airport

Switchboard 224 5555/
flight information 216 6666/
www.dubaiairport.com.

One of the most highly acclaimed airports in the world, DIA is currently undergoing an elaborate and extravagant expansion programme (scheduled for completion in 2006). This includes a new terminal (the airport's third) exclusively for Emirates airline flights.

Almost all major airlines arrive at the main Sheikh Rashid Terminal 1. Here the Dubai Duty Free (224 5004) is the last port of call for the purchase of alcohol before entering Dubai's 'hotel-only' licensing restrictions (*see p252* **Customs**). Airport facilities include internet and banking services, shops, restaurants, business services, a bar, a hotel and a regular raffle that gives you the chance to win a luxury car. Tickets cost Dhs500, but odds are favourable as there is a draw every time 1,000 are sold. The smaller Terminal 2 caters largely for charter flights, cargo and commercial airlines from Iran and the CIS countries. There is also a VIP terminal known as Al Majalis.

A card-operated E-Gate enables those who carry the relevant 'smart card' to check in and travel unhindered, using nothing more than their fingerprints for identification. For more information, see the airport website.

TO AND FROM THE AIRPORT

DIA is in Garhoud, about five kilometres (three miles) south-east of the city centre. If you're staying at one of the big international hotels, you'll get a complimentary **shuttle bus** or **limousine** transfer to and from the airport.

Otherwise, **taxis** are the most convenient and practical form of transport. There is Dhs20 surcharge on pick-up from the terminal (instead of the usual Dhs3). This means that the journey from the airport to the city centre costs around Dhs30, while the return journey is Dhs13 or so. It takes about ten minutes to get to Bur Dubai, while Jumeirah and the hotel beach resorts are about half an hour away.

There are **bus** links to and from both terminals every 20 or 30 minutes for around Dhs2, although timings are somewhat erratic and the routes can be lengthy. Route 401 goes from the airport to Al Sabkah bus station, while route 402 goes to Al Ghubaiba, running through the centre of the city. From Deira station, located opposite the Al Ghurair Centre on Al Rigga Road, the numbers 4, 11 and 15 will take you straight to Terminal 1, as will the 33 and 44 from Bur Dubai. Fortunately, all buses are fully air-conditioned. Call 227 3840 or 800 4848, or visit www.dubaipublictransport.ae for more details.

AIRPORT PARKING

There are short- and long-term parking facilities at the airport. Tariffs range from Dhs5 per hour in the short-stay car park to Dhs30 per day for up to ten days in the long-stay.

Airlines

Flight information 216 6666.

All airlines operating regular flights into DIA are listed on the airport website; some of the most popular are listed below. Note that some airlines ask you to reconfirm your flight 72 hours before departure, and that cheaper tickets will often incur a penalty fee for alteration or cancellation.

Air France *Information 294 0049/ reservations 294 5899/ticket sales 294 5991/www.airfrance.com.*
British Airways *Reservations & ticket sales 307 5777/ www.britishairways.com.*
Emirates *214 4444/ www.emirates.com.*
Etihad Airways *250 58000/ www.etihadairways.com.*
Gulf Air *271 3111/3222/ www.gulfairco.com.*
KLM *335 5777/www.klm.com.*
Lufthansa *343 2121/ www.lufthansa.com.*
Qatar Air *229 2229/221 4210/ www.qatarair.com.*
Royal Brunei *Information 351 4111/ticket sales 316 6562/ www.bruneiair.com.* (No alcohol served on board.)

By road

The UAE is bordered to the north and east by Oman, and to the south and west by Saudi Arabia. Road access to Dubai is via the Abu Dhabi emirate to the south, Sharjah to the north, and Oman to the east.

There is no charge for driving between emirates, but travel to or from Oman or Saudi Arabia requires your passport, driving licence, insurance and visa. Crossing the Oman border costs Dhs20

Getting on track

Dubai has no existing train system, but the government has announced provisional plans for the city's first urban railway. The final evaluation, estimated at Dhs2.8 billion, is currently being made for what will be a light rail metro system. The proposed 37 stations are due to open in 2009 with two lines: one connecting the airport to Jebel Ali via Deira, running along Sheikh Zayed Road to the Defence roundabout at Interchange 1; the other beginning at the Dubai Municipality behind the park, running acrosss the Creek and ending at the American University of Dubai.

per person, plus the price of a visa (Dhs13 for those with UAE residency, Dhs60 for those on a visit visa). Your car will be searched: carrying alcohol is prohibited and may mean you are turned away.

All the highways linking Dubai to other emirates and Oman are in good condition. Ensure your vehicle and the air-conditioning are in good working order, as it is inevitably hot and the drive through the Hajar Mountains to Muscat, the capital of Oman, takes around five hours.

Check with **Immigration** (398 0000) before you leave for any changes in travel policy. For traffic enquiries, contact the **Emergency Offices** (223 2323, www.dubaipublictransport.ae).

For more information, *see below* **Navigation**, *p248* **Driving** *and p249* **Road hog!**

By sea

The only sea access for passengers is from Iraq or Iran; journey time is more than two days and it costs around Dhs630 return. For schedules and details contact the **Dubai Ports Authority** (881 5000, www.dpa.co.ae).

Alternatively, you can call **Rashid Port** (345 1545), which operates sea routes to Port Bandar Abbas and Port Bandar Lankah in Iran, and Port Umm Qasr in Iraq.

Navigation

Thanks to its modern highway system, most of Dubai is fairly easy to get around. However, in some places the existing infrastructure has struggled to cope with the growth of the city, most notably the Garhoud and Maktoum Bridges, spanning the Creek, and the Shindagha tunnel underneath it. During rush hours (7-9am, 1-2pm, 5-7pm) serious tailbacks can develop. However, plans have now been announced for a third bridge over the Creek, which should ease congestion when it opens in 2006.

Despite the relatively good road system, Dubai can be a dangerous place to drive in. There are high numbers of road accidents and deaths, caused largely by speeding and poor lane discipline. Many drivers tailgate, chat away on their mobiles, and refuse to use either their indicators or their mirrors (*see p249* **Road hog!**).

The easiest way to get around is by taxi (*see below*). **Water taxis** or abras (*see p248*) are also available on the Creek, but they're an interesting tourist experience rather than a practical way of getting around the whole city.

Dubai's public buses (*see below*) are not very tourist friendly, and are primarily used by workers who are unable to afford cars or taxis.

The biggest problem with getting around Dubai, though, is the lack of an accurate system of street names. Some of the larger roads and streets are known by their name, but most are just numbered. This means your destination is usually identified by a nearby landmark, often a hotel or similar building.

See also p250 **Addresses**.

Public transport

Buses

The public bus system is rarely used by tourists, owing to the convenience of taxis. The service is extremely cheap, but routes can be convoluted and timings erratic.

Timetables, prices and route maps are available from the main bus stations of **Al Ghubaiba** in Bur Dubai (342 11130) and by the **gold souk** in Deira (227 3840). You can also call the main information line (6am-10pm daily; 800 4848) or visit www.dubaipublictransport.ae.

Should you brave a bus trip, try to have the correct money since change for larger notes is rarely available. All bus stops are request stops. Eating, drinking and smoking are not allowed on board; the front three rows of seats are reserved for women. Passengers without tickets are liable for prosecution.

Monthly bus passes (Dhs95, good value if you are going to use the bus more than three times a day) are available from the depots at **Al Ramoul** and **Al Qusais**.

Taxis

Official taxis are well-maintained, air-conditioned and metered. Fares are Dhs1.5 per kilometre (0.3 mile) with a Dhs3-Dhs3.50

cover charge, depending on the time of day. The two biggest companies are **Dubai Transport Company** (208 0202) and **National Taxis** (336 6611). Unofficial (unmetered) taxis are best avoided, as they tend to be older cars with poor air-con and may take you for a ride. If it's the only option available, be sure to agree a price before entering the car. Taxi drivers usually have a reasonable grasp of English, so you shouldn't find it too difficult to explain where you want to go.

If you're in an outlying area of the city you should consider booking a taxi online from www.dubaipublictransport.ae or by calling 208 0808. Fares for longer journeys outside Dubai should be agreed in advance (there is also a 12-hour service available, with petrol and driver included).

Drivers have a reputation for being honest, so if you leave something in a taxi, your driver might find a way to return it to you. Failing this, call the company you used and give the time, destinations (to and from) and taxi number, and they will do their best to help.

Water taxis

Abras are water taxis that ferry both Dubai workers and tourists across the Creek for about 50 fils (100 fils = Dhs1). The boats run between 5am and midnight, carry about 20 people and take just a few minutes to make the crossing from Bur Dubai on the south bank of the Creek to Deira on the north, or vice versa. *See also p67* **Abra rides**.

Driving

People drive on the right in Dubai. A vehicle licence may be secured at Dhs360 for the first registration, which is thereafter subject to annual renewal – following a road-worthiness test at a charge of Dhs290. The driving licences issued by some overseas governments may be used to obtain a Dubai licence.

Seatbelts are compulsory if you're in the front seats of a vehicle, highly recommended in the back. In residential areas, the speed limit is normally between 40kph (35mph) and 80kph (50mph). On the highways within the city the limit is 100kph (60mph); outside the city limits, it is 120kph (75mph).

Although there are, in theory, fines and bans for a whole series of offences, in practice the enforcement of these is pretty erratic. While you may have to pay up to Dhs1,500 if you're caught going through an amber or red light, don't expect much in the way of road rules or driving etiquette if you venture out by car.
See also p247 **Navigation** *and p249* **Road hog!**

Traffic fines & offences

A comprehensive official traffic police website (www.dxbtraffic.gov.ae) lists details on licence requirements, contact numbers and fines for offences. All offences are listed under 'Kiosk Locations and Violations'.

There is a zero tolerance policy on drinking and driving. If you are caught driving or parking illegally by the police, you'll be issued a *mukhalifaa* (fine). If caught by a speed camera you'll normally be fined Dhs200. When hiring a car, it's routine to sign an agreement of responsibility for any fines you may incur.

You can check whether you've racked up any traffic offences on www.dubaipolice.gov.ae or call 268 5555. Fines can be paid online, or at the Muroor (headquarters of the Traffic Police), near Galadari roundabout on the Dubai–Sharjah road.

Traffic accidents

If you are involved in a serious traffic accident, call 999; if it's a minor collision, call the police on 398 1111. If you do not report any scratch or bump to the traffic police, insurers will almost certainly reject your claim. Third-party vehicle insurance is compulsory.

If the accident was a minor one and no one was hurt, move the car to the side of the road and wait for the police to arrive. If there is any doubt as to who is at fault, or if there is any injury (however slight), do not move the car, even if you are blocking traffic. If you help or move anyone injured in an accident, the police may hold you responsible if anything happens to that person.

Breakdown services

There are two 24-hour breakdown services, the **AAA (Arabian Automobile Association)** (800 4900, www.aaauae.com) and **IATC Recovery (International Automobile Touring Club)** (800 5200, www.iatcuae.com). If you are driving when the car breaks down, try to pull over on to the hard shoulder. The police are likely to stop and will give assistance. If you're in the middle of high-speed traffic, it will be unsafe to get out of the car. Instead, use a mobile to call the police from the relative safety of your vehicle. Other breakdown services (not 24-hour) include:

Ahmed Mohammed Garage
050 650 4739.

Dubai Auto Towing Service
359 4424.

Vehicle hire

Most major hire companies have offices at the airport (11 companies have 24-hour outlets there, *see p249*) and hotels. Before renting a car, check the small print, especially clauses

Road hog!

The UAE has one of the world's highest death tolls from road accidents per capita, and if you drive along one of Dubai's highways it isn't hard to see why. Few people adhere to traffic regulations, and speeding, undertaking and use of the hard shoulder are frequent occurrences. All cars sold into the UAE have an audio warning when speeds exceed the 120kph (75mph) speed limit, but instead of detering the country's fast-living roadhogs, some simply have them illegally removed.

Bizarre manoeuvres such as reversing around roundabouts because drivers have missed their turning, or indicating right and then turning left are not unusual sights. One of the most unpleasant things you're likely to experience is extreme tailgating, with many motorists driving up behind you until they virtually touch your bumper in a bid to get you to move over and let them pass. If you're unable to move because the lane next to you is occupied, it's not unheard of for the driver behind to attempt to overtake by squeezing into the gap between your car and the central reservation.

Many resident expats opt to pay that little bit more and get a large, sturdy vehicle such as a 4x4, purely on the grounds of personal safety. Which is something you may wish to consider when hiring a car.

relating to insurance cover in the event of an accident, as this can vary considerably from company to company.

Drivers must be aged over 21 to hire a small car, or 25 for a medium (two-litre) or larger 4x4 vehicle. You'll need your national driving licence (an International Driving Permit is best, although it isn't legally required). You'll also need your passport and one of the major credit cards. Prices range from Dhs77 per day for a small manual car, to Dhs1,000 for something like a Lexus LS430. Motorbikes are not available for hire anywhere in Dubai.

Autolease 224 4900.
Avis 224 5219.
Budget 224 5192.
Cars 224 5524.
Diamond Lease 220 0325.
Europe 224 5240.
Fast rent a car 224 5040.
Hertz 224 5222.
Patriot 224 4244.
Thrifty 224 5404.
United Car Rentals 224 4666.

Fuel stations

At the time of writing, the cost of petrol was Dhs4.75 a gallon; so you should expect to pay less than Dhs60 to fill your tank. There are 24-hour petrol stations on all major highways. Most petrol stations have convenience stores on the premises, selling snacks and drinks.

Parking

Many areas in the city centre have introduced paid parking in a bid to reduce congestion. Prices are reasonable (Dhs1 or Dhs2 for a one-hour stay, depending on location), but this hasn't made it easier to secure a parking space. Paid parking areas are operational at peak times (generally from 8am to noon and 4pm to 9pm), and it's free to park there outside these hours and on Fridays or public holidays. If you park illegally or go over

your time limit, the penalty charge is Dhs150, increasing to Dhs165 if you don't pay within 14 days. Generally your car hire company will pay them for you and charge them to you at the end of your lease.

Particular black spots include the warren of streets in 'old' Bur Dubai, the stretch of Sheikh Zayed Road between the Crowne Plaza and Shangri La hotels and most of Deira.

Parking in shopping malls is free, but if you visit any of them on a Thursday or Friday evening expect huge queues and delays, particularly at the City Centre mall.

Most hotels have extensive parking facilities for visitors, including valet services.

Road signs

Road signs are in English and Arabic, which makes matters easier for Western visitors, but the sheer scale of the American-style highway system (up to five lanes on either side at some points) means you have to stay alert, especially at the junctions on Sheikh Zayed Road that have multiple exits.

Walking

Due to the intense heat and humidity, an outdoor stroll is out of the question between May and September. The city is simply not designed with pedestrians in mind; certain areas lack pavements and the sheer size of some highways can mean waiting up to 20 minutes just to cross – unless you're prepared to gamble with your life. You might even find yourself having to take a taxi journey just to get to the other side.

The best places to take a walk include the Creek-side areas of Bur Dubai and Deira, and the stretches of beach in Jumeirah and Umm Suqeim.

Directory

Resources A-Z

Addresses

Dubai is not divided into postcodes. While street addresses are slowly being introduced to the city, at present all official locations are simply given postbox numbers. The majority of roads are numbered, but not identifiable by anything other than nearby landmarks. Any resident here will happily point you in the direction of the Ritz-Carlton or the Jumeirah Beach Hotel, but few will know an actual address. Taxi drivers know most of the significant landmarks, but it's always worth carrying a map with you just in case. The most common reference points are hotels, shopping malls, restaurants and some of the bigger supermarkets, such as Spinneys.

It's not a bad idea to invest Dhs30 in a copy of the Dubai Municipality Map, which is available from **Book Corner** (*see p124*) or any Emarat Petrol station.

We've included a number of useful city maps at the end of this guide; *see pp273-287.*

Age restrictions

You must be aged 18 to drive in Dubai (21 to rent a small car, 25 to rent a large one) and to buy cigarettes, although the latter does not appear to be vigorously enforced. In restaurants and bars you must be 21 to drink.

It is illegal to buy alcohol from an off-licence without a licence. Issued by the Police Department to non-Muslims holding a residence visa, these are valid for one year only, but easily renewable. Alcohol can be bought from two suppliers; a+e and MMI. *See p87* **Buying booze** *and p178* **Authorised alcohol**.

Attitude & etiquette

A cosmopolitan city with hundreds of different nationalities, Dubai has a well-deserved reputation for being tolerant and relaxed. It is, however, a Muslim state and must be respected as one. Most 'rules' concerning cultural dos and don'ts are basic common sense and courtesy, with particular respect needing to be shown for Islam and the Royal Family.

GENERAL GUIDELINES

In formal situations it is polite to stand when someone enters the room and to offer a handshake to all men in the room on entering. Only offer your hand to an Arab woman if she does so first. It is courteous to ask Muslim men about their family, but not about their wives.

You may find yourself addressed by a title followed by your first name – for instance, Mr Tom – and it's not unusual for a woman to be referred to by her husband's name – Mrs Tom.

While the last ten years have seen attitudes relax, avoid offending locals with public displays of affection and flesh. This is particularly true in Ramadan (when everyone is expected to dress more conservatively) and at the Heritage Village, but in bars and nightclubs you won't find dress codes any different to those in the West. Topless bathing is not allowed, even on the private beaches, and some ask women not to wear thongs. Be respectful about taking photographs, and always ask for consent. Communication can at times be frustrating, but patience is crucial in a nation where time holds a different significance and civility is paramount.

For further information contact the **Ministry of Information & Culture** on 261 5500 or the **Sheikh Mohammed Centre for Cultural Understanding** on 344 7755. *See also p259* **Religion**.

In terms of getting by on a day-to-day basis, information, expansion and efficiency are buzzwords in Dubai. While

---

Travel advice

For up-to-date information on travel, contact your government's department of foreign affairs. Most have websites packed with useful advice for would-be travellers.

Australia
www.dfat.gov.au/travel
Canada
www.voyage.gc.ca
France
www.diplomatie.fr
Germany
www.auswaertiges-amt.de
India
www.meaindia.nic.in
New Zealand
www.mft.govt.nz/travel

Republic of Ireland
www.irlgov.ie/iveagh
Russia
www.dfat.gov.au/geo/russia
South Africa
www.dfa.gov.za
UK
www.fco.gov.uk/travel
USA
http://www.state.gov/travel

the personal services can sometimes astound, the all-too-common collapse in communication also can astonish. There is a tendency to be more keen to help than capable of carrying it through, with telephone conversations often leaving you more confused than when you started.

Far less harrowing is using the internet (*see p256* **Internet**), where countless sites offer straightforward facts and advice for tourists. In this guide, contact websites have been given in addition to the telephone number whenever possible.

Business

Dubai has been incredibly proactive in its bid to establish itself as the business hub of the UAE. Every effort is made to welcome new business and its corporate care is the envy of the rest of the world. Dubai's booming economy is aided by low labour costs, minimal taxes, free zones, a secure convertible currency and a liberal community.

This safe and secure environment has attracted international interest on a scale unrivalled elsewhere. The city's main economic activities are non-oil trade, oil production and export, and, more recently, tourism.

Airport business centres

All passengers using Dubai International Airport can use these 24-hour facilities:

Airport International Hotel Business Centre

216 4278/www.dubaiairport.com. **Map** p281 L2.
24-hour facilities comprising five meeting rooms (capacity: six to 18 people), one conference room (capacity: 60 people), eight workstations, state-of-the-art communication systems, and full secretarial and support services.

Global Link

Departures level, near Gate 16, Terminal 1, Dubai International Airport (266 8855/www.dubai airport.com). **Map** p281 L2.
This business centre provides passengers with six ISD booths, workstations, internet connection, fax and secretarial services.

Conference & exhibition organisers/ office hire

With large halls and spacious showrooms readily available in all the major hotels, Dubai is able to handle any kind of seminar, conference or trade exhibition. Comprehensive facilities will typically cater for small meetings through to major international conventions. Several public institutes have also been developed especially to host significant events; these include the recent **Dubai International Convention Centre** (332 1000, www.dicc. ae), which staged the annual International Monetary Fund convention in October 2003. Most of the city's hotels provide business facilities/ venues with all the necessary support services. Otherwise, the **Dubai World Trade Centre** or DWTC (info@ dwtc.com) and **Dubai Chamber of Commerce & Industry** (DCCI) (*see below*) are two useful points of contact for services and recommendations.

Dubai Chamber of Commerce & Industry

Baniyas Road, on the Creek, Rigga, Deira (228 0000/www.dcci.gov.ae). **Open** 8am-4pm Sat-Wed. **Map** p283 K4.
The DCCI exhibition halls and auditoriums are large, flexible spaces developed to accommodate exhibitions, trade and social fairs, and new product launches.

Dubai International Financial Centre

Emirates Towers (330 0100/fax 330 0311). **Open** 9am-6pm Sun-Thur. **Map** p282 H4.

The DIFC is an onshore capital market designated as a financial free zone. It's designed to offer financial services and to support new initiatives, with the focus on Banking Services, Capital Markets, Asset Management & Fund Registration, Islamic Finance, Reinsurance and Back Office Operations.

Dubai World Trade Centre

Sheikh Zayed Road, near Za'abeel roundabout, Satwa (332 1000/ www.dwtc.com). **Open** 8am-4pm Sat-Wed. **Map** p285 G9.
The DWTC incorporates the Dubai International Convention Centre. It comprises nine interconnected, air-conditioned exhibition halls covering 37,000sq m (14,285sq ft), which are available for lease either on an individual basis or in any combination of multiples.

Courier companies

The companies listed below provide freight-forwarding, domestic, logistical, catalogue-packing and moving services. They also offer source and delivery services (meaning they will find what you want and deliver it). Open 24 hours a day, they can be contacted by both telephone and internet. They all accept major credit cards. The UAE postal service, **EMPOST**, offers an express delivery service, which is known as Mumtaz Express (*see p258* **Postal services**).

DHL

800 4004/www.dhl.com.

FedEx

331 4216/www.fedex.com.

TNT

285 3939/www.tnt.com.

Hours

Working days vary hugely, owing to religious and cultural differences. Almost everyone outside the hospitality and retail sectors has Friday off, but some have a Thursday/ Friday weekend, others a Friday/Saturday weekend, and still others work a six-day week with only Friday off. Government offices have the Thursday/Friday weekend.

Working hours during the day can also vary, with a few firms still operating a split-shift system (normally 8am-noon and 4-8pm), though this is becoming increasingly rare.

Licences

The basic requirement for all business activity in Dubai is a licence (commercial/professional/industrial) issued by the Dubai Department of Economic Development. To apply, contact the **Ministry of Economy and Commerce** on 295 4000, www.uae.gov.ae.

Sponsors

The regulation of branches and representatives of foreign companies in the UAE is covered in the Commercial Companies Law. This stipulates that companies may be 100 per cent foreign-owned providing a local agent (UAE national) is appointed. These agents/sponsors will assist in obtaining visas in exchange for a lump sum or a profit-related percentage. The exceptions to this rule are the free zones, where no local sponsor is required.

Translation services

There are dozens of different communities in Dubai, covering many languages and dialects, but English is widely spoken, particularly in a business context. If you need something translated into Arabic you can try one of the following. (Note: none of them accepts credit cards.)

Eman Legal Translation Services
Room 104, 1st floor, above Golden Fork Restaurant, Nasr Square, Deira (224 7066/ets@emirates.net.ae). **Open** 9am-6pm Sat-Wed; 9am-2pm Thur. **Map** p283 L3.

Ideal Legal Translation & Secretarial
Room 17, 4th Floor, above Al Ajami Restaurant, Al Ghurair Centre, Al Riwqa Street, Deira (222 3699/ideal@emirates.net.ae). **Open** 8am-1pm, 4-8pm Sat-Thur. **Map** p283 K3.

Lotus Translation Services
Room 411, 4th floor, Oud Metha Office Building, Oud Metha Street, near Wafi Centre, Bur Dubai (324 4492/lotrnsrv@emirates.net.ae). **Open** 9am-5.30pm Sat-Wed; 9am-2pm Thur. **Map** p281 J3.

Useful organisations

American Business Council
16th floor, Dubai World Trade Centre, Sheikh Zayed Road (331 4735/www.abcdubai.com). **Open** 8am-5pm Sat-Thur. **Map** p285 G9.

British Business Group
BBG Office, Conference Centre, British Embassy, Al Seef Road (397 0303/www.britbiz-uae.com). **Open** 8.30am-5.30pm Sat-Wed. **Map** p283 J4.

Department of Economic Development
DCCI Building, next to Sheraton Hotel, Baniyas Road, Deira (222 9922/www.dubaided.gov.ae). **Open** 7.30am-2.30pm Sat-Wed. **Map** p283 K4.

Dubai Chamber of Commerce & Industry
DCCI Building, next to Sheraton Hotel, Baniyas Road, Deira (228 0000/www.dcci.gov.ae). **Open** 7.30am-2.30pm Sat-Thur. **Map** p283 K4.

Consumer

Although people flock to Dubai to shop, there are no statutory rights to protect consumers, except the right to recover the paid price on faulty goods. However, unless you are prepared to take it to court, exchange is as far as many stores will go. Tourists with consumer-related problems and enquiries can contact the **Department of Tourism & Commerce**

Marketing (223 0000). For complaints about purchased items, the **Emirates Society for Consumer Protection** in Sharjah (06 556 7333) may also be able to assist, while the **Dubai Economic Development Office** (222 9922) will try to help people who have problems with expiry dates and warranties.

Customs

There is a duty-free shop in the airport arrivals hall. Each person is permitted to bring into the UAE four bottles of alcohol (be they spirits, wine or beer), two cartons of cigarettes, 400 cigars and two kilograms (4.5lb) of tobacco.

No customs duty is levied on personal effects entering Dubai. For more extensive explanations on any duty levied on particular products, see the Dubai Airport website with links to the Municipality site: www.dubaiairport.com, 224 5555.

The following are prohibited in the UAE and import of these goods will carry a heavy penalty: controlled substances (drugs), firearms and ammunition, pornography (including sex toys, so be careful if trying to smuggle in your rampant rabbit), unstrung pearls, pork, raw seafood, and fruit and vegetables from cholera-infected areas.

For further information call the **Dubai Customs** hotline on 800 4410 or check out www.dxbcustoms.gov.ae. *See also p258* **Prohibitions**.

Disabled

Generally speaking, Dubai is not disabled-friendly. While things are starting to improve, many places are still not equipped for wheelchair access. Most hotels have made token efforts, but functionality still plays second

Directory

fiddle to design, meaning that wheelchair facilities have largely been swept under the carpet. Those that do have some specially adapted rooms include the Burj Al Arab, City Centre Hotel, Crowne Plaza, Emirates Towers, Hilton Dubai Creek, Hilton Dubai Jumeirah, Hyatt Regency, Jumeirah Beach Hotel, JW Marriott, Oasis Beach Hotel, Madinat Jumeirah, Ritz-Carlton Dubai, Renaissance, One&Only Royal Mirage and Sheraton Jumeirah. For reviews of most of these, see pp40-58.

The airport and major shopping malls have good access and facilities, and some **Dubai Transport taxis** (208 0808) are fitted to accommodate wheelchairs. There are designated disabled parking spaces in nearly all car parks; to use them you'll need disabled window badges, though many able-bodied drivers fail to respect this.

Drugs

Dubai adheres to a strict policy of zero tolerance for drugs. There are lengthy sentences and harsh penalties for possession of a non-legal substance, and there have been several high-profile cases of expatriates serving time for such offences. Drug importation carries the death penalty, although no executions have been carried out in recent years. But even association with users or importers carries a stiff penalty. For more information see the police website at www.dubaipolice.gov.ae.

Electricity

Domestic supply is 220/240 volts AC, 50Hz. Sockets are suitable for three-pin 13 amp plugs of British standard design; however, it is a good idea to bring an adaptor with

you just in case. Adaptors can also be bought cheaply in the local supermarkets. Appliances purchased in the UAE will generally have two-pin plugs attached. For queries get in touch with the **Ministry of Electricity** on 262 6262.

Embassies & consulates

For enquiries about visa, passport, commercial and consular services, as well as press and public affairs, contact your country's embassy or consulate. In Dubai, they are usually open 8.45am-1.30pm from Sunday to Thursday. If you need to contact an official urgently, don't despair; there is usually a number on the embassy's answer service for help outside working hours.

Your embassy provides emergency legal services (the stress being on 'emergency', since it has no authority over the UAE legal system if you are caught breaking the law), consular and visa services, and educational information and advice. For a list of all embassies in Dubai log on to www.dwtc.com/directory/governme.htm.

For embassies abroad, consult www.embassyworld.com. See also p250 **Travel advice**.

Australia
1st floor, Emirates Atrium Building, Sheikh Zayed Road, between Interchange 1 & 2 (321 2444/ www.austrade.gov.au). Open 8am-3.30pm Sun-Wed; 8am-2.45pm Thur. Map p280 G5.

Canada
7th floor, Juma Al Bhaji Building, Bank Street, Bur Dubai (314 5555/ www.canada.org.ae). Open 8am-3.30pm Sat-Wed. Map p283 J5.

France
18th floor, API World Tower, Sheikh Zayed Road (332 9040). Open 8.30am-1pm Sat-Wed; 8.30am-11am Thur, Fri. Map p285 G9.

India
Consulate area, near BurJuman Centre (397 1222). Open 8am-1pm, 1.30-4.30pm Sat-Wed. Map p283 J5.

New Zealand
15th floor, ABI Tower, Sheikh Zayed Road (331 7500/www.nzte.govt.nz). Open 8.30am-5pm Sun-Thur. Map p285 G9.

Pakistan
Khalid bin Waleed Road, near BurJuman Centre (397 3600). Open 8am-3pm Sat-Wed. Map p283 J5.

Russia
Al Maktoum Street (223 1272). Open 11am-1pm Sun-Wed; 10am-noon Thur. Map p283 J3.

South Africa
3rd floor, Dubai Islamic Bank Building, Bank Street, Bur Dubai (397 5222). Open 8am-4pm Sat-Wed. Map p283 J5.

United Kingdom
British Embassy Building, Al Seef Road, Bur Dubai (309 4444/ www.britain-uae.org). Open 7.30am-2.30pm Sat-Wed. Map p283 J4.

USA
21st floor, Dubai World Trade Centre, Sheikh Zayed Road (311 6000/http://dubai.usconsulate.gov). Open 8.30am-5pm Sat-Wed. Map p285 G9.

Emergencies

For **police** call 999, for an **ambulance** call 998 or 999, and for the **fire brigade** call 997. The **coastguard** can be contacted on 345 0520 and there is also a **helicopter service**. If you dial 999 or 282 1111, in an emergency Dubai Police will send a police helicopter, which they guarantee will be with you within eight minutes.

See also p258 **Police**; for a list of major hospitals, see p254 **Health**.

Gay & lesbian

Homosexuality is, in effect, prohibited in the UAE. While there is a small gay community in Dubai, it is not centralised

Directory

around a specific region and there is no official gay presence in the city.

Health

Dubai has well-equipped public and private hospitals. Emergency care for all UAE nationals, visitors and expatriates is free from the Al Wasl, New Dubai and Rashid hospitals (see below). All other treatments are charged to tourists, so it's advisable to have medical insurance as well as travel insurance.

The **General Medical Centre** *(349 5959)* on Jumeirah Beach Road is open 8am-7pm Sat-Wed and 8am-1pm Thur. Should you require further information call the **Ministry of Health (MOH)** on 306 6200 or the **Department of Health & Medical Services** (DOHMS) on 337 1160. Both are open during normal government hours, from Saturday to Wednesday. For people whose countries have a reciprocal medical agreement with the UAE, further treatments are available.

With high hygiene and cleanliness standards, the likelihood of picking up an infection or virus is low.

Accident & emergency

All the hospitals below have 24-hour A&E departments, but only emergency cases at the A&E of public hospitals are seen free of charge.

Contraception & abortion

Most pharmacies prescribe contraception over the counter, with relatively few contraceptives requiring a prescription. It is widely known (although officially illegal) that this includes the 'morning after' pill. The **American Hospital** has a Family Planning clinic (309 6877), and the **Canadian Hospital** offers consultation and an alternative to the 'morning after' pill. For both of these hospitals, *see below*.

Dentists

Good dentists are readily available in Dubai, including orthodontists and cosmetic dentists, though prices can be hefty. For a 24-hour emergency dental service, phone 332 1444. Both **Dr Michael's Dental Clinic** (349 5900) and the **Scandinavian Dental Clinic** (349 3202) come highly recommended.

Doctors

Most of the big hotels have in-house doctors, as do the majority of the hospitals. Alternatively there is the **General Medical Centre** (349 5959) or you can ring your local embassy for their recommendations (*see p253* **Embassies & consulates**).

Hospitals

The three main **Department of Health** hospitals in Dubai are listed below. For information on the services available, visit www.dohms.gov.ae.

New Dubai Hospital
Opposite Hamria Vegetable Market, after Hyatt Regency Hotel, Deira (271 4444/www.dohms.gov.ae). Map p282 H2.

Rashid Hospital
Oud Metha Road, near Al Maktoum Bridge, Bur Dubai (337 4000/A&E 337 1323/www.dohms.gov.ae). Map p281 J2.

Al Wasl Hospital
Oud Metha Road, south of Al Qataiyat Road, Za'abeel (324 1111/www.dohms.gov.ae). Map p281 J3.

Listed below are five private hospitals in Dubai that have Accident & Emergency departments. Note that all private health care must be paid for, including emergency care. Hospitals are required to display price lists for all treatments at reception.

American Hospital Dubai
Off Oud Metha Road, between Lamcy Plaza & Wafi Centre, Al Nasr, Bur Dubai (336 7777/www.ahdubai.com). Map p281 J3.

Canadian Hospital
Ground floor, Gulf Towers (336 4444). Map p281 J3.

Emirates Hospital
Opposite Jumeirah Beach Park, next to Chili's restaurant, Beach Road, Jumeirah (349 6666/www.emirates hospital.ae). Map p286 A15.
As well as an A&E facility, the Emirates Hospital has a 24-hour walk-in clinic (though you're required to pay Dhs150 for the first consultation).

Iranian Hospital
Corner of Al Hudeiba Road & Al Wasl Road, Satwa (344 0250/ www.irhosp.co.ae). Map p284 E9.

Welcare Hospital
Next to Lifco supermarket in Garhoud, Deira (282 7788/ www.welcarehospital.com). Map p281 L3.

Insurance

Public hospitals in Dubai (*see above*) will deal with emergencies free of charge. They have good facilities and their procedures (including the use of sterilised needles and the provision of blood transfusions) are reliable and hygienic.

Medical insurance is often included in travel insurance packages, and it is important to have it unless your country has a reciprocal medical treatment arrangement with the UAE.

While travel insurance typically covers health, it is wise to make sure you have a package that covers all

Directory

eventualities, especially as, for serious but non-emergency care, you would need to attend a private hospital or clinic, where treatment can be expensive.

Opticians

See p140.

Pharmacies

There is no shortage of extremely well-stocked and serviceable pharmacies in Dubai and no formal policy of prescription: all you need to know is the name of the drug you need.

Normal opening hours are 8.30am-1.30pm, 4.30-10.30pm Saturday to Thursday and 4.30-10.30pm Friday, but some open on Friday mornings as well. A system of rotation exists for 24-hour opening, with four chemists holding the fort at any one time for a week each. For a list of the 24-hour pharmacies on duty, check the back of the local newspapers or log on to www.dm.gov.ae. Alternatively, call the **DM Emergency Offices** on 223 2323: they will be able to point you in the direction of the nearest pharmacy.

Prescriptions

Most drugs are available without prescription. In rare instances when this isn't the case, pharmacists dispense medicines on receipt of a prescription from a GP.

STDs, HIV & AIDS

To secure residency in Dubai, you have to undergo a blood test and anyone identified as HIV positive is not allowed to stay in the country. Tourists do not have to be tested, but should you become ill and have to be hospitalised, expect to find yourself on the

next plane out if tested positive for HIV.

Despite there being no official figures, it's widely accepted that there is a genuine problem with sexually transmitted diseases, due in part to the large number of prostitutes in the city.

Sunburn/dehydration

The fierce UAE sun means heatstroke and heat exhaustion are always a risk. Sunglasses, hats and high-factor suncreams are essential, particularly for children, and the importance of drinking large quantities of water to stave off dehydration cannot be overemphasised.

Vaccinations

No specific immunisations are required for entry to Dubai, but it would be wise to check beforehand – a certificate is sometimes required to prove you are clear of cholera and yellow fever if you are arriving from a high-risk area. Tetanus inoculations are recommended if you are considering a long trip.

There are very few mosquitoes in the towns and cities, and since it's not considered to be a real risk, malaria tablets are rarely prescribed for travel in the UAE. If planning to camp near the mountains or to explore wadis in the evening, cover up and use a suitable insect repellent. If in any doubt, consult your doctor before your trip.

Polio has been virtually eradicated in the UAE and hepatitis is very rare.

ID

ID is necessary for car hire as well as in bars and clubs if they don't think you look over 21. Passports are the most

requested form, so have copies made in advance. Although no national ID card exists at the moment, plans are afoot to issue all residents of the UAE with 'smart cards', which are set to replace all other forms of identification (driving licence/labour and health cards etc) by 2006. Primarily being introduced to increase the speed and efficiency of public services and to provide a population census, it will link to all government departments and carry personal information like the individual's blood group, fingerprints and other biological characteristics. *See also p250* **Age restrictions**.

Insurance

While the crime rate in Dubai is exceptionally low, it is still worth insuring yourself before you travel. Travel insurance policies usually cover loss or theft of belongings and medical treatment, but be careful to check what is included, and any clause that might be disputed, especially if you're intending to take part in activities like desert off-roading and scuba diving.

Car insurance will be covered by any creditable, authorised car hire company and anyone holding a valid licence should be able to get insurance. However, do check whether you are covered for the Sultanate of Oman. Since many parts of the UAE have a 'porous' border, you may find yourself driving within Oman without warning (the road to Hatta, for example, will take you through Oman in several places).

Medical insurance is often included in travel insurance packages and it is vital to have it, since health care in private hospitals can be extremely expensive. Emergency care is available free of charge at the government hospitals (*see p254*

Health). Be careful to keep all documents and receipts of any medical payments you make, as you will have to claim them back later. For a list of insurance companies, check out www.yellowpages.net.ae.

Internet

Dubai is leading the way in the global movement towards electronic government. Not only is it often the most efficient way of gaining information, but you can now do seemingly do everything online, from paying a traffic fine to booking a taxi. The government organisation, **Etisalat**, controls the server and is the regulator of content. Consequently there is an element of censorship, with pornography, dating and gambling sites blocked. If the network fails, there can be no service at all for hours at a time, although thankfully this is uncommon. The only exceptions to censorship are the free zones in and around the city, which connect independently to the international web. You can contact Etisalat by dialling 101, or log on to www.etisalat.com.

The **EIM** (Emirates Internet and Multimedia) kiosks provide public access to email, news and business information, enabling users to access the net from anywhere, irrespective of their email provider. Kiosks can be found in airport waiting areas, shopping centres and hotel lobbies, and take various methods of payment. Costs range from Dhs5 to Dhs15 an hour. Most hotels have some form of internet access, and net cafés are dotted around the city.

Coffee Bean Café
Aviation Club, Garhoud (282 4122). **Price** Dhs15/hr. **Map** p281 K3.

Dubai Café.net
Sheikh Zayed Road, near Emirates Towers (396 9111). **Price** Dhs10-Dhs15/hr. **Map** p280 H4.

Giga Planet Café
Garhoud, near International School (283 0303). **Price** Dhs5/hr. **Map** p281 C3.

Al Jalssa Internet Café
Bur Dubai (351 4617). **Price** Dhs10/hr. **Map** p283 J5.

Language

English is widely spoken and understood in Dubai. *See also p264* **Language**.

Left luggage

There is a left-luggage storage facility at the airport, costing Dhs20 per bag per half day (12 hours). Call 213 3233 if you are flying with Emirates; passengers of all other airlines should call 216 1734.

Legal help

Dubai has strict laws, severe sentencing, no free legal aid and no equivalent of the Citizens Advice Bureau. Should you require legal help or advice, contact your country's embassy (*see p253* **Embassies & consulates**). Foreign embassies cannot override any law in the UAE and will not sympathise if you claim ignorance of those laws, but they can offer advice and support and give details of your legal status and options. Otherwise, contact the **Ministry of Justice** on 282 5999 for advice. The government has also established a **Department for Tourist Security** (800 4438), whose purpose is to guide visitors through the labyrinth of the law and to liaise between tourists and the Dubai police. For a full list of law firms, see www.yellowpages.net.ae.

Libraries

You must be a resident to borrow from Dubai's libraries, but most will be happy for you to browse or use the reading room, where there is usually a broad selection of English-language books. The **Dubai Municipality Central Library** allows the public to view its collections online, offering title searches, browsing and the capability to reserve books from home. They can be contacted on 226 2788.

British Council (BC)
BC Building, Al Maktoum Bridge, Bur Dubai (337 0109/www.british council.com). **Open** 8am-8pm Sat-Thur. **Map** p281 K2.

DM Library
Al Ras Street, opposite St George Hotel, near gold souk, Al Ras (226 2788/www.dpl.dm.gov.ae). **Open** 7.30am-9.30pm Sat-Wed; 7.30am-2.30pm Thur. **Map** p282 G3.

Dubai Lending Library
International Arts Centre, opposite the Mosque, Beach Road, Jumeirah (337 6480). **Open** 10am-noon, 4-6pm Sat-Thur. **Map** p284 D9.

Lost property

Theft in Dubai is a relatively uncommon occurrence, but if you are a victim of crime contact the nearest police station or report it to the special **Tourist Police** unit (800 4438) – necessary for the validation of your travel insurance claims.

If you lose something, most unclaimed items are taken to a general holding unit known as **Police Lost & Found**, which can be contacted on 216 2542. If you have lost something on a bus or abra, call the **public transport information line** on 800 4848 and ask for Lost & Found. If you leave something in a taxi, get in touch with the relevant company (*see p247*). The **airport** has a 24-hour lost property line (216 2542).

To minimise the aggravation caused by losing important documents, always make a copy. Should you lose your passport, report it immediately to the police and contact your embassy (for details of embassies, *see p253*).

Media

Despite the creation of **Dubai Media City** (complete with the slogan 'freedom to create'), the media in the UAE is still subject to government censorship, though direct clashes are rare as most organisations operate a policy of self-censorship. This means you'll never see anything that criticises the UAE royal families or the government, and there are no scenes of nudity in any films. However, in the past couple of years, censorship has become noticeably more relaxed, with references to alcohol and images of bikini-clad babes now allowed. Most international publications are available here, though the black marker pen of the censors ensures that overtly sexual images are covered up.

Newspapers & magazines

There are four English daily newspapers in Dubai: *Gulf News*, *Khaleej Times*, *Gulf Today* (Dhs2-Dhs3) and a free paper *7 Days* (Dubai's equivalent to London's *Metro*). All publish local and international news, though *Gulf News* is generally perceived as the strongest. It has a weekly magazine, *Friday*, and also publishes an entertainment guide on Wednesdays.

The city's magazine sector has become increasingly competitive in recent years and there is now a wealth of publications in Dubai. *Time Out Dubai* has gone weekly, but other monthly listings and entertainment magazines include *What's On* and *Connector*. Lifestyle mags include *Emirates Home, Viva* and *Identity* (interior decoration); *Ahlan!* (Dubai's answer to *Hello!*); and

Jumeirah Beach (coffee-table glossy). There are also free tourist magazines available in some hotels, though most of them are of dubious quality.

Radio

Dubai has five English-language stations, featuring a mix of British, Canadian and Australian DJs. Sadly, the quality of programming is generally pretty low.

Channel 4 FM, 104.8FM
Modern chart, dance and R&B tunes.
City 101.6 FM
Part Hindi, part English.
Dubai FM, 92.0FM
Government-run station that plays a mixture of older hits and contemporary chart music.
Dubai Eye 103.8
Bridges the gap between conventional music shows and talk radio.
Emirates 1 FM, 100.5FM
More modern chart, dance and R&B sounds.
Emirates 2 FM, 98.5FM
Easy listening.

Television

The Dubai government runs the English-language **Channel 1**, which shows dated programmes like *The Bold & the Beautiful*. Most residents and hotels have a satellite package of some form, with **Showtime** and **Star** among the most popular, thanks to offerings like the Movie Channel, BBC Prime and the Paramount Comedy Channel. In the past year, MBC has been making big waves as a free service, with MBC's **Channel 2** screening films 24 hours a day and **MBC4** showing the latest TV series and even UK Premiership football.

Money

The national currency is the dirham. As we went to press, UK£1 was equal to Dhs 6.9, and has been between 6.7

and 6.9 since 2004. The US$ has been pegged to the dirham at a fixed rate of Dhs3.6725 since 1980.

Bank notes come in denominations of Dhs1,000 (silver), Dhs500 (red), Dhs200 (blue), Dhs100 (red), Dhs50 (purple), Dhs20 (blue), Dhs10 (green) and Dhs5 (brown). There are Dhs1 coins and then 50, 25 and 10 fils, though you'll rarely use the lower denominations.

ATMs

The majority of banks and many hotels in the UAE have ATM machines, which are convenient for withdrawing UAE dirhams. Most credit cards, and Cirrus- and Plus-enabled cash cards, are accepted. Check with your personal bank for charges for withdrawing cash overseas.

Banks

There are a number of international banks in the city such as HSBC, Citibank, Standard Chartered and Lloyds TSB, as well as locally based operations such as the National Bank of Dubai and Dubai Islamic Bank. Opening hours are normally 8am-1pm Sat-Wed, and 8am-noon Thur. All are shut on Fridays. They offer comprehensive commercial and personal services and transfers, and exchanges are simple.

Bureaux de change

Rates vary and it's worth noting that the airport is the first place you can, but the last place you should, change your money. There are several money changers in the city centre (Bur Dubai and Deira) who tend to deal only in cash but whose rates (sometimes without commission) can challenge the banks', particularly with larger sums of money. Travellers' cheques are accepted with ID in banks and hotels and other licensed exchange offices affiliated with the issuing bank. There is no separate commission structure, but exchange houses make their money on the difference between the rates at which they buy and sell. As we went to press, they were buying UK£1 at Dhs6.734, and selling at Dhs6.777. Below are the main bureaux de change:

Al Fardan

Al Fardan Headquarters, Nasr Square, Maktoum Street, next to Citibank, Deira (228 0004/ www.alfardangroup.com). **Open** 8.30am-1pm Sat-Thur; 4.30-8.30pm Fri. **Map** p283 L3.

Al Ghurair

BurJuman, Halid Bin Walid Road, Bur Dubai (351 8895). **Open** 10am-10pm Sat-Thur; 4-10pm Fri. **Map** p283 J5.

Thomas Cook Al Rostamani

Next to Al Khajeel Hotel, Road 14, Al Nasr Square, behind HSBC bank, Deira (222 3564/www.alrostamani exchange.com). **Open** 9am-1pm, 6-9pm Sat-Thur; 5-9pm Fri. **Map** p283 L4.
Phone this branch for details of other locations in the city.

Wall St Exchange Centre

Near Naif Police Station, Naif Road, Deira (800 4871). **Open** 8.30am-10pm Sat-Thur; 8.30-11.30am, 4.30-10pm Fri. **Map** p283 J2.

Credit cards/cheques

All major credit cards are accepted in the larger hotels, restaurants, supermarkets and shops. Acceptance of cheques is less widespread. Bouncing cheques is a criminal offence and can result in heavy fines – even, in some cases, a jail sentence.

The UAE was slow to jump on the debit card bandwagon and no chip card service is available. A handful of the bigger chain stores accept Visa Electron and Switch cards; check with individual retailers.

Tax

Famous for its absence of direct taxation, meaning that thousands of expat workers enjoy tax-free salaries, Dubai does have some 'hidden' taxes, such as the ten per cent municipality tax included in food and hospitality costs, and, for those with a licence, a sales tax on alcohol from off-licences (often a steep 30 per cent). There is no corporate tax, except for oil-producing companies and foreign banks.

Opening hours

The concept of the Saturday/ Sunday weekend doesn't apply in the Middle East, since Friday is the holy day for Muslims. With so many different cultures living, working and praying under the same parasol, as it were, weekends in the UAE vary enormously: Europeans tend to take Friday and Saturday as their days off, whereas Thursday and Friday are the weekend for government departments.

Unfortunately, there are also no clear-cut rules when it comes to retail outlets either. The most common shopping hours are 10am-1pm and 4-9pm for stand-alone stores, but shops in malls open 10am-10pm. The exception is Friday, when most are closed until 2pm or 4pm.

Police

In an emergency call 999. If you just want information, www.dubaipolice.gov.ae is a good place to start. If you want to report something confidentially or think you have witnessed something illegal, there is a hotline (Al Ameen Service) on 800 4888.

Postal services

The Emirates post is run solely by Empost and works on a PO Box system, although a postal delivery service is planned for the future. All mail in the UAE is delivered to centrally located post boxes via the Central Post Office. With Dhs160 and an email address you can apply for a personal PO Box and will be notified by email when you receive registered mail or parcels. There is also a service that delivers parcels to your door for Dhs9.

Hotels will handle mail for guests and you can buy stamps at post offices, Emarat petrol stations and card shops. Shopping malls such as City Centre and Lamcy Plaza have postal facilities. Delivery takes between two and three days within the UAE but up to ten days or longer for deliveries to Europe and the USA. The service can be erratic, so don't be surprised if sending something to your home country takes longer than planned. All postal enquiries can be directed to the **Empost** call centre on 334 0033, 8am-8pm Saturday to Thursday. Alternatively, call the **Emirates Post Head Office** on 262 2222, 7.30am-2.30pm Saturday to Wednesday.

Central Post Office

Za'abeel Road, Karama (337 1500/ www.empostuae.com). **Open** 8am-11.30pm Sat-Wed; 8am-10pm Thur; 8am-noon Fri. **Map** p281 J3.

Prohibitions

The law is very strict with regards to the consumption of alcohol (other than in a licensed venue or a private residence), illegal drugs, gambling and pornography. Israeli travellers are not allowed into the UAE, and there is the possibility of complications arising if you have merely made a recent visit to Israel and have a visa stamp in your passport.

Religion

Islam is the official religion of the United Arab Emirates. Around 16 per cent of the local population is Shi'a Muslim and the remainder Sunni Muslims. Dubai is the most multicultural and therefore most tolerant of the emirates, and other religions (except Judaism) are respected, but it is still a Muslim state. The faithful congregate five times a day to pray and you will hear the call to prayer being sung from local mosques all over Dubai.

Tourists need to be extra sensitive if they are visiting during Ramadan, the ninth month of the Muslim calendar, lasting about one month, when Muslims fast during daylight hours to fulfil the fourth pillar of Islam. Determined by the lunar calendar, the dates vary annually, moving forward by roughly 11 days each year. During this period, bars will not serve alcohol before 7pm and clubs are shut, as no loud music or dancing are allowed. Eating, drinking or smoking in a public place during daylight hours is forbidden, though some restaurants erect screens to allow people to eat and drink in private. In 2005 Ramadan is expected to last for the duration of October. For details of how to behave, *see p250* **Attitude & etiquette**. *See also p262* **When to go**.

Owing to its relative tolerance, Dubai has a variety of Christian churches and Hindu temples. For details of places of worship, see www.yellowpages.net.ae.

The list below is a guide to **non-Muslim** places of worship in the city:

Church of Jesus Christ of Latter-day Saints
395 3883.

Emirates Baptist Church International
349 1596.

Holy Trinity Church
337 0247.

International Christian Church of Dubai
344 0828.

International Christian Fellowship (ICF)
396 1284.

New Covenant Church
335 1597.

Saint Mary's Church
337 0087.

United Christian Church of Dubai
344 2509.

Safety & security

Contrary to some perceptions of the Middle East, Dubai is one of the safest places in the world to visit. Indeed, the UAE has in recent years twice been designated the world's safest holiday destination by the international travel industry. Crime in Dubai is minimal, with problem issues restricted to areas such as money laundering that don't tend to impact directly on the tourist or resident. Security is high and accommodation blocks and malls are well-manned by private guards. Nevertheless, it is always a good idea for visitors to take out travel insurance, and to follow the normal precautions to safeguard themselves and their valuables.

Study

Dubai has developed an extensive and respected education system in only 30 years. Locals enjoy very high standards of free education,

while expats tend to send their offspring to private schools and colleges. There are more than 100 of these, catering for all nationalities.

If you wish to learn Arabic there are a number of language centres in the city, by far the most popular of which is the Arabic Language Centre.

Arabic Language Centre
Dubai World Trade Centre, Sheikh Zayed Road (308 6036/ info@dwtc.com). **Open** 8.30am-6.30pm Sat-Wed. **Map** p285 G9. Arabic courses for all levels are held on a termly basis throughout the year.

Telephones

The international dialling code for Dubai is 971, followed by the individual Emirates code: 04 for Dubai. Other area codes are Abu Dhabi 02, Ajman 06, Al Ain 03, Fujairah 09, Ras Al Khaimah 07 and Sharjah 06. For mobile phones the code is 050. Drop the initial '0' of these codes if dialling from abroad.

Operator services can be contacted on 100; directory enquiries are on 181 (or 151 for international).

Alternatively, consult the *Yellow Pages* online at www.yellowpages.net.ae, which in many cases can be quicker and less frustrating.

To report a fault call 170.

Making a call

Etisalat (www.etisalat.com) operates a monopoly on all telecommunications in the UAE, and on the whole the service is very good. Local calls are free and direct-dialling is available to 150 countries.

Cheap rates for international direct calls apply from 9pm to 7am and all day on Fridays and public holidays. Pay

Directory

phones, both card- and coin-operated, are found throughout the UAE.

To make a call within Dubai, dial the seven-digit phone number; for calls to other areas within the UAE, dial the area code (*see p259*) followed by the seven-digit phone number.

To make an international phone call, dial 00, then the country code (44 for the UK, Australia 61, Canada 1, the Republic of Ireland 353, New Zealand 64, South Africa 27, USA 1, France 33, India 91, Pakistan 92, and Russia 7), then the area code, omitting the initial 0, followed by the phone number.

Public telephones

There are plenty of public telephones, which accept either cash or phone cards. Phone cards for local and international use are available in two denominations (Dhs30 or Dhs45) from most Etisalat offices, supermarkets, garages and pharmacies. Coin-operated phones take Dh1 and 50 fils coins.

Mobile telephones

Dubai has one of the world's highest rates of mobile phone usage and practically everyone has at least one cellular phone. A reciprocal agreement exists with over 60 countries, allowing GSM international roaming service for other networks in the UAE. There is also a service (Wasel) that enables temporary Etisalat SIM cards (and numbers) lasting 60 days (or until your Dhs300 credit runs out) for use during your trip if your network is not covered or you do not have a GSM phone. Calls are charged at local rates, with good network coverage.

See also p256 **Internet.**

Time

The UAE is GMT + 4 hours, and has no seasonal change of time. So, for instance, if it is noon in London (winter time), it is 4pm in Dubai; after British clocks move forwards for BST, noon is 3pm in Dubai.

Tipping

Hotels and restaurants usually include a 15 per cent service charge in their bills; if not, adding ten per cent is normal if not obligatory. It is common to pay taxi drivers a small tip, just rounding up the fare to the nearest Dhs5 being the norm. For other services (supermarket baggers/bag carriers/petrol pump attendants/hotel valets) it is usual to give at least a couple of dirhams.

Toilets

There are well-kept free public toilets in malls and parks, and most hotels will let you use their facilities free of charge. Petrol stations have conveniences but their condition varies. Restrooms in souks and bus stations are usually for men only.

Tourist information

The Department of Tourism & Commerce Marketing (DTCM) is the government's sole regulating, planning and licensing body for the tourism industry in Dubai. It has information centres around the city, the most immediately useful being in the airport arrivals lounge (224 5252). Its one-stop information centres aim to answer any visitor queries, provide maps, tour guides and hotel information, as well as business and conference advice. Most of the larger shopping malls

(*see pp116-123*) have their own centres providing visitor information.

Department of Tourism & Commerce Marketing

10th-12th floor, National Bank of Dubai Building, Baniyas Road, Deira (223 0000/www.dubai tourism.co.ae). **Open** 7.30am-2.30pm Sat-Wed. **Map** p283 K4.

Visas & immigration

Visa regulations are always liable to change, so it is worth checking with your travel agent or the UAE Embassy in your home country before leaving. Overstaying on your visa can result in detention and fines (a penalty charge of Dhs100 per day that you're over). Nationals of Israel may not enter the UAE. Your passport must have at least two months left (in some cases, six) before expiry for you to be granted admission to the UAE, so do check before booking your flight.

The following nationalities will not need to obtain a visa before travelling to Dubai or the UAE; they will receive it on arrival at the airport.

Americas
USA, Canada.

Asia
Japan, Brunei, Singapore, Malaysia, Hong Kong, South Korea.

GCC (Gulf Cooperation Council) countries
Saudi Arabia, Qatar, Bahrain, Oman, Kuwait, UAE.

Oceania
Australia, New Zealand.

UK
Citizens of the UK will be granted a free visit visa on arrival in the UAE: passports will be stamped with the visa as you pass through Immigration at any airport in the UAE. Although the visa is usually stamped for 30 days, it entitles the holder to stay in the country for 60 days and may be renewed once for an additional period of 30 days for a fee of Dhs500.

Western Europe

France, Italy, Germany, the Netherlands, Luxembourg, Belgium, Switzerland, Austria, Sweden, Norway, Denmark, Portugal, Ireland, Greece, Finland, Spain, Monaco, Vatican City, Iceland, Andorra, San Marino, Liechtenstein.

To establish or confirm the permitted duration of your stay, you should contact the UAE Embassy or Consulate in your country at the addresses below. Failing that, the contacts given in **Travel advice** (*see p250*) will keep you up to date with the latest visa requirements – which seem prone to regular, unannounced changes. Any countries not listed above do require a visa.

UAE embassies abroad

Australia

36 Gulgoa Circuit, O'Malley ACT 2606, Canberra, Australia (2-6286 8802/uaeembassy@big pond.com/ www.users.bigpond.com/UAEEMBA SSY). **Open** 9am-3pm Mon-Fri.

Canada

45 O'Connor Street, Suite 1800, World Exchange Plaza, Ottawa, Ontario, K1P 1A4 (613 565 7272/ safara@uae-embassy.com/www. uae-embassy.com). **Open** 9am-4pm Mon-Fri.

France

3 rue de Lota,75116 Paris (45 53 94 04). **Open** 9am-4pm Mon-Fri.

India

E.P. 12 Chandra Gupta Marg, Chanakyapuri, New Delhi 110021 (687 2822). **Open** 9am-3pm Sun-Thur.

Pakistan

Plot No. 122, University Road, Diplomatic Enclave, PO Box 1111, Islamabad, Pakistan (279052). **Open** 9am-3pm Sun-Thur.

Russia

Ulofa Palme Street, 4 Moscow - CIS, (143 6414). **Open** 9am-4pm Mon-Fri.

South Africa

980 Park Street, Arcadia 0083, Pretoria, South Africa (342 7736-9). **Open** 9am-5pm Mon-Fri.

UK & Republic of Ireland

30 Prince's Gate, London SW7 1PT (020 7581 1281/embcommer@ cocoon.co.uk). **Open** 9am-3pm Mon-Fri. *Visa section* 9am-noon Mon-Fri.

USA

3522 International Court, NW Washington DC, 20008 (202 243 2400/New York office 212 371 0480/www.uae-embassy.org). **Open** 9am-4pm Mon-Fri.

Multiple-entry visas

Multiple-entry visas are available to business visitors who have a relationship with either a multinational company or other reputable local business, and who are frequent visitors to the UAE.

This type of visa is valid for six months from the date of issue and the duration of each stay is 30 days. The validity is non-renewable. The cost of such a visa is Dhs1,000 and the visitor must enter the UAE on a visit visa and obtain the multiple entry visa while in the country. The visa is stamped on the passport.

96-hour visa for transit passengers

As a way of promoting Dubai city tours, passengers who stop at Dubai International Airport in transit for a minimum of five hours are eligible for a 96-hour transit visa which enables them to go into the city for that period of time. Passengers wanting to find out about this are advised to go to the City Tours desk in the airport arrivals lounge to make a booking on one of the several tours on offer. The visa is issued free, but the tour service is not. This visa is available only to those travelling onwards from Dubai and not returning to their original country of departure.

Water & hygiene

The tap water in Dubai comes from desalination plants, and while technically drinkable, it doesn't taste great. Most choose to buy their drinking water, which costs only Dhs1-Dhs2 for a litre bottle; though do be wary of the ridiculous mark-ups at certain bars and restaurants. Outside Dubai avoid drinking water from the tap – you might even want to use bottled water for brushing your teeth.

General standards of food hygiene are extremely high in Dubai, though caution should be shown if trying some of the smaller roadside diners. If in doubt, avoid raw salads and *shoarmas* (meat cooked on a spit and wrapped in a pitta).

Outside the city limits, milk is often unpasteurised and should be boiled. Powdered or tinned milk is available, but make sure it is reconstituted with pure water. You may also want to avoid dairy products, which are likely to have been made from unboiled milk.

Weights & measures

The UAE uses the metric system, but British and US standard weights and measures are widely understood. Road distances are given in kilometres.

What to take

Lightweight summer clothing is ideal in Dubai, with just a wrap, sweater, or jacket for cooler winter nights and venues that have fierce air-conditioning. The dress code in the UAE is generally casual, though guests in the more prestigious hotels such as the Ritz-Carlton and the Royal Mirage do tend to dress more formally in the evening.

Directory

Average monthly climate

Month	Temp °C/°F	Rainfall (mm)	Relative humidity (%)
Jan	23/32	11	71
Feb	25/77	38	72
Mar	29/84	34	68
Apr	33/89	10	65
May	38/100	3	62
June	39/102	1	65
July	40/104	2	85
Aug	40/104	3	85
Sept	39/102	1	69
Oct	35/95	2	70
Nov	30/86	4	69
Dec	26/79	10	72

For links to the latest satellite images of weather conditions in the Middle East and Europe, go to http://www.uaeinteract.com/uaeint_misc/weather/index.asp.

Since you are visiting a Muslim country, bikinis, swimming costumes, shorts and revealing tops should be confined to beach resorts. Bars and clubs are really no different from in the West, with tans shown off to the max.

With such a wealth of shopping facilities, there is precious little you can't get hold of in Dubai. That said, visitors cannot buy alcohol from off-licences – so be sure to stock up at Dubai Duty Free (see p246) when you arrive at the airport.

When to go

Climate

Straddling the Tropic of Cancer, the UAE is warm and sunny in winter and hot and humid during the summer months. Winter daytime temperatures average a very pleasant 24ºC, though nights can be relatively cool: perhaps 12-15ºC on the coast and less than 5ºC in the heart of the desert or high in the mountains. Local north-westerly winds (shamals)

frequently develop during the winter, bringing cooler windy conditions as well as occasional sandstorms.

Summer temperatures reach the 40s, but can be higher inland. Humidity in coastal areas averages between 50 and 60 per cent, reaching over 90 per cent in summer – even the sea offers no relief as the water temperature can reach 37ºC.

Rainfall is sparse and intermittent. In most years it rains during the winter months, usually in February or March. Winter rains take the form of short, sharp bursts, and the very occasional thunderstorm. Generally appearing over the mountains of the south and east of the country, these rumbling cloudbursts can give rise to flash floods, but on average rain falls only about five days a year.

In terms of when to go, you really can't go wrong if you visit any time between November and March, as you're virtually guaranteed beautiful weather every day. June to September can be

unbearably hot and humid during the day, although hotel bargain deals can still make it an attractive proposition. Also bear in mind when Ramadan is taking place (see p259 Religion).

Public holidays

There are two different kinds of public holidays: those that are fixed in the standard calendar, and those religious days that are determined by the lunar calendar and therefore vary from year to year. The precise dates are not announced until a day or so before they occur, based on local sightings of phases of the moon.

The fixed dates are: **New Year's Day** (1 January), **Mount Arafat Day** (11 January), **Accession of HH Sheikh Zayed as Ruler of the UAE** (6 August), and **UAE National Day** (2 December).

The variable dates are: **Eid Al Adha** – a three-day feast to mark the end of the hajj pilgrimage to Mecca (January/February/March); **Ras al-Sana** – the start of

Islamic New Year (February); **Mawlid al-Nabi** – the Prophet Mohammed's birthday (May); Lailat al **Mi'raj** – the accession day of the Prophet Mohammed (September); and Eid Al Fitr – three days marking the end of **Ramadan** (currently October).

Women

The cultural differences between locals and expats in Dubai are obvious, and the traditional advice for women in any big city – catch taxis if you're unsure about the area, don't walk alone at night and so on – should still be heeded, but all women here tend to enjoy a high standard of personal safety.

If you are wearing revealing clothing in a public place you will attract stares, some of simple condemnation and others of a more lascivious nature. That said, physical harassment is rare, particularly as the local police are swift to act against any offenders.

The traditional combination of abaya (long black robe) and sheyla (head scarf) worn by Emirati women is something you are less and less likely to see on younger women, who tend to wear Western-style clothes in the city. The metal face masks (burkha) are largely reserved for more conservative women in rural areas.

This development in itself goes some way to illustrate the changing roles of women in the UAE, championed by its multicultural epicentre: Dubai. With the instigation of an education system available to women (female students now outnumber male) and the government's active encouragement of women in the workplace, attitudes have clearly evolved and statistics claim that women now fill some 40 per cent of jobs in the civil service.

Dubai International Women's Club (DIWC)

Opposite Mercato mall, Beach Road, Jumeirah (344 2389). **Open** 8am-5pm Sat-Thur. **Map** p286 C12.
This is a social club, with around 150 members, that meets four times a month. The club organises charity events, not only in Dubai but also overseas.

International Business Women's Group

345 2282/www.ibwgdubai.com.
The IBWG is an organisation for women in the business world, and meets on a monthly basis to exchange ideas and offer advice. Call or check the website for details of forthcoming meetings; you can also call Jane Drury on 050 659 8634 or check **www.expatwoman. com** for advice and information on meeting other female expats.

Working in Dubai

Dubai holds many attractions for prospective newcomers, especially the enticing tax-free salaries. If you are considering working in Dubai, it is worth visiting first to get a feel for the lie of the land. Dubai is a relatively small business community, so even a week's worth of well planned networking can be fruitful in terms of making contacts – there is a real 'who you know' attitude here, so come armed with your very best first impressions and plenty of friendly pushiness. There are also several employment agencies and recruitment consultants online to help you; try www.yellowpages.ae for a full list of Dubai-based agencies. While UK-based recruitment organisations can be hit and miss, a company like www.itprecruitment.com maintains its sound reputation, as do the South African-based www.ananzi.co.za and the local giant www.bayt.com.

To be able to work in Dubai, either you must get sponsored by an employer or your spouse must do so. If you managed to secure

employment from home, the process of becoming a fully fledged Dubaian is a little smoother, but it can still take some time.

New recruits generally arrive on a 60-day visit visa. This entitles you to work for the stipulated period, while your employer gets the residency ball rolling with the Immigration Department. It's advisable to have several copies of your passport with you, as well as plenty of passport photos for the numerous forms. Your employer should provide a comprehensive list of the paperwork is required – check before you fly out in case you need to bring along original education certificates or other proofs of qualification.

In order to gain residency in Dubai you'll also need to pass a medical test for HIV/AIDS, hepatitis and other infectious diseases. It is fairly standard to be offered extra medical insurance as part of your package, but once you have received your health card you are entitled to use any of the public hospitals in Dubai. Health cards need to be renewed every year, residency visas and labour cards only every three years.

For further general information and advice about setting up in business in Dubai, visit www.uae interact.com or check out the business website and directory www.ameinfo.com.
See also p251 **Business**.

Dubai Naturalisation & Residency Administration (DNRA)

Trade Centre Road, near Bur Dubai Police Station, Bur Dubai (398 0000/www.dnrd.gov.ae). **Open** 7.30am-2.30pm Sat-Wed. **Map** p285 H8.
The DNRA presides over procedures and laws related to expatriate entry to and residence in the United Arab Emirates (including tourist visas).

Directory

Language

Arabic is the official language of Dubai, and both Urdu and Hindi are widely spoken and understood, but English is the predominant language. However, while attempting them might be grammatically challenging, using a few Arabic phrases is always appreciated. Some basic words and phrases are given below, written phonetically. Capitals are not used in Arabic, but are used below to indicate hard sounds.

With Arabic possessing so many dialects and sounding so different to English, such transliteration is never easy. We've opted for a largely classical option, with a few of the more useful colloquial phrases thrown in.

Getting by
Hello *marhaba*
How are you? *kaif il haal?*
Good morning *sabaaH il khayr*
Good evening *masaa' il khayr*
Greetings *'as-salamu 'alaykum*
Welcome *'ahlan wa sahlan*
Goodbye *ma' 'is-salaama*
Excuse me *afwan*
Sorry *'aasif*
God willing *insha'allah*
Please (to a man) *min fadlak*
(to a woman) *min fadlik*
Thank you (very much) *shukran (jazeelan)*
Yes/No *na'am/laa*
I don't know *lasto adree* or *laa 'a-arif*
Who?/What? *man?/matha?*
Where?/Why? *ayina?/lematha?*
How much? (cost) *bekam?*
How many? *kam?*
The bill please *alfatourah min faDlak*

Advanced pleasantries
Do you speak English? *titkallam inglizi?*
I don't speak Arabic *ma-atkallam arabi*
Nice to meet you *yusadni moqapalatak*

What's your name? *ma esmok?*
My name is... *esmei...*
How old are you? *kam amrk?*
What's your job?/Where do you work? *ma heya wazefatuk?/ ayna tam'al?*
Where do you live? *ayna taskun?*
I live/I work in Dubai *askun/a'amal fi Dubai*
How is the family? *kayfa halou l'a ila*
Congratulations *mabrook*
Happy birthday *eid meelad sa'eed*
You are very kind *anta lateef jedan*
With pleasure *bikul siroor*
Good luck *ha'z'zan sa'eedan*
Have a good trip *atmna lak rehla muafaqa*
Thanks for coming *shukran limajee, ak*
Best wishes *atyab al-tamniyat*
When will I see you? *mata sa'araak?*
Wait a little *intazarni kaliln*
Calm down *hadia nafsak*
Can I help you? *hal astateea'i musaa'adatuk?*

Numbers & time
Zero *sifr*
One *waahid*
Two *itnain*
Three *talata*
Four *arba'a*
Five *khamsa*
Six *sitta*
Seven *sab'a*
Eight *tamanya*
Nine *tis'a*
Ten *'ashra*
Eleven *heda'ash*
Twelve *itna'ash*
Thirteen *talata'ash*
Fourteen *arba'atash*
Fifteen *khamista'ash*
Sixteen *sitta'ash*
Seventeen *sabi'ta'ash*
Eighteen *tamanta'ash*
Nineteen *tis'ta'ash*
Twenty *ishreen*
One hundred *me'ah*

Sunday *al-ahad*
Monday *al-itnayn*
Tuesday *al-talata*
Wednesday *al-arba'a*
Thursday *al-khamees*
Friday *al-jum'a*
Saturday *al-Sabt*
Day *yom*
Month *shahr*
Year *sanah*
Hour *sa'aa*
Minute *daqiqa*
Today *al-yom*
Yesterday *ams/imbarah*
Tomorrow *bukra*

People
He/She *houwa/hiya*
I/Me *ana*
We *nahnou*
You (to one male) *anta*
(one female) *anti*
(to a group) *antom*
(to several women) *antonna*
They (male and female) *hom*
(female only) *honna*
Father *ab*
Mother *umm*
Son *ibn*
Daughter *ibnah*
Husband *zauj*
Wife *zaujah*
Brother *akh*
Sister *ukht*
Child *tifl*

Getting around
Airport *matar*
Post office *maktab al-barid*
Bank *bank*
Passport *jawaz safar*
Luggage *'aghraad*
Ticket *tath karah*
Taxi *Taxi*
Car *say-yarra*
City *madina*
Street *share'h*
Road *tareeq*
Bridge *jisr*
Mosque *Jame'h* or *messjed*
Bazaar *souk*
Boat *markab*
Beach *il-shat'i*
Customs *jumrok*
Library *maktabeh*
Shop *mahall*
Museum *mathaf*

Further Reference

Books

For a full list of Arabic authors and bookshops, see www.uaeinteract.com.

Frauke Heard-Bay
From Trucial States to United Arab Emirates
In 1971, the seven sheikdoms at the southern end of the Persian Gulf, the Trucial States, formed the state of the United Arab Emirates; it was soon a member of the UN, OPEC and the Arab League. This academic volume examines the historical and social movements that have shaped the UAE.

Denys Johnson-Davies (translator) and **Roger MA Allen** (editor)
Arabic Short Stories
A charming and insightful collection of tales from the Middle East.

Alan Keohane
Bedouin: Nomads of the Desert
This photographic portrait pays tribute to the ancient tribal customs that survive among those who continue to make the annual journey across the desert. A timely reminder of the importance of preserving the UAE's ancient traditions.

Martin Lings
Muhammad, His Life Based on the Earliest Sources
A fascinating account for those wishing to learn more about the origins of Islam.

Alistair MacKenzie, Pamela Grist and **Christopher Brown**
Images of Dubai and the United Arab Emirates (Explorer Series)
This coffee-table tome comes highly recommended. Stunning photographs are divided into four categories: landscapes, seascapes, cityscapes and escapes.

Edward Said
Reflections on Exile & Other Essays
Powerfully blending political and aesthetic concerns, Said's writings changed the field of literary studies.

Jeff Sampler
Sand to Silicon
Geared towards those with a more business-orientated interest in Dubai, Sampler examines how this tiny emirate transformed itself into a major player on the international stage, internally through bold decision-making and externally by its openness to outside influence.

Jeremy Williams
Don't They Know It's Friday? Cross-Cultural Considerations for Business & Life in the Gulf
Another business handbook, this one addresses the cultural aspects of life in all GCC countries, dealing with the realities of business practice, as well as the stresses and strains of operating in the Gulf as a Western visitor or expatriate.

Daniel Yergin
The Prize: The Epic Quest for Oil, Money & Power
These 800 pages on the historical role of oil are certainly not everybody's cup of tea, but for those with an interest in the greasy stuff and its role in power politics, business, diplomacy and world history, this is an exceptionally detailed, well-informed account.

Magazines

For a weekly preview of top events, meal deals, hot tickets and local listings, pick up *Time Out Dubai*. Otherwise, free magazines *Connector* and *Aquarius* are distributed at various malls and public places around town; they carry listings and discount vouchers.

Travel

As well as consulting the following web resources, it's well worth checking out the **Dubai Explorer** series of guides. Top titles include the Family Explorer, Off Road Explorer and Underwater Explorer.

Dubai City Guide
www.dubaicityguide.com.
Guide to Dubai shopping, events, hotels, restaurants and sightseeing.

UAE Internet Yellow Pages
www.uae-ypages.com.
Invaluable resources, full of local listings.

Maps
www.geocities.com/fayarus/dubailinks.

Websites

www.timeoutdubai.com
For an insider's glimpse of what's happening, when and where.

www.uaeinteract.com
Official website of the Ministry of Information & Culture, providing general information on the United Arab Emirates.

www.dubaipolice.gov.ae
Local police website.

www.dubai-e.gov.ae
Official government website.

www.dubaitourism.co.ae
Handy for general tourist information.

Transport

www.dubaiairport.com
News from Dubai International Airport.

www.dpa.co.ae
Messages about water transport from the Dubai Ports Authority.

www.dubaipublic transport.co.ae
Bus timetables and schedules.

Directory

Index

Note: page numbers in
bold indicate section(s)
giving key information
on topic; *italics* indicate
illustrations.

a

abra rides **67**, 149, **248**
Abu Dhabi *212*, 213-224
accommodation 222-
224, 225
background & history
10, 11, 12, 14, **15**, *15*,
213-216
beaches & islands 217-
219
etiquette 216
Grand Mosque 63
map *214-215*
nightlife 221-222
racetrack 187
resources 224
restaurants 219-221
shopping 222
sightseeing 216-217
tourist information 224
transport 224
accommodation
budget 57-58
self-catering 55, 57, 58
see also hotels; youth
hostels
addresses 61, 247, **250**
affection, displays of 35,
37
age restrictions 250
Ahmadiya School, Al 69
Ahmed bin Hasher Al
Maktoum, Sheikh 188
Ain, Al 224-225
Ain Al Gamour 240
airlines 246
Airport, Dubai
International 246
business centres 251
Dubai Duty Free 119
left-luggage 256
lost property 256
airports (outside Dubai)
216, 224, 237
Ajman 230-232
alcohol 35, 36-37, 178
in Abu Dhabi 216
age limit 178
bar prices 167
buying 87, 178
drunkenness 178
in Sharjah 230
Ali Ibn Ali Taleb
Mosque 63

ambulance 253
antiques 119, 120,
123-124, 165
apartments 57, 58
Aqah, Al 243
archery 191
architecture 25-31
coming attractions 31
early 26-27
arish see *barasti*
art
children's activities
154-155
galleries 58, 64,
162-165
showrooms 165
Awalah 240
Ayurveda 208, 209
ayyalah 159

b

Bach Flower Remedies
208
Badiyah 242
badminton 191
balloon rides 68, 191
Bani Yas clan 10, 11, 26,
213
Bank of Credit &
Commerce International
22
banks 257
barasti 26, 27
barbecue sets 140
bars & pubs
in Abu Dhabi 221-222
the best for… 109, 167
DJ bars 169, 174,
175-177
drinking 166-167, 171-
175, 178-181
with food 110, 111, 113
Irish bars 172, 174, 175
live music venues 169,
171, 172, 174, 177-178
members-only policy
168
see also p271 Bars,
Pubs & Clubs index
basketball **191-193**, 197
Basta Art Café 64, 106,
107
Bastakia 11, **64**, 65
architecture 27
children's attractions
149
galleries 162
mosques 63
restaurant 84
souk 63

walking tour 64
see also Dubai Museum
BCCI *see* Bank of Credit &
Commerce International
beach clubs 202-204
Beach Road 69
beaches 72, 151, 152, 205
Abu Dhabi 217-219
east coast 238-244
see also Jumeirah
beauty products 135-137
beauty salons 137
Bedouin 13, 14, 15, 26,
27, 217, 231, 244
exhibition 66
belly-dancers 85, 93
Big Red 77, *77*
billiards 198
Bin Madiya Mosque 63
birdwatching 49, 72, 74,
240
Bithnah, Al 240
boat trips
abra rides **67**, 149, **248**
dining cruises 85, 92
fishing 194-195
Wonder Bus 78
Bollywood 156
bookshops 124-125
Bowen Therapy 208
bowling alleys 119, **193**
British role (history)
10, 11, 12, 13, 14, 16,
18, 213, 226, 235
Brush & Bisque-It 155
bull butting 239
Bur Dubai 60, 62-66
accommodation
40, 44-45, 51, 57-58
architecture 27, 28
cafés & bars 107-110
nightlife 169-174
restaurants 84-92
shopping malls 116-119
souks 62
bureaux de change
257-258
Burj Al Arab 25,
28-29, **47**, 68
Assawan Spa & Health
Club 207
restaurants 97, 101
Sky View Bar 181
tearoom (Sahn Eddar)
112
Burj Dubai 31
BurJuman Centre
116, 117
cafés 107, 109
Yo! Sushi 90
buses 212, **247**, 265

airport 246
to places outside Dubai
224, 230, 232, 233,
236, 240
tours 78
business & commerce
18, 23, 24
licences & sponsors 252
services 251-252
successful families 20
women's group 263
Bustan Rotana Hotel, Al
53, 53
Oxygen 95, 174
restaurants 93, 95, 96

c

cable car 68
Café Céramique **111**,
151, **154**, **155**
cafés 106-113
the best for… 109
internet 256
see also p271
Restaurants
& Cafés index
camel farms 75
camel racing **74-75**, 146,
186, **187**
camel rides 49, 72, 79, 153,
205
camel souk 75
camping equipment 140
camping trips 49, 237
carpets 119, **139**, 239
cars & driving 61,
246-247, **248-249**
accidents & breakdown
248, 249
hire 248-249
parking 249
petrol 249
road signs 249
women 35
see also 4x4 vehicles
CDs 120, **139-140**
censorship 124, 156-157,
256, 257
ceramic art 154, 155
Chamber of Commerce
251, 252
children's attractions
148-155
activity centres 119,
153-154
by area 149-151
arts & crafts centres
154-155
clothes shops 129-130
parks 152-153

Advertisers' Index

Please refer to the relevant pages for
contact details

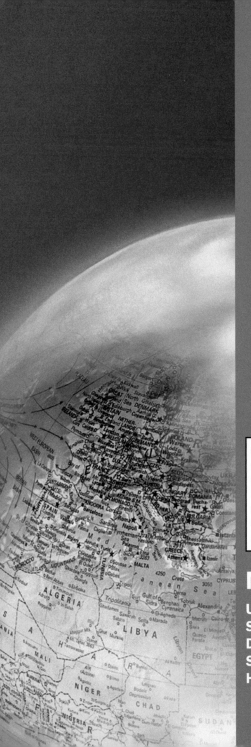

Place of interest and/or entertainment	
Bus station	
Park	
Hospital	
Hotel	■
Restaurant	●
Area name	AL RAS

Maps

United Arab Emirates

SWEDEN
EIRE UK
POLAND BELARUS
RUSSIA
GERMANY
UKRAINE
FRANCE
ROMANIA
KAZAKHSTAN
SPAIN
TURKEY
SYRIA
TURKMEN-
ISTAN
IRAQ
IRAN
ALGERIA
LIBYA
EGYPT
SAUDI
ARABIA
UAE
MALI
NIGER
CHAD
SUDAN
OMAN
YEMEN

Jazireh ye Lavan

A r a b i a n

*Hawar
Islands*

*Al Matbakh
Cape*

Salwah Gulf

QATAR   ○ **DOHA**

Das

Dayyina   *Qarnein*

Zirkuh

Arzanah

Udeid Bay

Al Qaffay

Dalma

T r u c i a l

Ghemeis Cape

Al-Ifzi'iyyah

Sir Bani Yas

Merawwah

Al Yasat

Jananah

Jebel Dhanna   ● **Al Mirfa**

Gheweifat   ○ Ruwais

As Sila   *Jabal az
Zannah
114 m*

Baynuna'h   **Habshan** ○

Madinat Zayid ○

Baynunah ○

Ghayathi ○

Bu Hasa ○

Al Maghrib   **Al Ma'alla** ○

Meziyrah

Taraq

Khannur   **Qatuf**

Kharimah

Umm Hisin   *Al*

SAUDI ARABIA

Mukhayriz ○

To Riyadh & Kuwait ↗

0   100 km
0   50 miles

© Copyright Time Out Group 2005

IRAN

Jazireh ye Hormoz

Jazireh ye Qeshm

Jazireh ye Larak

Strait of Hormuz

Jazireh ye Kish

OMAN

Musandam Peninsula

Jazireh ye Forur

Ash Sham

Khaymah Cape

Rams

G u l f

Ras Al Khaimah

Digdagga

Haffah Cape

Umm Al Quwain

Dibba

Rul Dibba

Hamriya

Idhn

Badiyah

Fakkan Bay

Ajman

Manama

Jabal Adham 1,128 m

Khor Fakkan

Sharjah

Sir Abu Nu'ayr

DUBAI

Al Dhaid

Fujairah

Gulf o Oman

Al Awir

Mileiha

Al Haba

Fili

Al Liseli

Margham

Hatta

Ghanadah Cape

Al Samha

Al Faqa

Ash Shu'ayb

C o a s t

Abjan

Al Haiyir

Sweihan

At Khatam

ABU DHABI

Al Saad

Sa'diyyat

Mafraq

Bani Yas

Al Ain

Abu al Jirab

Al Khatam

Bu Samarah

Tarif

Ayn Al Faidah

At Taff

Al'Arad

Al'Qua'a

OMAN

Al Humrah

Sabkhah

Al Khis

Jarrah

Je'eisah

Liwa

Hamim

At Rabbad

Umm a Zummul

Street Index

Dubai Overview

0 ————————————— 5 km
0 ————————————— 3 miles
© Copyright Time Out Group 2005

ARABIAN

GULF

Port
Rashid

AL
RAS

AL HAMRIY

Dubai
Dry Docks

MANKHOOL

Dubai
Marine
Beach
Club

AL HUDAIBA

AL BADA'A

AL QATAMI

JUMEIRAH

SATWA

ZA'ABEE

Jumeirah
Beach
Park

AL WASL

SHEIKH ZAYED ROAD (E-11)

E-44

Safa
Park

JUMEIRAH

Interchange 2

Dubai
Offshore
Sailing
Club

AL MARQADI

AL
SAFA

Oasis Centre
Mall

AL
QUOZ

Nad Al Sheba Camel
Souk & Racecourse

Oasis Restaurant

Nad Al Sheba Club,
Nad Al Sheba Racecours
& Godolphin Gallery

Kite Beach

The Chalet

UMM
SUQEIM

Jumeirah
Beach Hotel

Interchange 3

Burj Al
Arab

Wild
Wadi

AL MANARA

Mina A' Salam
Souk Madinat

UMM
AL SHEIF

AL QUOZ
INDUSTRIAL AREA

Al Qasr

Interchange 4

Mall of the Emirates

Palm
Island

AL SUFOUH

Knowledge
Village

Marina Gulf
Trading

One&Only
Royal Mirage

DMC &
DIC

SHEIKH ZAYED ROAD (E-11)

AL BARSHAA

Jebel Ali
Sailing Club

Le Meridien Mina Seyahi

Conservation
Area

Le Meridien Grosvenor House

Dubai
Marina

Interchange 5

Le Royal Meridien

Emirates Golf Club

Ritz-Carlton Dubai

Oasis Beach

Hilton Dubai Jumeirah

AL MINA
AL SEYAHI

Sheraton Jumeirah Beach Resort

To Jebel Ali Hotel

E-11

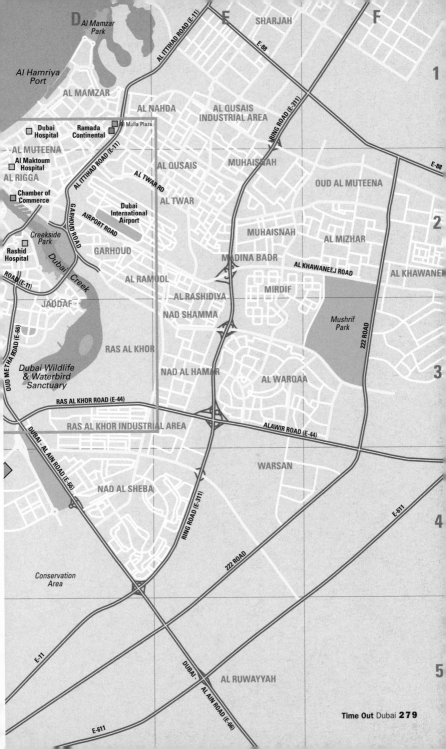

D Al Mamzar Park

E SHARJAH

F

Al Hamriya Port

1

AL MAMZAR

AL ITTIHAD ROAD (E-11)

E-88

AL NAHDA

Al Mulla Plaza

AL QUSAIS INDUSTRIAL AREA

RING ROAD (E-311)

E-88

Dubai Hospital

Ramada Continental

AL MUTEENA

AL QUSAIS

MUHAISNAH

OUD AL MUTEENA

Al Maktoum Hospital

AL RIGGA

AL ITTIHAD ROAD (E-11)

AL TWAR RD

AL TWAR

MUHAISNAH

AL MIZHAR

Chamber of Commerce

GARHOUD ROAD

AIRPORT ROAD

Dubai International Airport

2

MADINA BADR

AL KHAWANEEJ ROAD

AL KHAWANE

Creekside Park

Rashid Hospital

GARHOUD

MIRDIF

Dubai Creek

AL RAMOOL

ROAD (E-11)

JADDAF

AL RASHIDIYA

Mushrif Park

222 ROAD

NAD SHAMMA

OUD METHA ROAD (E-66)

Dubai Wildlife & Waterbird Sanctuary

RAS AL KHOR

NAD AL HAMAR

AL WARQAA

3

RAS AL KHOR ROAD (E-44)

RAS AL KHOR INDUSTRIAL AREA

ALAWIR ROAD (E-44)

DUBAI - AL AIN ROAD (E-66)

WARSAN

NAD AL SHEBA

RING ROAD (E-311)

222 ROAD

E-611

4

Conservation Area

E-11

DUBAI - AL AIN ROAD (E-66)

AL RUWAYYAH

5

E-611

F

G

H

0   2 km

0   1 mile

© Copyright Time Out Group 2005

1

Port Rashid

AL DAGHAYA

AL SINNDAGHA

AL RAS

AL KHALEEJ ROAD

AL SOUQ AL KABEER

ARABIAN

2

Dubai Dry Docks

AL MINA

AL RAFFA

AL MANKHOOL ROAD

GULF

MANKHOOL

AL HUDAIBA

AL MINA ROAD

AL ADHID ROAD

Dubai Marine Beach Club

AL JAFILIYA

AL WASL ROAD

AL KIFAF

3

BEACH ROAD

AL BADA'A

AL SATWA ROAD

2ND ZA'ABEEL ROAD

Dubai Zoo

JUMEIRAH

AL SATWA

Emirates Towers

Towers Rotana Hotel

4

Jumeirah Beach Park

Dusit Dubai

AL WASL

RAS AL KHOR ROAD (E-44)

5

BEACH ROAD

AL WASL ROAD

Safa Park

SHEIKH ZAYED ROAD (E-11)

JUMEIRAH

Al Safa Complex (Park'n'Shop)

Metropolitan Hotel

AL MARQADH

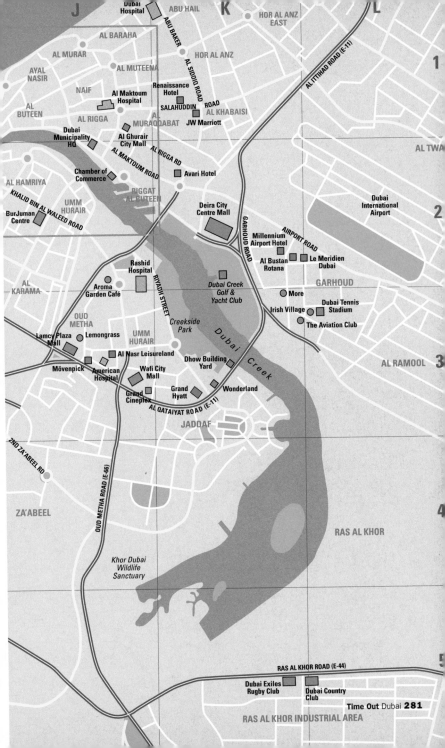

ARABIAN GULF

F   G   H

0   500 m
0   500 yds
© Copyright Time Out Group 2005

1

Container
Terminal

UAE Frontier
& Coast Guard

Deira Fish, Meat
& Vegetable Market

2

12 ALDAGHAYA ST. 33 20
AL
DAGHAYA
10J AL SABKHA ROAD

26A 4B 40
AL SOUND ST. 33B 4B 46B
11A 39A

Deira
Covered
souk

Gold souk
OLD 43 4A
BALADIYA ST. 4B 33A
AL KHALIL STREET
Food 10 4A
souk 21 16C
Heritage &
Diving Centre
33 33A 12B
16A 20 AL SOUK AL KABEER ST

AL SHINDAGHA

AL
SHINDAGHA
TUNNEL

AL BUTEEN

Spice
souk

Sheikh Saeed
Al Maktoum House

10 AL KHOR STREET
12 AL AHMADIYA ST
70S SIKKAT AL KHALI
27A
11A
3

24 BANIYAS ROAD

AL RAS

3

PORT

5 AL HADD ST
34

5B

RASHID

Coaster
Berth

Grand
Mosque
Bur Dubai
souk
11 C

Bastakia
Quarter

304 AL KHALEEJ ROAD

Basta
Art Café

XVA

Al Shindagha
Market

51 A

Textile
souk

34

Dubai
Museum

AL FAHIDI ST

Majlis
Gallery

25E
7A 4A

Bus & Taxi
Station
11 A

28A

19

24 AL GHUBAIBA ST

26

AL SOUK
AL KABEER

62B
25D
40B
44 33B

11A

Astoria
Hotel

13B 16

21A

India House

4

33 C 64

AL MUSALLA ROAD

12 27A 81
8 22
2 37B 37C
43A 45B
32

29A
25B 30

301 KHALID BIN AL WALEED ROAD (BANK STREET)

Ascot
Hotel
5E
7E

Rush Inn

4C

Four Points
Sheraton

3C 24A

26

301 KHALID

AL MINA

10A 7B
11A

9B

11D

1 A

3 A

Cemetery

15 AL ROLLA RD

17 A

AL RAFFA

5 A

10 A

21A
12B
14 B
23

16 A

21 B
20 B

17B

24 B

4 B

9 A

8 A

304 AL MINA ROAD

306 MANKHOOL ROAD

MANKHOOL

Sea View
Hotel

Cemetery

Cemetery

Cemetery

11A

4 B

8 B

10 B

12 A

16 A

25

5 A

13 A

12 A

13 B

11 B

27

12 C 29

16 A

19 A

page
285

15 A

17 A

13 B

15 C

13 C

28B

5

AL RAS

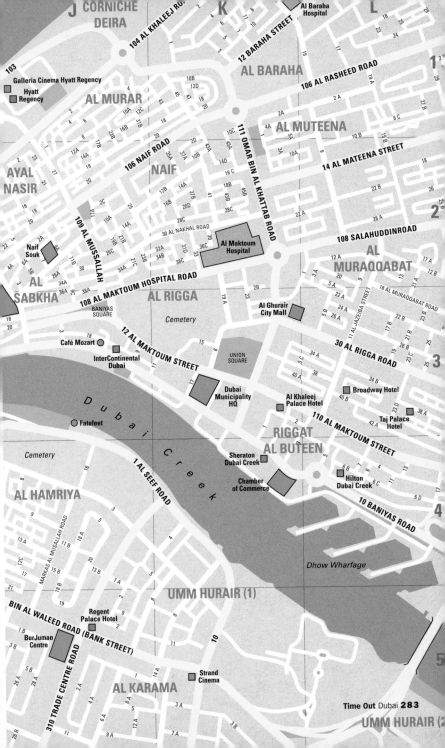

C   D   E

6

Dubai Dry Dock

0   500 m
0   500 yds
© Copyright Time Out Group 2005

AL MINA

7

ARABIAN

GULF

304 AL MINA ROAD

Capitol Hotel

9

2 C
21

4 B

305 AL DHIYAFA ST

8

5 A
7 A

1

10 A 18 A
30 A

3 A
4 A
7 A

Jumeirah Rotana

7 C
3 B

JUMEIRAH (1)

5 B
7 B

AL BADA'A

2 A

9

12 A 18 A
14 A 20 A

Dubai Marine Beach Resort & Spa

13 A Palm Strip Mall

17 A

21 A

Russian Beach

23 A

27 A

Jumeirah Mosque

The One Café

21 B AL HUDAIBA ROAD

11
12 A
16 B
22 A
30 B

2 A

17 A

13 B
15
17 B

6 A 8 A

4

12 A 14 B
16 B 18 B
20 A
24 A

17 B

11

302 JUMEIRAH ROAD

Lime Tree Café

Magrudy Centre

Jumeirah Centre Mall

23 C

25

27 C

23

21

29 A

29

31

306 AL SATWA ROAD

9

2 A 4 A

17 B

Johnny Rockets

Dubai International Arts Centre

35 A

Jumeirah Plazа

Century Plaza

12 B
31 A

18 C

10 C

12 C

Iranian Hospital

304 AL WASL ROAD

8 B

2 B

27 A

4 A
6 C
8 C

29

30 C

29

31

31 B

22 A

33

2 B

6 B

33

35 A
37 A

24 B

39 A

26 A 35 B
37

39 B

30 D

45 A

39
41

8 C
10 B
29

35 B
39

43 B
45

8 C
24 B

23

10

43 A

47 A

4 A

Beach Centre Mall

41 A

Sheikh Mohammed Centre for Cultural Understanding

12 D

45 A

22 D

41 B

26 B
28 B

43 A

45
47
49

45

10 C
12 C

53

6 C
33 A
35 A
39 A
41

284 Time Out Dubai

53 A

47 A

12 D

16 D

47 C

45 A

32 A

57

page 287

Dubai Zoo

8 A 51

Green Art Gallery

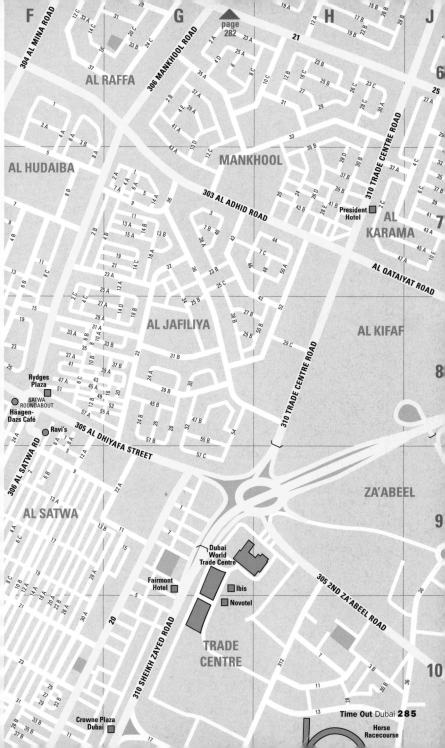

F

304 AL MINA ROAD

AL RAFFA

306 MANKHOOL ROAD

G

page 282

MANKHOOL

303 AL ADHID ROAD

AL HUDAIBA

AL JAFILIYA

President Hotel

H

310 TRADE CENTRE ROAD

AL KARAMA

AL QATAIYAT ROAD

J

6

25

7

Rydges Plaza

SATWA ROUNDABOUT

Häagen-Dazs Café

Ravi's

306 AL SATWA RD

305 AL DHIYAFA STREET

AL KIFAF

310 TRADE CENTRE ROAD

8

ZA'ABEEL

AL SATWA

310 SHEIKH ZAYED ROAD

Dubai World Trade Centre

Fairmont Hotel

Ibis

Novotel

305 2ND ZA'ABEEL ROAD

9

TRADE CENTRE

Crowne Plaza Dubai

Horse Racecourse

10

A

B

C

0   500 m
0   500 yds
© Copyright Time Out Group 2005

11

A R A B I A N

G U L F

12

13

14

15

302 JUMEIRAH ROAD

311 AL UROUBA STREET

304 AL WASL ROAD

302 JUMEIRAH ROAD

Mercato
Mall

Creative Art
Centre

Town Centre
Mall

JUMEIRAH (2)

Jumeirah Beach
Park

Jumeirah
Beach Club

JUMEIRAH (3)

286 Time Out Dubai

Majlis Ghorfat
Um Al Sheef

313 ALATHAR

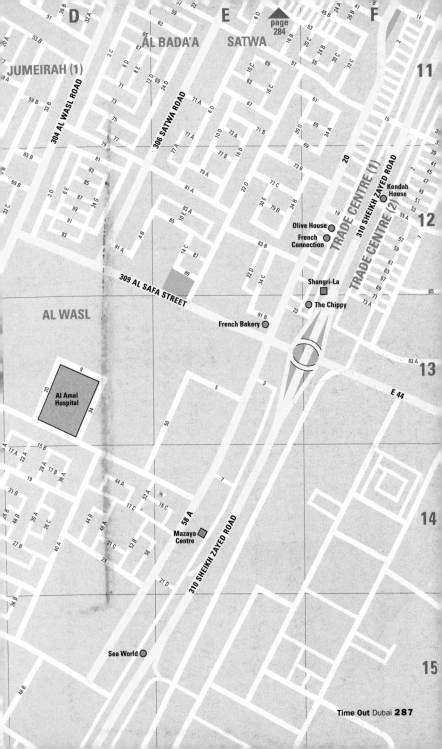

D
E
F

28 B
51
32 A
59
22
45 A
24 A
41
11
6 D
6 B

AL BADA'A
53
18 B
20 C
41
11
20 A
53 B
63
SATWA
57
24 B
30 C
32 C
2

JUMEIRAH (1)
2 C
65
67
10 C
69
55
11
73
6 D
8 E
12 D
69
24 D
83
16 C
15

71
71 A
6 D
61

59 B
32 B
75
77 A
10 D
73 A
65
34 A

65 B
79
77 A
77 B
18 D
69
39

69 B
2 D
81
79 A
73 B
20
41

32 C
6 E
85
81 A
22 D
47

24 G
87
83 A
10 E
30 E
79 A
34 B
310 SHEIKH ZAYED ROAD
Kendah House ●
49
55 A
53
12

89
85
32 D
34 C
83 B
Olive House ●
57

93
91 A
4 B
14 C
87
French Connection ●
59

309 AL SAFA STREET
89
32 D
34 C
Shangri-La ■
61
65

AL WASL
91 B
23
The Chippy ●
67

French Bakery ●
73 A
71

9
5
3
83 A
13

20
Al Amal Hospital
50
E 44

34

15 B
44 A
52 A
7

17 A
22 A
17 C
15 C

19
28 A
17 B

38 A
21 B
30 A
26 C
17 C
52 A
58 A
14

46 B
48 B
44 B
48 A
21 C
52 B
Mazaya Centre ■

27 B
40 A
23
58
310 SHEIKH ZAYED ROAD

38 B
21 D

48 B
Sea World ●
15

306 SATWA ROAD
304 AL WASL ROAD
TRADE CENTRE (1)
TRADE CENTRE (2)
page 284

Highlights

Our guide to the best itineraries…

FOR INDULGENCE

Check out the **Gold & Diamond Park** (*p134*) or **gold souk** (*p122*) for tailor-made jewellery, and Dubai's latest purveyor of swank, **Saks Fifth Avenue** (*p128*). Shopaholics can bet their bottom dollar that a new mall has opened since their last visit too (*pp116-123*). Spend a blissful afternoon of pampering at Madinat Jumeirah's **Six Senses Spa** (*p210*), then head to Gordon Ramsay's **Verre** (*p96*) for an ultra-romantic evening of fine dining. You won't go wrong with the fairytale setting of **Pierchic** (*p103*), finished off with a lazy drink or two on the jazz-fuelled **Rooftop** (*see p179*) at the One&Only Royal Mirage. For a dream-like desert escape, find time to stay over at **Al Maha** (*p49*). And if that's stretching the budget a little too far, console yourself at **Boudoir** (*p175*) – on selected nights women can party like royalty on free bubbly.

FOR ENLIGHTENMENT

Scratch beneath the surface of Dubai's glitz and glamour by taking an educational tour around the **Jumeirah Mosque** (*p71*) and exploring the Creek by **abra** (*p67*). Make time to taste Arabic cuisine at **Bastakiah Nights** (*p84*), or jump aboard the **Bateau Dubai** (*p85*) for a boat-bound supper tour. For an insight into the city's history, take a trip to the **Dubai Museum** (*p64*) before wandering the narrow alleyways of **Bastakia** (*p64*). When it's time to rest up, opt for tobacco with real flavour in one of the city's **shisha bars** (*p107*). If you've time to take a trip out of town, the museums of **Sharjah** (*p226*) are second to none, while the capital **Abu Dhabi** has a preserved **Dhow Harbour** and **Heritage Village** (*p217*).

FOR FAMILY FUN

Visit the imaginative educational zones of **Children's City** (*p153*) and the less instructional but equally entertaining rides of **Encounter Zone** (*p153*). Big kids and little ones alike will enjoy the thrilling waterslides of **Wild Wadi** (*p153*). For something more sedate, take a leisurely stroll (or drive) around **Mushrif Park** (*p205*) before unpacking the picnic basket. You might even bury dad in the sand at **Al Mamzar Park** (*p152*). Kids in need of more artistic stimulation should be entertained at the new **Jam Jar** studio (*p154*) or **Café Céramique** (*p110*).

FOR EXCITEMENT

The UAE's monster dune **Big Red** (*p77*) will challenge any desert driver, although less stomach-churning but equally picturesque fun can be had at **Hatta Rock Pools** (*p74*), where you can swim by the waterfalls. Back in the city, there's no better sight than thoroughbreds pounding the turf in winter at **Nad Al Sheba** (*p74*). If you'd rather be in the thick of the action, consider taking a high-powered kart for a spin at Dubai's new **Autodrome** (*p198*) or get your skin on and learn how to **dive** (*p200*). The best views of the city can still be had from **Vu's** (*p86*) on the 50th floor of the Emirates Towers. After dark, Dubai's clubbers flock to the **MIX** (*p169*) if there's a big-name DJ in town – otherwise everybody heads to the city's newest superclub, **Trilogy** (*p175*).

FOR RELAXATION

Dubai is rapidly emerging as a golfer's paradise, and many visitors let go their frustrations on the emirate's pristine fairways. Of the many new developments, the **Dubai Creek Golf & Yacht Club** (*p196*), reopened in 2005, is a sight to behold. Non-sporty types will want to unwind amid Dubai's rich café culture: we recommend **Shakespeare & Co** (*p109*) or the perma-packed **Lime Tree** (*p112*). If it's Friday, forget about the waistline and enjoy one of the city's bargain **brunch** deals (*p97*). To truly get away from it all, consider a dhow cruise of the **Musandam** (*p237*), a half-day **fishing** excursion into the Gulf (*p194*) or a sun-drenched wind-down on the unspoilt beaches of **Fujairah** (*p238*). Return to Dubai to tell your tales over a chilled beer at dusk – the **Barasti** (*p178*) is a perfect spot for a sundowner.

The wetter, the better: **Wild Wadi**. *See p153.*